Michael Trimble

RURAL REBELS

Map of Western Kenya showing the spread of the
Cult of Mumbo and Dini ya Msambwa.

AUDREY WIPPER
Department of Sociology
University of Waterloo

RURAL REBELS

A Study of Two Protest Movements in Kenya

1977
OXFORD UNIVERSITY PRESS
NAIROBI LONDON NEW YORK

Oxford University Press

OXFORD LONDON GLASGOW
NEW YORK TORONTO MELBOURNE WELLINGTON
IBADAN NAIROBI DAR ES SALAAM LUSAKA CAPE TOWN
KUALA LUMPUR SINGAPORE JAKARTA HONG KONG TOKYO
DELHI BOMBAY CALCUTTA MADRAS KARACHI

Oxford University Press, P.O. Box 72532, Nairobi

© OXFORD UNIVERSITY PRESS 1977

Made and printed in East Africa

Dedication

*To my parents and to those DyMers who stubbornly
refused to sever ties with the past.*

Contents

Page

Part IV APPENDICES

Preface

It is a pleasure to witness the appearance of Professor Wipper's ambitious and well-executed study of two cases of a phenomenon that is important, intriguing, and still too little understood, politico-religious protest under colonial conditions. Her research on the Cult of Mumbo and the Dini ya Msambwa movement—research which necessarily included extensive inquiry into Kenyan society as a whole—has extended over a decade, and this volume reveals clearly the fruitfulness of her long labour.

Any student of collective behaviour knows how difficult it is to secure a proper 'handle' on phenomena so complex as nativistic cults and nascent movements of political protest among colonial peoples. Their socio-cultural context is inevitably complex and fluctuating; the factors shaping their careers are inevitably multiple; their agendas are inevitably complicated; and their histories typically yield a zigzag pattern of development. Given this complexity and denseness of the phenomena to be analysed, the investigator scarcely knows where to begin.

Given this circumstance, the reader must admire the strategy of Professor Wipper's analysis. In the case of both movements, Professor Wipper provides, as a first step, an organized historical description of the movement, paying particular attention to the authenticity of her often distorted and otherwise unsatisfactory data. To follow this—again in both cases—she retraces her steps, but this time in more analytic fashion, locating the multiplicity of historical events and situations according to an organized framework of causal factors. The result is an ever expanding, ever more general, more analytic sequence of argumentation.

For this reason, Professor Wipper's study yields something of interest to everyone. The Africanist will find that the depth of her

x

coverage brings to light a great deal of new historical material on a part of the world whose history is so relatively untold. The methodologically-minded anthropologist will profit from her sensitive account of the difficulties in both the archive-retrieving and interviewing phases of her research, as well as the strategies by which she attempted to render these data more nearly representative and accurate. There is much in the study for the theoretically-minded as well. Early in the introductory chapter Professor Wipper lays out a number of past efforts to account for religious and political protest in colonial societies, and convincingly lays most of these to rest. (It should be added, however, that this task was not altogether a mighty one, since those past accounts are so shot through with oversimplifications and transparent ideological preferences.) More important, she infuses her on-going discussions with reference to a variety of more serious theoretical formulations. Witness, for example, her salient critique of mass society theory in Chapter 13, in which she brings both historical data and persuasive interpretations of them to suggest that communal integration is a *resource* rather than an *obstacle* to mobilization for political protest; this discussion provides an interesting supplement to Maurice Pinard's similar critique of mass society theory in his *The Rise of a Third Party*, Englewood Cliffs, Prentice-Hall, 1971.

In re-reading Professor Wipper's accounts of the Mumbo and the Dini ya Msambwa movements, I could not help being forcefully struck by what might be called the 'totalism' of the colonial situation in many of its aspects. The colonial power typically attempts to dominate the colonized, directly or indirectly, in all respects, economically, politically, and religiously. Partly as a result of this domination, the strains imposed on colonial peoples are always multiple, as Professor Wipper documents in Chapters 8 and 17. They suffer economic deprivation, exclusion from political life, loss of status, and the imposition of unfamiliar and disruptive beliefs and norms. And, under colonial government—at least in its vital phases—the colonial power has an armoury of instruments for political repression. As a result, colonial peoples can scarcely contest their rulers politically. If one keeps in mind the overwhelming impact of this totalistic character of colonial domination, it is not difficult to appreciate the fact that many of the responses of colonial peoples display a corresponding totalism of their own. Their ideologies envision the most sweeping political reversals; their agendas are multiple; and they typically promise the birth of a new society, a new self, a new life, whether those be rooted in an idealized past or a utopian future. In sum, totalistic domination breeds totalistic response, largely because specific, piecemeal, and incremental responses are effectively unavailable in the prototypical colonial situation.

Neil J. Smelser,
University of California,
Berkeley.

Acknowledgements

This project, which has spanned more than ten years, has involved a large number of people. During that time I have acquired a host of debts that can only partially be acknowledged. Many people in Kenya helped in the various stages of the research. In particular I would like to thank R. D. McLaren, the Assistant Registrar of Societies; Nathan Fedha of the Kenya National Archives; the members of the History Department at the University of Nairobi; Charles Onyango, my research assistant; and the *East African Standard* and *Daily Nation* for the use of their libraries.

Without the cooperation and forbearance of the rural people this study would have been impossible. Benjamin Wekuke, Samson Wafula and Pascal Nabwana arranged access to people and helped me navigate unfamiliar surroundings. Local government personnel—district commissioners, district officers, chiefs and police officers—generously gave of their time. The warm hospitality of the Nabwana family, of the fathers and sisters of Misikhu Roman Catholic Mission, and of Edith Ratcliffe of the Friends Mission at Lugulu was much appreciated.

Many of the ideas in this book I owe to friends, fellow students and teachers in two geographically distinct, though in some ways similar places—the University of California at Berkeley and Makerere University in Kampala. Both were academic communities in the true sense of that term—places where people committed to the quest for knowledge provided stimulating contact, encouragement and constructive criticism. I would like to express my gratitude to Neil Smelser, who directed the original research and gave support and suggestions all along; to David E. Apter who encouraged me to go into African studies and helped to make my research stint in Africa a reality; to Herbert Blumer for a perspective, a 'way of seeing', and to Carl G. Rosberg, Wolfram Eberhard, Robert A. LeVine, John Lonsdale, Robert Rotberg, Frank Furedi and Jan J. de Wolf for their valuable comments.

Colleagues from the Department of Sociology at the University of Waterloo—Edmund Vaz, Harold Fallding, Powhatan Wooldridge, Margrit Eichler and Sally Weaver—read and commented upon different sections of the manuscript.

Grants from various institutions funded this research for three different periods in Kenya — the Canada Council, the International Federation of University Women, the Social Science Research Council of Canada, and the Woodrow Wilson Foundation. This book has been published with the aid of a grant from the University of Waterloo. Sanford S. Elberg, the former Dean of Graduate Studies at Berkeley, J. R. Kidd formerly of the Social Science Research Council of Canada, and W. F. Forbes of the University of Waterloo were particularly helpful with the funding.

Ethel Robinson, Audrey Meyer, Evelyn McGillivray, Samson Otieno and Reta Lienhardt took on the task of typing a manuscript with many quotations and footnotes and some almost illegible insertions. Reta Lienhardt, who did the bulk of the typing, deserves special mention for being as much an editorial assistant and friend as a typist. I am indebted to Jamini Vincent for editorial work and to Jane Hartley who did the final editing and processing of the manuscript for publication. Finally, I thank my mother, who quietly gave the right kind of support at the appropriate times.

The author and the publishers gratefully acknowledge permission to quote from the following:

Audrey Wipper, Elijah Masinde—A Folk Hero, Chapter 10 of *Hadith 3*. Proceedings of the 1969/70 Conference of the Historical Association of Kenya, East African Publishing House, Nairobi, 1971, pp. 157-191.

R. I. Rotberg and Ali A. Mazrui (eds.) *Protest and Power in Black Africa*, Oxford University Press, New York, 1970, pp. 377-423.

C. W. Hobley, *Kenya from Chartered Company to Crown Colony*, H. F. and G. Whitherby Ltd., London, 1929, pp. 83-86.

PART I

Introduction

Chapter 1

INTRODUCTION

T H E colonization of Kenya began in the late nineteenth century. The British government, involved at that time in Egypt, entrusted the territory from Uganda to the East African coast to the jurisdiction of a chartered agent, the Imperial British East Africa Company. It soon became apparent that the Company did not have the resources to bring this enormous area under its administration and so the Foreign Office took control of Kenya in 1895 and declared it a Protectorate.[1]

British efforts to consolidate their influence beyond a few scattered forts met opposition from the indigenous people. Expeditions to establish administrative posts were attacked by tribesmen whose terrain had been invaded. The building of the railway from the coast to Uganda was hampered by raids from angry pastoralists whose grazing grounds had been disturbed. Caravan routes were plundered for booty. Sometimes it was only after a series of clashes extending over a period of years that particular tribes were subdued.

Pacification was accompanied by the extension of administration into the hinterland. The British made use of indigenous leaders at the local level as agents of imperial rule. The problem in Kenya was the absence of kings and powerful chiefs with authority over political units large enough from the British point of view, to administer effectively. In the absence of such, the heads of powerful clans and other locally recognized leaders were appointed as agents.

Closely following the military, sometimes even preceding it, were the missionaries intent on winning converts to Christianity. From 1899 to 1906, no less than eleven Protestant denominations and Roman Catholic orders opened up mission stations in Kenya. The missionaries had little success among the scattered nomadic pastoralists so they concentrated their efforts on the agriculturalists in two areas of dense settlement now known as Central and Western Provinces.[2]

Against this background of Christian evangelism, a number of messianic and millenarian movements, breakaway sects and independent churches made their appearance. The earliest recorded was Nomiyo Luo which arose in 1912, followed by the cult of Mumbo in 1913. By 1971 there were 157 independent denominations with 5,650 congregations giving a rough average of 36 congregations per denomination. The membership of the independent churches of 1,694,840 near equalled the membership of all the Protestant churches in Kenya and was not far below the Roman Catholic membership of 1,998,000.[3]

Many of these movements originated by secession from Christian missions, although some arose independent of any direct affiliation with a particular mission. A large number were short-lived. Others showed a surprising tenacity despite rudimentary organization, the death of the charismatic leader, and in some cases, severe repression. In general, their message combined old and new beliefs, religious, political and economic aspirations. Their tactics varied from militant revolt at one extreme to ritualistic prescriptions at the other. British administrators, uncertain about their nature, vacillated in how they handled them. If the movement was 'truly religious', they felt its practice should be allowed. On the other hand, if it was subversive, it should be repressed. What puzzled British and later African administrators was that many appeared to be both.

This study examines two of these movements, the cult of Mumbo and Dini ya Msambwa. Mumbo and Msambwa originated in the early and late colonial period, respectively. First, since little is known about them, they will be described in an effort to answer a basic question, what is their nature.[4] Second, the major determinants of Mumbo and Msambwa in the colonial period will be delineated in order to explain not only *why these movements arose but why they took a particular form. That is, why a passive millenarian movement*[5] (*Mumbo*) *appeared at one time and an active movement* (*Msambwa*) *at another*, bearing in mind the qualification that since movements shift their orientation through time, the explanation seeks to explain *dominant phases only rather than end states*.

No attempt will be made to rigorously compare these two movements. There is simply a vast difference in the amount of material available on Mumbo and Msambwa which will lead (unless much

material on Msambwa were omitted) to their uneven treatment.
While this element of disequilibrium may jar some readers, I feel
it is worthwhile because the data do provide some insight into that
intriguing question of the ingredients of active and passive millenarianism.

For purposes of this study, no sharp line dividing movements
called millenarian, prophetic and messianic, cargo and crisis cults,
separatist sects, and even some independent churches will be drawn.
I hesitate to call the movements being studied by any of these names
since each name has a long association with particular phenomena
remote from the movements under examination. Occasionally one
of the aforementioned terms will be used to draw attention to a
particular component.

The term religious-political movement most accurately reflects
the essential nature of these movements, at least in the colonial
period. A religious movement exemplifies collective mobilization
with the objective of redefining man's relationships to questions
of ultimate concern—the purpose of life, of death, his relations to
the cosmos and to his fellow men. A political movement, in turn,
exemplifies collective mobilization with the objective of maintaining,
restoring, modifying or changing the institutionalized structure of
power in a social system.[6] However, since 'religious-political
movement' is rather cumbersome, the term 'protest movement'
will be used (even this hopefully neutral term is not without its
problems) with the understanding that *such movements contain both
religious and political components, have both instrumental and
expressive significance for their adherents, may be both forward-
looking and backward-looking, and may have both 'active' and 'passive'
tendencies*.

Protest movements are important to study for various reasons.
Since they are concerted efforts by large numbers of people to promote or to resist change they are significant both as vehicles of,
and as obstacles to, change. By studying movements in the past as
well as in the present, in the Third World as well as in the western
world, we can broaden our knowledge of social movements in
general and perhaps throw some light on the study of contemporary
movements. The bringing of cross-cultural data to bear on hypotheses originating in western, industrial societies may serve to
free them from cultural and historical limitations.

The term 'peasants' will be used in this book to mean populations that are involved in cultivation at the subsistence level and make autonomous decisions regarding the processes of cultivation. This category covers tenants and sharecroppers as well as owner-operators as long as they are the key decision-makers on how crops are to be grown. In the area we will be discussing, peasants are predominantly owner-operators. They tend to keep the market at arm's length as unlimited involvement in it threatens their hold on their source of livelihood. Products are sold in the market to produce that extra margin of returns with which to buy goods one does not produce in the homestead. The peasant tends to cling to traditional arrangements which guarantee his access to land and labour.

The farmer, in contrast, enters the market fully. He subjects his land and labour to open competition, explores alternative ways to best use his resources in order to maximize returns, and favours the profitable product over one entailing the smaller risk.[7] Squatters, the other category of rural people of major concern to this study, are discussed in Chapter 9.

The Etiological Question

Protest movements have proliferated in other parts of Africa, North and South America, Europe and Oceania. Many exhibit an extraordinary similarity despite their geographical, historical and cultural differences. The Kenyan movements are related to the cargo cults, apocalyptic, millenarian movements, primarily of Melanesia, which promise a millennium in the form of material and spiritual cargo. Dini ya Msambwa is similar to the Mau Mau movement and the Maji Maji rebellion in some of its religious and political elements. The nativism of Mumbo and Msambwa recalls the Ghost Dance of the North American Indians.

What causes these movements? Here I will examine various determinants delineating broad classificatory types rather than individual theories *per se* which vary in the emphasis given to different factors and could not be adequately covered in a short space. Explanations range from low level empirical generalizations pertaining to a single movement, to explanations that seek to explain the occurrence of movements in particular areas, to general theories that try to explain their occurrence anywhere in Africa, or the occurrence anywhere of particular kinds of movements. Cross-cultural literature will be utilized with an emphasis on East and

Central African movements. This survey by no means covers all the important work but uses particular studies to illustrate various kinds of explanations.

Political Protest

During the colonial period, these movements were often interpreted as pre-nationalistic or as primitive forms of protest. Lanternari's survey of prophetic and messianic movements in colonial countries presents them as primarily 'cults of liberation' seeking freedom for their oppressed peoples.

> The birth of these movements can only be understood in the light of historical conditions relating to the colonial experiences and to the striving of subject peoples to become emancipated. Premonitory religious movements of revival and transformation usually lie at the origin of every political or military uprising among the native peoples and take the form of messianic cults promising liberation.[8]

The links between movements led by Simon Kimbangu, André Matswa and Simon Mpadi in the former Belgian Congo and the national independence struggle have been spelled out by Andersson, van Wing and Balandier.[9] Balandier, although he does not deny their sociological and cultural aspects, writes: 'Although they are outwardly religious, these movements rapidly develop a political aspect; they are at the origin of nationalisms which are still unsophisticated but unequivocal in their expression.'[10] Shepperson, Coleman, Welbourn and Mair likewise see them as a religious strand of African nationalism.[11] According to Worsley and Hobsbawm, they will disappear with the development of more specialized vehicles for articulating political grievances such as political parties and labour unions.[12]

Rosberg and Nottingham in *The Myth of 'Mau Mau'* discuss the growth of nationalism in Kenya that emerged in the Mau Mau movement. They examine the long history of social, economic and political grievances not adequately remedied by the authorities and highlighted by two major controversies over land alienation and female circumcision. They reject the view held by the settlers, missionaries and colonial administrators that Mau Mau was merely another of the earlier religious movements that had proliferated in Kenya from the earliest colonial times.

Few would argue that there has not been a close association in

Africa between these rural-based movements and the development of modern nationalism. But if colonial oppression was their *raison d'etre* one would expect that independence would witness the end of these movements or, at the most, the survival of a few with a drastically changed orientation. Far from dying out, however, these movements have flourished. Obviously explanations which gave primacy to nationalistic aspirations have not told the full story.

An important question, in no way adequately dealt with so far, is whether or not protest movements existed prior to the advent of colonial rule. The question becomes more intriguing when it is admitted that there is indeed evidence that they did. Hence alien domination, whether white or black, may be a more crucial determinant than colonialism *per se*.

Economic and Social Causes

Mooney's study of the causes of the Ghost Dance, a chiliastic movement among the Plains Indians of the American Southwest that culminated in the Sioux rebellion of 1890, examines the plight of the Indians resulting from their contact with the white man.[13] Distress caused by an epidemic of black leg in 1888 was aggravated when crops failed in 1889. The buffalo, the Indians' chief source of food and clothing, had been wiped out. A nomadic people, accustomed to roaming the plains, they were confined to reservations and made totally dependent upon government rations. The government periodically reduced both the size of the reservations and the rations. Promises concerning the provision of education and compensation for appropriated lands were never honoured. Other epidemics, measles, whooping cough and gripe, further ravished their numbers. And at the time of the outbreak, the presence of troops in Indian areas had increased their apprehension.

Mooney's excellent analysis pinpoints the multiple causes of distress but not all severely deprived people form millenarian movements. The question remains, given conditions of severe deprivation, why did such a movement arise rather than some other response?

Most African separatist religious movements have originated, according to Fernandez, for non-religious reasons such as instrumental acts by the leaders to gain more status and power.[14] Schlosser, on the basis of her survey *Propheten in Afrika*, takes the position, 'Apart from purely personal ambition, the reasons for the appearance

6

of prophets are predominantly of an economic and political nature, exclusively religious only in the rarest cases.'[15]

Massive inflation and insecure squatters were the factors that garnered support for Dini ya Msambwa according to Jan de Wolf, an anthropologist, who studied religious innovation among the Bukusu.

> Most important of these [circumstances that gave rise to Dini ya Msambwa] was a massive inflation. There were large amounts of money in circulation because of remittances from people serving in the army, compulsory wage labour on European farms, and compulsory cattle sales. Yet this medium of exchange was useless for acquiring the traditional symbol of wealth, cattle, because it has all been sold, or for buying modern western consumer goods, imports of which were strictly limited. At the same time there was a large scale eviction of unwanted squatters, occupation of farms along the borders of the White Highlands which had been used by Africans, and a severe limitation of the number of cattle, sheep and goats which African labourers were allowed to keep in the White Highlands . . . I shall attempt to show that *the mass appeal of his* [*Masinde, the leader*] *preaching must have been based on the run-away inflation and the insecurity of the squatters as the major causes.*[16] (Italics mine.)

Such an explanation omits a number of determinants that were equally, some even more, important, as will be shown in Chapters 13 and 17.

Economic explanations have been criticized. On the basis of his study of medieval millenarianism Cohn notes that poverty, hardship and oppression cannot in themselves account for millenarianism.

> For most peasants life must always have been a ceaseless struggle, and for many a losing struggle. In every village there were numbers of peasants living near or at subsistence level; and agricultural surplus was so small and communications so precarious that a bad harvest often meant mass famine . . . If poverty, hardships and an often oppressive dependency could by themselves generate it, revolutionary chiliasm would have run strong among the peasantry of medieval Europe. In point of fact it was seldom to be found at all.[17]

Hobsbawm makes the same point about millenarianism in Andalusia in the late 1860s. 'The rise of revolutionism was not simply a reflex of bad conditions, for conditions may have improved, though only to the point of eliminating the actual catastrophic famines.'[18]

Andersson, from his study of messianic movements in the Lower Congo, in particular Kimbanguism and Khakism, concludes that economic crises can contribute to an outburst of these movements but that they do not serve as an actual cause. He noted the presence of many *evolués* (who would tend to be among the most prosperous Africans) in the Kimbanguist movement.[19]

If, as Worsley contends from his study of cargo cults in Melanesia, millenarian beliefs have recurred again and again throughout history because they have a strong appeal to the lower classes, to 'the dispossessed, the disinherited, and the wretched,'[20] one would expect the lower classes to be over-represented in the membership of such movements. Was it the poorest Melanesians who joined cargo cults? This proposition needs more empirical testing. Data on recruitment to millenarian and other movements indicate that there is no simple correlation between economic deprivation and recruitment. Specific propositions relating economic factors to support for protest movements require investigation. Representative samples of memberships and populations need to be examined quantitatively in order to discover the different factors involved in support and non-support. Only then will we begin to get some definitive answers.

Psychological Stress

Theories of psychological stress emphasize the frustrations, anxieties, fears and insecurities that find outlets in religious ecstasy—trances, states of trembling, speaking in strange tongues and hysterical dancing. Many of these interpretations stress the pathological aspects of this motor activity.

Ralph Linton's 'Nativistic Movements', published in 1943, was an early effort at a general explanation on a comparative basis of a particular type of movement, nativism, defined as 'any conscious, organized attempt on the part of a society's members to revive or perpetuate selected aspects of its culture.'[21] According to Linton, the roots of nativism lie in situations of culture contact where one group dominates another, and where there is widespread nostalgia on the part of the subjugated people to return to an idealized version of the indigenous way of life. Linton delineates some important conditions that foster nativism although the literature gives ample evidence of others. Again, what he fails to explain is why these conditions give rise to nativistic movements and not to, say, political movements or to sheer apathy.

Though they emphasize the religious nature of the independent churches, Welbourn and Ogot characterize them as 'accommodative' institutions that came into being when mission churches failed to meet *African needs for community, personal identity, and a place to feel at home.*[22]

Lewis Feuer would even go so far as to explain the Mau Mau rebellion in terms of the Oedipus complex, sons reject the traditional life and rebel against their fathers. He reduces Kenya's complex independence movement, dating back to the nineteenth century when Africans first tried to repel the foreign invaders, centreing upon social, economic and political grievances, taking various forms in its development, and supported by different tribes although the militant last stage was Kikuyu dominated, to President Kenyatta's hatred of, and rebellion against, his substitute father, the British colonialists. In his analysis the nationalist struggle gives way to the primacy of inter-generational revolt.[23]

Religious Expression

The emphasis upon political, economic and psychological explanations has led Turner, Baeta, and Shepperson to take scholars to task for subsuming the religious under other factors. Turner, author of a two volume study on the Aladura movement in West Africa, questions the importance given to non-religious factors which he feels have obscured the primarily religious orientation of many movements. He sees these movements as attempts to create a new and more satisfying religious life that reconciles old and new religious beliefs and reunites the sacred and secular so fundamental to tribal society and lost by the older mission churches as they become larger and more bureaucratized.[24]

Baeta, in discussing prophetic movements in Ghana, states:

In my opinion it would be very wide of the mark indeed to suppose that the people forming the core of these churches are persons suffering from any psychological malaise, or extraordinary emotional strains and stresses. Rather they appear to be perfectly normal, even "relaxed" men and women, taking the new developments in their stride. It appears to me that in recent studies of new cults and other movements of a religious nature among African peoples, the presumed background element of

9

psychological upheaval, tensions and conflicts, anxieties, etc., due to "acculturation, technology and the Western impact" has tended to be rather overdrawn.[25]

One of the largest movements for moral reform in East Africa was the Revival, originating in 1929 in southern Uganda and spreading eastwards into Kenya, northwards into the Sudan, and southwards into Tanzania. It indicted Christian society for its moral laxity and attempted to reform the Anglican church. Inextricably linked with religious-moral motives was resentment of European 'superiority' and paternalism.[26]

The Leader as Mobilizer

The dominant presence of some prophet or messiah whom the followers believe holds divine power is another mode of explanation. In areas of Christian penetration, the native messiah may be pattern-ed on the New Testament messiah, though it would be naive to suppose that all native messianism is so patterned since many native messiahs have never heard of Jesus Christ—the 'messiah' being a common figure in the world's history.

Nativistic cults may await the return of ancient heroes, great kings, warriors and other ancestors. The legendary 'Barbarossa' motif—the belief that the king or hero never died but still lives and will one day return to lead his people to a utopian order—is found in many indigenous belief systems and probably provides a theme that in some ways parallels the Christian resurrection. André Matswa of the Kimbinguist movement died in 1942, according to historians, but legend has it that he is still alive and will return. Similarly when the founder of South African Zionism, Isaac Shembe, died, rumours circulated that he would rise again.[27] This took a slightly different turn in the Lenshina movement of Zambia where the prophet, Alice Lenshina, claimed to have died and to have arisen again.[28]

In contrast to de Wolf's economic explanation, Benjamin Kipkorir singles out the charismatic leader as the prime cause in the rise of Dini ya Msambwa among the Pokot which culminated in the violent Kolloa Affray. 'I am convinced that it was the personality of Lukas Pkech which was instrumental in spreading DyM among the Pokot.' According to him, Pkech had 'extraordinary charisma' which enabled him to spread his proscribed doctrine, in part, because of a 'spell which . . . [he] cast on the Pokot. Those who came into his presence were overawed by his eyes. His personality was gripping if not frightening.'[29] Yet the only evidence to back up this assumption of charisma except for the fact that Pkech had some followers (as do a hundred other leaders of prophetic and messianic movements in Kenya) is hearsay—a district commissioner reported a tribal policeman's reaction to Pkech.[30] Completely lacking are any opinions of Pkech's followers. Did they believe him to be endowed with extraordinary powers, to have a special mission? We are not denying that Pkech may have had charisma, but only suggesting that the evidence is rather meagre, and that if the concept is not used more sparingly, it may lose its meaning and usefulness.

This concept has been increasingly criticized for giving too much importance to the qualities emanating from the leader and too little to the believers' contribution in creating 'charisma'. La Barre notes that the many instances of the 'failed messiah' tend to cast doubt on the 'great man' theory.[31] No matter how attractive the leader is, the social-structural conditions must be propitious for a movement to originate.

Combination Theories
Sundkler accounts for the proliferation of independent churches in South Africa by political, religious, economic, social and psychological variables. The two general causes are the colour bar and the example of Protestant denominationalism. Specific causes are conflicts over church discipline in the missions and personality conflicts between Africans and missionaries. Additionally, there is the Africans' search for economic security by securing land or a church colony. In some instances, the deepest cause is a nativistic-syncretistic interpretation of Christian religion.[32] The fact that African leaders continue to secede from their own African churches shows that other causes are at work, such as the struggle for leadership, status and power.

Iliffe's explanation of the Maji Maji rebellion in southern Tanzania concentrates on religious, economic, and tribal factors and explains not only the causes of unrest but how this unrest was mobilized and channelled into a rebellion. Maji Maji originated as a mass response to peasant grievances, was sanctified and extended by prophetic religion, and finally crumbled as crises compelled reliance on the oldest and most fundamental loyalties to kin and tribe.[33]

Iliffe suggests that the rebels made use of common grievances resulting from the economic pressures of German rule; that they organized according to prior political and cultural groupings, and that an attempt to mobilize on a basis wider than tribe employed either traditional religious beliefs or created new religious forms.

The most ambitious theory to date is that of Barrett who tries to explain the origins of six thousand religious movements from all over Africa.[34] He asks, why are separatist movements found in some tribes and not in others? His scale of religious tension called the 'tribal *zeitgeist*' is designed to measure the 'strength' of traditional society, the 'strength' of the European impact on it, and to predict when similar movements will arise. Since this scale, composed from eighteen questions, includes such important dimensions as the length of the colonial period, land alienation, *per capita* income and the density of Protestant missions, it is disappointing to find that, in the end, Barrett cannot resist the temptation to reduce his multi-dimensional explanation to a single root cause—the failure on the part of the missionaries to extend brotherly love to Africans, that is, their prejudice towards Africans whom they failed to treat as equals. This failure became widely perceived when the Bible was translated into the vernacular and Africans could see for themselves the discrepancy between scriptural teachings and mission practices.

The Negative Stereotype of Kenyan Movements

In Kenya, these movements have been described, at least in the colonial period, from the viewpoint of westerners. Journalists and novelists fascinated by their exotic aspects have played up the sensational. Sex and superstition, magic and witchcraft, have been given a prominent place. This picture has been reinforced by European administrators and missionaries who, because they 'lived' for years among Africans, supposedly held an accurate view. (European is used here as it is in East Africa to refer to white people in general.) Sir Philip Mitchell, Kenya's Governor from 1944 to 1952, a man who had spent much of his career in East and Central Africa, described the followers as 'deluded, hysterical' people under the sway of a leader whose 'diseased brain' was centred upon self-aggrandizement. Their actions were said to be motivated by 'the black and blood-stained forces of sorcery and magic stirring the vicious hearts of wicked men.'[35] A description that is not too different from that provided by journalists.

Carothers, a government medical doctor, argued that the Mau Mau movement was the product of demagogic leadership exploiting anxiety-ridden people with a magical mode of thinking:

> It arose from the development of an anxious conflictual situation in people who, from contact with an alien culture, had lost the supportive and constraining influences of their own culture, yet had not lost their "magic" modes of thinking. It arose from the exploitation of this situation by relatively sophisticated egotists.[36]

Did the two movements under study fare any better? Colonial administrators and missionaries saw the cult of Mumbo as an atavistic, irrational movement grounded in perversions and superstitions.[37] The work of scholars, both western and indigenous, has to some extent supported the views of the administrators and missionaries. Bethwell Ogot, a Kenyan historian, described Mumbo as 'fanatical and non-programmatic . . . a cult whose leaders preached the complete rejection of everything European and a return to the African way of life.'[38] John Lonsdale, another historian, wrote of the cult's 'reactionary appeal . . . the rebellion had to be backward-looking, rejecting all things European . . . Mumbo was a political aberration. A return to the Old Africa was not yet the key to the future.'[39] And M. P. K. Sorrenson concluded, 'Mumbo was an atavistic movement, an attempt to reject the Europeans and all their works.'[40]

As for Dini ya Msambwa, it was summed up as 'one of those back-to-the-primitive religious movements.' C. T. Stoneham, an early administrator, assessed Msambwa rioters as follows:

> A word may be said for such administrative officials whose duty it is to guide and cherish wild, superstitious and bloodthirsty black people in places where there is little to depend on but their own courage and a reputation for fairness and sympathy. It is no joke to deal with a frenzied mob of 500 tribesmen with no support other than a handful of native police who know they will be overwhelmed at the first onset. But the District Commissioner reasoned with those lunatics and persuaded them to disperse.[41]

Elspeth Huxley characterizes two contrasting responses on the part of Africans to the European incursion as 'the way of the Zealot, and the way of the Herodian.' 'The first looked back to a glorious past, the second forward to a realistic future . . . Africans have seen very clearly that they must master Western techniques

13

if they are to compete on equal terms with Europeans . . . The rise of the Zealots is making itself felt . . . in the spontaneous appearance of many fanatical, half-crazy quasi-religious cults, each under a crackpot leader who preaches a return to ancient ways.' Dini ya Msambwa, she depicts as an example of the Zealot response. 'The leader of this sect was an epileptic released from a mental hospital who claimed to be Elijah come again. . . . An obvious danger is that folk who like to fish in troubled waters will at first encourage and then manipulate for political ends these simple-minded, confused and in a sense pathetic Zealots.'[42]

The manipulative theme is also evident in Kipkorir's analysis of Dini ya Msambwa among the Pokot:

> There can be no doubt that Pkech *understood the "plight" of the Pokot people and exploited it to the full*. This plight did not arise from European economic exploitation but from age-old maladies and disasters; drought, eye-diseases, early old-age, barrenness and concern for stock . . .Above all *he capitalized* on the Pokot love of song and dance.[43] (Italics mine.)

From the above as well as from other statements,[44] a stereotype emerges of these movements with the following characteristics:

a) They completely reject the modern world and advocate a return to the traditional life.

b) They are the antithesis of reason. Ecstasy, ritual and 'hysterical mobs' are seen as evidence of irrational, even pathological behaviour.

c) The members are capricious, excitable people not fully in control of themselves or simple people easily duped by their leaders who manipulate them through Machiavellian tactics for their own evil ends. Interestingly, one view presents the members as irrational while the leaders, in contrast, are wickedly rational.

d) The members suffer major character defects. They are immoral, especially sexually, and even 'vicious' and 'bloodthirsty'.

This stereotype grossly oversimplifies these movements, though its usefulness for the authorities is obvious. For if these movements were reactionary, then they should be suppressed since they were negative forces standing in the way of modernization. Although some of the above characteristics are exhibited, it is a one-sided interpretation that serves to exonerate the administration, bypass the important questions of whether, in fact, there are genuine grievances, and completely omits the members' perspectives. What are their ideas of justice and injustice, fair and unfair obligations? Their definitions of the social world in which they live are essential to an understanding of what the movement is all about. By quoting them, I will try to give their perception of the situation, in particular, of the movement and of the authorities.

The emphasis upon aberrant, irrational, volatile elements implies that mysterious, non-rational forces generate these movements and hence their determinants are beyond empirical investigation. But even a quick glance at their distribution shows that they occur among some clans, tribes, and in some places and periods and not in others and are supported by people in particular social categories. This clustering by clan, tribe, place and in time, invites investigation. We discard the perspective that movements are products of irrational, psychological factors.[45] Psychological factors are not dismissed as determinants, for some form of psychological stress is a necessary ingredient, but they are seen as only one of a number of determinants that have their roots in social conditions.

Conclusions

1) A question still to be answered adequately about many movements is, what is their nature? Of what elements are they composed? Too many researchers have assumed they knew what the movement was all about, and, working on certain assumptions, the expected was indeed found. Much controversy has involved discussions of essentially different phenomena. Until we have more factual data on particular movements, general discussions of etiology, high level theories, and complex measurement scales are of limited value.

2) Behaviour labelled 'traditional' and 'regressive' and assumed to be resistant to change needs to be much more closely examined in the context of specific situations. Of what does 'traditional behaviour' consist? If a movement is 'reactionary', what is the specific content of its reaction? Who is trying to introduce what kind of change and for whom? The colonial situation tended to be equated in 'colonial minds' with modernity and when Africans rejected the former they were seen to be rejecting the latter.

3) In accounting for causation, there has been much reductionism. Too much emphasis has been given to one set of causal factors to the neglect of others. It is more useful to assume that many factors

15

are involved and later to reduce the number of variables than to look for prime causes.

4) Some explanations are more ideological than empirical. 'Wretched', 'oppressed' and 'disinherited' tend to be used with little attempt to operationalize them. In many instances, a sizeable proportion of the members are not the most wretched people in the country (if measured in economic terms); or the disinherited (if measured by loss of land); nor does hardship explain much if there are non-members suffering from even greater hardship. Without being operationalized and without showing the ways in which these factors interact with others to produce recruits, these concepts are not sufficiently discriminating and are not subject to empirical testing. The study of these movements has now reached the stage where specific propositions require testing with cross-cultural data.

5) Many explanations have focussed on causes of unrest and discontent but have made little attempt to explain why and how these were expressed in a particular form.

The Frame of Reference
Data on the following dimensions were gathered, where possible and appropriate, for the cult of Mumbo and Dini ya Msambwa and organized under the headings:
1) background of the movement
2) origins and development
3) beliefs and activities
4) basis of support
5) attitudes of agents of social control and
6) a later phase of the movement

The basic theoretical perspective found to be most useful for our analysis is that of Neil Smelser as set forth in his *Theory of Collective Behavior*. Smelser's value-added approach identifies six general determinants that taken together and in various combinations— the *accumulation* and *interaction* of variables is emphasized— can account for any episode of collective behaviour. Briefly they are:
1) *Structural conduciveness*. The most general structural features that permit or encourage collective behaviour to develop.
2) *Structural strain*. Tensions, ambiguities, conflicts and discrepancies that accumulate in a situation of structural conduciveness.
3) *General beliefs*. Before collective action can be taken shared

beliefs must be present that identify the sources of strain and advocate particular responses.

4) *Precipitating factors.* The episode or episodes that set off the accumulated tensions often by focussing them upon a particular group or goal. It is an event that sharpens or exaggerates a condition of conduciveness and strain and provides concrete evidence for the general beliefs.

The term '*exacerbating*' will be used, since it pinpoints the function of this determinant in relation to social movements more accurately than 'precipitating' which is more appropriate for collective outbursts such as riots and crazes. This determinant crystallizes emotions, ignites frustrations, inflames passions thereby pushing people into taking sides. In short, it 'draws up the battle lines'. Pride, humiliation, anger, hate, bitterness, and righteous indignation are among the strong emotions involved.

5) *Mobilization of participants for action.* Those affected begin to act on the basis of a shared belief. Here the role of leadership is particularly important.

6) *The operation of social control.* Those counter determinants that act to inhibit, interrupt, deflect or prevent the accumulation of the above mentioned determinants. In this study we mean by the agents of social control persons acting in official or semi-official capacities whose task is to maintain the established system. They include government ministers, members of parliament, administrators, chiefs, missionaries, social workers, the press, and in the colonial period, the settlers and the Home Government. Their perceptions determined the course of action that was taken towards the movement which in turn influenced its development. Since the agents have a preponderance of power, it is their definitions of situations which officially prevail. Distinct similarities in perspective will be noticed among the agents regardless of whether it is the colonial or post-colonial period.

This framework, though implicit in the description of each movement, is not explicit in the analysis because it is easier to organize the data using descriptive categories. (A serious defect in this taxonomy as far as social movements are concerned is its lack of a time factor.) It will be used when the major determinants of each movement are summarized in Chapters 8 and 17. The methodology is discussed in Appendix A.

RURAL REBELS

Notes

1. This section on colonial penetration and pacification relies heavily on Carl Rosberg and John Nottingham, *The Myth of 'Mau Mau', Nationalism in Kenya*, (Praeger, New York, 1966), pp. 7–16.
2. Kenya's diversified population of 10,942,705 is composed of 42 tribes of varying sizes. The five largest, Kikuyu, 2,201,632; Luo, 1,521,595; Luhya, 1,453,302; Kamba, 1,197,712 and Gusii, 761,679 comprise 64 per cent of the total population (*Kenya Population Census, 1969, Volume 1*).

   The vast semi-desert lands of the north and northeast which occupy three-fifths of Kenya's total land and the southern plains crossed by the Tanzanian border are occupied by nomadic pastoralists, the Hamitic and Kalenjin peoples, who use these arid lands to graze their cattle. The large majority of Kenya's tribes, the Bantu and Nilotic peoples, are agriculturalists who inhabit the smaller but more fertile areas on the coast and in the central and western regions. The Kikuyu and Kamba tribes who together represent one-third of the population dominate the central region. The Kikuyu live to the north of Nairobi, the capital city, on the thickly populated slopes of the Aberdare Range of mountains.

   The other concentrated area of settlement is the basin of the great inland lake, Victoria. This region is populated by various Bantu and Nilotic tribes who together compose another third of the population. The Nilotic Luo live on the eastern shores of the lake and the two large Bantu groups, the Luhya and the Gusii live in the highlands to the north and to the south of the Luo respectively. To the east on a strip of land that parallels the Rift Valley are the Kalenjin of which the Nandi, 261,969 and the Kipsigis, 471,459 are the largest. The Pokot also of this grouping live northeast of the Luhya in the northern part of the Rift Valley Province.

   The many name changes this western area has undergone present the reader with a confusing picture. See Carole DuPre's discussion of the various changes in the boundaries and naming of this area in *The Luo of Kenya: An Annotated Bibliography*, ICR Studies 3 (Institute for Cross-Cultural Research, Washington, D.C., 1968), p. 13.

   Prefixes are attached to distinguish different forms, for example from the stem *Luhya*, *Muluhya* means a person; *Baluhya* or *Abaluhya* means the people; *Luluhya*, the language, and *Buluhya* the country. However, I have used simply *Luhya* to mean a person or the people and so on throughout.
3. These figures are from David B. Barrett, George K. Mambo, Janice McLaughlin and Malcolm J. McVeigh (eds.), *Kenya Churches Handbook*, (Evangel Publishing House, Kisumu, 1973), pp. 184–88.
4. Several articles describe these movements: Nyangweso [Pseud.], 'The Cult of Mumbo in Central and Southern Kavirondo', *The Journal of East African and Uganda Natural History*, X, 38, May–August, 1930; J. D. W. Welime, 'Dini ya Msambwa', a paper read at East African Institute of Social Research (henceforth EAISR) Conference, Makerere University, Kampala, Uganda, January 1967; L. C. Usher-Wilson, 'Bishop's Study of 'Dini ya Misambwa': First Published Account of a Dangerous African Movement', *East Africa and Rhodesia*, 1414 and 1416, November, 1951; J. S. La Fontaine, 'Notes on Ancestor Worship Among the Babukusu and its Difference from Dini ya Msambwa', typescript copy, EAISR Library, Makerere University, Kampala, Uganda; Jan Jacob de Wolf's thesis, 'Religious Innovation and Social Change Among the Bukusu', unpublished Ph.D. thesis, University of London, 1971, discusses the Dini ya Msambwa movement; G. S. Were, 'Dini ya Msambwa: A Reassessment', University of East Africa, Social Science Conference, (henceforth EASSC) December, 1966; and 'Politics, Religion and Nationalism in Western Kenya, 1942–1962: Dini ya Msambwa Revisited', Bethwell A. Ogot (ed.), *Politics and Nationalism in Colonial Kenya*, (East African Publishing House, Nairobi, 1972), pp. 85–104.

5. Millennium in an earlier and narrower sense meant the ushering in of a literal thousand-year reign of Christ on earth. Now, millenarian simply refers to movements which promise the imminent coming of an earthly paradise through a total, cataclysmic transformation accomplished by supernatural agencies, and that is the sense in which it is used here.
6. Neil Smelser, 'Collective Protest and Political Outcomes', unpublished manuscript, p. 2.
7. Eric R. Wolf, *Peasant Wars of the Twentieth Century*, (Harper and Row, New York, 1973), pp. xiv–xv.
8. V. Lanternari, *The Religions of the Oppressed*, (Mentor Books, Toronto, 1963), pp. vi, 19.
9. E. Andersson, *Messianic Popular Movements in the Lower Congo*, (Kegan Paul, London, 1958); G. Balandier, 'Messianismes et Nationalismes en Afrique Noire', *Cahiers Internationaux de Sociologie*, XIV, 1953, pp. 41–65; Balandier, *Sociologie Actuelle de l'Afrique Noire*, (Presses Universitaires de France, Paris, 1955), pp. 417–504; J. van Wing, 'Le Kibangisme vu par un témoin', *Zaire*, XII, 6, 1958, pp. 563–618.
10. Balandier, 'Messianismes et Nationalismes', p. 41.
11. G. Shepperson, 'Ethiopianism and African Nationalism', *Phylon*, XIX, 1, 1958, pp. 9–18; and 'The Politics of African Church Separatist Movements in British Central Africa, 1892–1914', *Africa*, XXIV, 3, July 1954, 233–246; James S. Coleman, *Nigeria: Background to Nationalism*, (University of California Press, Berkeley, 1958), p. 175; F. B. Welbourn, *East African Rebels: A Study of Some Independent Churches*, (SCM Press, London, 1961); L. P. Mair, *New Nations*, (Chicago University Press, Chicago, 1963), p. 181.
12. Peter Worsley, *The Trumpet Shall Sound*, (MacGibbon and Kee, London 1957), pp. xlii–xlviii; E.J. Hobsbawm, *Primitive Rebels: Studies in Archaic Forms of Social Movements*, (W. W. Norton and Co., New York 1959), p. 65.
13. James Mooney, *The Ghost-Dance Religion and the Sioux Outbreak of 1890*, (University of Chicago Press, Chicago, 1965).
14. J. W. Fernandez, 'African Religious Movements: Types and Dynamics', *Journal of Modern African Studies*, II, 4, December, 1964, pp. 531–49.
15. K. Schlosser, *Propheten in Afrika*, (Braunschweig, 1949), p. 401.
16. de Wolf, 'Religious Innovation', p. 34.
17. N. Cohn, *The Pursuit of the Millennium*, (Harper and Row, New York, 1961), pp. 23–4.
18. Hobsbawm, *Primitive Rebels*, p. 79.
19. Andersson, *Messianic Popular Movements*, p. 232.
20. Worsley, *The Trumpet Shall Sound*, pp. xlii, 225.
21. Ralph Linton, 'Nativistic Movements', *American Anthropologist*, 45, 1943, pp. 230–40.
22. F. B. Welbourn and B. A. Ogot, *A Place to Feel at Home*, (Oxford University Press, London, 1966), p. 141.
23. Lewis S. Feuer, *The Conflict of Generations*, (Basic Books, New York, 1968). See pp. 221–31 and in particular, pp. 223–24.
24. H. W. Turner, *African Independent Church: The Life and Faith of the Church of the Lord Aladura*, (Clarendon Press, Oxford, 1967); and 'African Prophet Movements', *Hibbert Journal*, LXI, 242, April, 1963, pp. 112–16.
25. C. G. Baeta, *Prophetism in Ghana*, (SCM Press, London, 1962), p. 6.
26. J. V. Taylor, *Process of Growth in an African Church*, quoted in F. B. Welbourn, *East African Rebels*, p. 9.
27. Bengt G. M. Sundkler, *Bantu Prophets in South Africa*, (Oxford University Press, London, 1961), pp. 111, 126.
28. Shepperson, 'Nyasaland and the Millennium', in Sylvia L. Thrupp (ed.), *Millennial Dreams in Action*, (Mouton & Co., The Hague, 1962), pp. 144–59.

29. Benjamin E. Kipkorir, 'Colonial Response to Crisis—The Kolloa Affray and Colonial Kenya in 1950', *Kenya Past and Present*, II, (1), 1973, pp. 23–35 and 'The Kolloa Affray 1950', *Transafrican Journal of History*, II, (2), 1972. The first and third quotes are from the *Transafrican Journal of History*, p. 119, p. 124, and the second quote from *Kenya Past and Present*, p. 24.

30. District commissioner A. B. Simpson at the inquiry that followed the affray stated that a policeman sent to arrest Pkech, noted for his courage, returned frightened. 'The tribal policeman's eyes were bulging and he said that he had been almost bewitched by the powers of the leader's eyes and he said that the leader pointed at him with a specially weighted stick which seemed to glitter.' (p. 124).

31. Weston La Barre, 'Materials for a History of Studies of Crisis Cults: A Bibliographic Essay', *Current Anthropology*, XII, 1, February, 1971, p. 20.

32. Sundkler, *Bantu Prophets*, p. 295–97.

33. John Iliffe, 'Organization of the Maji Maji Rebellion', EASSC Paper, Dar es Salaam, December 1966.

34. David B. Barrett, *Schism and Renewal in Africa*, (Oxford University Press, Nairobi, 1968).

35. Sir Philip Mitchell, *African Afterthoughts*, (Hutchinson, London, 1954), pp. 242–48, 254–55, 260–68. The words in quotation marks were all used in Sir Philip's account of African cults.

36. J. C. Carothers, *The Psychology of Mau Mau*, (Government Printer, Nairobi, 1955), pp. 12–15.

37. See below, pp. 65–71.

38. B. A. Ogot, 'British Administration in the Central Nyanza District, 1900–1960', *Journal of African History*, IV, 1963, pp. 249–73.

39. John Lonsdale, 'A Political History of Nyanza 1883–1945', unpublished Ph.D. thesis, Cambridge University, pp. 190, 363.

40. M. P. K. Sorrenson, *Origins of European Settlement in Kenya*, (Oxford University Press, Nairobi, 1968), p. 280.

41. C. T. Stoneham, *Mau Mau*, (Museum Printer, London, 1953), p. 114. See also the *East African Standard*, articles entitled, Police Fire on 1,000 'Religion of Good Spirits' After Threat to Burn Mission, 12 February 1948 and Police Held Fire as Long as They Dared, 8 March 1948, and *The Times, London*, Africans Clash with Police, 12 February 1948, for additional statements demonstrating the negative stereotype.

42. Elspeth Huxley, 'The Rise of the African Zealot', *Corona*, II, 5, May 1950, pp. 163–65.

43. Kipkorir, 'The Kolloa Affray', pp. 125–26. I am not implying that all dimensions of this stereotype are present in the writings of any one person, but only elements of it.

44. For further statements by the agents of social control see pp. 65–71 and pp. 254–60.

45. The emphasis upon irrational factors in the field of collective behaviour is consistent with a deeply entrenched bias. Early theorists interpreted collective outbursts in terms of unconscious forces. See Gustave Le Bon, *The Crowd*, (The Viking Press, New York, 1960) and Sigmund Freud, *Group Psychology and the Analysis of the Ego*, (Bantam, New York, 1960). These early assumptions about the nature of crowds and other manifestations of collective behaviour have increasingly come under attack. See George Rudé, *The Crowd in History 1730–1848*, (Wiley, New York, 1964). For other critiques of the traditional social-psychological approach Neil Smelser, *Theory of Collective Behavior*, (The Free Press, New York, 1962), pp. 1–22; Ralph H. Turner and Lewis M. Killian, *Collective Behavior*, (Englewood Cliffs, Prentice-Hall, 1957), pp. 3–19.

The Cult of Mumbo

PART II

The Cult of Mumbo

Chapter 2

BACKGROUND OF THE MOVEMENT

RESISTANCE to the British in southwestern Kenya was first
demonstrated in 1905 and 1908 when the Gusii tribe staged
two uprisings. Only after disastrous confrontations with modern
weapons did the indigenous people change to more passive forms
of resistance. Prominent among these were millennial movements.
They formed a loose network of small, locally organized groups
with little or no coordination except for shared anti-European
sentiments and a belief in a millennium when their prophets would
return and banish the foreigners forever.

Of special significance was the earliest on record in the area, the
cult of Mumbo, which had its beginnings during the first decade
of British administration. Mumboism prophesied the early departure
of the Europeans and the coming of a Golden Age during which the
elect would be blessed with abundance and the wicked overthrown.
In its symbolism, Mumboism was nativistic. It rejected European
customs and advocated a return to the old prophets and the old
ways. Its message stressed the lost glory and dignity of the tribe
that were to be re-established in the millennium. From another and
more revealing perspective, Mumboism was both revolutionary and
utopian, rejecting the colonial regime, tribal authority and mores,
and introducing new values and leadership. Although it engaged
in sporadic protest, the cult was concerned primarily with prophecies,
dreams, ritual and ecstatic behaviour.

Separated from the main arteries of communication and cut off
from contact with the British by the absence of settlers, South
Nyanza was an area whose inhabitants continued their traditional
ways longer than those in the more accessible regions. They were
slower than either the Luo in Central Nyanza or the Kikuyu in
Central Province to articulate political opinion. By 1938, for example,

23

there were still no political associations. Even in 1949, Philip Mayer noted that 'outside the immediate neighbourhood of the township and of the two main mission stations, Christians are few and literacy is rare among adults.'[1]

It was into this isolated area, in the early 1900s, that the British attempted to extend their control. The reaction was a protest which found its centre in the Kisii Highlands also known as Gusiiland. Located some fifty miles south of the equator and some thirty miles inland from Lake Victoria, the Highlands were bordered on the south by Tanzania, on the east by the District of Kericho, the tea growing country of the Kipsigis tribe, on the southeast by the vast plain of the nomadic cattle people, the Maasai, and on the west and north by the Nilotic Luo. Softly rolling hills, a pleasantly cool climate and fertile, rain-drenched valleys make the Highlands a delightful green oasis amid the semi-arid lowlands of the west and the hot savannahs of the east.

The Gusii, a pastoral-agricultural people numbering in 1969 more than seven hundred thousand belong to the Bantu-speaking language group.[2] Composed of seven autonomous sub-tribes: Kitutu (Getutu), Mugirango (Mogirango), Wanjare (Nchari), Bassi, Nyaribari, Majoge, and Mukseru (Mogusero) that recognized Mogusii as their ancestor, they formerly banded together to wage war on the Kipsigis.[3] Otherwise, each sub-tribe went its own way fighting over cattle, women and territory. The Kitutu were, in the period immediately prior to the establishment of British rule, by far the strongest of the sub-tribes, and were much involved in raiding nearby peoples, especially the Luo and Kipsigis, for cattle.

Three factors, in particular, contributed to the region's gradual awareness of the outside world, undermined the basis of traditional life, and set the stage for the development of millennial movements: (1) British penetration and political reorganization, (2) the missions and (3) the Carrier Corps and forced labour.

Punitive Expeditions and Political Reorganization

British administration was not established in South Nyanza until 1908. Their first efforts sparked local rebellions which led to the 1905 and 1908 punitive expeditions.[4] These dealt harshly and effectively with the rebels, and both ended in the Gusii's total defeat.

Up to 1905, the British had had little contact with the Gusii.

It appears that the Luo chief's clan of Karachuonyo location was on good terms with the administrators.[5] Its members willingly paid their hut tax and because they were cooperative, the administration established its first post on their territory at Karungu. The missionaries, likewise, were welcomed and they, in turn, opened a mission station nearby. (Here is an early example of the type of alliances made between clans, missions, and the administration that were to characterize early British rule and to play a large part in determining political alignments.) Reportedly, a major motive behind the 1905 expedition was to gain restitution for stolen Luo cattle and to punish the raiders, the Kitutu, thus demonstrating that tribes under British protection were indeed protected.

When a message arrived in 1905 of a Kisii revolt (Europeans at that time referred to the Gusii as 'Kisii'), a detachment of a hundred African police under W. Robert Foran and a company of the Third King's African Rifles (KAR) under Captain Jenkins were immediately despatched to quell it. Foran described the encounter:

> Then came word that the Kisii were in open revolt. Almost immediately a small punitive force was sanctioned, though reluctantly by Sir Charles Eliot. [The Commissioner of Kenya from 1901 to 1904.] It was stated that he had declared that, if every officer on appointment to the KAR was given the East African General Service Medal with several bars on landing at Mombasa, there would be no occasion found for military expeditions against local tribes. . . .
>
> The tribesmen did not understand the power of modern weapons and had yet to encounter the white man in combat. They boldly attacked the small force of 200 askaris [local policemen] with masses of spearsmen. Captain Jenkins formed [a] square and gave battle. He let the attack have a good dose of lead, but this did not halt their more determined advance. They ran straight up to the rigid walls of fixed bayonets. Their losses were great. The machine-gun was kept in action so long during this sharp engagement that it became almost red-hot to the touch. Before the Kisii warriors were repulsed, they left several hundred dead and wounded spearsmen heaped up outside the square of bayonets. This was not so much a battle as a massacre, but wholly unavoidable under the circumstances. It was an urgent case of decimating that determined attack or else being completely wiped out by the Kisii warriors.[6]

Foran goes on to report that British casualties were negligible and that on the following day the leading chiefs surrendered unconditionally and the tribe was fined heavily in cattle and sheep.

Early in 1907 the site for the district headquarters was chosen and Northcote spent the rest of the year overseeing the construction of the buildings and laying the foundation for administration among the Gusii. Chiefs and headmen had to be selected and the Gusii encouraged to bring civil and criminal cases before the administration.[7] In this period, a series of incidents occurred that increased the antagonism towards the Europeans of certain Kitutu clans, later responsible for the 1908 uprising.

Northcote had great difficulty in making contact with prominent individuals in several parts of Kitutu. Many remained hostile to, and refused to accept, the idea of British administration. Nor did it help matters that he felt compelled on several occasions to take provisions from the local people by force. Considerable food was needed to feed the numerous porters and policemen engaged in constructing the headquarters. Grain, goats and sheep were taken on one occasion, and later paid for, but this seizing of personal property could not have endeared him to the local populace nor decreased their apprehension about the British presence.

The Kitutu continued their cattle raiding and Northcote's intercession on behalf of the Luo further exacerbated relations between them. In June 1907 he visited Kitutu elders demanding that they turn over to him cattle allegedly stolen from the Luo and threatened them with reprisals if they didn't. They refused. Nor would they pay the fine he levied on them for the killing of two Luo men. Cattle rustling continued. In July of that year, Northcote dispatched thirty-five police to recover stolen cattle in a dawn attack which surprised the inhabitants and netted the administration one thousand head of cattle. Later when the police were attacked, they killed four Kitutu before returning to Kisii station. Eventually Northcote kept only sixty-five cows, returning the rest to the Kitutu.

The administration started to collect the hut tax in December 1907. Because the tax had to be paid in money, the Gusii were forced to sell their livestock in order to get rupees needed for the tax. Otenyo, a Gusii, stole some money from one of the Swahili cattle traders who had moved into the area. The theft was reported to Northcote who decided to investigate the matter. Northcote went to Otenyo's home and, when he didn't appear, took two of his cows. Muraa, a renowned prophetess, who, ever since the British had shown any designs on Gusiiland, had agitated against them, was furious. She ridiculed the young men for permitting Northcote to take the cows, saying they were like women, afraid of one white man. At her urging, Otenyo picked up his spear and went off. He ambushed Northcote, spearing him in the back as he was passing on his horse. This incident sparked off the 1908 uprising.[8]

Foran, head of one of the relief patrols sent to Northcote's aid, provides this account of part of the revolt:

> [In Gusiiland] every village was deserted and the warriors massed on the hilltops; but they made no attempt to interfere with our advance. They had not forgotten their experience when attacking the 1904 [correctly 1905] column under Captain Jenkins. The closer we got to the Boma [Swahili for a compound, in this case it refers to the administrative headquarters] the denser became the masses of Kisii spearmen; yet they still hesitated to dispute our progress. . . .
>
> [Later, after the Gusii had asked to surrender] we were astonished to see heavy clouds of smoke arising from the neighbourhood on the road to Kendu, followed by the sputtering of machine-guns and rifle-fire . . . [Foran had sent a message to the commander of the Kisii Expeditionary Force en route to Kisii informing him of the tribe's willingness to surrender and that they were now peacefully returning with their livestock to their villages. To his amazement this information was ignored. 'Another medal cheaply won', remarked a British officer on learning that the Expeditionary Force was going to fight anyway.] We made our way towards the headquarters of the Kisii Expeditionary Force to report ourselves and receive instructions. The African Rifles were putting in some strenuous work—burning villages, devastating standing crops, capturing live-stock and hunting down the bolting warriors. It was tough luck on the latter, for I have no doubt they were under the impression that the tribal surrender had been accepted and no war would take place . . . .[9]

W. Lloyd-Jones, another participant in the 1908 expedition, recalls the clash:

> The longed-for counter-attacks were never made, though everything was ready to give the enemy a warm reception . . . .
>
> However, the operations continued, and more cattle were brought in and more homes and gardens destroyed . . . A deputation of Kisii to the camp was met by machine-gun fire. They retired hurriedly, and sent a message to say that they did not like it and to request that it should not occur again.
>
> The rains now broke, and life in the zaribas [stock enclosures] with several thousand head of stock became intolerable. To make matters worse, a case of beer, the property of a senior official, had been broken. Woe to the porter who was responsible for it! The Kisii had by now disappeared altogether, and taken refuge with their hereditary enemies, the Kavirondo so in the absence of the enemy peace was declared. A dinner party was held and flattering speeches exchanged, but the staff was

rather depressed by the receipt of a telegram from the Secretary of State, deploring the slaughter and ordering the operations to be suspended forthwith. Thus ended the "war" in Kisii.

No decorations were awarded for these operations, thereby causing much heart-burning and disgust amongst the fire-eating staff; but the men who had speared the District Commissioner were collected, and another blow had been struck for the honour of the British Empire and freedom of trade under the Union Jack.[10]

A series of telegrams conveyed the results of the expedition to the Colonial Office in London, where, for some time, there had been concern over the handling of punitive expeditions which, in the absence of official policy, had been left pretty much to the man on the spot.[11] On 1 February 1908, a telegram received by the Colonial Office read, 'Result of operations in Kisii to 28 January cattle captured 5,636 sheep and goats 3,281. 100 Kisii killed. No further casualties on our side. Operations suspended as several clans wish for peace. Kisii reported generally demoralized.' Two days later another telegram reported the number of Gusii dead had risen to a hundred and sixty and that the commanding officer soon hoped to meet the main body of Gusii. At that point Winston Churchill, then Colonial Under-Secretary, intervened:

> I do not like the tone of these reports. No doubt the clans should be punished; but 160 have now been killed outright—without any further casualties, and the main body had not yet been encountered . . . . It looks like butchery and if the H. of C. [House of Commons] gets hold of it, all our plans in E.A.P. [East Africa Protectorate] will be under a cloud. Surely it cannot be necessary to go on killing these defenceless people on such an enormous scale.

Churchill then sent the following telegram to Sir Donald Sadler, the Governor of Kenya:

> Much regret to observe large numbers of Kisii killed in recent operations. Rely on you to confine bloodshed within narrowest limits consistent with safety of force and restoration of order. Impress immediately upon O.C. [Officer Commanding] that every effort should be made to induce the enemy to submit peacefully after the most severe lesson they have received and mercy should be extended to all personally concerned in original outbreak. I shall expect a full report upon any causes of discontent which may have provoked rising.

Churchill's suspicions turned out to be correct. A letter from Northcote to his father two days after his spearing stated that the incident had been exaggerated—it was only the Kitutu who had attacked—and that far too severe repressive measures had been used.[12] Lieutenant Colonel MacKay, the commanding officer, later sent in a report that confirmed what the previous telegrams had indicated:

> From the date I commenced active operations to the end of the expedition on 6 February 1908, the enemy suffered heavily. They lost over 7000 cattle captured and 5000 sheep and goats were taken, many living and cattle Bomas were burnt while over 200 casualties were inflicted on the enemy, who were completely demoralized fleeing with their families into the Kavirondo country for personal safety.

At the termination of the expedition, a large *baraza* (a public gathering, often called to make official announcements) was held on 12 February 1908, attended by most of the leading Kitutu elders. At this *baraza* it was announced that cattle taken in the military operations would be returned to the Kitutu if they worked for the administration building roads. (In fact a large number of cattle were returned in payment of road work.)[13]

This controversial episode was not allowed to drop with Churchill's admonitions but was carried on by R. Popham-Lobb, an official who had for some time been incensed over the tactics employed by punitive expeditions. He despatched a long report to the Colonial Office a year after the event, in which he urged the close scrutiny and supervision of military operations. He attacked the colonial administration and used the 1908 expedition as a prime example of needless slaughter. 'The whole episode betrays a degree of administrative ineptitude and a vicious misuse of force on the part of the Administration which deserves the greatest censure, and a Governor so lacking in a sense of his responsibilities with regard to native races under his care that he is able to see in the result of such methods only a "complete success" . . . '

Despite Popham-Lobb's attack, no investigation was undertaken and no punishments meted out. This was due in part to the lateness of his report, for it was considered unwise after a year to reopen the whole question. Instead, a set of Lugard's 'Instructions for the Control of Expeditions' was sent to the East African authorities for their consideration.

From the above documents, the following conclusions can be drawn.

1) The Gusii suffered the humiliation and demoralization of

complete defeat. Pacification showed the futility of armed resistance and closed off the possibilities of revolt and direct challenges to the colonial power.

2) These military expeditions must have proved a shattering experience for the Gusii. They furnished a rude awakening to the realities of foreign conquest and left a legacy of bitterness that remained for many years. Not only did they lay the basis for British rule in South Nyanza but they gave Africans their first contact with Europeans which must have made the Europeans appear to be objects both of fear and hate.

3) Since the Gusii had indicated a desire to surrender, the very need for the 1908 expedition can be seriously questioned. Northcote's spearing appears to have been used as an excuse to perpetuate widespread destruction against a whole community, regardless of its participation in the disturbance.[13] Evidence suggests that the military seized upon a minor incident to establish the insurgents' powerlessness, thereby clearly demonstrating who was master.

4) The location of the revolts indicated the likely involvement of the Bogonko clan. Kisii station was situated in Kitutu location, an area occupied by the Kitutu sub-tribe. Ainsworth's reports singled out the Kitutu as the protagonists. 'In a few words, it is evident that the Kitutu did not want a station near them. They resented the white man intruding amongst them.'[14] Foran and Maxon likewise refer to the Kitutu as the insurgents. In the Kitutu sub-tribe, the Bogonko was the largest clan, comprising more than half of the location's population.[15] Since it was also the most powerful, its warriors probably led the attack. Subsequently this area became the centre of Mumbo activity. (The various links between the uprising and the possible reasons for Bogonko support of Mumboism will be traced in a later section.)

With the advent of the British, Gusii society was politically re-organized. Villages where the young warriors had lived while making forays upon a neighbouring tribe's cattle were abolished; allegiance to clan and tribe no longer entailed military duties; territory was divided on the basis of tribal units with the result that the seven Gusii sub-tribes were allocated to seven sub-units known as locations—an administrative unit about the size of a county—and central authorities were introduced into a traditionally chiefless society. In making these changes, the British utilized the indigenous structure, placing chiefs and headmen responsible to them in charge of areas roughly coinciding with sub-tribal units. Usually the chiefs were chosen from traditionally powerful clans whose right to rule was accepted by the people. Sometimes, however, the British would appoint an individual who had secured their favour but who was not highly regarded by Africans. At other times, rival contenders from within the same clan or between two powerful clans contested the chieftainship.[16] Thus a basis for inter- and intra-clan rivalry was established.[17]

Under the new system, the chiefs had extensive powers and considerable autonomy in the management of their locations. Each reported directly to the district officer and the district commissioner. During Mumboism's most active period, the chiefs also held judicial powers until the African Tribunal Courts were established in the 1930s. Even after that they informally exercised judicial powers providing not only advice and warnings but meting out punishments.[18]

Most chiefs were wealthy before taking office, but if they weren't they soon rectified this condition. While a chief did not have the actual right to appoint personnel, he was in a key position to influence choices. Nor did chiefs fail to exercise this influence as can be seen by the many officials who were their kinsmen. This concentration of power meant that the chiefs could act autocratically and few would dare to challenge them.[19] A chieftainship was viewed as a political plum, a position that could be used to enhance an individual's as well as a clan's power, prestige, and wealth. Thus the office of chief was much sought after, and its loss could well foster envy and bitterness on the part of the unsuccessful.

The Missions
The missionaries' arrival followed the extension of administration into the hinterland. The first missionaries, the Seventh-day Adventists, opened a mission station at Genia in 1907. The second, the Mill Hill Fathers, founded a mission near Kisii in 1911. Besides introducing Christian teachings which challenged tribal beliefs, the missionaries opened schools and hospitals. Their educational efforts produced a group of young men who became increasingly divorced from indigenous social control. Year after year, the annual reports noted the growing rift between the students and tribal authority. The 1924 Report complained that the mission adherents 'are too much inclined to consider themselves as a class apart

and consequently entitled to different treatment from other natives and to a certain extent to be outside the authority of ordinary native law and custom.' In 1926, S. O. V. Hodge, the acting district commissioner, wrote that the elders 'complain of the lack of respect shown by mission boys to their elders and betters. This is repudiated by the boys themselves who in their turn complain of the drunkenness, laziness, and unprogressiveness of the older generation.' Many new converts believed that in becoming Christian they had rid themselves of communal obligations and tribal control.

No doubt the rivalry between the Adventists and the Fathers was still another factor that disturbed Africans since their differences were often more obvious than their common ground of Christianity, and, although open disagreement among the missionaries themselves rarely came to the fore, disagreement among their converts was often violent.[20]

The Carrier Corps and Forced Labour

The recruitment of men to the Carrier Corps was another event that aroused the inhabitants of Nyanza to events in the larger world and gave thousands of men new experiences and ideas. With the progress of World War I, it became necessary to recruit porters to transport equipment for the German East African campaign.[21] Carrying heavy loads through the tsetse- and mosquito-ridden swamps and over sun-baked savannah in humid tropical weather was one of the toughest, most gruelling assignments of the war. It was estimated that of the one hundred and sixty-two thousand Africans recruited for military labour, twenty-four thousand died—although other estimates of the dead were much higher and the government's conservative figure was strongly criticized.[22]

The experience of the Carrier Corps, which was not forgotten, had a profound effect upon the Africans' attitudes toward employment. A district annual report, states, for example, that in 1914 many young men had been tricked into coming to the district station to 'cut grass', whereupon they had been seized and sent off to the Corps.[23] When rumours spread in 1938 of an impending second world war, the Gusii displayed anxiety and hardly anyone turned up for the annual administration sponsored sports meet. Even after a lapse of twenty-four years no Gusii intended to be so deceived again!

It was also no secret that the administration, under pressure from the settlers who needed farm labourers, forced young men to leave the district and seek work in other areas. Although leading colonial officials attempted to stop this practice, individual district commissioners appeared to have had considerable leeway in the administering of their areas.[24] In 1915 the district commissioner of South Nyanza wrote, 'Lately in order to fulfil labour requisitions, force has had to be applied, i.e. the young men have been rounded up during the night.' Nor was this an isolated incident.[25]

Recruiting was also done through labour agents, which again played into the hands of the chiefs and members of powerful clans. Needless to say, the men recruited tended to come from the poorer, weaker clans that had no means of resisting.

Notes

1. Philip Mayer, *The Lineage Principle in Gusii Society*, (Oxford University Press, London, 1949), p. 4.
2. *The Kenya Population Census 1969.* According to the 1948 Census they numbered 237,000.
3. The spellings in parentheses are tribal names commonly used today.
4. W. Robert Foran, *A Cuckoo in Kenya*, (Hutchinson, London, 1936); F. H. Goldsmith, *John Ainsworth, Pioneer Kenya Administrator 1864–1946*, (Macmillan, London, 1955); G. H. Mungeam, *British Rule in Kenya 1895–1912*, (Clarendon Press, Oxford, 1966); *Nyanza Province Annual Report 1909*, written by John Ainsworth; W. Lloyd-Jones, *K.A.R., Being an Unofficial Account of the Origins and Activities of the King's African Rifles*, (Arrowsmith, London, 1926); Robert A. and Barbara B. LeVine, 'Nyansongo: A Gusii Community in Kenya', *Six Cultures*, Beatrice B. Whiting (ed.), (Wiley, New York, 1963); Philip Mayer, *Gusii Bridewealth, Law and Custom*, (Oxford University Press, London, 1950).

   There is some confusion over the dates of these expeditions. The LeVines (p. 71) and Mayer (p. 2) refer to a 1907 punitive expedition. However, Ainsworth, Foran and Lloyd-Jones who participated in it, and the carefully documented study of Mungeam, together with *The London Times Index* confirm beyond doubt the date of the revolt as 1908.

   There is also some confusion about a third revolt. I have found no actual description of the revolt. Mayer refers to a 1916 expedition, 'Two punitive expeditions (1907 and 1916) served to break resistance, and administration since then has gone on smoothly enough with a notable expansion of services since the beginning of the 1930's.' LeVine, on the other hand, speaks of a 1914 expedition ('An Attempt to Change the Gusii Initiation Cycle', *Man*, LIX, [1959], p. 120). Neither LeVine nor Mayer document their sources. The district records of South Kavirondo and the district and provincial annual reports for that period do not mention a punitive expedition. I also checked *The London Times Index* and found no reference to either a 1914 or 1916 expedition. The LeVines' reference may pertain to the time the Mumboites mistook the British evacuation of Kisii upon the advance of the Germans for the millennium whereupon they ransacked the government offices and missions.

5. John Lonsdale, 'A Political History of Nyanza 1883–1945', unpublished Ph.D. thesis, University of Cambridge, 1964, p. 176; R. M. Maxon, 'The Gusii Uprising of 1908', EASSC Paper, Nairobi, December 1969, p. 2.

6. Foran, *A Cuckoo*, pp. 178–79.

7. This section on Northcote setting up the administration in South Nyanza is drawn from Maxon, The Gusii Uprising of 1908.

8. This account is taken from Maxon. Both Foran, *A Cuckoo* and Lloyd-Jones, *K.A.R.* p. 108, claim that Muraa's preaching incited the Gusii to revolt.

9. Foran, *A Cuckoo*, p. 338.

10. Lloyd-Jones, *K.A.R.*, pp. 111–12.

11. The following account of the Colonial Office's reaction has been taken from Mungeam, *British Rule*, pp. 171–80. For the individual documentary references, see Mungeam.

12. Northcote was deeply upset about the indiscriminate use of force, not only against the Kitutu but against tribes that had in no way opposed the administration. 'It would take too long,' he wrote his father, 'to describe the absolute idiocy, obstinacy and want of knowledge of military operations in this country which they showed.' KNA (Kenya National Archives): DC/KSI/4/2. Diary of G. A. S. Northcote, 12 February 1908. Quoted in Maxon, 'The Gusii Uprising 1908', p. 7.

13. Maxon, 'The Gusii Uprising 1908', p. 8.

14. Mungeam, *British Rule*, pp. 175.

15. See below, pp. 58–60.

16. Lonsdale, A Political History, p. 27.

17. See Carl Rosberg and John Nottingham, *The Myth of 'Mau Mau'* pp. 80–4, for a similar explanation.

18. Robert A. LeVine, 'The Internalization of Political Values in Stateless Societies', *Human Organization*, XIX, 2, 1960, p. 52.

19. For a fuller discussion of the role of chief in Kisii District see LeVine, 'Nyansongo', pp. 89–94.

20. *South Kavirondo District Annual Reports*, *1913*, *1921*, *1922*, *1924*, *1926* and *1928*.

21. Lord Bertram Francis Cranworth, *Kenya Chronicles*, (Macmillan, London, 1939) pp. 73–4.

22. Goldsmith, *Ainsworth Pioneer*, p. 100, simply mentions that other figures are higher but he does not provide them. Norman Leys, a medical officer in Kenya, wrote in 1924 that the British recruited in all 350,000 porters for the German East Africa campaign, of whom 150,000 were from Kenya. The officially recorded deaths totalled 46,618. 1,743 were killed and 44,875 died of disease. The relatives of 40,645 dead men went untraced. Norman Leys, *Kenya*, (Hogarth Press, London, 1924), p. 287. See also Rosberg and Nottingham, *The Myth of 'Mau Mau'*, pp. 30–1.

23. *South Kavirondo District Annual Report 1938*.

24. For an example of intervention by higher officialdom, see below pp. 66–8.

25. *South Kavirondo District Annual Reports 1915* and *1920*.

Chapter 3

ORIGINS AND DEVELOPMENT

T HE exact date of Mumbo's origins as a movement among the Gusii is hard to pinpoint. There is a legend about Onyango Dunde, a Luo of Alego location (which lies on the eastern shore of Lake Victoria), who in 1913 was accosted by a gigantic snake one evening when sitting in his hut. The snake was so big that when it stood on its end in the lake, its head reached into the clouds. (One version has the snake coming from the clouds.) The snake swallowed Onyango and then regurgitated him, unhurt but shaken. This probably was the snake's way of obtaining Onyango's attention, because immediately it began to speak:

> I am the God Mumbo whose two homes are in the Sun and the Lake. I have chosen you to be my mouthpiece. Go out and tell all Africans—and more especially the people of Alego—that from henceforth I am their God. Those whom I personally choose and also those who acknowledge me, will live forever in plenty. Their crops will grow of themselves and there will be no more need to work. I will cause cattle, sheep, and goats to come up out of the lake in great numbers to those who believe in me, but all unbelievers and their families and their cattle will die out. The Christian religion is rotten [*mbovu*] and so is its practice of making its believers wear clothes. My followers must let their hair grow—never cutting it. Their clothes shall be the skins of goats and cattle and they must never wash. All Europeans are your enemies, but the time is shortly coming when they will all disappear from our country. Daily sacrifice—preferably the males—of cattle, sheep, goats, and fowls shall be made to me. More especially do I prefer black bulls. Have no fear of sacrificing those and I will cause unlimited black cattle to come to you from the Lango, Maasai, Nandi and Kipsigis. Lastly my followers must immediately slaughter all their cattle, sheep and goats. When this is done, I will provide them with as many more as they want from the lake.

Having spoken the snake disappeared into the lake and Onyango set out to spread Mumbo's words.[1] He soon gathered a fairly large following.

Although the cult apparently originated among the Luo, it appeared to get its start and direction among the Gusii from Mosi, a headman from Kabongo location. Mosi claimed that Onyango introduced him to Mumboism. He was converted sometime before World War I when he had a vision of a great snake. In his vision God took him to heaven and showed him all kinds of food which would be showered upon the faithful at the advent of the snake. He returned to earth in a shower of blood and at first people were afraid of him. Mosi claimed divine instructions were revealed to him through visions.[2]

From Alego location in Central Nyanza, Mumboism spread quickly to neighbouring locations and thence to South Nyanza, carried by some mission trained men in the absence of the Adventist missionaries. (The Adventist mission, though staffed mainly by Canadians, had its headquarters in Hamburg, Germany. During World War I, the missionaries were all interned.) Mumboism's millennial message fitted in well with such Adventist teachings as 'Watch and pray, for the end of the world is at hand.' The district commissioner of Kisii spoke of a new religion, 'Mumbo', making its appearance in his district in 1914 −15.[3]

The sect's existence became patently evident on 19 September 1914, when the Germans invaded Kisii from what was then German East Africa and the British vacated the town in order to mobilize resistance and return. Believing Mumbo's prophecy that the British would soon depart, the local inhabitants mistook their temporary exodus for the millennium and looted the town and the neighbouring missions. They ransacked government buildings and houses, the missions of Nyaribari, Nyanchwa, and Asumbi, and the trading centres of Riana and Rangwe. District officer P. M. Gordon recorded the event:

> Thus it was that the Africans who gathered on the surrounding hills to watch the battle of Kisii, and as evening fell, saw the rival forces draw off to the north and south, felt assured that the prophecy was fulfilled. The Europeans had gone forever! . . . Their works, their offices, and Missions must be cast out. In this spirit of frenzy the empty Missions and trading centres, and offices were plundered, sacked and burned. The sight of the African Rifles marching back in good order the following morning must have been a severe shock.[4]

Even the heavy fine of three thousand head of cattle levied by the administration and the dispatch of many Gusii to work outside the location did not kill the movement. In the years 1915 to 1920 it spread rapidly.

In 1920 another group, closely resembling Mumbo, was reported. It had been started by an old woman, Bonairiri of Kitutu location, and its adherents believed in the return of the prophet Zakawa. Zakawa was a great Gusii medicine man and prophet who, when the Uganda Railway was begun, had collected the Gusii, gone to the site of the present district headquarters, and prophesied where the police lines, the hospital, the office, and the district commissioner's house would be built. He had prophesied that over the course of years the young men would be disarmed and proved a a greater source of revenue to their parents than the girls (who brought bridewealth), because they would receive wages for their work. He also predicted the departure of the Europeans. When most of his prophecies came true, Zakawa's reputation as a seer was established. Whether he had actually uttered these prophecies is immaterial, since everyone believed that he had.[5] Later his influence was enhanced by a belief that he was still alive. Apparently he had died during a great beer-drink around 1902 but because he had not had a regular funeral, it was thought that he had not truly died and would return.

At the outset, Bonairiri sought permission from the chief to start a school where she could instruct her followers. The chief took her to the district commissioner who refused her request. In mid-October 1920, the chief reported that Bonairiri had collected a few people to whom she was preaching Mumboism. The administration dispersed her school.

With the addition of Zakawaism, the movement was strengthened. In December 1920 district commissioner H. E. Welby reported that all the people of Kitutu location were attending Bonairiri's school and that most, especially the old men, believed in Zakawa's return.[6] Two days before the predicted reappearance of Zakawa and the departure of the white man, the district commissioner, worried about Mumboism's rapid growth and the restlessness that it was causing, disbanded Bonairiri's school and rounded up the leaders. Bonairiri was found insane and confined to a mental institution. Her husband, Owura, whom Welby described as 'chiefly responsible for the ready adoption of the dangerous part of the teaching', her son, Marita, said to be 'the most active agent in spreading the dangerous part of his mother's and father's teachings', and Ongeri, the son of Muraa, the prophetess responsible for the spearing of Northcote, together with another woman, were all deported to Lamu in 1921, an isolated island just off the coast of Kenya, some five hundred miles away.

Repression, however, did not mean the end of the movement. During the 1920s there were outbreaks of Mumboism in Karachuonyo, Kasipul, and Kochia locations of South Nyanza. In 1927, the district commissioner of Kisii wrote that the natives of Majoge location were resurrecting Mumboism and that it was spreading rapidly to Bassi and Nyaribari locations. (These locations form the northeastern section of South Nyanza and border on one another.) The administration made the leaders move their huts into Kisii village where they could be watched. In 1931, the Local Native Council passed a resolution forbidding the practice of Mumboism.

The district commissioner expressed the fear that should there be a serious famine or some other calamity the cult would recruit many followers and trouble would ensue. And as predicted, it was in the early 1930s during a serious economic depression brought on by drought, famine, and an invasion of locusts, that the last widespread resurgence occurred and spread into all areas of South Nyanza. The climax was reached in November 1933 at the District Sports Meet when twenty armed young Mumboites defied an order of the senior Gusii chief to disperse. The nine leaders were promptly arrested and after a judicial inquiry deported to Kipani, another isolated settlement on the Kenyan coast. Within a few months, little was heard of Mumboism.

The movement did not die out completely, however. There was evidence of its activity in 1938 and 1947. Finally, in 1954 during the Mau Mau emergency, it was again proscribed.[7] In 1963 Ogot estimated that there were still about five hundred practising Mumboites.[8] My own investigation in June 1966 suggested that the cult was extinct. Local people could recall its existence but none knew of any recent activities. When asked whether any members were still alive, several mentioned Marita, Bonairiri's son, but no other name was given.[9] Ex-chief Musa Nyandusi wrote in January 1967, 'Marita Ogwora is the only survivor who is alive, others were old and died. Since they were arrested by the British Government, they never practised their cult.'[10] It is difficult to say whether repression actually brought an end to the movement or whether it died out simply because of the attrition of older members and its failure to attract new and younger members.

The centre of Mumboism was in the District of Kisii in the locations of Kitutu, North Mugirango, Nyaribari, Bassi, Majoge, and Wanjare. The neighbouring locations of Gem, Kasipul, Kara-chuonyo, Kochia, and Kaniamwa were also affected. It even recruited members as far away as the Luo location of Gwassi on the shores of Lake Victoria.

Two observations can be made about Mumboism's pattern of development. First, its growth coincided with years of agricultural depression. Its greatest activity occurred during the early 1920s and the early 1930s, both periods of serious hardship when people pressed by drought and famine may have sought supernatural help in controlling the elements.[11] The seeking of supernatural aid in times of hardship or when one feels misfortune is imminent fits in well with Gusii religion, described not as an object of daily attention but rather 'a set of beliefs and practices which spring into action during an emergency when supernatural punishment is feared' and in periods of stress 'when the desire to try anything that might help is very strong.'[12]

Second, the movement developed spasmodically. There were periods when membership expanded greatly, churches were built, schools opened, and feasts held. These florescences sparked government concern and it would respond with repression, causing Mumbo to lie dormant for some time only to blossom forth in a nearby area with another leader.

Little is known about the actual organization of local groups. Sometimes the Mumboites built their meeting places on hilltops, at other times they met in their home compounds in a hut set aside for this purpose. The following describes such a meeting place:

> The meeting place of the cult consisted of a beautifully swept enclosure adjoining the High Priest's Boma and capable of seating some two hundred people. From the next boma to that of the High Priest ran a path, four feet wide and trenched at the sides. . . . The enclosure was surrounded by a well-built dry stone wall. In the centre was a little semi-open hut about six feet in diameter, finished with white mud . . . There was no door, it appeared symmetrical all round.[13]

The members were divided into two orders. The first order, the priests, were older, established men, usually the head of a *boma*, who were called—by being possessed—in a way similar to Onyango, the founder. It was believed that the spirit of Mumbo wandered the land until it found a suitable person to enter. Supposedly invested with supernatural powers that enabled them to cure all kinds of illnesses and even to resurrect the dead, such people were local leaders. The second order consisted of the priests' dependents and any others who wished to join.[14] Members were distinguished on the basis of their tasks, be it evangelist, food provider, teacher, prophet, or any other of various ritual specialists.[15]

Notes

1. 'The Cult of Mumbo in Central and South Kavirondo', by Nyangweso in *The Journal of the East Africa and Uganda Natural History Society*, XXXVIII, XXXIX, May, August 1930, pp. 13–14. 'Nyangweso' must have been a British administrator since he had access to administrative files. He might have been district commissioner S.O.V. Hodge who was the district commissioner of South Nyanza at that time.
2. KNA: PC/NZA4/5/7, Intelligence Reports of the provincial commissioner, Nyanza.
3. KNA:KSI/27: District of South Kavirondo Administrative Records.
4. An Outline of the History of the District of South Kavirondo—Kenya Colony 1870–1946, in *South Kavirondo District Annual Report 1946*.
5. Zakawa's repute has grown with the attainment of independence for time confirmed his prophecies about the white man's departure. I talked with two ex-chiefs and they both spoke admiringly of how Zakawa had been proven correct.
6. KNA:CN/43. Letter, 5 December 1920, H. E. Welby, district commissioner of Kisii to acting provincial commissioner of Nyanza, Central Kavirondo Political Records.
7. *East African Standard*, 17 September 1954.
8. B. A. Ogot, 'British Administration in the Central Nyanza District from 1900–1960', *Journal of African History*, IV, 2, 1963, pp. 249–74.
9. I located Marita with some difficulty, having to drive over miles of narrow, hilly, dirt roads muddied from the 'long rains' and so eroded that the car often straddled a deep gully. Eventually what were called roads petered out to trails, and finally driving had to be abandoned. After hiking across country, I found Marita's home. Marita was absent and a boy was sent to find him. Marita returned but refused to talk to me, feigning tiredness, although it was early afternoon. Despite my plea that we could have a 'restful talk', he insisted, 'I'm very tired, I must have my rest.' Aside to his companions he said, 'What's a European doing here? We're going to die.' My guide, a young welfare worker, was amused at the old man's fears. He explained: They're afraid. They've never seen a European come to this primitive place.' This statement was surprising since Marita lived only fifteen miles from Kisii. It served, however, to underline the remoteness of the Highlands.
   Although Marita's refusal was exasperating, it was understandable. His contact with whites had been limited to the British who had deported and imprisoned him and his parents. Even though Kenya had achieved independence, he still feared and distrusted white people.

10. Personal letter to the author from ex-chief Musa Nyandusi, 23 January 1967.
11. Lonsdale, A Political History, p. 14; *South Kavirondo District Annual Reports 1921, 1933*.
12. LeVine, 'Nyansongo', pp. 77–78. LeVine was writing about a sub-tribe of the Gusii. There is no reason, however, why other Gusii would not share the same religious behaviour.
13. Nyangweso, 'Cult of Mumbo', pp. 15–16.
14. *Ibid.*
15. KNA:DC/NZA4/5/7. Based on a letter 8 December 1933, Intelligence Reports, South Kavirondo District.

Chapter 4

BELIEFS AND ACTIVITIES

M umboism articulated an aggressive stand against foreign domination: 'The Christian religion is rotten; all Europeans are your enemies.' The movement proclaimed a set of values to which all 'true Africans' should adhere, and it attacked the administrators as bearers of false values. The British were charged with being alien intruders and corrupters of the traditional way of life, and the chiefs with being agents of the intruders and traitors to that way of life.

The chiefs were treated with particular contempt. For example, at the District Sports Meet, after twenty Mumboites in warriors' garb openly defied both the senior Gusii chief and an important Luo chief sent to stop their dancing, district commissioner E.R.S. Davies reported:

> I believe that they have all intrigued against the authority of the chiefs and headmen and deliberately hindered them in carrying out their duties by insults and threats, and claiming greater powers . . . When I arrested Muchirongo the day after the meeting of Mumboites at Kisii, I heard him abusing the chiefs, some of them individually by name and all of them collectively in a way that showed me that such teaching was dangerous to peace and good order, and inciting enmity between his followers and government. He and those who thought like him were without doubt intriguing against constituted power and authority . . . Moreover the chiefs are evidently afraid of it and realize that they are the special objects of hatred and scorn.[1]

Given the powerful position of chiefs, the authoritarian structure of Gusii society,[2] and the fact that the order had come directly from the district commissioner, this defiance was particularly bold. Also, its conspicuous style—the men were decked out in fighting attire (perhaps symbolizing the former revolts) and participated in tribal dances (perhaps denoting loyalty to tribal values)—

42

suggests premeditated action designed to antagonize as well as to convey a message.

The millennial dream, derived from the prophecies and visions of the leaders, was the movement's chief tenet and with minor variations was held in common by the different local groups.[3] It promised the destruction of the colonial order: the present world was soon to undergo a great cataclysm at which time a terrible vengence would befall the enemies of the Mumboites, all of whom— the administrators, missionaries, and chiefs—would be overthrown and a kingdom of the Mumboites established.

Several versions recounted how this transformation was to proceed. In one, water would be turned into blood and only Mumbo's followers would have drinking water provided by him. All white people would disappear leaving only Africans. In another, the founder was to be snatched up into heaven by fire from whence he would dispense food to his followers. A third story recited how a certain Abachi tribe (an unknown tribal name) would descend from the north and exterminate the white man with sharp knives. Even the exact number each Abachi would kill (twenty white men apiece) was specified. Another story that circulated during World War I, and had some basis in fact, predicted that the Germans would soon invade and cut off the arms of men in clothes, presumably Europeans and westernized Africans, and particularly chiefs and mission converts. The Mumboites would escape unscathed because they were the Germans' friends. Still another story recounted that Zakawa's return was to be followed by days of darkness and a plague of locusts, after which the white man would be no more, and Zakawa, together with a priestess, would occupy the district headquarters. Given the frustrated ambitions of the Bogonko clan it is not surprising that the apocalypse they envisioned was both catastrophic and violent.[4]

What was the utopia to be like? As with the Marxian utopia only the barest outlines were specified, but in contrast to that utopia, work was not given a prominent place. There was to be an abundance of material goods, a relaxed happy life free from worry in which the Mumboites could smoke bhang (Indian hemp) as much as they wanted. They would be blessed with an unfailing supply of sheep, cattle, and goats and their unattended crops would grow plentifully. Food would be showered upon them from heaven or arise of its own accord from Lake Victoria.[5] They would be reunited with their dead, especially their great warriors and prophets, and their god Mumbo. The crippled would be cured. What the members wanted was not the old way of life but a utopian version of the old life freed from famine, death, and the drudgery involved in daily work.

The Mumboites showed a deep admiration for western goods and technology. The underlying theme in visions, stories, and comments was their longing for 'all those wonderful things' which Europeans possessed. In his vision of heaven, Mosi, a priest, found his entry announced by an explosion of light after which he approached God on a motor bike accompanied by five Europeans.[6] When the new order arrived, Muchirongo, Bonairiri and Zakawa were not going to live in their mud and wattle houses, they were going to collect the tax and occupy the district headquarters.

When was this paradise to occur? Although the date was not usually specified, it was believed to be near at hand. There were reports that Mumboites were buying lamps in preparation for the end of the world when all would be dark. Some followers, believing Mumbo's promise of food in the millennium, stopped cultivating their gardens; a few killed all of their livestock as he had ordered; and others refused to comply with the government demand for road construction, saying that since the Europeans would soon leave, roads would no longer be needed.[7] (Road work may have been disliked because of its past connection with punishment for the 1908 uprising, apart from it being hard work and roads being seen to be of little use to Africans.)

One of the most revealing aspects of this dream was its reversal theme. In the promised land the superior-inferior positions of Europeans and Africans were to be reversed, the poor were to become rich and the weak, strong. The Europeans would suffer terrible punishments. They would die, be damned, be turned into monkeys, have their arms cut off, or be eaten by the great snake Mumbo. This theme appeared in a number of stories. For instance, part of the myth stated that actually the black man had been created first and the white man second but that Zakawa and Mumbo had purposely put the whites over the blacks. Zakawa's sorceries were also credited with originally bringing the whites to Africa. This situation was soon to be righted with the return of Zakawa and other prophets who would banish the whites forever. No information is available as to why this topsy-turvy state of affairs had originated, but in similar sects it came about, so the explanation goes, to test the black man by trials and tribulations—a purification through suffering. Only those who had truly followed Mumbo's edict—'Go tell all Africans . . . that henceforth I am their God'— would be saved.

This theme appeared not only within the movement but similar stories circulated elsewhere in South Nyanza. For example, a rumour that gained some currency among the Gusii and Kipsigis during World War II was that of the 'Queen's dream'. The Queen of England was said to be really a prophetess who dreamt that a black baby with wings would be born. The social order would then be reversed and the black races would take command. In an effort to prevent the baby from being born, the government was supposedly trying to make Africans sterile by distributing European blankets and tea which were believed to possess magical properties that could cause sterility.[8] What the movement did was to take such rumours and stories and give them form and coherence by linking them to a set of related ideas.

Whatever else they did, these stories certainly portrayed the blacks' dislike of whites, and they transferred the power to determine men's destinies to the black man. Since he will soon occupy his rightful position, he will control instead of being controlled. The reversal theme can be viewed as an effort to come to terms with the fact that the British possessed superior ability to cope with the physical environment and had far greater material wealth than Africans. This myth transformed the humiliating aspects of defeat into virtues, for Mumboism credited its own prophets with having put the Africans into a subordinate position. The colonial era, soon to be terminated, was to be considered merely an interlude in the chain of events leading to the Mumboites assuming their predestined superior position.[9]

Mumboism turned to the past for inspiration: fresh meaning was imbued into tribal ways, old dreams were animated with a new vitality. Since Mumbo had ordered a return to the old ways, the converts were directed to reject the new religion of Christianity, to sacrifice daily, let their hair grow long, wear skins, and never to wash. Tribal dances were encouraged. The most venerated Gusii warriors and prophets were claimed by the movement. Zakawa the great prophet, Bogonko the mighty chief, and Muraa became its symbols, infusing the living with the courage and strength of past heroes.

Furthermore, leaders bolstered their own legitimacy by claiming to be the mouthpieces of deceased prophets, an effort in which their descendants were especially successful. Nyamachara and Uriogi, the sons of Zakawa, for example, revived a belief in their father's return, as a result of which pilgrims came to their village bearing gifts of livestock and some even reported that they had seen Zakawa. In a similar vein, Ongeri, the son of Muraa, spread his mother's teachings, and Nyakundi, the son of Bongonko, established himself as the medium of communication with both his father and Zakawa. Thus, with the progeny of Gusii heroes supporting the movement, blood ties as well as symbolic links with the past were established. Here was an especially powerful group whose prestige and authority could well be used to arouse and weld the various disunited groups into solid anti-British opposition. The legitimacy conferred by the ancestors, especially Gusii heroes, was of particular significance because among the Gusii, ancestor spirits are the major supernatural beings.

The movement's advocacy of a return to the old ways may have another implication. Identifying with indigenous values obviously meant the rejection of Europeans, especially of the missionaries who insisted upon the wearing of clothes and on cleanliness. But the rejection of European clothes was probably also connected with the chiefs' practice of employing as assistants young men who dressed in European or Swahili apparel, 'the donning of which is popularly supposed to increase their cerebral powers.'[10] Usually these men had obtained an elementary education, a knowledge of Swahili, and were converts to Christianity. They were useful to the chiefs on two accounts: first, they could translate from the vernacular into Swahili (many chiefs, at least at that time, could not); second, they had become acquainted with Europeans, and chiefs in working with the British preferred assistants who had some knowledge of the white man's ways. Consequently these young men held positions of status as associates of chiefs, missionaries, and administrators. Thus, if the chiefs were viewed by the Mumboites as European lackeys, doubtless the mission converts were viewed as equally contemptible. In addition, their behaviour was not likely to endear them to their tribesmen. With their knowledge of the outside world they could qualify as sophisticates among their illiterate countrymen. There were countless complaints about their 'swelled heads' and one can imagine how obnoxious some were in lording it over their fellows. Therefore, Mumbo's rejection of European clothing may also have been tied up with its refusal to recognize these youths' claims to superiority.

In spite of Mumboism's blatant rejection of Christianity and whites, Christian influence is, however, evident in its teachings. Bonairiri preached that woman came from the rib of man. The millennial concept appears to be derived from Christian eschatology since there is no mention in either Gusii or Luo religion of a Day of Judgment, there being rather the principle of retribution whereby evil doers were punished here and now. The belief that the Mumboites would be provided with food by their god during the millennium is reminiscent of the Lord supplying manna to the Children of Israel during their progress through the wilderness to the promised land. Though a traditional custom, the sacrifice of animals may well have been reinforced by the Old Testament practice. A number of precepts, such as one will go to heaven by praying to Mumbo, one should not steal, one should not insult people, one should honour the aged, and one should not go about naked, have a Christian flavour about them. Although some of these practices were part of traditional life, the very fact that they were singled out as explicit rules suggests Christian contact.

The origins story (Mumbo, the sea serpent, swallows Onyango Dunde) sounds as if it came straight from the Old Testament account of Jonah and the whale. A Luo tale, however, tells of an important elder being swallowed by a sea serpent and later regurgitated safely on the shore.[11] Another tale tells of a Luo, Obondo, who was possessed by Mumbo spirits. He stayed for some time in Lake Victoria and Mumbo showed him various herbs for treating people possessed by Mumbo spirits and gave him the power to cure all kinds of illnesses. When he returned to his home in 1912, there was widespread possession among the Luo by Mumbo spirits.[12] The date coincides with the movement's origins around 1913.

The lake region of Kenya has a history of possession cults dating back at least to the early years of Luo settlement in the late nineteenth or early twentieth century. Spirit possession among the Luo, according to Owuor, is connected with foreign contact. Widespread possession developed during the fearsome Lango raids, and it appeared again shortly after the Europeans began to administer southern Nyanza. (Owuor writes: 'Spirit possession among the Luo today seems to be of quite recent origin and it has been . . . very

47

much connected with foreign contact.' I would think that he is referring to only the latest florescences, as possession cults have been noted in other parts of East Africa much earlier.) Mumboism seems to be derived from a Luo spirit cult and since there were parallels between Luo and Christian myths, they became the basis for a new one.

The concept of the God Mumbo may have been composed of ideas found in Gusii but particularly Luo and Christian religions. According to LeVine, the word *Nyasaye*, which is equivalent to our concept of 'luck' or 'fortune', was often heard among the Gusii who say that it is a Luo word diffused via the missionaries. Events over which an individual has no control are attributed to *Nyasaye*. However, the Gusii, the main supporters of Mumboism, did not appear to have any well developed ideas of a creator-spirit or of a sea serpent spirit.[13]

Of more relevance, did the Luo, the tribe in which the myth originated, have such an idea? Whisson maintains that the concept of a creator-spirit was indeed present in Luo cosmology before the Christian idea of a creator was introduced. *Nyasaye* was believed to be the origins of the universe and of life. To some extent *Nyasaye* was equated in Luo thought with the sun. It was considered a good thing for all people to be out of bed by dawn, when simple supplicatory prayers were offered to the rising sun. An old man might say 'Rise well for me that I may be at peace.' Similarly, prayers were offered at night as the sun set. *Nyasaye* was seen not only in the sun but in other large and extraordinary phenomena—in the moon, in large rocks, in *big snakes*, in elephants, and in awe-inspiring objects of nature. *Nyasaye* belonged to the cosmology of a nomadic people to be worshipped wherever men were, not only in a temple or in a sacred grove.

Nyasaye's attributes were those of a moral God who rewards and punishes people (brings health and wealth or misfortune) according to whether they uphold or break tribal customs. He supervised the universe generally, his primary function being the maintenance of good.

Mumboism seems to have taken from Luo religion the idea of a creator-spirit that dwells in a sea serpent and in the sun. In Mumboism, the traditional view of a vague life-force that fills wondrous objects gives way to an omnipotent figure that promises eternal life to his followers and damnation to unbelievers. The

Luo creator-spirit who punishes those who break the rules has been accentuated and made into a personal god with the attributes of the God of the Old Testament. He is a commanding and demanding patriarch who requires exclusive worship from his children and lays down rules that must be followed, 'I am the God Mumbo . . . go and tell all Africans . . . that henceforth I am their God. Those whom I choose personally, and also those who acknowledge me, will live forever in plenty . . . but all unbelievers and their families and their cattle will die out . . . .'[14] The very wording of Mumbo's commands bears such a strong resemblance to the Old Testament patriarch that the Old Testament appears to be a main influence. On the other hand, the article on Mumbo (from which this quotation was taken) was written by 'Nyangweso', obviously a British administrator, and he may well have translated Mumbo's edicts into the Christian idiom. Anyway, a new culture item has emerged from apparently combining indigenous and western ideas.

To sum up, Mumboism's stories, myths, and prophecies represented the wishes and dreams of peasants for wealth, happiness, freedom, and the punishment of their enemies. Overwhelmed by a new force over which they had no control and for which their traditional beliefs had no answers, they were at pains to explain it. Beginnings of doubts about the efficacy and veracity of traditional beliefs were met by Mumbo's provision of answers to the pervasive questions of the times. The answers, concocted of traditional and Christian teachings, claimed legitimacy by rejecting Christianity and turning to the old prophets and heroes, yet at the same time certain attractive ideas were utilized from what was considered the west's powerful religion. Mumboism's message was a skillful attempt to revitalize traditional beliefs by combining traditional and western ideas and thereby obtaining the best of two belief systems.

These new beliefs also attempted to restore pride in traditional ways and promised a new self-respect based, in part, upon downgrading Europeans and upgrading Africans. They provided a ray of hope in a promise of a better tomorrow. In the words of one district commissioner: 'The melancholy fact remains to be stated, that a large number of men and women in this district do find, at any rate, spiritual and physical satisfaction in these base fraudulent practices.'[15] Hence, Mumbo's message represented first and foremost a way of rejecting the colonial system with all of its inequalities and injustices, and thus provided a means to adapt to a rapidly changing social order.

Given these beliefs, what means did the Mumboites employ to bring their millennial dream to fruition? They appeared to rely heavily upon magic and ritual to solve their problems. If the proper rites were performed Mumbo would bless them. Priests sacrificed to Mumbo to ensure protection against drought and locusts. The usual practice was to present a priest with a sheep or goat which he sacrificed to Mumbo with the prescribed oblations. Sometimes it was specified that such offerings should be black, at other times white. Feasts were held periodically. Together with their integrative function, they may have symbolized the disappearance of economic privation during the millennium. The priests also performed ceremonies to appease the spirits, control the elements, cure sickness, and restore life.

This concern with magic was rooted in indigenous beliefs. Illness, death, and various kinds of disaster were dealt with by sacrifices and oblations carried out by different supernatural specialists: sorcerers and witch-smellers in the area of medicine, rain-makers and hail-stoppers for weather protection, magical detectors for theft control, and other experts who executed rituals for removing different kinds of curses and providing protection against specific misfortunes.[16]

Resistance to the British appeared to be largely symbolic, as in the refusal to wear European clothes or to eat European food. It was believed that no harm could come to anyone protected by a Mumbo cloak and cap of skins. District commissioner Campbell obviously understood the significance of Mumbo garb when he wrote:

> As regards the men . . . I personally interviewed them all and they professed Mumboism. Each was wearing a "mumbo" cloak of goat skins sewn together also a hat of skins . . . I am glad to say that for the time being my action has squashed the movement as those who foolishly paid cattle etc. to the teachers now see those men in prison awaiting trial and in consequence of my having burnt their cloaks and hats before their eyes I do not anticipate any immediate recrudescence among the Kisii.[17]

Because of government repression, resort was taken to less obvious signs of membership. One chief, for example, who would not be able to admit membership and keep his job, wore a badge of goatskin under his ordinary clothes. This was a most appropriate symbol, since the British disapproved of the wearing of skins. These tactics were probably encouraged by Muraa's counsel. Muraa, after the 1908 revolt, apparently changed her tack and exhorted people not to fight the Europeans by force any more because God had told her that they would go. God himself was going to fight them and the people should trust in Him. They should also try new ways—of talking and cleverness—to rid themselves of the foreigners.[18]

This 'passive' orientation may have been indirectly abetted by Mumbo's derivation from a Luo possession cult. While these cults have been known to militantly oppose the established order, as for example the Nyabingi cult of Ruanda and Uganda which was the main vehicle for active opposition to the established authority structures throughout the region—first, the indigenous elite and then the colonial powers[19]—the Luo cults apparently did not mobilize opposition to the authorities but concentrated rather on healing and possession. Owuor mentions only one instance where there was any action taken against foreign things, and even then it was symbolic as when a woman was told that the *juogi* (spirits) wanted her to dress as in the old days.[20]

Luo reaction to foreign things seemed to be largely handled through accommodation rather than opposition. An example of this approach, of maintaining the old ways yet pursuing the new, is the story Owuor recounts of ritual specialists who refuse to heal on Sundays. 'Come tomorrow,' they will tell the prospective patient, 'for now we are off to Church [a Christian church] !' The Luo, unlike the Gusii, did not attack the source of strain, the foreigners, but cooperated with them and utilized instead a 'coping' mechanism, the complex institution of possession. This approach seems to have been borne out on a broader scale as Ogot states that on the whole, the establishment of administration in Luoland was a peaceful affair.[21]

Possession was much in evidence. A member, Ayuka Achieng, stated: 'I was possessed by a spirit long ago—the spirit of my mother. It is now about one and a half months since I took the Mumbo religion. Nobody taught me . . . . One night I trembled and I knew that it was Mumbo. I was lying down at the time.'[22] Assistant district commissioner S. H. Fazon reported that an informant had described possession as follows: 'Mumbo comes when dark clouds are in the west. He possesses people and makes them tremble. Sometimes he comes at night when a man is asleep. Signs of possession are trembling and speaking unintelligible words.'[23] Possession was linked to sun worship. At sunrise and sunset all Mumboites faced the sun with the first finger and thumb of each hand forming a circle which was held to the eyes like binoculars. They gazed intently at the sun until they become completely dazzled, stretched their arms towards it, and simultaneously broke into gibberish.[24]

Traditionally it was Gusii and Luo women who were possessed. Evidence suggests that the cult changed this practice to permit men to be possessed as well. Chief Orinda, in giving his objections to Mumboism, listed male possession as a new practice of which he disapproved.

Possession among the Mumboites could also have been influenced by its Luo membership. According to Luo beliefs, free spirits live in people most of the time but when not possessing people return to their several homes, in the sun, in trees, in rivers, or in the water snake, Mumbo, whose home was Lake Victoria. These spirits, *juogi*, were believed to give the person possessed the power to prophesy and, after suitable experience, the power to cure people possessed by the same kind of spirits. In all likelihood, possession was reinforced by the Christian practice of 'receiving the spirit', and the traditional powers given the possessed extended to include the miraculous powers of Jesus Christ. Although I have no direct evidence of this connection such is the case in a present day sect, Mario Legio, which originated in a nearby area.

The Mumboites were great smokers of bhang and consequently were harassed by law enforcement officers. It was said that they smoked secretly during specific hours set aside each day—4 and 5 a.m. and 7 and 9 p.m.—and hid their pipes on the mountain during the day.[25]

It is interesting to note that the movement made several attempts to abolish both female and male circumcision,[26] in 1920 ordering that it be suspended for several, some say nine years. One version included the idea that any children circumcised during the nine year period would die. Apparently the order was carried out, at least in Kitutu and North Mugirango locations, for the year 1921. But dissatisfaction with this arrangement led to its resumption the following year. When in 1922, many children died during the period of seclusion, their deaths were attributed to the violation of custom in 1921.

Circumcision is among the most important events in the life of the Gusii. The ceremony marks the assumption of an adult role with its rights, duties, and higher status. It is an integral part of the whole fabric of mores, customs, and practices that order Gusii society. Philip Mayer, in a detailed study of the initiation rites, describes the community's involvement:

> The initiation cycle is woven into the life of the neighbourhood in such a way that nobody remains altogether unconcerned. Children too young to be initiated themselves are occupied in carrying food or running errands. . . . The older boys and girls, who have already been initiated but are not yet married, play a very important part, indeed, apart from the actual operation and the adults' beer parties, they organize and carry out most of the rites and celebrations themselves . . . . The young married people are less closely involved, but maturity brings the right to be entertained at the beer-drinks with which all parents celebrate their respective children's entry into and emergence from seclusion. Among the old people, some will be needed to take part in the ritual, for instance, in blessing the novices at the end of seclusion and burning the bedding.[27]

This we suggest was an attempt at a radical innovation, especially when it was tried as far back as 1920. Writing about the Gusii in 1959, LeVine stated:

> Although fairly progressive agriculturalists, they are behind other Kenya Bantu tribes in westernization, owing partly to isolation and partly to cultural conservatism. One of the major foci of this conservatism is the initiation cycle, involving genital operations for boys and girls. . . . Although missionary activity and the use of European clothing have altered the ritual content of the initiation to some extent and school attendance limits its duration for some boys, there has been no general trend against initiation in Gusiiland, no long-term indication that its universality and cultural significance have been impaired.[28]

Had this order been followed, important changes in Gusii culture and social relations would have ensued. Boys and girls well below the usual age might have been circumcised, and if they had failed to fulfil kinship and other obligations of adult status the meanings of initiation for the child and his family could have been substantially altered. The age-grading of children would also have been disturbed and, if a considerable number of prepubertal boys and girls had waited the nine years to be circumcised, some would have indulged in sexual relations and offspring would have resulted, thereby violating the mores that initiation must precede sexual activity. Besides, Gusii distinctiveness is maintained by their language and culture rather than administrative autonomy. Circumcision is one of the most important customs integrating all Gusii and setting them off from the surrounding Luo. Therefore, the order to abolish circumcision was *strongly anti-traditional*.

It is also possible that incest and the 'communal enjoyment of women' may have been practised as these activities are mentioned in five separate accounts.[29] The most reliable data came from an old man convicted of incest with his daughter in 1938 and sentenced to two years' imprisonment with hard labour. He gave as his reason his membership in Mumbo.[30]

A strong argument can be made for dismissing such allegations. First, there is a paucity of evidence. Second, the Gusii lived in a generally hostile and suspicious environment where malicious gossip was rife.[31] And third, given this milieu, together with the administration's need to justify Mumbo's repression, it would not be surprising if many accusations were exaggerated. On the other hand, to dismiss the accusations *prima facie* might lead to over-looking a significant dimension in the development of protest. What is needed, is to look beneath the rhetoric to investigate each accusation for whatever truth there may be in it. In reference to sexual practices the questions to be answered are, first, did the population in general regard them as deviant and second, did the Mumboites engage in them to a greater extent than non-members?

The answer to the first question can be stated quite simply: for the Gusii, marriage provided, and still does, the only acceptable sexual outlet. All other relationships were regarded as deviant, although viewed with varying degrees of disapproval.[32] Feelings of sexual avoidance and embarrassment between persons of adjacent generations were at the core of Gusii morality. They were strongest between father and daughter or daughter-in-law, next strongest between father and son, less between mother and son, and weakest between mother and daughter or daughter-in-law. LeVine does not spell out the taboos governing the father-daughter relationship, but having elaborated on the father-son relationship, he states that the former is even stricter. Hence, father-daughter incest would be abhorrent to the Gusii. It was viewed as an affliction caused by ancestor spirits which must be propitiated by sacrificing an expensive animal like a sheep or a goat.

No information is available on what the ambiguous phrase the 'communal enjoyment of women' entailed. However, according to custom, sexual relations were surrounded by norms of privacy.

Adultery, especially on the part of the wife, was believed to bring severe supernatural sanctions, and premarital sex, though engaged in, was not approved by the older people. Girls had misgivings and feared gaining the reputation of a 'slut' and young men did not consider it proper to fornicate with girls whom they intended to marry. Thus both incest and communal sex would be regarded as deviant by the Gusii.

As for the second question, evidence suggests that at least some Mumboites indulged in these practices. Scholars have written about sex as an area of particular tension for the Gusii. LeVine and Mayer have noted the aggressive sexual behaviour of both men and women.[33]

Obviously not all Gusii were satisfied with the established norms, least of all youths whose sex life was stringently curtailed and whose sources of adventure and status had been cut off. Since young people were prominent in the cult, it is reasonable to expect that they would push for new arrangements. Therefore, given a culture area with less than satisfactory norms which impinge, in particular, upon an age group prone to experimentation, it would not be at all surprising if deviant practices had developed.

No data are available on how widespread these practices were, whether they were carried out as part of the ritual, and if so, what were the accompanying beliefs. Since the movement was composed of small, autonomous groups, it provided ample scope for each to go its own way. The possible significance of this behaviour will be discussed later.

Notes

1. KNA:PC/NZA4/5/7. Intelligence Reports of the provincial commissioner, Nyanza.
2. LeVine, 'Nyansongo', pp. 39–40, 84–94 for a discussion of the authoritarian nature of Gusii society.
3. See above, p. 35.
4. See below, pp. 58–60.
5. This vision of the wealth-to-come is not surprising since among the Gusii a man's social status and influence in community affairs largely depended upon his wealth. A rich man was respected and listened to, while a poor man was despised and ignored. LeVine, 'Wealth and Power in Gusiiland', P. J. Bohannan (ed.), *Markets in Africa*, (Northwestern University Press, Evanston, 1962), p. 523.
6. KNA:PC/NZA4/5/2. Intelligence Reports of the provincial commissioner, Nyanza.
7. KNA:KSI/27. Letter 2 December 1927 from the district commissioner of

South Kavirondo to the provincial commissioner, South Kavirondo Political Records.

8. KNA:PC/NZA4/5/2. Intelligence Reports of the provincial commissioner, Nyanza.
9. The functions of salvation beliefs and the themes of just compensation and vengeance against one's enemies, found in the religions of the 'non-privileged classes', are discussed by Max Weber in *Sociology of Religion*, (Beacon Press, Boston, 1969), pp. 106–117. He states, 'This hope for and expectation of just compensation, a fairly calculating attitude, is, next to magic (indeed, not unconnected with it), the most widely diffused form of mass religion all over the world.' p. 108.
10. *South Kavirondo Annual Report 1910–1911.*
11. Goldsmith, *Ainsworth Pioneer*, p. 74. In Luo religion, free spirits are believed to live in Mumbo, a mythical water snake found in Lake Victoria. M. G. Whisson, *Change and Challenge*, (Christian Council of Kenya, Nairobi, 1968), pp. 8–9.
12. Henry A. Owuor, 'Spirit Possession Among the Luo of Central Nyanza', Kenya, typescript copy, EAISR, no date. The following discussion of Luo possession is based on Owuor's account.
    Snakes and mythical serpents were a common element in traditional African cosmologies. For instance, a water snake appeared in the mythology of the Maji Maji Rebellion. See George Shepperson and Thomas Price, *Independent African*, (Edinburgh University Press, Edinburgh, 1958), p. 420.
13. Our discussions of Gusii and Luo religion must necessarily be limited. For a fuller discussion of Gusii religion see LeVine, *Nyansongo*, pp. 73–78. Ex-chief Ooga, who was a chief during the period of active Mumboism, maintained that the Gusii were sun worshippers. He said that they looked at *Engora* (the sun) and asked *Engora* to help them. To my question whether all the Gusii worship the sun or only the Mumboites, he replied, 'all people of Gusii'. 'The word "Mumbo" or "Nyamumbo" means God', he said. 'When the missionaries came they translated the word God into "Ombamumbo", or the abbreviated form "Mumbo". From an interview with ex-chief Ooga, 28 June 1966. See the following paragraph in the text which discusses the sun in Luo religion.
    According to district commissioner Gordon, the Gusii have a snake god called *Kiboyi*. Gordon is not the most authoritative source and this statement was mentioned only and not documented. KNA: Gordon, An Outline of the History of the District of South Kavirondo-Kenya Colony, 1870–1946, *South Kavirondo District Report 1946*.
    For more detailed discussions of Luo religion see Whisson, *Change and Challenge*, pp. 1–21 and *The Will of God and the Wiles of Men*, Proceedings, EASSC, January, 1962, p. 3.
14. Nyangweso, 'Cult of Mumbo', pp. 13–17. I am grateful to John Lonsdale for bringing this to my attention.
15. KNA:PC/NZA4/5/7. Intelligence Reports, South Kavirondo District, 8 December 1933.
16. LeVine, 'Nyansongo', p. 77.
17. KNA:KSI/27. Letter, 26 November 1918, District of South Kavirondo Political Records.
18. Interview with ex-chief Ooga on 28 June 1966.
19. Elizabeth Hopkins, 'The Nyabingi Cult of Southwestern Uganda' in Robert I. Rotberg and Ali Mazrui (eds.), *Protest and Power in Black Africa*, (Oxford University Press, New York, 1970), pp. 258–336.
20. Owuor, Spirit Possession Among the Luo.
21. B. A. Ogot 'British Administration in the Central Nyanza District of Kenya', *Journal of African History*, IV, 2, 1963.
22. KNA:KSI/27. Statement taken on 19 July 1915. District of South Kavirondo Political Records.

23. KNA:KSI/27. His informant is anonymous. Report of Investigation Made Concerning the Worship of Mumbo, 31 July 1915, District of South Kavirondo Political Records.
24. Nyangweso, 'Cult of Mumbo'; Henry A. Owuor, 'Spirit Possession Among the Luo'.
25. KNA:CN/43. Central Kavirondo Political Records.
26. The material used here on the attempt to abolish circumcision is taken from LeVine's, 'Gusii Initiation Cycle', pp. 117–20. I have drawn extensively from his article both here and later in the book.
27. Philip Mayer, 'Gusii Initiation Ceremonies', *Journal of the Royal Anthropological Institute*, LXXXIII, 1953a, pp. 9–10.
28. LeVine, 'Gusii Initiation Cycle', p. 117.
29. At first, I was inclined to view these allegations as only that. There were, however, five separate accounts that reported the same practices. Granted, hearsay forms the bulk of the evidence but then it would almost have to be, given this kind of activity. I realise also that such newsworthy accusations are liable to be repeated without any fresh evidence.
   The evidence comes from government documents. District commissioner Kenyon-Slarey in a letter dated 16 April 1920, wrote: 'It is said that they enjoy all women in common and regard incest as natural.' Assistant district commissioner Bond wrote 6 July 1930 about a particular cult leader who was believed to be committing incest with his daughter. (CN/43: Central Kavirondo District Political Records). District commissioner Gordon stated that incest was often practised among the Mumboites. (*South Kavirondo District Annual Report 1946*). And the article by Nyangweso mentions both incest and communal sex.
30. *South Kavirondo Annual Report 1938*. This evidence is the best because it came directly from a member and was not merely someone's opinion.
31. Robert A. LeVine, Socialization, Social Structure and Intersocial Images, in Herbert C. Kelman (ed.), *International Behaviour: A Social-Psychological Analysis*, (Holt, Rinehart and Winston, New York, 1965), p. 64.
32. I use LeVine's description of sex in 'Nyansongo', pp. 50–2, 57–72, as typical of Gusii. Granted it is a study of only a single community but unless special factors exist that would make it non-representative, there is no reason why it should not provide a satisfactory guide to distinguishing deviant from non-deviant practices.
33. Robert A. LeVine, 'Gusii Sex Offences: A Study in Social Control', *American Anthropologist*, LXI, 1959, pp. 965–90; Philip Mayer, 'Privileged Obstruction of Marriage Rites Among the Gusii', *Africa*, XX, 1950, pp. 113–25.

Chapter 5

BASIS OF SUPPORT

TRIBAL support for Mumboism came mainly from the Gusii and a few Luo and Kuria.[1] Aside from tribal affiliation, were there any special categories or strata of people for whom the movement had special appeal?

The core of support for Mumboism appears to have come from the Bogonko clan, the largest and wealthiest clan of the Kitutu sub-tribe. This tribe consisted of seven alien clans linked to the dominant Bogonko lineage, whose allegiance had been bought by providing their members with cattle for bridewealth. The political structure of the Kitutu developed from mutually benefitting patron-client relationships founded on the warrior tradition. In the era immediately prior to the British occupation, the Bogonko clan was at the peak of its prestige, having subordinated the seven clans to itself and having formed the beginnings of a 'state' system with a hereditary chieftainship. This was the most advanced system of political authority, in the sense of a centralized, hierarchical structure clearly demarcating the political from other spheres, to be found among the seven Gusii sub-tribes. Some of its elders were even recognized as authorities not only within the clan itself but throughout the whole tribe.[2] Bogonko, the founder of this lineage, was the Gusii's greatest warrior-chief.

> Old men enjoy relating tales of the awe in which people held Bogonko, a nineteenth-century hero and leader of the Getutu tribe. It is said that when he walked out of his home area people fled from their houses until reassured that he would do them no harm. Songs in praise of his wealth, power, and accomplishments were composed. When he attended his grandson's wedding, woven mats were laid down so that he should not have to walk on cow dung.[3]

It is submitted that the position and influence of the Bogonko clan suffered under colonialism. In choosing a chief for Kitutu location, Bogonko's heirs were bypassed and a man chosen from another clan. Nyakundi, Bogonko's son, believed that he should have been chosen. Ex-senior chief Musa Nyandusi recalled this rivalry. (Nyandusi was appointed chief of Nyaribari location in 1927 and was a strong opponent of Mumboism.)

> Nyakundi was a very big man like a chief. The Europeans were here and they did not appoint Nyakundi chief. They chose Nsungu, the brother of ex-chief Ooga instead of Kitutu location. . . . Nyakundi said to Nsungu "You are appointed by the *wazungus* [Swahili for white people]. You are a small chief. I, the son of Bogonko, am the leader of the location."[4]

The British, in not appointing Bogonko's son, aroused the hostility of this lineage already unhappy over their presence and assured itself of their opposition. It is also submitted that they became the leaders of protest against the colonial regime as the centre of Mumbo activity was in Kitutu location where, as previously stated, more than half of the population belonged to the Bogonko clan. Furthermore, the clan was well represented in Mumbo, Bogonko being an important symbol and his son, Nyakundi, having been imprisoned for Mumbo activities. Ex-senior chief Nyandusi explained Nyakundi's arrest:

> Nyakundi was a secret follower of Mumbo. Nsungu, the chief, went to the DC [abbreviation for district commissioner] and told the DC that Nyakundi was a follower of Mumbo. Nyakundi was arrested and taken to Kisumu Prison. Nyakundi wouldn't eat European or Asian food. He would only eat Kisii food. The guards struck him. He went on a fast and died.[5]

This could explain the Mumboites' hatred of particular chiefs. What could be more abhorrent to a proud clan than to have to take orders from a member of a rival clan and one who at the same time was responsible for the jailing of their revered Nyakundi? Their hatred of chief Nsungu not unexpectedly extended to his relatives. An intelligence dispatch reported the Mumboites were spreading the story that the great snake was coming to destroy all chiefs, Ooga being singled out by name.

The administration's anxiety over the repercussions that might result from Nyakundi's death was reflected in the precautions taken to prevent any myth from arising. The district commissioner discussed Nyakundi's death:

Nyakundi derived his great influence, an influence far greater than any other Kisii from the fact that he is the son of Bogonko who was the most influential and most feared chief who died before the British arrived. Nyakundi himself was of a very forceful character and a commanding figure and as he always took the line of opposing government he naturally had a large following. . . . Now Nyakundi is dead and Chief Nsungu fears and so do I that no one will believe in his death and he will become an oracle like Zakawa. It will then be easy for some relative with sufficient wit to become the mouthpiece of both Nyakundi and Zakawa. Nyakundi having always been anti-government during his visible life time may safely be assumed to continue anti-goverment indefinitely in his invisible state. As an illustration from what the Kisii will believe about Nyakundi it is interesting to note that when the locusts recently flew across Kitutu, . . . the natives jumped to the conclusion that the locusts had brought Nyakundi back from prison. They refused to kill or eat the locusts which at another time would have been considered a delicacy. Some even saw Nyakundi standing on a hilltop talking to people. It is considered that the only possible means of convincing the people that Nyakundi is really dead is to bring his body back for burial. . . . [6]

Doubtless, the clan's bitterness increased with the death of Nyakundi. Now another name could be added to the martyrs' roster.

Finally it is submitted that the resentment of the Bogonko clan was primarily *political*, arising from their resentment over the administration's by-passing of their chief (possibly because of the clan's role in the revolts). This has also been noted by LeVine, Ogot and Ochieng'.[7] Indeed, the Bogonko's lack of other grievances has been pointed out by several others. In contrast to the Kikuyu situation, for example, there was no acute land shortage among the Gusii and the Luo of South Nyanza.[8] And general anti-British sentiments cannot serve as a sufficient explanation because all Kenyan Africans experienced the same system of colonial rule and some protested and others did not.

But it can be argued that alien rule impinged on some to a greater extent than on others, and that those who felt its burdensome aspects more, were consequently more highly motivated to protest and, if need be, to suffer the consequences of their militancy. In the case of the Bogonko clan, the members appear to have used general anti-British sentiments to further their own political purposes.

In addition, other support for Mumboism came from people who had something to lose under the British system, for example, the tribal ritual specialists for whom there was no room in the mission churches. Though the missions could provide a place for the priest-like head with a set of customary duties, they excluded the charismatic prophet who sought to cure psychological and physical disorders.[9] In Mumboism, where there was an emphasis on communicating with the supernatural, possession, and the curing of illnesses, there was room for this type of leader. Old people, especially old men, may have felt similarly threatened if new values and new ways were widely accepted. Hence their support for a movement advocating a return to traditional ways and the rejection of the aliens.

There were also those who aspired to new roles in a changing society. A surprisingly large number of leaders were women, Bonairiri, the chief exponent of Zakawaism; Kibiburi, considered a dangerous agent by the administration and deported to Lamu; Obondo, mentioned in administrative correspondence as a future priestess; and Okenyuri, the wife of a cult leader described as 'the most attractive agent who works the mystical and oracular interviews with Mumbo', and Muraa. Gusii society had many middle-aged or elderly female diviners. This was the most important role a woman could occupy outside the family and, although a respected position, it did not endow her with extraordinary powers or prestige.[10] The cult may have adapted this role to that of priestess.

Young men were especially prominent. Chief Orinda, in charge of a location where the cult was strong, said, 'The sect consists only of young men. There are no old men in the sect or practically none.' Chief Mahangain reported that the elders were refusing to attend *barazas* and 'that the young men are preaching to the effect that it will only be a short time before white men go, that they will have a free fight, and it will be a case of the survival of the fittest.[11] This sounds as if the young were openly challenging the elders' authority.

There is an apparent inconsistency here. Earlier, we noted that the district commissioner had stated in 1921 that Zakawaism was especially attractive to the old men and that almost all in Kitutu location had joined. Here (in 1919), we note that chiefs say that only young men joined and hardly any older people. How is this discrepancy to be explained? It could be that the composition of the membership varied by area or by time, or that Zakawaism had a particular appeal for older people, giving more emphasis to the nativistic elements, while Mumboism stressed the new order the millennium would usher in and a break with certain aspects of the past. Lacking evidence, we can only conjecture.

Why did women and youth support the movement? What was there in it for them? Young men, as mentioned earlier, had reasons to be particularly dissatisfied with the colonial system that, in banning cattle raiding and inter-tribal fighting, had eliminated their main occupations. (Cattle villages where the young men spent much of their time were officially abolished in 1912. Proscription by no means signalled the demise of these pastimes as amply demonstrated by present day cattle rustling and tribal clashes. However, the number of men thus engaged declined greatly.) The virtual closing off of these avenues of mobility fell hardest on the young men who had used these raids to acquire kudos and cattle needed for bride-wealth, both requisites of adulthood. Effectively unemployed, they were becoming increasingly restless.

At the heart of the traditional authority system were the ancestors and the elders. In death as well as in life, the ancestors were regarded as being intimately bound up with the welfare of the clan. Only the elders, because of their close lineage relationship to the ancestors, were able to ascertain the ancestors' will and, when necessary, make the required propitiations.[12] This gave them much power and permitted them to exercise strong social sanctions. One of the functions of ancestor beliefs was to keep respect and power in the hands of the elders who, because of their age, were believed to possess the necessary attributes of authority.

But the cult established other criteria for leadership. In keeping with its reversal theme, youth and women, both of whom occupied relatively low status in the traditional structure, figured prominently as leaders. They communicated with the ancestors, interceded on behalf of the members with other supernatural agencies, and made many of the decisions that in traditional society belonged to the elders. Thus, in rejecting age and sex, two major attributes of traditional leadership, and in introducing new norms and leadership roles, Mumbo, in essence, rejected tribal authority.

Both mission and Mumbo youth were rebelling against tribal authority, and some of the latter were engaging in activities highly disapproved of by the older generation. Joining either the movement

or a mission provided new activities, and both supported, even if
unintentionally, rebellion against tribal authority. Both groups
attracted young people and, although the Mumboites clearly disliked the educated mission students, the cult recruited some of them.
Two choices were presented to young people, first, to join the Mumbo
movement which was to take an aggressive stand against the
foreigners and to defy the chiefs and elders, or second, to join a
mission where one could become literate and perhaps acquire a
job with the administration. Joining a mission had the added
advantage that one was not forced to leave the district to work.[13]
One group of young people chose to accommodate to the colonial
system while another chose to reject it. Although any number and
combination of factors could have accounted for the difference
in choice, is it possible that distance was the crucial factor? Did
it simply depend on whether a mission or a branch of the movement
was closer to the individual's home? Again, to answer this question,
we need more data.

Mumbo recruited a clan with political grievances, people whose
positions were threatened by the incipient order, and those who,
like women and youth, were laying claims to new roles. No doubt
as in any amorphous, heterogeneous movement, the psychologically
unstable, the shiftless, and the malcontents joined, but they do not
appear to have formed its mainstay.

Notes

1. KNA:PC/NZA4/5/7. South Kavirondo Intelligence Reports 1930–1936-
2. Even today this clan is quite exceptional. Its size is enormous: eighteen
   sub-clans (none of the other clans have more than four) and more than
   thirty thousand people. Mayer, *The Lineage Principle*, pp. 11–15, 28–31.
3. LeVine, 'The Internalization of Political Values', p. 53.
4. Interview with ex-senior chief Nyandusi, 24 June 1966.
5. *Ibid.*
6. KNA. Letter from the district commissioner of South Kavirondo to the
   acting provincial commissioner of Nyanza, August 1928. South Kavirondo
   Political Records.
7. LeVine, 'Gusii Initiation Cycle', p. 118; B. A. Ogot and W. R. Ochieng',
   'Mumboism—an Anti-Colonial Movement', in B. A. Ogot (ed.), *War
   and Society in Africa*, (Cass, London, 1972), pp. 174–75. Ogot and
   Ochieng' agree that in bypassing Bogonko's heirs for the chieftainship,
   the British secured the resentment of the whole lineage and that Nyakundi, disgruntled, led an anti-government movement expressed in both
   Mumboism and Zakawaism. They disagree that the Bogonko clan furnished the greatest support for Mumboism but since they fail to document
   their evidence, I have no way to assess it.

8. Cmd. 4556: *Report of the Kenya Land Commission*, (1934), pp. 292, 297.
9. Lonsdale, A Political History, p. 354.
10. LeVine, 'Nyansongo', p. 76.
11. KSI/27: Letter from district commissioner Campbell, 6 February 1919, District of South Kavirondo Political Records.
12. LeVine, 'Nyansongo', pp. 75–7, 92–4.
13. *The South Kavirondo District Annual Report 1915* notes that 'it is often the case that a lad describes himself as a "mission" boy merely that he may escape being sent out to work.'

Chapter 6

ATTITUDES OF AGENTS OF SOCIAL CONTROL

IN examining the nature of Mumbo and its development, a crucial dimension is the way in which the agents of social control — administrators, chiefs, headmen, tribal police, and missionaries — perceived it and dealt with it.

Administrators were particularly anxious during the years 1915 to 1920 when the movement was spreading rapidly. In 1915, the district commissioner noted that if left unattended 'in an affair of this sort incalculable harm may be done and the position in time become so bad that the whole district be utterly inflamed and disorganized.'[1] Not knowing with what it was dealing, the administration questioned the chiefs and missionaries and sent informers into Mumbo's schools.

Some administrators even feared another uprising. The district commissioner wrote in 1918: 'There is no question but that Mumboism may become an extremely dangerous political force. . . . If such warnings are totally neglected there is a possibility of the events which occurred at Blantyre being repeated in this Protectorate.'[2] (In 1915, Africans led by John Chilembwe had revolted near Blantyre, formerly Nyasaland, now Malawi. The revolt had lasted less than two weeks and had been completely crushed, yet it was a portent for other colonial administrations.) The following year the district commissioner was still apprehensive, being convinced that the movement was preaching sedition and fearing that it might lead to another 'Kitutu War.'[3]

Some administrators viewed the leaders as exploiters of credulous peasants, immoral people who manipulated an environment of fear and superstition for their own ends. The district commissioner of South Nyanza, E. R. S. Davies stated in 1934:

The general opinion which I form on the present evidence is that the promoters of the movement and their devotees are parasites addicted to bhang smoking who want to obtain food for nothing and have used unscrupulously certain prophecies of the past and a fear of locusts, over which they are believed to have power. They on the other hand claim to be teachers of a true religion persecuted by the chiefs who attribute evil and sedition to them.[4]

As late as 1953 the movement's reappearance was being explained by a district commissioner in terms of particular leaders, who, having had their cattle confiscated earlier for their Mumbo activities, saw in its reorganization an opportunity to amass stock. 'The fee for becoming a Mumboite is a goat—a higher grade in it requires a cow.'[5]

Once Mumbo had established itself as anti-British, the administration used imprisonments, fines, forced labour and various harassments to suppress it. Mumboites were arrested, detained, and deported on charges that would not have been upheld under normal conditions in British and American courts of law. For instance, a district commissioner in a letter to his provincial commissioner admitted that he had insufficient evidence to have four people deported. Nevertheless they were deported.[6]

Assistant district commissioner Bond reported how he destroyed a place of worship together with its sacred symbols:

In the centre of the hut (or tabernacle) was a phallic altar post bearing traces of bloodstains. I had this uprooted and have brought it in. . . . In the western corner of the enclosure a bush plant (nyaluthkoth) had been planted. I had it uprooted. In the eastern corner a small length of inner wall covered with dry grass from which a shrub (bwombwe) was growing so to leave a covered but hollow space between the walls. I burned the grass and bush. From the above it would seem probable that Mumboism has a debased connection with sun worship. According to the elders this is the old religion (if any) of the Luo but there were in their days no such rites as incest or what appeals to them most, the feeding of crocodiles with good meat.[7]

This hostile reaction on the part of the administration naturally hardened the movement's view toward it.

In spite of its repressive tactics, the administration did not present a monolithic front in its handling of the cult. It stressed a pragmatic approach and attempted to abide by the rule of law, even though often disregarding civil liberties. An interesting case occurred in 1918, when district commissioner Campbell sent some Mumboites out of the district on a project using compulsory labour and the provincial commissioner ordered their return:

> The Assistant District Commissioner here reports that you have sent in a batch of 28 men under escort for work at Magadi. As you are aware labour is not to be forced even for Government purposes without the sanction of His Excellency. Neither Chiefs nor District Commissioners can deport men from their Districts except they are being transferred from one jail to another under warrant. In the circumstances, I am ordering the return of the men and shall be glad of an explanation.

In defending his action, district commissioner Campbell wrote:

> In this matter I feel bound to say that I consider the headman acted with extraordinary loyalty and energy. It requires some pluck on the part of a chief to boldly tackle a wholesale and vicious movement such as this, surrounded by superstition, illwill and mysterious "dawa" [magic]. In acceding to their suggestion to send the riff-raff out to work and try the teachers it seemed to me and still does that in the interest of Government, the step taken was a wise one and that under the Native Authority Ordinance Section 5 (1) and (2), 6 (1) a legal one. I cannot agree that sending men such as these to Magadi for six months work for good wages can be described as "deportation" and when natives in a reserve are misbehaving themselves I do not understand how the operation of sending them out for a few months work can be placed on the same footing with "forcing labour" when all and sundry have to be called upon. . . .

Higher authorities were sought. The chief native commissioner (the highest official in charge of native affairs) John Ainsworth, supported the provincial commissioner's reprimand as he too viewed the district commissioner's action as *ultra vires*. Ainsworth did not see Mumbo as particularly dangerous and suggested a wait-and-see stance and ridicule instead of repression:

> Personally I failed to detect in it any disloyal or harmful tendency and formed the opinion that to take official notice of the matter was likely to do more harm than good. Sometime ago, I saw some of the so-called teachers and followers when I came to the conclusion that the best way to deal with the subject was to ridicule rather than take serious notice of it. . . . Personally I deprecate any repressive action by the Government until and unless we are satisfied that the cult has become such as to lead to disloyalty or that it is dangerous to peace and order in the districts concerned.
>
> Any hasty or ill-considered action in a matter of this description is likely to create an impression in the native mind that the Government fears the teaching when it becomes imbued with exaggerated importance and may on that account alone become highly desirable.

I believe that the best policy is to keep in touch with any such movement as this and allow it to have full scope until we are satisfied that it is necessary to take steps to deal with it. . . .[8]

For their part, acting as agents of the administration responsible for law and order, the chiefs and headmen viewed the sect with hostility. If it disrupted the community, they were required to deal with it and it was they who were blamed for not forewarning the district commissioner. Administrative records report: 'All the Kisii chiefs and many of the Luo chiefs . . . were unanimous in advising the suppression of the cult' and 'The trial [of Mumboites] was well attended by the general public. About 150 assessors (chiefs and tribal elders) recommended the deportation of the eight accused and the imprisonment for six months of another.'[9] The chiefs tended to favour more drastic measures in dealing with Mumboism than the British. And even though the odd chief might sympathize with Mumbo's goals or even be a member, they were, in the main, against it. They had much to lose if its goals were achieved. Mumbo's elect and not British appointees were to be the potentates in the new order. Having successfully exploited British rule by reaching the top of the native authority structure they tended to look askance at any group that advocated radical change.

Not unexpectedly, the missionaries were against the movement. For example, Father Scheffer of the Asumbi Catholic Mission fully supported district commissioner Campbell's ordering of the Mumboites out of the district on work projects. His view was consistent with the missionary perspective of that time:

I have heard reports to the effect that Mumbo people, taken by you, have been sent back from Kisumu. What a pity! Mumbo people were responsible for all the looting in September 1914.[10] They were responsible for a good amount of trouble to their respective chiefs at the time the latter were recruiting government labour.

At the present they still are opposed to the progress of civilization and from information received they are an immoral and drunken lot.

One of their many prophecies was that in 1914 when the crops would be in the *wazungu* would leave the district. This very prophecy made some people think that Mumboism was of German origin and if I had anything to say in the matter, I would stamp out anything of that kind, and the manner I would try to stamp it would be to make them see something of the world. It would convince them that the *wazungu* had come to stay and they would have to submit to the higher authority.[11]

It is not surprising that the missionaries were against Mumboism since the missions probably lost some members to it. Although no figures are available, if the situation is at all like that posed by other independent sects, Mumbo may have posed a serious threat or at least been perceived as such by the missionaries.

By and large, then, the agents of social control viewed the cult negatively. They wanted peace and stability, whereas Mumboism continually provoked unrest and lawlessness. It upset established ways. Youth challenged chiefs and elders, and the sect challenged foreign domination and, possibly, traditional life.

Whether or not any of these accusations is true, it should be noted that the history of sects and other nonconforming groups shows that new and different groups whose ways and motives are unknown tend to be regarded by the established order with suspicion and, at times, outright hostility. That such suspicion was largely inappropriate in the instance being studied here is clear for the following reasons.

1) Doubts about the truthfulness of many accusations were voiced from the lowest to the highest administrative levels. Chief Orinda stated frankly that he did not like the Mumbo people but added:

> On the other hand much that has been said against them is not true. They cultivate like other people and they do not kill stock, and they give no trouble at all when they are wanted for work. They come to work at once. Their teaching is good. They teach men not to steal, or use insulting language, or to laugh at old men, or to walk about naked.[12]

An informant, sent to one of the sect's schools, reported:

> I don't know that they do any harm except to say that the *wazungus* will soon return to their own country. They do not kill all their cattle in preparation for the millennium. They have little feasts at their bomas for 10 days to monthly intervals and occasional big ones for which they foregather at Betis' boma. [They had been accused of killing all their cattle in preparation for the millennium. Some of the more fervent believers probably did, but the more prudent did not.][13]

While most administrators viewed the sect as dangerous, retrogressive, and a menace to law and order as well as to morals, a few refused to characterize it as all bad. Assistant district commissioner Fazan, after investigating it, wrote:

> Most of them have stock, and they cultivate shambas [farms]. They all either wear clothes, or more than one goat skin, so that they live up to

69

the percept not to go naked. A man called Wadi, who is the chief of Chief Orinda's retainers and has most of the actual work of collecting porters to do [for the Carrier Corps], states that the Mumbo people give no trouble whatever, and that their readiness to turn out for government labour is conspicuous. For my part I can add the testimony that I have more than 40 of them confined in my camp at the present moment. None of them are reported to have resisted the summons to appear, and nobody has made any attempt to escape. Therefore they do not seem to me to be intractable.

I investigated a charge of assault (or grievous hurt) against them and found that the persons who brought the charge were more culpable than the persons charged. The persons who brought the charge were mission boys.

By the foregoing remarks I do not mean to vindicate Mumboism. I am aware that a large amount of damage has probably been caused by it. But it is possible that the attitude of the persons concerned may be loyal in one place and disloyal in another.

I should not even like to say they are not disloyal here, but I have found no evidence of it.[14]

2) The administration's accusation that Mumboite rituals exploited credulous Gusii does not stand up to examination. A comparison of their fee with those charged by the *omari* (witch-smellers, the traditional practitioners) shows that the Mumboites charged the usual fee, a cow (worth about $42 or 300/-) or a goat or goat meat ($5 or 35/-).[15] On the other hand, the issue of who was a true or false prophet, a true or false witch-smeller, is complex and beyond the scope of this book.

3) While it is true that the Mumboites smoked bhang, so did many others in Nyanza. John Ainsworth, provincial commissioner of Nyanza in 1908, commented on this practice:

All the Kavirondo, particularly the Luo are great smokers of tobacco which is grown in this country. . . . It is also a custom amongst the men at times to smoke bhang obtained from a species of Indian hemp which is cultivated in the country for this purpose. Bhang smoking produces a state of semi-madness or intoxication. . . . Some few months ago I instructed all DC's to call in all chiefs and inform them of the dangers of bhang smoking and point out to them that a great deal of crime in the country was due to its use.[16]

In 1921 senior commissioner H. R. Tate wrote: 'Bhang smoking and witch-craft are prevalent all over the District and are difficult to stop.'[17] Anyway, the administration's belief that bhang encouraged the outbreak of hostilities because of its aggression-arousing tendencies is debateable.[18] Bhang may release aggressive tendencies or it may produce a state of euphoria.

4) As for the charge that the movement was regressive and irrational, it is true that it looked to the past for support and inspiration so that in one sense it was regressive. Mumbo could not banish the Europeans, but it could, at least symbolically, reject them by paying homage to old heroes. As for incest and communal sex being indices of regressing to past ways, there is no evidence that these were ever part of approved Gusii life. And if they were indulged in by the Mumboites, the evidence is too weak to suggest that any more than a faction were involved. (Later we will suggest an explanation for their possible occurrence.) But, by and large, what does seem clear is that the Mumboites were not on these grounds, at least, particularly different from the population at large. Indeed instead of regressing to old ways, the movement rejected or attempted to reject several important mores, circumcision, possibly privacy in sexual relations, and traditional authority.

Failure to consider the time perspective in interpreting actions can sometimes lead to error. The Gusii were defeated in battle. For them to persist with this tactic would have been futile. Obviously an alternative to the spear had to be found. Groping for ways to cope with the formidable intruders, they turned to a belief in the millennium which had been promised by the powerful white man's religion. Under the circumstances this can hardly be construed as irrational conduct.

Notes

1. KNA:KSI/27. Letter, 21 July 1915, District of South Kavirondo Administrative Records.
2. KNA:KSI/27. Letter, 26 November 1918, District of South Kavirondo Political Records.
3. *Ibid.*, Letter, 6 February 1919.
4. KNA:PC/NZA4/5/7. 8 January 1934. Intelligence Reports, South Kavirondo District.
5. *Ibid.*, 8 December 1953.
6. KNA:CN/43. Letter, 5 December 1920, by district commissioner H. E. Welby, Central Kavirondo District Political Records.
7. 'Nyangweso', who uses assistant district commissioner Bond's description of the Mumboites' tabernacle in his article already referred to, pressed on with his phallic argument. He discussed at length whether the altar post was or was not a phallic symbol. Since all his informants denied

71

RURAL REBELS

any such connection and since he observed similar posts to which cattle were tied at night he regretfully concluded that the similarity must be accidental and that it was simply a custom to carve posts in that way. KNA:CN/43, Letter, 6 July 1930. Central Kavirondo District Political Records.

8. KNA:KSI/27. This correspondence can be found in District of South Kavirondo Political Records.
9. KNA:PC/NZA/4/5/1. See reports dated 8 December 1933 and 8 January 1934. Intelligence Reports, South Kavirondo District.
10. See above, p. 36.
11. KNA:KSI/27. Letter, 1 December 1918. District of South Kavirondo Political Records.
12. KNA:KSI. Statement, 19 July 1915, District of South Kavirondo Political Records.
13. Ibid., Statement, 23 August 1921.
14. KNA:KSI/27. Report, 21 July 1915, District of South Kavirondo Political Records.
15. Robert LeVine, 'Omoriori: Smeller of Witches', Natural History, LXVII, 1958, pp. 142–47.
16. Nyanza Provincial Annual Report 1907–1908.
17. Nyanza Province Annual Report 1920–1921.
18. KNA:CN/43. Letter from district commissioner H. W. Welby to the provincial commissioner 5 December 1920 expresses this fear. Central Kavirondo Political Records 1920.

72

Chapter 7

A LATER PHASE OF THE MOVEMENT

DURING the 1950s, groups similar to Mumbo appeared sporadically. But none had any lasting impact. In 1952, a millenarian movement inspired by the Adventists emerged in various parts of the Highlands.[1] At the time Mumboism was banned in 1954, another sect in the same area known as *Dini ya Mariam*, was also banned. (*Dini*, or some variation thereof, is used widely in Kenya to mean, religion. More specifically, it refers to the immigrant religions and, by extension, such new religious movements as are here described.) Mariam Rogot of Kabondo location was its chief protagonist. Accompanied by her husband, Paul Adika, she walked the countryside proselytizing. She spoke of the imminent end of the world, carried out baptisms, and incited ecstatic behaviour among her followers. *The South Nyanza Annual Report, 1954* described the group as follows:

> Led by a half crazy woman named Mariam Rogot, this sect which originates from a small group of renegades from the Roman Catholic missions, displays a marked similarity to the Mumbo religion which had with difficulty been stamped out many years before. In June Mariam Rogot, her husband and one other were removed from the District on Detention orders, and this prompt action had the required effect so that by the time the sect was formally proscribed in September the movement had almost died out and gave no trouble during the remainder of the year.

In 1958 Mariam and her husband were sentenced to a month's imprisonment for holding illegal meetings. On release they recommenced their preachings, whereupon they were restricted to Nyamira station in the Kisii Highlands. Despite the optimistic note in the 1954 report of the sect's imminent demise, the 1959 report concluded with: 'There is no doubt that Mariam still has disturbance potential particularly among the very emotional and less stable bodies of fanatical religious thought.' And in 1960 it was reported that Mariam and Paul had been de-restricted early in the year and had remained relatively quiet. Their activities included preaching on a number of occasions and attempting to amalgamate three other sects.[2]

Of a different order were the visionary experiences and efforts to abolish circumcision originated by the Bogonko clan in and before 1957.[3] LeVine discusses the short-lived 1957 attempt and states that it was only the most recent example. Information is not available on earlier ventures except for the already discussed 1921 effort.

The 1956 initiation ceremonies began as usual in October, but instead of stopping as was customary in December, they continued on into January. The Gusii explained this strange occurrence by telling how a youth from the Bogonko lineage saw three old men with long hair, sitting in the middle of the Echarachani River drinking beer. They ordered him to return with his father and when he did, the old men said:

> We are tired of living in the water. You tell the people of Bogonko and Kitutu to resume circumcision of their children and continue until seeding time [April-June] then stop. After that do not circumcise children for nine years. This is to give us, the people of the water, a chance to circumcise our own children. Go tell all people in Gusiiland to obey that rule.[4]

The old men disappeared and the father and son spread the story in Kitutu. This order was plausible because it came from a source that commanded respect: the old men appeared to be a composite of ancestor spirits and living lineage elders which would make them particularly powerful wielders of supernatural sanctions.[5]

The following evidence links this episode to Mumboism and to the Bogonko clan,

1) The order was reported by a Bogonko youth and directed to the Bogonko clan.

2) This attempt to change the initiation cycle was opposed by the chiefs because of its association with Mumboism. When the chief of Kitutu location heard of the vision, he immediately said it was an attempt by the Bogonko people to resuscitate Mumboism and the elders took the same view. Since this occurred during the time Mau Mau posed a severe threat both to the British and to the chiefs as civil servants, it is understandable that the chiefs should

frown upon any renewal of a movement that had overtones of militant Mumboism. Furthermore, it is likely that the chiefs saw the instructions to abandon circumcision as a threat to the established order in much the same way as they regarded Mumboism.

3) This event was not unique and bore a striking resemblance to earlier Mumboism.

a) The order to suspend circumcision was the same as that ordered by the Mumboites in 1920. Then the nine year period was also mentioned. Thus inspite of previous disastrous consequences, the 1957 suspension of initiation was patterned on an earlier effort.

b) The 1957 attempt was carried out in a manner reminiscent of the origins' myth. In both cases, spirits making their home in the water issued instructions that if followed would have introduced a radical change in tribal ways. Besides, the instructions were issued through a medium. This pattern of oracular presentation was deeply rooted in tradition.

c) Geographically, both places where the events occurred were historically significant. Kitutu is a traditional source of cultural innovation. The Echarachani River flows through an area where the heroes of Kitutu are celebrated in myth and song, and it is the region where Gusii military success and civil leadership reached their greatest heights in pre-British days. Furthermore, visions had been experienced at the particular river before. And Lake Victoria, the site of the previous revelation, has a prominent place in tribal folklore.

d) The mouthpiece of the ancestors was a youth, and youth were important in the sect.

In the following chapter, the possible significance of this behaviour will be discussed.

Notes

1. Robert A. LeVine, Witchcraft and Sorcery in a Gusii Community, in J. Middleton and H. H. Winters (eds.), *Witchcraft and Sorcery in East Africa*, (Routledge and Kegan Paul, London, 1963), p. 230.
2. *South Nyanza District Annual Report 1960.*
3. LeVine, 'Gusii Initiation Cycle', pp. 117–18.
4. *Ibid.*, p. 118.
5. The attitude of Gusii towards the ancestor spirits is one of fear and deference, involving an unquestioning obedience to their demands. 'The ancestor spirits are always considered to be right no matter how unreasonable their behaviour might seem.' LeVine, 'Nyansongo', pp. 74–5.

Chapter 8

THE MAJOR DETERMINANTS OF THE CULT OF MUMBO—INTERPRETATION AND CONCLUSIONS

HAVING discussed the determinants of Mumboism with their qualifications, and having considered the available evidence, the following interpretation of the historical processes involved in its development emphasizes the delineation of broad variables. It generalizes going beyond strict adherence to facts, drawing inferences where necessary, especially in the section on loss of status and power where, because the evidence is patchy and insufficient, the explanation is speculative. Although the dimensions of Smelser's model are analytically distinct, they are so closely related that empirical discussions of any one determinant tend to involve others. In order to avoid unnecessary repetition, factors will be somewhat arbitrarily allocated to one or another category, the emphasis being upon providing a satisfactory explanation.

The Structurally Conducive Conditions

These factors set the stage for the movement that developed and determined its most general characteristics.

The Cultural Heritage

A warrior tradition expressed primarily in cattle raiding led to the first British-Gusii encounters, as the British felt that Gusii aggressiveness towards tribes they considered their friends could not go unpunished.

Among the Gusii, as with peoples of pre-European Africa, there was no clear separation of the religious and political, sacred and secular spheres of activity. Religious-moral values were associated with political offices and religious beliefs normally included a metaphysic, a cosmology, and a moral and political theory. In the words of Thomas Hodgkin, 'The language of politics was at the same time the language of religion.' Thus, it followed that movements which sought to arouse Africans, still largely religious in their mode of thinking, to a new conception of themselves, of their rights and duties, would use religious symbols for the task.

Societies that lack advanced technological and scientific knowledge—where there is ignorance of the findings on the etiology of disease or of the meteorological processes involved in fluctuations in rainfall—have little power to predict or control the occurrence of natural disasters such as floods and famines, and few reliable measures with which to combat disease and sickness. When the elements involved in one man's good fortune and another's bad fortune are largely unknown and uncontrollable by practical means, men have at all times rationalized their fate by assuming the presence of mysterious powers in the universe and among their fellow beings. Gods, spirits, and magical forces outside the community, together with witches and sorcerers within it, are postulated to explain societal strains and the workings of the universe.[1] When the Gusii were confronted with the world of the white man, which they did not understand and could not control, they brought into play magical devices and supernatural explanations. Christianity's emphasis upon the supernatural fitted in well with this kind of interpretation.

The Colonial Experience

A liberal government policy which permitted many Christian missions to enter Kenya and to establish mission stations and, in turn, put no obstacles in the path of later secession movements, promoted the formation and spread of these movements. As long as a movement could convince the authorities that it was religious, it was allowed to practise, but if it was defined as subversive, it was repressed. In neighbouring Uganda, where only Roman Catholics and Anglicans were allowed to establish churches, and where these religions were adopted early in the colonial period by the indigenous elites, there were far fewer movements.

The Gusii were sufficiently settled on the land for the missionaries' teachings to make some impact. Mission education, which stressed the religious aspects of western culture, strongly influenced Africans' understanding of white society.

The presence in South Nyanza of the Seventh-day Adventists with their doctrine of the imminent coming was a factor congenial to millenarianism. Millenarianism has appeared mainly in countries that have had some contact with the Judeo-Christian messianic hopes, for it requires some familiarity with the idea of the attainment of a perfect state, of a paradise here on earth. Religions that have an 'other-worldly' orientation, that put all the emphasis upon the hereafter or upon a purely spiritual salvation, and that see history as composed of repetitive, ever recurring cycles, are not conducive to millenarianism. Judeo-Christian contact is not, however, a necessity. Traditional belief systems frequently contain some idea of the return of ancestors or of a culture hero, and these concepts, upon contact with Christianity, may develop into fully fledged millenarian beliefs. No traces of millenarian ideas, however, were found in either Gusii or Luo cosmology.

By disseminating the 'one and only true religion' the missionaries introduced a severe strain into Gusii society. But mission teachings would likely have had far less impact if the punitive expeditions had not already severely jolted the society, creating doubts about indigenous beliefs and leadership. Some Gusii seemed to reason that since the whites' military had proven itself so powerful, their religion must be likewise. The missionaries, intent on their 'Christianising and civilizing' mission, held out rewards to converts, such as literacy, western knowledge, and jobs.

A factor that appears to have had independent effects on the creation of conduciveness is the stateless tribal structure. Stateless societies have no central political organs that unite the tribe as a whole. Although clans may share a common language and culture, they are self-governing units that conduct their own political affairs. Power tends to be widely dispersed through a number of independent religious-political offices. Such highly segmented societies were incapable of offering any unified resistance to the invaders and, in many cases, permitted them to play one group off against another.

The absence of a centralized authority structure, while offering little resistance to the invaders, may have had another quite different effect in promoting the development of Mumboism. In affording local groups greater freedom for action, it probably abetted local level initiative, as evidenced in the proliferation of many Mumbo and similar groups. Individuals appeared to have had little compunction about forming their own groups, which operated quite independently of each other, giving them a tenacity in the face of government repression.

Another dimension that made for compatibility between the tribal structure and mission teachings was role similarity. In tribal society, there were a number of ritual specialists whose roles paralleled in certain respects Christian prophetic and messianic roles. In addition, the missionary in charge of a mission station acted in the Africans' eyes like a chief. He was the 'owner' of much land, many buildings, and he had many people in his entourage. Thus, he appeared to have the power, status, and wealth required of a chief. This similarity in roles permitted the merging of traditional and Christian forms.

Absence of Means to Rectify Grievances
Particularly important in creating the appropriate conditions for Mumboism were the two crushing defeats which left the Gusii at a loss as to what to do, and closed off for the time being any efforts to expel the foreigners by force.

Multiple Strains
A basic premise of this study is that structural conduciveness in itself is not a sufficient condition for the rise of a protest movement. It only lays the framework within which other factors must interact to produce a particular type of movement. Strains vary in their intensity and combine in different ways. For instance, the government's efforts to recruit Africans for the Carrier Corps, and the Africans' experience in the Carrier Corps, act as separate determinants and at different times in the sequential recruitment to Mumboism.

The following strains were evident in South Nyanza. Some affected the population at large, others impinged with particular sharpness on certain segments helping to recruit members.

Enforced Change
Although there were many aspects of their life they would like to see changed, Africans tended to oppose changes forced on them. The government's drafting of labour for the Carrier Corps and wage employment evoked their hostility, and with good reason. The Carrier Corps subjected them to such severe hardship that many died, and not even for a cause of their own. Wage employment, aimed at supplying the settlers with labour, gave them few rewards. They had to leave their families and migrate considerable distances

for paltry wages, and when they resisted, government agents often resorted to coercion. The government interfered in their life in other ways as well. For instance, cattle rustling and inter-tribal fighting were proscribed.

Economic Hardship

Economic hardship in the form of famine and drought periodically affected the inhabitants of South Nyanza and exacerbated underlying tensions. Mumbo's membership appeared to increase in periods experiencing a sharp decline in the standard of living. This strain was not, however, one of the root causes, but acted as a determinant only on specific occasions.

Role Strains

Conflict between the younger and older generations, eased in Gusii society by sending youth off cattle raiding, was exacerbated by the government's ban on it, and by the missions providing youth with skills that made them far less dependent on tribal authority. Mumbo's nativistic element may well have been particularly attractive to old people who joined because they felt that tribal values and hence their power and status, were being threatened by mission teachings and unruly youth.

In any society, there are people dissatisfied with their share of the system's rewards. Situations of unrest, where established values are being questioned, offer an opportunity for the discontented to better their position. Mumbo's status reversal theme attracted people from less favoured positions. Young men and women, both low in power and prestige compared to mature men, saw in Mumbo an opportunity to acquire more satisfying roles.

Loss of Status and Power

Colonial domination was experienced with particular sharpness by different sectors of the population. Although military defeat was humiliating for all Gusii, it was even more so for the Bogonko clan which probably suffered the brunt of the destruction. It lost not only lives and possessions but, to add insult to injury, in the political reorganization that followed, this proud clan lost its dominant position to a rival clan. Loss of power, prestige and 'face' involved pride and humiliation — powerful ingredients of discontent. These deprivations appear responsible for recruiting the core support.

At the same time, members of the Bogonko clan were in a highly structured situation that provided few legitimate channels for the expression of grievances. Their protest was at first channelled into Mumboism's millennial hopes, but when these failed to materialize, it was redirected into attempts to abolish circumcision and other acts of defiance. The effort to abolish circumcision, closely linked as it was to tribal identity, was particularly aggressive, attention-gaining, and extreme, and perhaps mirrored the desperation of a clan long bedevilled by feelings of bitterness and long prevented from asserting itself. At first, its aggression was directed toward the foreign rulers, but later it acquired a negativistic strain, lashing out at the tribal system itself, and was marked by a shift from collective goals to more individualistic, hedonic values.

This negativism may have been encouraged by growing land pressures that had begun to be felt by the 1950s. *The Kenya Population Census 1962* showed that the district of Kisii was one of the country's most densely populated areas. Hence, the tensions that gave rise to earlier protest may have been exacerbated by economic pressures, well known to be particularly potent fomenters of unrest.

The general patterning of activities supports this interpretation. Drugs, ecstasy, visions, and passivity fit together and reinforce each other. Escapism and passivity were encouraged by the smoking of bhang which, in turn, promoted visionary states. Religious ecstasy or possession was seen, in part, as communicating with ancestral spirits. Sexual passion may also have been given a religious meaning. In all ages, the literature of religious mysticism has viewed religious ecstasy as closely related to, and often intertwined with, sexual passion. Members of some cults have even practised incest in the belief that special powers were thus acquired. Nevertheless, the breaking of mores is not done without psychic cost and evidence shows that usually the costs are high. In regard to the Gusii, it seems likely that smoking bhang palliated status frustrations as well as guilt feelings derived from having flouted mores.

The argument that support for Mumbo came from those with strong anti-British feelings needs to be qualified. It is a facile generalization that obscures both the complexity of the colonial relationship and the *quid pro quo* realities of the day-to-day struggle for power. It presents a one-sided view of the African-British relationship which underplays the Africans' dexterity in dealing with the British. It is perhaps too obvious to point out that Africans, like people everywhere, are interested in power, wealth, and prestige. It should be borne in mind that British administrators were few in number and that they had to rely upon support from the indigenous leaders. From the first days of colonial occupation alliances were made between the British and the African chiefs who often helped the British bring areas under their control, while enhancing their own position by the subjugation of their enemies with the help of the British.

In South Nyanza, it was not just a case of the British using Africans, but of particular African rivals for chieftainships securing their positions by acquiring British backing. The British provided a new structure of power and rules within which the age-old struggle continued. Those chiefs who learned early how to handle the British in order to achieve their own ends came out on top. Tribal and clan rivalry continued as it had for centuries, only now another dimension, foreign domination, set the stage. Consequently, those clans and sub-clans whose positions were enhanced and whose claims were supported by the administration tended to be pro-British. One can hypothesize that had the British supported the Bogonko clan's claims to the chieftainship, the Bogonko would probably have worked with the administration and, being dominant, would not have protested.

Exacerbating Factors

In any movement that extends over time, there are a number of events or severe strains that are decisive in recruiting particular groups. Here are two possibilities.

The German invasion of Kisii and the temporary exit of the British may well have changed the conditions of conduciveness and attracted a significant number of adherents. This dramatic event probably confirmed for some the Seventh-day Adventists' prediction of a coming millennium as well as Mumbo's similar prophesy, cast doubts about the invulnerability of the British, and stimulated interest among the populace in Mumbo.

The active cooperation of a chief or headman with the administration in deceiving his own people, as is likely to have occurred when young men were enticed to the district headquarters where they were shanghaied into the Carrier Corps, could well have incensed the population and, in particular, already rebellious youth, leading them to join.

General Beliefs

Mumbo's beliefs reflect the character of conduciveness and strain, and focus on removing the main sources of strain, the foreigners and the Africans under their influence. The movement held aloft a vision of a future life in which the oppressed would be elevated and the oppressors put down. It advocated radical change. It would reverse the power structure, abolish circumcisions, and broaden clan and tribal allegiances. This ideology, formed from Christian and indigenous ideas did not aim to change the present order, but to abolish it and to usher in a new social order.

When the Gusii saw that there was no way to fight the aliens militarily, the thoughts and hopes of some turned to the 'other world', of which the missionaries had spoken: if only they worshipped the true god and followed the proper rituals, their problems would be solved. Hence their protest advocated a withdrawal from the world of action and pragmatic solutions and a reliance on ritual to evoke supernatural forces to punish and eliminate their enemies.

As for specific action directed toward ousting the British or acquiring an education, or engaging in any concrete projects that would provide the means for the desired goals, there was little. Some evidence suggests passive resistance. There were complaints that the Mumboites refused to comply with compulsory labour or to pay their taxes. But, by and large, anti-British activity was limited to sporadic protest like the looting of Kisii, agitation, and the symbolic rejection of the foreigners.

Rituals stressed traditional symbols and practices. Advocating in a few specific ways a return to the past, the cult nevertheless rejected much of the past. The 1957 attempt to abolish circumcision may not only have indicated a deep dissatisfaction with the tribal system, but it may also have signalled preparations for a new order that the millennium would usher in. Thus the cessation of ties with the old order shown by the breaking of mores. Lanternari seems to have missed an important dimension of these movements when he maintains that they 'always adhere to native tradition and reject western beliefs.'[2]

Mobilization for Roles

Conduciveness, strains and beliefs are not in themselves sufficient to produce a new movement. Leaders must appear and people with grievances mobilized.

An important figure in determining Mumbo's choice of means was Muraa, who, after the 1908 rebellion, counselled her people not to fight the British any more but to rely upon prayer to oust them. This orientation may have been influenced by mission teachings but the stronger influence was probably Luo possession cults that also relied largely upon magical solutions.

The loosely structured movement was composed of small, autonomous groups clustered around local readers who articulated deeply held sentiments. The peasants' hopes, wants, fears, and resentments persisted despite the appearance and disappearance of leaders. These sentiments usually remained dormant until a spokesman brought them to the fore by giving them some form, even if a rather loose one, and, to our minds at least, full of contradictions. In large part this explains Mumbo's tenacity and the administration's difficulty in stamping it out for whenever the administration tried to chop off its head it found itself battling a Hydra. Groups sprang up here and there wherever a local prophet appeared. When one set of leaders was deported, others came to the fore, there being little organization for the administration to seize. People were bound together by an amorphous structure of shared sentiments and beliefs with little formal organization or programme.

Agents of Social Control

Once Mumbo had originated, government repression, whenever it appeared to be gaining strength, continued to create conditions compatible with millenarianism. As the government proceeded to stamp out any appearance of Mumboism and as millenarian hopes receded, protest turned to hedonism and hostile acts directed against the tribal system. Thus protest moved from armed opposition to millenarianism, from outright militancy to symbolic militancy, and finally, perhaps, to accommodation and withdrawal.

*   *   *

The first challenge to colonial authority in South Nyanza came from the Mumbo movement, composed of autonomous groups borne along by a millennial dream. Its objection to alien rule indicated an uncompromising position. Its attempts to find new ways to cope with the invaders were fumbling, experimental, and ineffectual. Compared with the Kikuyu and Luo who, by the 1920s and 1930s, were pressuring and petitioning the administration and the Home Government to redress their grievances, the Gusii were politically unsophisticated. And, although Mumboism's protest eventually fizzled out because of severe repression and the dissipation of its energies upon individualistic, hedonistic goals, still it represents the beginnings of political protest among the Gusii, the articulation of grievances, and the building of embryonic trans-tribal allegiances.

Notes

1. Daryll Forde (ed.), *African Worlds*, (Oxford University Press, London, 1954), pp. x–xii.
2. Lanternari, *The Religions of the Oppressed*, p. 20.

PART III

The Dini ya Msambwa Movement

Chapter 9

BACKGROUND OF THE MOVEMENT

A movement called Dini ya Msambwa first made its appearance in the remote western region of Kenya bordering the foothills of Mount Elgon in the early 1940s.[1] Its leader, Elijah Masinde, a fiery Bukusu, ordered the foreigners to leave the country and his people to return to their traditional religion.[2] Masinde's words were backed up with militant action, defiance of chiefs and district commissioners, riots, the burning down of mission churches, schools, and administrative buildings. Dini ya Msambwa spear-headed an amorphous popular movement that aroused the colonialists' fears — reports of secret meetings, underground activities and fanatical passions seemed portents of a general insurrection.

Dini ya Msambwa represents a distinct turning point in Luhya nationalism. Previously, the Luhya had sought to remedy their grievances through reform measures. Msambwa combined new, revolutionary ideas with radical tactics. 'Masinde was the first nationalist', a respected leader of the community said. 'He was the first person to tell the British to get out'.

Before examining Msambwa's origins and development, we will briefly describe the context in which it arose and some pertinent historical background.

Punitive Expeditions

Msambwa's main support and leadership came from the Luhya, a people of Bantu stock, who, at the time of the British entry, composed a loose grouping of twenty-one politically independent, though culturally and linguistically related, sub-tribes. Seventeen of the sub-tribes occupied what was then known as the North Nyanza District of Nyanza Province, and four, the Bukedi and Bugisu Districts and a little of the Busoga District of Uganda.[3]

The sub-tribe, composed of numerous clans, thirty being about average, was the basic political unit. The clans operated more or less autonomously. Big clans appeared to exercise minimal direction over small clans. For instance, if a big clan was going on a cattle raid, members of a small clan would be invited to participate. Among the clans, a state of semi-warfare, primarily cattle raiding, existed. There is little evidence of wars on a wider trans-tribal scale.[4]

The two Luhya sub-tribes of particular interest to this study are the Wanga and the Bukusu. At the outset, the Wanga cooperated with, and the Bukusu opposed, the British, and these contrasting positions were maintained well into the colonial period.

In the late nineteenth century, the Wanga were the most politically advanced, in terms of a centralized political structure, and cohesive sub-tribe among the Luhya. They were the only ones with hereditary chiefs and a well established chieftainship. Their *nabongo* or chief, Mumia, is one of Kenya's legendary figures. Born around 1849 into an old dynasty, he was approximately twenty-three years old when he succeeded his father, Shiundu, killed in battle in 1883. His village, known as Mumias, was situated on an important trade route opposite a vital ford in the Nzoia River. Mumia, as his father before him, was friendly with the Arab traders who used to stop with their caravans to rest and replenish their food supplies before proceeding into the interior in search of ivory, hides and slaves. Mumia, with help from the Swahili traders Abdullah bin Hamid of Mombasa and 'fat' Sudi from Pangani as well as from Maasai mercenaries of the Uasin Gishu District, was busy in the last half of the century expanding Wanga hegemony.

After the Arab traders came British explorers and missionaries. By the 1890s, Mumias had become an important British base. Joseph Thompson, the first white man to traverse Nyanza, reached there on 3 December 1883, and was welcomed by Mumia. Soon afterwards, Bishop James Hannington arrived *en route* to Uganda. Although Mumia tried to discourage him from continuing his journey, the bishop ignored his advice and went on to meet his death at the hands of the Baganda.

The Church Missionary Society was given land by Mumia on which to build a mission. The Reverend W. A. Crabtree, who arrived in 1894 to begin work on the site, described Mumia, 'All the Kavirondo chiefs I have known hitherto have been clad in skins a simple and scanty garment. Imagine, then, my intense surprise when a tall man greeted us, wearing a long white *kanzu* [an Arab garment that looks something like a caftan] and over that a long black coat reaching to the feet, embroidered in silver; and on his head a Turkish cap, black velvet embroidered in blue and silver.'[5]

Mumia's position was strengthened with the pacification of unruly tribes and the establishment of administration. Mumia continued to ingratiate the Wanga with the British by supplying them with warriors, equipment, guides, and a base from which to launch attacks. The British, in turn, provided Mumia, harried by dynastic rivals and tribal enemies, with invaluable military aid. In 1896 they even mounted a punitive expedition against the Kager clan of Ugenya for him. Two hundred Luo were killed.[6] Mumia, friendly first with the Arabs, then the British explorers and missionaries and later the administrators, established a pattern of cooperation with the aliens that served their mutual interests.

About the beginning of the nineteenth century, the Bukusu were subjected to endless raids by the Teso, who were moving from the Tororo and Mbale regions of Eastern Uganda into Bukusu country. Their homes were razed, crops destroyed, cattle looted and whole villages abandoned. These attacks forced the Bukusu to move continually. Some migrated to what are now the locations of Samia, Bunyala and Marachi, some to Luo country, and some moved westwards across the Uganda-Kenya border. At one time, only six clans defied the Teso and remained. A legend tells of the Bukusu being chased around Mount Elgon three times by the Teso.[7]

The next threat to the Bukusu came from the slave traders. The exact date when Swahili and Arab traders entered Nyanza for the first time is unknown, but by 1878 they were raiding Luhya country from their headquarters at Mumias. The Bukusu suffered from these raids as they were geographically vulnerable:

> It would appear that for many years past Ketosh [meaning Bukusu] had been the happy hunting ground of the Swahili and Arab traders, particularly on those occasions when they arrived from Karamoja via Baringo, after an unsuccessful quest for ivory and with plenty of trade goods on hand; or when the easy acquisition of a batch of slaves was too tempting to forgo on their leaving Mumias on their way coastwards.[8]

Once again the Bukusu were forced to defend their lives and property.

Joseph Thompson the explorer, accustomed to receiving a warm welcome from the peoples of Nyanza, was to his surprise, rebuffed by the Bukusu. Later he was told the following story which he related:

> [Several years previous] the traders had lost a few men through murder or otherwise. In revenge for this the traders, five years previous to our arrival, had decided to "tengeneza" [straighten out] the natives. For this purpose a combined caravan of some 1500 men stationed at Kwa-Sundu [Mumias] was marched upon them. Dividing into sections, they entered the district at different points, and crossed it, devastating every village on the way, killing thousands of men and women, committing the most horrible atrocities, such as ripping open women with child, making great bonfires and throwing children into them, while the small boys and girls were captured as slaves. . . . Indeed there is no monster more savage and cruel than the Swahili trader, when the demon nature within him is set loose.[9]

The slave traders referred to in the above passage were organized by 'fat' Sudi from his base at Mumias. This episode would explain the Bukusu's hatred of the Wanga as well as their suspicious and hostile attitudes towards aliens in general.

The Bukusu who practised a mixed pastoral-agricultural economy with families living on their own land, drastically changed their way of life in order to survive. Under the leadership of their great hero, Mukite wa Nameme, they built fortified villages where they lived together and they reorganized their military. New offensive and defensive tactics were adopted.[10] These changes proved effective. Their cattle raiding became so ruthless that they were hated by neighbouring sub-tribes. The Nandi called them Ketosh (enemies), a name adopted by colonial officials, though resented by the Bukusu.[11] In time, the Teso, Wanga, Tachoni, Samia, Maasai, and the Luo of Ugenya location were all defeated. The Bukusu not only recovered but enlarged their territory, taking Itesio location at the expense of the Teso. Through these experiences, they developed patterns of behaviour, military prowess and hostility towards strangers, that were to play an important role in their future relations with the British.

In the latter part of the nineteenth century, the British began to pacify the various tribes of North Nyanza. During those years, the administration was mainly concerned with protecting the important caravan route from Eldama Ravine to Mumias, improving transportation facilities, and ensuring a steady supply of food for their stations and caravans en route. It protected friendly tribes which accepted its authority and punished those which opposed it. This tactic, it was hoped, would convince the recalcitrant of the futility of their resistance and deter potential trouble-makers.[12]

C. W. Hobley of the Imperial British East Africa Company was posted to Mumias as sub-commissioner in 1895 for the purpose of setting up what was to be the first permanent administrative district in North Nyanza. The Bukusu, not unexpectedly, did not welcome him and it was not long before they were at odds. The last straw as far as the administration was concerned came when it sent twenty-five Sudanese soldiers to retrieve rifles that the Bukusu had purchased from deserters and the Bukusu annihilated them to a man. Then it was decided that the defiant Bukusu must be punished. Frederick Jackson sums up the reasons behind the punitive expedition:

> As Mr. Grant reports that these people [Bukusu] have been for several years past a source of endless trouble not only to the surrounding natives who are friendly towards us, and have considered themselves under the protection of the white man . . . but also to Europeans and traders, as they have been in the habit of raiding the former, and harbouring deserters from the latter, from whom they have acquired 50 to 60 breach loading rifles . . . and as they are also in league with the people of Kikelelwa . . . who killed the man who . . . disappeared with the mail bag, it is a matter of expediency that they should have been brought to task, and I trust that the punishment they have received will have a deterrent effect on them and others.[13]

Hobley, the expedition's leader, provides a firsthand account. Though lengthy it will be quoted because it provides a glimpse of some important Bukusu traits and of early tribal relationships, as well as a vivid description of an event later enshrined in Dini ya Msambwa's folklore:

> North of the Nzoia, between the river and the lower slopes of Mt. Elgon dwelt a powerful tribe called the Ketosh, in descent very much the same as the Wa-Wanga but with a strain of Hamitic blood. They were not on good terms with Mumias people, and the tribe contained many wild and turbulent spirits. . . .
>
> During the previous twelve months the desertion of men with rifles had increased and the Ketosh chiefs had notably encouraged it, paying cattle for every rifle received. Mr. Spire, with laudable intentions, had insisted on the surrender of the rifles as being government property, and considerable palaver had taken place with but little result. He then . . . despatched twenty-five Sudanese soldiers from the garrison of the station . . . to demand the arms. . . . As might have been expected under such circumstances no European officer being present, a gun went off during the palaver with the chief. The Ketosh tribesmen then emerged and attacked the detachment of Sudanese. They fought gallantly, but were

speared one by one and eventually annihilated. Here was a nice kettle of fish to fry, and my first task was to endeavour to get in touch with the Ketosh leaders and extract some reparation for this slaughter. . . .

I was reluctantly forced to appeal to Uganda for an expeditionary force to subdue the tribe. Accordingly, William Grant of Busoga was sent down in command of a company of Sudanese troops, and a levy of armed Baganda, about 1000 strong, under the Kakunguru, an important chief of Uganda. Hearing of the preparation, Mumia asked to be allowed to attach a column of spearsmen and the Uasingishu Masai also volunteered about a couple of hundred warriors. . . . [It is interesting to note the number of tribes willing to help the British subdue the Bukusu and probably indicates the intensity of anti-Bukusu feeling.] A march of about ten miles brought us near to a great walled village and directly our fan of scouts approached it the tribesmen retired inside, barred the gates and opened fire, so there was no doubt that a fight was staged. . . .

When the main body arrived . . . we opened fire on one of the gates with a small Hotchkiss gun. This had no effect on the stout logs which barred it, so we shelled the huts. The Kakunguru then sought permission to storm the gate with his levies, and sanction was accorded. They advanced with great elan and succeeded in forcing an entrance, but the Ketosh spearsmen massed inside the village, counter-attacked and drove out the Baganda with considerable loss. . . . We then cut down a section of the mud wall by maxim fire and advanced to the attack. The defence then concentrated on this sector; the spears came over like rain and the Sudanese were held up by the ditch. The Baganda were then ordered to renew the attack at the original gate, and eventually the village was taken and burnt, the survivors streaming out by still another gate. The Masai during the night stormed another fortified village about half a mile away, first creating confusion by firing burning arrows into the thatch of the huts. There were no cattle in these villages so we knew that the enemy had really been preparing to make a stand on this spot which was the scene of the attack on the Sudanese detachment. The fact that we had about ninety killed and wounded was a measure of the severity of the contest. . . .

[He describes the expedition's advance into Bukusu country.] One day we were joined by several hundred Elgumi warriors from the plains to the south-west of Elgon, who had seized the opportunity of revenging themselves on the Ketosh for former raids. . . . We declined their assistance, and told them that this was not their quarrel. . . .

Two days later another battle occurred. The following morning we commenced to march along the foot of the scarp in a northerly direction, and very shortly our scouts reported that the enemy were in force in a great walled village about a mile or so away. . . . It was quite a fortress, about 250 yards in diameter, with loop-holed mud walls nine feet high, a ditch six feet deep and low gates at intervals. [This is Chetambe's fort near Lugulu to which the Bukusu had fled.] As our force approached, the Ketosh opened fire from a variety of firearms but luckily with little idea of markmanship. The attitude of the enemy, however, showed that this was probably their great stand, and such it proved to be.

A storming party of Baganda was organized, supported by a half company of Sudanese, the nearest gate was shelled and a section of the mud wall on each side of the gate was undercut by machine gun fire, until it collapsed. An advance was ordered. The Baganda and Sudanese stormed the breach with great dash, but once amongst the crowded huts the advantages of their fire was lost, and the Ketosh with great gallantry counter attacked and our force experienced considerable loss, two Sudanese officers being killed or wounded, and the survivors driven out of the village. The situation was then critical, so Grant, Sitwell and I took in the balance of the Sudanese and, instead of advancing into the middle of the village, fought our way along the inside of the wall, opening fresh gates as they were reached. As each gate was opened, contingents of our force poured in; and eventually resistance was overpowered. We all had some very narrow escapes from warriors who charged up with spear and shield nigh to the rifle's muzzle and afterwards learnt that the fighting men had primed themselves with beer and Indian hemp for the action. . . .

After about an hour's desperate struggle the resistance collapsed, and the broken remnants of the enemy force fled by gates on the far side of the village. . . .[14]

The Bukusu were daring, tough and tenacious fighters who gave the British, with their formidable support, a hard battle. Hobley noted the 'gallantry' with which they fought.

There is conflicting evidence as to the extent of losses. Hobley reported ninety members of his force either killed or wounded in the first encounter, so we can assume that with the preponderance of modern weapons on his side, the Bukusu suffered much greater losses. The surviving Bukusu composed a sad song about the battle which contains the sentence, '*Khwafwa khwabuna eee nga lumerera! Wa Chetambe eee nga lumerera ee!*' ('We died like the *lumerera* [very small ants which travel by the thousands] at Chetambe's fort.') Ansorge, a British doctor serving with the expedition, on the other hand, wrote that 'comparatively few' Bukusu were killed, but that villages were burned to the ground, crops destroyed, grain stores consumed by the victors, and their cattle divided up with half going to the government and the other half to their allies.[15] Captured Bukusu women were taken by British soldiers back to Mumias and subsequently ransomed by chief Mumia to the Bukusu for goats, cattle and hoes.

Although the expedition inflicted great hardship on the Bukusu, it did not quell their opposition. As early as 1904 they had recovered sufficiently to oppose chief Mumia when he appointed a headman who tried to collect a hut tax of two rupees or to exact the equivalent in labour. The dishonesty of Swahili tax collectors led to the burning down of two administrative huts and to a demonstration in 1905.[16] They continued to cause trouble in 1907 and 1908 over these and other matters.[17] They destroyed bridges in order to hinder the visit of the tax collector and even went so far as to try to move north eastward into the Trans Nzoia to escape the government.[18]

Hobley observed, 'They [Bukusu] are assertively independent, and to such a degree that it is rarely that one finds a chief who has any real control over his people, and it is this independent and pugnacious nature which has rendered our task of reducing this area to a state of law and order a slower process than in Buganda.'[19] In sum, the pacification of the Bukusu was a long drawn out process. The British, through force of arms, had to demonstrate time and again their sheer power.[20]

The Bukusu's response to the foreigners was in keeping with the way they had confronted similar problems in the past. They displayed an ability to adapt themselves to new situations even when it entailed drastic changes in their lives. They began acquiring guns as soon as they possibly could. Earlier they had given up living scattered across the plain for the safety of walled villages and had reorganized their military into a more effective unit. Not only were they resourceful, but once set upon a specific course, they showed a determination and resilience in the face of obstacles.

Political Reorganization

When the British began to rationalize the political processes,[21] they employed Mumia and his relatives in much the same capacity as the Baganda had been used in the administration of Uganda. In 1909 Mumia was made paramount chief of North Nyanza. This meant that all other location chiefs took orders from him, at least up to 1920, when the district headquarters was transferred from his village to Kakamega, some twenty miles distant. After that his authority declined, although until the establishment of a district appeal court in the 1930s he performed his judicial function.

Mumia's relatives were appointed chiefs and headmen in a number of locations in the North Nyanza District. Though the following chart is incomplete, it provides an idea of the extensiveness of Wanga jurisdiction.[22]

Personnel	Location	Period
Chitechi	Buholo	1895–1905
Kadiima (half brother of Mumia)	Bundo	1905 onwards
	Samia	1912–1927
Mahero	South Bukusu	1900 onwards
Shiundu	Kabras	1909 onwards
Mulama (half brother of Mumia)	Marama	1910 onwards
Wambani	Butsotso	1910 onwards
Murungu (half brother of Mumia)	Kimilili, Itesio and Malakisi	1910–1934
Were (half brother of Mumia)	Bundo	
Tomia	Butsotso	

The securing by any one sub-tribe of a favoured position was bound to cause problems with the others, particularly when its members exercised authority over formerly autonomous, chiefless, sub-tribes. But the Wanga were particularly unacceptable since the Bukusu harboured an old grievance dating back to 1895. 'The Kitosh were defeated and brought to order . . . but the Babukusu never forgave Mumia', noted John Osogo.[23] So intense were their feelings, that some Bukusu migrated to the White Highlands, preferring employment with white farmers to life under Wanga rule.[24] We will not attempt here to evaluate Wanga rule but rather to examine some of the problems it created and its legacy for future Luhya politics.

Chiefs, in administering tribes that had hitherto not had any centralized direction, had to assert themselves and a number of chiefs did so by resorting to physical coercion. A district commissioner, in discussing chief Murungu's methods, stated:

> Unfortunately he does not rise to his position. He is handicapped first by being a stranger in his sub-district and when he was appointed he tried to administer the country by means of armed retainers who were practically uncontrolled. The men were disbanded and all arms confiscated a year ago and now Murungu has orders to use the council of elders in each location and administer through them only . . . . He uses too much or too little force and either bullies his people or shows himself very much afraid of them.[25]

In the eyes of many Luhya, the government and Mumia became identified as one. 'Whenever headmen or chiefs were appointed, he [Mumia] was believed to have been responsible for it, not the government. Equally, whenever the government attacked some community, as they did in many places during the first twelve years, the local people always said it was Mumia who sent the government forces against them.'[26]

The chiefs were accused of undermining the clan elders' authority. They tended to surround themselves with fellow tribesmen and to by-pass local councils of elders in matters that had traditionally belonged to the elders. When they met opposition, they relied on the government to back them up.[27] In the area of land rights the issue became so contentious that the government instituted an investigation. *The Report of the Committee of Native Land Tenure in the North Kavirondo Reserve* in 1930 concluded:

> Our investigations have revealed certain conditions which appear to us to require the immediate attention of Government. . . . Natives appointed solely for the administration purposes . . . have usurped the authority and function of *liguru* [head of the council of elders] in respect of land. . . .
> We are informed that in many cases headmen and sub-headmen have allotted holdings on clan lands to their chosen friends and supporters with total disregard of the real *liguru*, thus trampling on proper native law and custom.[28]

Some chiefs used their position to increase their own wealth and power. Wanga chiefs, in demarcating locational boundaries gave generous slices of other clans' territory to their kinsmen.[29] In addition, the distinction between government and personal property was not clear to all chiefs. Chief Murungu, for one, had to be reminded by the administration that he was not entitled to fees collected at a *baraza* or to cattle obtained from a fine.[30]

The government made efforts to curtail the arbitrary powers of chiefs. They were forbidden in 1924 to require people to work on their private farms.[31] They were ordered to use the council of elders in each location and to administer through them. Opposition grew. Year after year, District Reports noted the 'growing discontent' over Wanga suzerainty.[32] *The Native Affairs Annual Report 1923* stated:

> Among the Bantu of North Kavirondo there has been a marked tendency to strive for appointment of local petty chiefs as official headmen as against those of the Wanga sub-tribe which has been the ruling family in the past. The more prominent of the Wanga chiefs such as Mumia, Mulama and Murunga have, however, maintained their prestige and authority; it is to be hoped that they will continue to do so. Mumia is getting very old, but Mulama and Murunga are two of the most intelligent and capable and progressive chiefs in the colony.

97

The administration, realizing that agitation would continue until the Wanga were removed gradually replaced them as they died or retired with men from within the location. Wanga power took a definite decline in 1925 when Mumia retired and all of his powers were taken away, although he retained his title nominally. Several chiefs were deposed in 1926 and 1927 for corrupt practices. By the late 1920s and early 1930s, the locations of Kimilili, Bunyala, Kabras, Elgon, Samia, Wamia, Butsotso, Bunyore, Kisa and South Marama had become independent. Only chief Murungu remained over a non-Wanga location until 1936.[33]

Once the process started, the government had difficulty in stopping it. In 1930, C. S. Thompson attributed the district's undercurrent of unrest to grievances which coalesced around the issue of clan autonomy:

> The movement had manifested itself in the continued effort of the natives to get rid of any headman who can in any way be regarded as an outsider, in the desire of certain clans who were scattered abroad by internecine war, famine, pestilence many years ago to come together again and with existing boundaries which in some cases divide certain numbers of natives from the rest of the clan with which they claim affinity. . . .[34]

In 1933, the district commissioner declared, 'The process of de-volution . . . is now complete.'[35] In 1934, the administration again stated it would countenance no further splitting up of locations or the appointment of assistant chiefs. These declarations had little effect. The district commissioner wrote with some exasperation in 1935 that 'some individuals . . . do not think it has gone far enough and would hardly be satisfied until every clan or sub-clan had a puppet chief of no more importance than a *minyapare* or *mlango* [headman]. Most of the clan agitators are individually respectful and pleasant, but *are fanatical on this one subject.*' (Italics mine.) Even in 1938, the same issue was being voiced. 'In North Kavirondo almost every dispute has its origins in inter-clan jealousies', wrote the district commissioner.[36] Thus in granting some locations their own chiefs, a veritable Pandora's Box had been opened: clan autonomy became the goal and clans whose members had been separated continued to agitate.

Protest also centred on the issue of the paramount chief. Mumia was getting old and the British had let it be known that with his death the institution would end. Most Luhya favoured such an appointment in the belief that it was a step towards greater political autonomy on the lines of the Kingdom of Buganda. Paramountcy was seen as a way of gaining more independence and status for chiefs, of changing their position from being merely agents executing British policy (in particular from being labour recruiters for the settlers) to being genuine African leaders with decision-making powers in their own right. Chiefs were behind the campaign as they wanted to acquire more control over land and local resources for development, as well as to increase their own legitimacy in the eyes of Africans.[37]

On this issue the agitators were divided into two main groups. Chief Mumia knew he did not have long to live and was anxious that his son, Abdullah, should succeed to the title. The second faction was that of chief Mulama backed by the North Kavirondo Central Association. An ambitious man, Mulama began to intrigue for the paramount chieftainship. When the Central Association's petitions to the administration on his behalf were refused, the Association called together a *baraza* in 1935 and proclaimed Mulama paramount chief alluding to sanctions from England or Nairobi. The Governor immediately denounced it and Mulama was dismissed from his headship of Marama location.[38]

A less determined or less militant group would probably have been dissuaded by the Governor's rebuke, but not the Central Association. In 1945 it thought the circumstances were propitious since Rapando, a Wanga chief, had died, a successor had not yet been named, and chief Mumia's health was failing. The Association staged a second démarche by suddenly calling a *baraza* to elect a chief and presented Mulama again as a candidate. Chief Mumia and the administration were furious. The district commissioner forbade the holding of the *baraza*, and the provincial commissioner remarked, 'It was evident that had they succeeded in their purpose, the Association would have advanced this as a first stage in their demand that the Nabongo [chief] should be proclaimed Paramount Chief.'[39]

Mumia, by skillfully cultivating the foreigners, maintained and strengthened Wanga power during the first years of British occupation.[40] His support helped the British bring one area under their control and thus worked against wider African interests. But at this stage in Kenya's history loyalties were tied to the sub-tribe or clan, in only a few instances had broader groupings emerged. It was to be expected that individual chiefs would manoeuvre to promote their own sub-tribe at the expense of rivals. Mumia, in keeping with the perspective of that period, was advancing Wanga interests. The great weakness of Luhya and other Kenyan tribes in their opposition to the invaders lay in their lack of tribal and inter-tribal unity—loyalty was owed to a unit too small to provide effective opposition. Instead of the tribes banding together in a united stand against the invaders, they, in fact, did much of the fighting for them.

To summarize, British intervention led to the intensification of clan conflict. It placed government appointed chiefs and headmen in positions of jurisdiction over sub-tribes that had formerly been autonomous and approximately equal. Thus clan rivalries were exacerbated as warring clans intrigued over boundaries and manoeuvred and petitioned over appointments. Commenting on this intense interclan hostility, the district commissioner concluded, 'This means there is a perpetual spark that is liable at any time to light a blaze of trouble. . . . There is no doubt that *North Kavirondo is not only the most politically minded of the Districts but also due to clan partisanship the most prone to local disturbance.*'[41] (Italics mine.) Thus, early in the colonial period, the pattern of North Nyanzan politics was established.

The Missions

Heading the movement that challenged Wanga overlordship and pushed for a paramount chief was a new generation of mission-educated young men who wanted a share in the decision-making, prestigious positions. These years saw a struggle between the old chiefs to maintain their privileged position and men representing new interests who were no longer content with the status quo.[42]

The opportunities for young men were few. The missions provided an opportunity to acquire a rudimentary education and a few skills, literacy, knowledge of English and familiarity with European ways, that might lead to a job in a mission as a school teacher or catechist, or in the administration as a tax collector, census taker, member of the Local Native Council, or some other minor official. The administration needed Africans to fill the lower echelons as there were relatively few European officials. For instance, the 1937 African population of Nyanza was 354,000 and it was administered by forty-one Europeans and forty-nine Asians. Before pursuing the role of mission converts, let me backtrack to briefly discuss the missions.

North Nyanza attracted many Christian denominations. Its higher elevation meant a healthier, more invigorating climate than the lowlands of Central Nyanza. The Church Missionary Society (CMS, Anglican) began to work in the Maragoli Hills in 1905 and opened a station at Maseno in 1906. The Roman Catholic Mill Hill Fathers settled in Kisumu in 1904 and at Mumias in 1905. The Friends Africa Mission (FAM), an American Quaker group, arrived in 1902 at Kaimosi. The Church of God, originally the South African Compound and Interior Mission, was another evangelical American group which established itself at Kima in Bunyore after 1906.[43] The Pentecostal Assemblies of East Africa started a mission at Nyang'ori in 1924, and the Salvation Army opened their first mission at Malakisi in 1936.[44]

The missions opened schools and as early as 1911 had enrolled a fair number of Luhya.[45] By 1918 there were more than seven thousand students.[46] Jomo Kenyatta explained the Africans' desire for education. 'The education, especially reading and writing, was regarded as the white man's magic, and thus the young men were very eager to acquire the new magical power.'[47]

The competition among the missions for the allegiance of Africans aggravated a situation already fraught with hostilities. Rivalries surfaced in the overzealous activities of mission converts. In one year a Roman Catholic received six months for threatening to burn down an Anglican school, six members of Friends Africa Mission were fined 21/- for assaulting a Roman Catholic teacher, five others received six weeks for assaulting elders, and so on.

The unforeseen consequences of education, as discussed for South Nyanza, was to liberate youth from tribal control. They demanded the right to regulate marriage dowries, a traditional prerogative of the elders. They accused the chiefs of bribery and of smoking bhang.[48] They refused to obey their parents, the missionaries, the chiefs and in time, some would reject the colonial system itself. District commissioner C. B. Thompson of the North Nyanza District wrote in 1929: 'Unfortunately the mission adherents, in many cases got completely out of hand. The large number of out-schools and in the case of the Friends Africa Mission the shortage of missionaries in the Reserve have made it easy for *politics to usurp the place of religion and for these schools to become in some cases centres of sedition*.'[49] (Italics mine.)

Not only did the missions free youth from the customary

constraints but they recruited youth already in conflict with the traditional order who found a kind of sanctuary in the missions. The *North Kavirondo District Annual Report 1925* commented:

> Four CMS natives who had been brought up in *baraza* before the District Commissioner by Chief Mulama for holding meetings likely to be subversive of authority refused to return to their seats after their affair had been dealt with and resisted the efforts made to remove them. In the course of the fracas one of the two police present was assaulted; and ultimately the four got away (while the police were mobbed by a crowd of Church Missionary Society natives) and fled for refuge to Archdeacon Owen's house at Maseno where they were arrested the same day.
>
> Later in the year the Honourable Acting Chief Native Commissioner had reason to complain of the insolence and indiscipline of Church Missionary Society natives who went down to work on his farm; so that it is evident that there is something wrong in the Church Missionary Society system of teaching.

Some administrators attributed this rebelliousness to the rapid growth of missions and the shortage of European supervisors. To expand their mission work, many Protestant denominations had trained Africans quickly and put them in charge of local groups and schools.[50]

Alliances between particular missions and chiefly families were formed. For example, chief Murungu initially reserved his area for the Protestants and chief Sudi did the same for the Roman Catholics.[51] Local church elders and teachers sometimes came from the same clan as the chief, and chiefs sat on mission councils. The first pupils to join mission schools were often the sons of chiefs, sub-chiefs, headmen and their relatives. Having acquired an elementary education these young men, in time, entered the mission hierarchy or became chiefs themselves.[52] Here was the beginnings of a self-perpetuating elite.

The missions contributed in the following ways to creating the appropriate circumstances for the development of Dini ya Msambwa:
1) Religious heterogeneity and conflict weakened the influence of any one denomination and led to a skeptical attitude on the part of many Africans to any one denomination's claim to have the religious truth.
2) New values introduced by the missionaries early in the twentieth century helped to undermine indigenous ways and authority.
3) Chief-mission alliances strengthened the position of an emerging

local elite, associated religion with politics, and exacerbated cleavages, between chiefly and non-chiefly clans. Young men from non-chiefly clans had to seek other avenues of advancement among them, the voluntary associations and the independent churches.

Early Colonial Land and Labour Policies

Up to World War I the settlers of British and Boer descent were overwhelmingly from South Africa. After the war, ex-servicemen, many of them former officers, increased the non-South African element. Kenya became less of a South African 'colony' and more of a retreat for aristocrats, gentleman farmers and pensioned officers of the Crown. But irrespective of their origins, British settlers quickly formed a community of interests bent on consolidating settler power. They feared they would be swamped by the Asians or massacred by the Africans of the countryside. It was for these reasons that the settlers living in the Central Highlands attempted to found a white man's country patterned after South Africa:

> The South Africans . . . called it a "white man's" country but it was to be a white man's country founded in the South African image, with no "nonsense" about equal rights for black and white. Their farming methods, their control of labour, their political techniques and objectives were all founded on South African precedents. . . . The part Africans were expected to play in this hierarchical society was essentially the same as that performed by servants and rural labourers in England. The masters were, on the whole, kind and charitable to their African servants but, like the South African frontiersman, they believed that Africans should be kept in their place.[53]

Once the decision had been made to build Kenya's economy on the basis of European owned plantation agriculture with Africans supplying the labour, ways had to be found to expand the labour supply, for Africans had shown a reluctance to leave the reserves for wage labour.[54] The settlers pressured the government to establish a policy that would provide them with the needed labour, even though instructions from the Secretary of State for the Colonies in 1908 forbade the government to directly assist in labour recruitment. Instead, Africans were to be encouraged by 'suggestion' to seek work.

The Native Labour Commission of 1912-13 composed of settlers, missionaries and administrators made a number of recommendations designed to expand the supply of labour. It suggested that the size of the reserves be limited and that taxes based on number of wives be instituted. The desertion of labourers was recognized as a serious problem and the Commission recommended some form of registration similar to that of Southern Rhodesia. Put into effect in 1919, the *kipande* required African males over sixteen years of age to carry registration certificates, usually worn on a string around the neck. Africans had to obtain the signature of their employer when they wished to seek work elsewhere or return to the reserves. The settlers used the *kipande* to control their labourers, since by refusing to sign it a settler could prevent a labourer from leaving, or he could blackball a particular worker whom he disliked. The *kipande* was seen by Africans as a blatant mark of second class citizenship, as they and not Asians or Europeans had to register.

African farming of cash crops was discouraged for the settlers did not want any competition, and they felt that it might cut the flow of labour to their farms. Prohibitions against the growing of coffee and other crops were not lifted until 1953 when Africans first began to produce for the market.

During World War I, there was a severe labour shortage. It was clear to both officials and settlers that the expansion of European plantations could only be supported by pursuing a policy that came close to compulsory labour for the private gain of individual Europeans. In 1919 Sir Edward Northey, the governor, issued the most severe of a series of labour circulars instructing government officials 'to exercise every possible influence to induce able-bodied male natives to go into the labour field.'[55] Women and children were to be encouraged as well.

Liberal forces in Britain and Kenya challenged Northey's policy and the colonial government's close identification with settler interests. The Bishops of Mombasa and Uganda and Dr. Arthur of the Church of Scotland Mission in a public memorandum strongly criticized the Northey circular on the grounds that the 'encouragement envisaged' would really be compulsion for the benefit of the settlers. They argued that compulsory labour was not in itself wrong. It would be acceptable if properly organized and used for legitimate national purposes such as building roads for all the people. Arthur, in defending their stand, stated, 'There is not a missionary or a Government administrative official in the country who does not know that *unauthorized compulsory labour had been in force through pressure on the chiefs by officials and labour recruiters*.'[56]

(Italics mine.) The home authorities of the Church of Scotland refused, nevertheless, to sanction any legalized compulsion and told their Kenyan representatives to withdraw their support from the statement.

Continued pressure upon the Home Government by humanitarian forces in Britain suceeded in 1921 in getting the British Government to forbid the Kenyan Government to engage in recruiting labour for private employment. Anyway, that year was the first time in the Colony's history that the labour supply had exceeded the demand and from then onwards labour became less of a problem as Africans moved voluntarily into the labour force for varying periods of time. In actual practice recruitment seems to have been left largely in the hands of the chiefs and individual district commissioners and, despite official policy, to have continued. Government officials let the chief know what was expected and left it to his ingenuity to acquire the needed men.

From as early as 1904 squatters had been encouraged to settle on European farms where they were allowed to cultivate crops and pasture livestock in return for part of their labour. In the early days, arrangements were made individually between European farmers and squatters and these amounted to a loose tenancy whereby the African and his family occupied an undeveloped portion of the settler's farm and worked part-time for him. (In 1918 it was not more than three or four months' work per annum.) There was generally an understanding that at certain times of the year, for instance the harvest, the squatter's family would work for the settler. During the time he worked, the squatter received a monthly wage of 4/- and a ration of *posho*.[57] By the end of World War I, squatting had become an established part of the socio-economic structure of the White Highlands and up to 1930 provided its most important source of labour.

The movement of Africans onto settlers' farms has been portrayed in much of the literature in terms of pressures on Africans to accommodate to the settlers' needs. This perspective underplays the attractions of squatting up to 1920, during which time there was a labour shortage and squatters were able to extract rather favourable terms from the settlers. Headmen from the estates would go to the reserves and advertise the advantages of life on particular farms 'mentioning that in his area the squatters could have as many sheep, cattle and goats as they liked, that there was water near and that *posho* would be free for the first three months.'[58] By moving onto settlers' farms, Africans could avoid compulsory labour, recruitment to the Carrier Corps and the 'arbitary' rule of chiefs and their agents.[59]

According to Wambaa and King, the basic appeal of squatting lay in the abundance of land and in the freedom to live the traditional life:

> They did not mind some wage labour provided they could continue their old social life and get space for their stock and cultivation. In any case, the *mzungu* at that time was a very good man from their point of view. He only wanted a few men actually to work for him. The rest could live in their little settlements all over his great estates, and had their dancing and singing just as before. In fact they had a reserve to themselves within these large farms—and it was a quiet reserve, unlike those back in Central Province. . . . Many of the people therefore wanted to go up to avoid some of the restrictions upon their life in the Reserves. . . .
>
> Many thought it the best estate of all—because it came nearest to the old life they had once known. Delamere [Lord Delamere, the owner] allowed no trousers and no schools on his estate; he said these would just make Kikuyus and his Maasai workers into prostitutes. He provided instead as much red ochre as they wanted, and posho also, and free milk—as much as you could drink. You lived in a separate reserve within his farmlands and your herds could multiply.[60]

In this early period, since there was more than enough land for everyone, the squatter could cultivate as much land as he liked and could choose any area on the estate except that which the settler himself farmed.

During the first quarter of the century life was better for the squatters in the Rift Valley than the life they left behind in the reserves. Some became quite prosperous and accumulated much livestock. But the rapid increase in African population and stock began to alarm the settlers. By the 1920s it had become clear to both them and the government that if the Highlands were to remain a white man's country, regulations and restrictions had to be placed on the squatters.

Once there was no longer a labour shortage, the settlers moved quickly to consolidate their advantages and to extend the paramountcy of European interests in Kenya. In conjunction with the government and through direct and indirect means, they subordinated the squatters' interests to their own. By 1922 the squatters' fate had turned and from then onwards their standard of living deteriorated. The settlers made attempts from 1923-25, rejected by the Colonial Office, to change the squatters' status from tenant to labourer. The acreage a squatter could cultivate was reduced, and by 1925 their cattle had been banned from most areas in the Rift Valley. Goats were next to go and then a limit was placed on the number of sheep, eight to ten being about average in the Molo area. (These limitations varied from place to place and with the individual settler.) Sometimes labour officers would confiscate and kill hundreds of sheep until the limit had been reached. This caused much enmity towards the government and the 1925-29 period is remembered with great bitterness, being referred to as the time when settlers 'started shooting our animals.'[61] An Ordinance was passed making it compulsory for squatters to have a legal contract with the farmer and many without contracts were returned to the reserves.

Under the Native Authority Ordinance, all adult males could be, and commonly were, required to do six days unpaid work every three months. No equivalent labour was demanded from Europeans or Asians. The usual penalty for refusal was a fine of up to £7 10/-, but Sir Edward Grigg, the Governor, said in 1925 that a fine was not enough and from that time on a magistrate could add a two month prison sentence.

At this time the Kikuyu Central Association (KCA) was making headway in the reserves as the champion of Kikuyu nationalism. The squatters' deep frustrations provided it with an opportunity to move into the Highlands. As the squatters' conditions grew worse, more and more joined the KCA and by 1929 it had a considerable following in the Rift Valley. In that year there were further reductions in the number of livestock squatters could keep and the situation grew tense. Rumours circulated predicting calamities. There was a series of strikes on the farms followed by a campaign of passive resistance. Squatters refused to work for the settlers and many returned to the reserves. This exodus caused officials to fear that another labour shortage might develop.

Around 1930, faced with an economic depression, the settlers again attempted to get rid of extra squatters and their families. Once more they pressured the administration for favourable legislation regarding the squatters and at the same time began to evict them. The *North Kavirondo District Annual Report, 1932* stated:

> Natives have had difficulty in finding work in any of the neighbouring white areas and those who were fortunate enough to do so have had to

107

be content with a modest wage. In Kaimosi in the early part of the year
there seemed good reason to believe that squatters on the farms were hard
pressed even for the necessities of life.

We will leave the topic of squatters and pursue it later in Chapter
13. Their grievances were to become an important source of Dini
ya Msambwa's most militant protest.

Before the settlers arrived, African land was secured by the
Protectorate Regulations of 1897 which stated that alienation could
not proceed on land regularly utilized by Africans. It could only
occur if this condition was not being met and the government was
satisfied that Africans would not be adversely affected. The Orders-
in-Council of 1901 and 1902 and the Crown Lands Ordinance of
1902 drastically changed this situation. The Protectorate government
was given jurisdiction over all lands. Only the *occupation and use
of land entitled Africans to it for there was no provision for African
ownership*. The ordinance of 1902 stated that land could not be
sold or leased to settlers if 'in actual occupation'. The term 'actual
occupation' was not clearly defined and the decision was left to
the administration. Many cases are on record of land being acquisi-
tioned despite Africans' occupancy or claims to land rights.
This occurred particularly among the Kikuyu, many of whom ended
up being squatters on land they regarded as their own.

The Crown Land Ordinance of 1915 stated that Africans had no
inherent or legal rights to land. What had happened was that the
provisions of the 1897 Regulations which had protected African
holdings against land grabbing had disappeared and land could
now be confiscated if the Governor and the Secretary of State for
the Colonies were convinced that it was not being 'beneficially
occupied'. This clause gave considerable leverage to the
administration in deciding what land was 'beneficially occupied'.

At the same time the government recognized that Africans
required some security of land in view of the settlers' continual
demands for more. It believed that African lands should not be
encroached upon to the extent, at least, of jeopardizing the tribe's
immediate needs. To effect this, a system of tribal reserves was
established. At first, these areas were under the authority of the
Outlying District Ordinance which prevented non-Africans from
entering. Even though the Crown Land Ordinance of 1915 recognized
'native reserves', it required ten more years of agitating on the
part of Africans before the boundaries were gazetted in 1926.

Africans continued to press for the security of their land. They wanted the same rights, individual title deeds, as Europeans. Land ownership was legally defined in 1921 by a Supreme Court decision known as the 'Barth Judgement' which defined African reserves as Crown Land. The African was not to be allowed to own land on the same basis as the European but was to be a 'tenant-at-will of the Crown' and could be removed individually or *en masse* by an order of the government with permission from the Secretary of State for the Colonies.[62]

Thus, it is easy to see why Africans felt uneasy, for although the administration had promised to protect their rights, it deprived them of the very rights of ownership that the settlers enjoyed. By 1932 the Kikuyu were experiencing a severe land shortage due to an expanding population and the loss of land to the settlers. The issue had become emotion-ridden and was expressed in the demand for the return of 'our stolen land'. By 1934, some 6,543,360 acres of land had been alienated for occupation by 2,027 white settlers, an average of 2,534 acres per settler, of which only 274 acres were actually under cultivation. Less than .7 per cent of the entire population of Kenya, a figure which includes all Europeans, held what has been estimated to be 20 per cent of the Colony's best land.[63]

Of all issues, land evoked particular bitterness on the part of the dispossessed. Senior chief Koinange poignantly expressed the feelings of a squatter working for a settler on land he regarded as his own. 'When someone steals your ox, it is killed and roasted and eaten. One can forget. When someone steals your land, especially if nearby, one can never forget. It is always there, its trees were dear friends, its little streams. It is a bitter presence.'[64] While the Kikuyu were the tribe most seriously affected, the Luhya were aware of what could happen to them. Settlers had begun to farm adjacent areas of the Uasin Gishu Plateau as early as 1908.[65]

Space does not permit any further discussion of policies that gave a major advantage to the European over the African farmer, and policies that were to be increasingly attacked by Africans. Although the issue is far from settled, considerable evidence indicates that Africans paid heavily for a system in which they stood to lose their land and had to work for low wages. *The Report of the East African Commission* in 1925 had this to say:

> The Chief Native Commissioner of Kenya in a paper submitted to us estimated that in 1925 the maximum amount that could be considered to

have been spent on services provided exclusively for the benefit of the native population was slightly over one quarter of the taxes paid by them. As a concrete example, we were informed that in the last ten years the Kitui Akamba have paid 207,749 pounds in direct taxes alone, and that "you can travel through the length and breadth of Kitui Reserve and you will fail to find in it any enterprises, building or structure of any sort which the Government has provided at the cost of more than a few sovereigns. . . . If we left the district tomorrow the only permanent evidence of our occupation would be the buildings we have erected for the use of our tax-collecting staff."[66]

The government expenditure on African education in 1929 was £22,000 compared to £23,600 for the education of less than one thousand European children.[67]

E. A. Brett assessed the allocation of resources as follows:

If settlement was to succeed (and success was measured in terms of building up a new South Africa), a very large percentage of these resources would have to be diverted into the settler sector. This became the major objective of the settler group, so that a continuous political campaign was mounted by the settler lobby to ensure that this would be done. . . .

By the 1930s the effect of these policies . . . had been to create a large and virtually permanent proletariat in Kenya . . . and to guarantee the settlers the labour which they required . . . .

As a whole the African producer and wage-earner was heavily taxed and received few administrative services in return (apart from the largest police, prison and court services in East Africa), the settler community paid relatively little and received the bulk of the services provided out of total internal revenue.[68]

Early Luhya Voluntary Associations

By the end of the first decade of the twentieth century, armed resistances to colonial intrusion had ended. The years from the end of World War I until 1940 saw the beginning of Luhya protest politics. Senior commissioner R. W. Hemsted noted in 1925, 'In spite of a general state of peace and contentment, the natives are not becoming easier to administer. A new spirit has grown up amongst them, and they are becoming great politicians.'[69] In 1930 the district commissioner commented that the year had been 'characterized by acute political unrest in many locations, while in others the elements of disorder have merely been waiting to see how far it would be safe to go.'[70]

The introduction of voluntary associations by the missions established a pattern that Africans quickly adapted to their own ends. Several associations were formed in the 1920s and 1930s. Although these associations were nominally open to anyone, they followed tribal and religious distinctions—usually recruiting members from a single tribe and/or from a particular denomination. These divisions were promoted by both the Africans' and the missionaries' inclinations.

The North Kavirondo Taxpayers' Welfare Association was founded in 1922 by Archdeacon W. E. Owen at Maseno, the Church Missionary Society headquarters. It was a Luo organization and recruited young mission converts and 'progressive farmers'. It had a northern branch among the Luhya that made little headway. District reports from 1925 to 1930 note its existence and yearly meetings but state that it was not very active and was slowly dying a 'natural death'.

The Roman Catholics, in order not to lose converts to the North Kavirondo Taxpayers' Welfare Association, started their own association called the Native Catholic Union in 1925 with Monsignor Brandsma as president. The district commissioner remarked approvingly upon the discipline that the Catholics had over their members.

The North Kavirondo Chamber of Commerce was an association of maize growers drawn from the Kimilili-Broderick Falls area which was active in the late 1930s. According to the government, its members were 'progressive', meaning they were ready to cooperate with the agricultural staff in soil conservation and marketing measures.[71]

Converts from the Friends Africa Mission at Kaimosi organized the Luhya's first 'modern' political association, the North Kavirondo Central Association (NKCA), in 1932. It was modelled after the Kikuyu Central Association, one of the earliest and most important vehicles of Kikuyu nationalism. Its first president, Andrea Juma, was a Maragoli school teacher who had lived for some years in Nairobi. So had its first secretary, Erasto Ligalaba, who worked as a compositor on the government Swahili newspaper, *Habari*. John Adala, the master of the government African school at Kakamega, replaced Ligalaba as secretary, and he was, in turn, succeeded by Herbert Moses Lubanga in 1938.[72]

The fact that Archdeacon W. E. Owen was the 'father' of the Kavirondo Taxpayers' Welfare Association probably also stimulated Dr. Bond of Friends to support the North Kavirondo Central

Association because the Friends had not been happy over the Archdeacon's strong influence with the Kavirondo Taxpayers' Welfare Association and its Luhya branch. In 1936 the North Kavirondo Central Association had a membership of some three hundred. The majority were Quakers, together with some Anglicans and a few Islamised Wanga.[73] It was strongest in the district's most densely populated locations of Maragoli and Bunyore, although its membership grew until it had branches in almost every location.

The Association found a *cause célèbre* when gold was discovered in the Kakamega reserve in 1931 and a minor gold rush ensued. Substance was given to African fears of land confiscation by the high-handed actions of a few prospectors who began to dig prospecting pits without permission from the owners of the land, sometimes destroying their crops and huts. Several leaders of the Association were fined for obstructing the miners and uprooting their claim stakes. Africans defended their land and clashes between them and the Europeans became so serious that the prospectors considered forming a unit of the Kenya Defence Force.

The government found itself in an acutely embarrassing situation. It was unthinkable, at least in European circles, that prospecting for gold should be prohibited. Yet only a few months before gold was found, the Native Land Trust Ordinance had set aside reserves 'for the use and benefit of the native tribes of the Colony for ever'. An important cause had stipulated that if any land was excluded from the reserves for any public purpose other than communications, an equal amount of land both in area and in value, if possible, should be added. In addition, no lease was to be granted without consulting the Local Native Council and the Local Land Board in the area concerned and no lease could be granted in an area under 'beneficial occupation'. The area of the gold fields, thickly populated and closely cultivated, was obviously under 'beneficial occupation'.[74]

An Amendment incorporating major changes to the main Ordinance was rushed through the Legislative Council with scarcely a dissenting voice. This Amendment provided monetary compensation to Africans for land taken instead of allocating them equivalent land elsewhere. The government argued that since mining operations were likely to be short-lived, to give Africans equivalent land in exchange would be unnecessarily cumbersome.

The publication of the Amendment raised a storm of protest. The English press and parliament were shocked at the betrayal of imperial pledges to consult African landholders and to add land to the reserve if any was excluded. The Africans interpreted the Amendment to mean that the miners could take over all areas covered by their claim pegs merely by paying their owners a few shillings. They felt that the government had reneged on its promises and had taken sides with the miners against them. The Local Native Council was shown to be utterly powerless to do anything and, in fact, had not even been consulted.[75]

The Association sent several petitions to the Secretary of State and made a number of accusations, some of which had no substance. For instance, it contended that:

> Many women, children, and domestic animals have lost their lives by falling into prospecting pits. When a man falls into a pit and dies his relatives receive 3 shillings compensation. Trespassers on mining property are flogged to death . . . natives dispossessed by mining would be removed to the top of Mt. Elgon.[76]

At a meeting between representatives of the Association and the administration, John Adala asked why the dependents of a European killed in the mines received 15,000/- when the dependents of an African killed received a mere 360/-. The district commissioner replied that in each case the payment equalled three years salary and that since Africans were only drawing 10/- a month (roughly $1.40) and Europeans £20 a month ($56.00), it was fair! The Association rejected this, arguing that 15,000/- compensation should be paid to dependents regardless of race.[77] The district commissioner's reply illustrates the inequalities of a racist society, but of more significance was the Africans' rejection of this system. An important step had been taken in the politicization of the Luhya. The Europeans' 'right' to a superior position with all its accompanying rewards was no longer accepted, if indeed it ever had been, and Africans were insisting on equality.

During the controversy, the government clarified its policy. Prospectors were warned to be more careful in their dealings with Africans, and a system of compensation for damage to African property was established. The issue of land claims was looked into by the Local Native Council and it was decided that copies of leases would be deposited with the chairman of the Council, chief Murungu. In this way, African property rights would be protected despite the frequent turnover of administrative officers.

These measures helped alleviate the acute tensions and conditions subsequently improved greatly. In fact, Archdeacon Owen, one of the severest critics of the Mining Ordinance, congratulated the government on its handling of the situation.[78] If the Archdeacon, a champion of African rights and a tough watchdog of government policy, was satisfied, an equitable settlement must have been reached. Still the district commissioner admitted in 1933 that 'while individually natives looked upon mining with a more friendly eye than hitherto, *it must not be assumed that collectively they are reconciled to being deprived of even a single acre of their land*, and the prospect of leases being granted still causes consternation.'[79] (Italics mine.)

By 1936 mining operations had slowed down. The individual alluvial worker had almost disappeared and the administration reported few disturbances. After this flurry the land issue was not to raise its head again until after World War II.

In 1939 a significant event occurred in the development of tribal identity. The North Kavirondo Central Association invented the name Abaluhya, meaning 'fellow tribesmen', for the Bantu tribes of North Nyanza and changed the name of the Association from Kavirondo to Abaluhya Central Association. 'Kavirondo' had never been liked since it did not distinguish them from the Luo who lived in the region then known as Central Kavirondo. (In order to avoid confusion the name North Kavirondo Central Association will continue to be used here.)

The Association's role in the controversy over the paramount chieftainship has already been discussed. Its involvement was an attempt to broaden its basis of support as well as to legitimize the concept of a united Luhya nation.[80]

The Central Association began to develop links with groups inside and outside of Kenya. Several intelligence reports mentioned that money had been collected to send students to England and America for education and for a correspondence course provided by Marcus Garvey, the organizer of the militant Back-to-Africa movement among American Blacks.[81] These projects, however, appeared to come to little. This contact with America is reminiscent of similar movements in Zambia and Malawi in the late nineteenth and early twentieth centuries where tenuous links were established between Garvey's movement and John Booth's Seventh-day Adventists and his pupil, John Chilembwe, and his Providence Industrial Mission.[82]

Links betweeen the North Kavirondo Central Association and the Kikuyu Central Association began to be established in the 1930s. Several members of the Kikuyu Central Association had come to North Nyanza with the white miners and they introduced the Luhya to their Association. Several joint meetings were held. Three members of the Kikuyu Central Association, including the honourable member of parliament, Isher Dass, a militant Indian who supported African causes, and Jesse Karioki, its vice-president, visited the Kavirondo Central Association in 1938 and warned the Luhya about the alienation of land to Europeans.[83]

Joint associational action was given an impetus in 1938-39 when the government, alarmed at the serious soil erosion in the reserves, decided to implement soil conservation measures. These measures evoked a strong outcry throughout the country and support for the North Kavirondo Central Association rapidly expanded in the North Nyanzan locations. Following the fencing off of a pilot soil conservation scheme, seen as a prelude to a European takeover of their land, even some chiefs joined. In November 1938, the Central Association, together with the Kikuyu Central Association and the Kavirondo Taxpayers' Welfare Association, issued a joint protest to the Secretary of State against compulsory destocking instituted to help alleviate soil erosion.[84]

Other causes the Central Association espoused were the non-payment of war gratuities to the dependents of Africans killed in World War I,[85] tax exemptions, and high taxes. The Association tried to collect funds to send chief Mulama to England to present their grievances directly to the British Government but was refused permission to collect funds by the district commissioner.[86]

It accused the missionaries of 'stealing African land', took issue with the one thousand acres granted the Friends Mission at Kaimosi, queried the size of government grants to Friends as well as to the Roman Catholics, and told the missionaries 'now it's time you went home'. In spite of the administration's accusation that the Association did nothing useful and only stirred up trouble, it did improve the water facilities in 1940 by constructing more wells than the Medical Department.[87]

Some administrators took time to instruct the Association's officers in the correct way to petition. 'For me time was spent with Andrea Jumba, the President of the Central Association', said the district commissioner in 1936, 'showing him exactly how a petition must be presented to the House of Commons. The time spent seems to have been wasted as, in the first place, he sent a typewritten document in quadruplicate to me, and then said as "father of the district" I should find an M.P. to present it to the House.'[88]

The Association annoyed local administrators as it did not hesitate to circumvent them and go directly to the Governor, the Secretary of State or members of parliament in England. An exasperated provincial commissioner decried this practice:

> The President of the Central Association presented yet another petition direct to the Secretary of State naively enough enclosing 1 shilling in stamps for favourable reply. He has been told before, I think the sixth time, the proper method of approaching the authorities at Home, but he has scored by the very fact of his letter, incorrectly presented, having been noticed at Home. . . . I hear that there is yet another petition on the way Home protesting at the setting aside of ten acres at the various Courts for Social Centres. The Local Native Council have approved of this, but, alas the Association does not.[89]

With the advent of World War II the Kikuyu Central Association long suspected by the government of subversion, was proscribed. Taking heed, the North Kavirondo Central Association agreed to disband until the end of the war. The government's reason for its 'request' was that the tribe would be more united to help in the war effort if certain controversial issues were temporarily shelved. Two months later a relieved district commissioner wrote:

> The decision of the North Kavirondo Central Association to close down has produced a peaceful and friendly atmosphere in North Kavirondo. Formerly it was almost impossible to hold a *baraza* without a number of questions being asked which reflected a subversive attitude towards government policy and one of hostility towards government designed to prejudice adversely the position of chiefs and others. No such attitude has been noticed during the last two months.[90]

The Central Association was revived after the war but failed to become a vital force again.

Conclusions

Skilled neither in the use of the English language nor in the methods of modern politics, some of these early efforts by the 'new men' at articulating grievances were crude and groping, yet they represented a growing political awareness and a developing pattern of dissent. Their presentations, at times inaccurate and exaggerated, led the administration to slough them off as the fulminations of trouble-makers. To ignore them, however, was dangerous for at the same time the administration was well aware of the district's acute unrest.

Efforts to build modern political institutions gave young Africans practice in the tactics of pressure politics. They gained experience in writing petitions, handling funds, and in managing western-type organizations. People were stirred up, issues defined, hostility focussed upon the Europeans, and redress demanded.

The North Kavirondo Central Association, though it contacted groups outside its own area and had a sprinkling of members from other tribes, was essentially tribal in character. It helped to develop tribal identity among previously hostile sub-tribes. The Association's direct and aggressive approach, its demands for equal rights, and its willingness to by-pass colonially prescribed tactics heralded a coming era. Dini ya Msambwa would soon push further in all these directions. This period saw the development of two opposing forces, clan solidarity and Luhya nationalism. Because of divisive issues, Luhya nationalism was to remain centred around the location and fragmented by inter-clan disputes.

With this we come to the end of a discussion of some background conditions from which Dini ya Msambwa arose, necessary in order to understand the issues facing it and other political associations in the 1940s. We have seen that the Luhya's initial responses to the foreigners varied from militancy to cooperation. Next, mission converts formed voluntary associations which tried to work within the constitutional framework. We shall now turn to a third response, a militant prophetic movement led by ex-mission converts. This chronology of responses cannot be interpreted with too much exactitude, as sometimes the second and third type responses occurred simultaneously, but it is apparent that there is a rough correlation between the type of response and the historical period.

Fifty years after the 1895 confrontation, the Bukusu were ready to fight the British again. The members of this sub-tribe with its warrior tradition had in the intervening years been struggling against Wanga hegemony. By 1936 all the Wanga chiefs had been replaced by locally born chiefs. Thus in 1943 the Bukusu were free to renew their struggle against the foreigners, only this time, instead of a head-on clash, guerrilla tactics would be employed.

Notes

1. The name of the movement as given in its constitution is 'Dini ya *Musam-bwa*'. However, in order to avoid confusion, the conventional spelling, *Msambwa*, will be followed.

2. As with most tribes there are alternate names and spellings. Bukusu is used here although Bugusu and Vukusu are used elsewhere. The Gisu are also referred to as Gishu and Gesu and the Wanga as Hanga.

3. This area has been subjected to many name and boundary changes. (Not to mention country, for at the turn of the century much of Luhyaland was then in the Eastern Province of Uganda and governed from Entebbe. In 1902 the Eastern Province was transferred to Kenya, then the East Africa Protectorate.) At the time of World War II, Nyanza Province was broken into North Nyanza, Central Nyanza, South Nyanza and Kericho Districts. After the War, and this is the period of our major concern, Nyanza was divided into Elgon Nyanza and North Nyanza (prior to 1950, known as North Kavirondo) Districts in the north; Central Nyanza, South Nyanza, and Kisii Districts in the south. This terminology will be used in discussing Dini ya Msambwa, though the reader should be aware that documents from other periods will be using a different terminology. In 1956, the government created Elgon Nyanza District in which the Bukusu formed the majority. It comprised what are today Busia and Bungoma Districts. Before 1959, there were only four locations in Bungoma District: Malakisi (presently known as North and South Malakisi), Kimilili (today comprising Kimilili, Bokoli, and Ndivisi locations), Elgon, and South Bukusu (now East and West Bukusu). Up until 1951, South Bukusu was known as South Kitosh. In 1962, the boundaries of Nyanza Province were again changed. North Nyanza and Elgon Nyanza Districts became Western Province and were divided into Bungoma, Kakamega and Busia Districts, with Bungoma being the home of the Bukusu.

4. For a discussion of the Luhya's political structure see Gunter Wagner, 'The Political Organization of the Bantu of Kavirondo', *African Political Systems*, M. Fortes and E. E. Evans-Pritchard (eds.), (Oxford University Press, London, 1940), pp. 197–236; Gunter Wagner, 'The Abaluyia of Kavirondo', *African Worlds*, Daryll Forde (ed.), (Oxford University Press, London, 1954), pp. 27–54; Gideon S. Were, *A History of the Abaluyia of Western Kenya c. 1500–1930*, (East African Publishing House, Nairobi, 1967); J. Osogo, *A History of the Baluyia*, (Oxford University Press, Nairobi, 1966); J. Osogo, *Nabongo Mumia*, (East African Literature Bureau, Nairobi, 1967).

5. Elizabeth Richards, *Fifty Years in Nyanza, 1906–1956*, (Acme Press, Nairobi, 1956), p. 8.

6. B. A. Ogot, *History of the Southern Luo*, (East African Publishing House, Nairobi, 1967), pp. 232-33.

7. Osogo, *A History*, pp. 80–1.

8. Frederick Jackson, *Early Days in East Africa*, (Edward Arnold, London 1930), p. 231.

9. Joseph Thompson, *Through Masailand*, (Low, Marston Searle and Rivington, London, 1885), p. 506.

10. Were, *A History*, pp. 135–36.

11. Osogo, *A History*, p. 81.

12. Were, *A History*, p. 165.

13. *Ibid.* Originally from manuscripts at the Public Record Offices, London, FO2/92, No. 12. Jackson to Kimberley, 7 February 1895.

14. C. W. Hobley, *Kenya from Chartered Company to Crown Colony*, (Witherby, London, 1929), pp. 82–8. For slightly different versions see Osogo, *A History*, pp. 130-31, and Were, *A History*, pp. 166–67.

15. W. J. Ansorge, *Under the African Sun*, (Heinemann, London, 1929), p. 72. The information on the ransom of the women and the quotation

118

about dying like ants came from Osogo, *A History*, pages 85 and 131, respectively.

Professor Gideon S. Were, Dean of Arts at the University of Nairobi, in his book, *A History of the Abaluyia of Western Kenya c. 1500–1930*, appears to have presented these events in order to make the British look ruthless. Were presented the capitulation as follows:

> As Ansorge who took part in the expedition observed the Babukusu suffered more severely because '*every adult male captured is put to death*' and also because their 'villages were burnt to the ground, a severe matter in a district where wood for rebuilding the huts had to be fetched from a considerable distance; standing crops were destroyed; vast stores of corn found in the villages were used up by the invading army; and cattle, their most valuable possession captured by the hundred.' (p. 167, Italics mine).

The sense of this passage as Were has constructed it is that the British killed every captured male. Yet in Ansorge's book from which the quotations are taken they are separated by two pages. The first quote in its original context merely referred to the killing of captured adult males as a tribal rule of war, while the second longer one was part of a sentence that began with the observation that relatively few Bukusu were killed. By piecing together these two quotations Were has made the British rather than their native allies, especially the Maasai, the culprits, and has stressed the great loss of Bukusu life whereas Ansorge stressed just the opposite. See Appendix B for the contexts from which these quotations were taken.

16. de Wolf, 'Religious Innovation', p. 81.
17. Moyse-Bartlett wrote that two small expeditions of the King's African Rifles were sent to restore law and order in the Kitosh and Kabras Districts in 1907 and 1908. Lt. Col. H. Moyse-Bartlett, *The King's African Rifles: A Study in the Military History of East and Central Africa*, (Gale and Polden, Aldershot, 1956), p. 208.

    Foran, probably referring to the same incidents commented, 'In 1907 a small body of the Kisumu Police, under my command was dispatched to deal with the truculent Kitosh and shortly afterwards with the Kabras tribe. No Military was engaged in these minor operations which achieved all that was desired.' W. Robert Foran, *The Kenya Police 1887–1960*, (R. Hale, London, 1962), p. 27.

    Carl Rosberg and John Nottingham in *The Myth of 'Mau Mau'* (p. 10) state, 'Large military expeditions, reinforced by auxiliaries from Mumia and other client chiefs, were sent out against the Vugusu (Kitosh) on the slopes of Mt. Elgon in 1895, 1907, and 1908, while there were also five campaigns against various other Luhya people in Nyanza between 1895 and 1907.'

    In checking their sources I can nowhere find that three large expeditions were launched against the Bukusu. There was the one large 1895 expedition but the other two appear to have been skirmishes. Foran and Moyse-Bartlett write of minor expeditions to put down inter-tribal squabbles.
18. Osogo, *A History*, p. 132.
19. de Wolf, 'Religious Innovation, p. 80. The original source is noted as Hobley's 'RAI paper' (1902), and in the bibliography the only 1902 work of Hobley's is *Eastern Uganda, an Ethnological Survey*, (Royal Anthropological Institute, Occasional paper No. 1, London, 1902).
20. de Wolf, 'Religious Innovation', pp. 81–3.
21. In 1908, the District of North Nyanza was divided into eight administrative units known as locations. The present Luo locations of Gem, Alego, and Buholo and part of Ugenya were included. Later, additional locations were created with the boundaries generally following the existing clan

and sub-tribal divisions. These new units, however, represented a definite departure from the traditional where the clan and sub-clan were the effective administrative units. The sub-location now became the smallest administrative unit and above it the location composed of different clans which until then had been self-governing. This reorganization into larger and more manageable units strengthened local government.

22. Osogo, *A History*, p. 132.
23. Osogo, *Nabongo Mumia*, p. 27.
24. de Wolf, 'Religious Innovation', p. 89.
25. *Ibid.*, p. 84.
26. Were, *A History*, pp. 163–64.
27. John Lonsdale, 'Some Origins of Nationalism in East Africa', *Journal of African History*, IX, 1, 1968, p. 156.
28. Report prepared 9 October 1930.
29. *Nyanza Province Annual Report, 1932;* Were, *A History*, p. 175. Jan de Wolf reports an incident that eventuated in fighting when chiefs Mulama and Murungu decided to start a coffee plantation on Bukusu land. The district commissioner told them to confine such endeavours to their own locations and he acknowledged that in the past boundaries had been made very much under Mulama's guidance. Religious Innovation, p. 95.
30. *Nyanza Province Annual Report, 1922–1923;* KNA:NN/23, Character of Chiefs, 1927.
31. de Wolf, 'Religious Innovation', p. 86.
32. KNA:DC/NN/1/16, *North Kavirondo District Annual Report, 1922.*
33. Let me elaborate a little on the agitation over chief Murungu. In 1929 demands for the removal of chief Waluchio of Kimilili and chief Murungu of Malakisi were voiced. Waluchio tendered his resignation and Amutalla Mayuko, an ex-headman, was appointed. (Later we shall see how Pascal Nabwana and the Bukusu Central Association tried to have him replaced.) Murungu also submitted his resignation, but the government felt it had gone far enough in meeting Bukusu desires for self-determination. Consequently, Murungu retained his post as nominal overlord of the whole of North Nyanza. In 1933 agitation continued over Murungu. A petition to the Colonial Secretary for his removal received a resounding 'no'. Sixteen agitators, mostly Church Missionary Society youth, were required to execute bonds to keep the peace owing to a letter they had written drawing a parallel with the French Revolution! In 1935 Mumia's sons, contrary to his wishes, tried to oust Murungu, their uncle, in order to draw his pay as they themselves frankly admitted. See the *North Kavirondo District Annual Report, 1935.*
34. KNA:PC/NZA/1/25. *Nyanza Province Annual Report, 1930.*
35. KNA:DC/NN/1/18. *North Kavirondo District Annual Report, 1933.*
36. KNA:DC/NN/1/18. *North Kavirondo District Annual Report, 1938.*
37. Lonsdale, 'Some Origins of Nationalism', pp. 127–128.
38. KNA:DC/NN/1/18. *North Kavirondo District Annual Report, 1935.*
39. KNA:KSI/24. *Nyanza Province Annual Report, 1945.*
40. There is controversy over the position of the Wanga at the time of the British entry into Kenya. Wagner, Were, and the district commissioner of North Nyanza for 1935 maintain that the Wanga were in a precarious position and that it was through Mumia's manoeuvrings that they achieved dominance. The district commissioner writes, 'It will be recalled that the advent of settled government made a startling difference to the fortunes of the Wanga. From being in desperate danger of being crushed between the Kitosh in the North and the advancing Luo in the South, Mumia's astuteness in making allies of the British and his loyalty and intelligence made him the right-hand man of the early administrators and it was natural that they should nominate members of his family to take charge of

areas. . . .' (KNA:DC/NN/1/14–1/16. *North Kavirondo District Annual Report*, 1935.)

Were contends that '. . . by the second half of the 19th century, the Wanga Kingdom was in decline and its frontiers were progressively contracting. Also, unlike Buganda, Wanga was a small state both territorially and in terms of population. . . . The decision of the Administration to rely on Abawanga agents and headmen for the opening up of the as yet unadministered regions of Buluyia brought the Wanga Kingdom, once more, to the centre of the early colonial and foreign activities in which they had played a leading role from the very beginning. It was a key role which, if skillfully manipulated, could yield great benefit.' (Were, *A History*, pp. 174–75.)

Wagner states, 'The only tribal group which attained a certain political ascendancy over some of their neighbours was the Wanga. Their ascendancy was, however, rather limited, and it is even doubtful whether it existed before the opening of the direct trade route from the coast to Uganda, which passed through the residence of the Wanga chiefs. Their political influence over their neighbours was further strengthened when the British administration established its first headquarters and a small garrison of Sudanese soldiers in the Wanga country, and when, in recognition of the loyalty shown by the Wanga chief, it bestowed upon him the honourary title of paramount chief.' (Wagner, 'The Abaluyia', pp. 35–6.)

In contrast to the above writers, Osogo asserts, 'Mumia's empire extended over a very wide area with a population of more than a million people. This would take in all the Luyia peoples, and even more. . . . One indication of the vast territories Mumia and his ancestors ruled is the number of wives they married from widely separated areas.' (Osogo, *Nabongo Mumia*, p. 6.) Osogo's hypothesis of an empire is poorly documented and his evidence ambiguous.

The stronger argument lies with the former group who claim that Wanga dominancy was limited prior to British occupation and that it was Mumia's skillful bargaining with the British that bettered Wanga fortunes.

41. KNA:DC/NN10/1/8, *North Kavirondo District Annual Report*, *1936*.
42. See below, pp. 186 – 87.
43. Rosberg and Nottingham, *The Myth of 'Mau Mau'*, p. 17.
44. Osogo, *A History*, p. 134.
45. KNA:PC/NZA/1/6. *Nyanza Province Annual Report, 1910–1911*.
46. KNA:DC/NN/1/1. *North Kavirondo District Annual Report, 1917–1918*. By 1930, mission schools numbered 557. They were divided up as follows: Church Missionary Society 106 with 3,709 conversions; Friends' Africa Mission 202 with 700 conversions; Mill Hill Brothers 237 with 1,074 conversions; Church of God 7 with 214 conversions; and the Salvation Army 5 with 350 conversions. As of 1938, some 16 per cent of the population were mission adherents. Thus a relatively large number of young people acquired at least some elementary education. (E. M. Chilver, Native Administration and Political Change in North Nyanza District, typescript copy, Kampala, Uganda.)
47. Jomo Kenyatta, *Facing Mount Kenya*, (Mercury Publications, London, 1961), p. 272.
48. KNA:PC/NZA/1/20. *Nyanza Province Annual Report, 1925*.
49. KNA:DC/NN/1/18. *North Kavirondo District Annual Report, 1930*.
50. KNA:DC/NN/1/18. *North Kavirondo District Annual Report, 1936*.
51. de Wolf, 'Religious Innovation', pp. 116, 128.
52. Examples of sons succeeding their fathers as chiefs are given by de Wolf, 'Religious Innovation', p. 134.
53. M. P. K. Sorrenson, *Origins of European Settlement in Kenya*, (Oxford University Press, Nairobi, 1968), pp. 232, 238, 102.

54. Rosberg and Nottingham, *Myth of 'Mau Mau'*, pp. 61, 111. The following discussion of the government's land and labour policies draws heavily from Rosberg and Nottingham's *Myth of 'Mau Mau'*; papers by Frank Furedi, 'The Kikuyu Squatter in the Rift Valley: 1918–1929', Historical Association Conference, Nairobi, August 1972; and Rebmann M. Wambaa and Kenneth King, 'The Political Economy of the Rift Valley: A Squatter Perspective', Historical Association Conference, Nairobi, August 1972.

55. Roland Oliver, *The Missionary Factor in East Africa*, (Longman, Green and Co., London, 1952), p. 248.

56. Dr. Arthur to the Secretary of Foreign Missions Committee, Church of Scotland, October 1920. Quoted in F. B. Welbourn, *East African Rebels*, p. 125.

57. Furedi, 'The Kikuyu Squatter', p. 4.

58. Wambaa and King, 'The Political Economy of the Rift Valley', p. 3.

59. Furedi's study, based on a sample of seventy-four squatters, found that these were the three main reasons given.

60. Wambaa and King, 'The Political Economy of the Rift Valley', pp. 1–3.

61. *Ibid.*, p. 5, and Furedi, 'The Kikuyu Squatter', p. 9.

62. *Report of the Kenya Land Commission*. Cmd. 4556, 1934, p. 418.

63. Donald L. Barnett and Karari Njama, *Mau Mau from Within*, (Mac-Gibbon and Kee, London, 1966), p. 32.

64. Rosberg and Nottingham, *Myth of 'Mau Mau'*, p. 74.

65. Goldsmith, *John Ainsworth*, p. 93.

66. *Report of the East African Commission*. Cmd. 2387, 1924, 1925, p. 185.

67. Leys, *Kenya*, p. 243.

68. E. A. Brett, 'Economic Policy in Kenya Colony: A Study on the Politics of Resource Allocation', EAISR Paper, Kampala, Uganda, 1965. Also see his book, *Colonialisation and Underdevelopment*, (Heinemann, London, 1973).

69. KNA:PC/NZA/1/20. *Nyanza Province Annual Report, 1925*.

70. KNA:DC/NN/1/18. *North Kavirondo District Annual Report, 1930*.

71. KNA:PC/NZA/4/5/5. North Kavirondo District Intelligence Reports. 1935.

72. KNA:DC/NZA/4/5/2. Intelligence Reports of the provincial commissioner, North Nyanza.

73. KNA:DC/NN/1/18. *North Kavirondo District Annual Report, 1936*.

74. This section on the gold rush relies on: Lonsdale, 'Political Associations in Western Kenya'; Robert I. Rotberg and Ali A. Mazrui (eds.), *Protest and Power in Black Africa*, (Oxford University Press, New York, 1970), p. 626; KNA:DC/NN/1/18. *North Kavirondo District Annual Report, 1933;* and Rosberg and Nottingham, *Myth of 'Mau Mau'*, pp. 163–164.

75. Lonsdale, 'Political Associations', p. 621.

76. KNA:PC/NZ/4/5/6. North Kavirondo District Intelligence Report, March 1936.

77. KNA:PC/NZ/4/5/5. North Kavirondo District Intelligence Reports, 1937.

78. KNA:/NN/1/18. *North Kavirondo District Annual Report, 1934.*

79. KNA:DC/NN/1/18. *North Kavirondo District Annual Report, 1933.*

80. Rosberg and Nottingham, *Myth of 'Mau Mau'*, p. 162.

81. KNA:PC/NZA/4/5/2. Intelligence Reports Nyanza Province, 5 June 1939.

82. George Shepperson, 'The Politics of Church Separatist Movements in British Central Africa, 1892–1916', *Africa*, XXIV, 1954, pp. 233–46.

83. KNA:PC/NZ/4/5/6. North Kavirondo District Intelligence Report, September 1939; and PC/NZA/1/33. *Nyanza Provincial Annual Report, 1938.*

84. Rosberg and Nottingham, *Myth of 'Mau Mau'*, p. 163.

85. KNA:PC/NZA/4/5/5 and PC/NZA/4/5/6. North Kavirondo District Intelligence Reports 1935–1937.
86. KNA:DC/NN/10/1/2. Letter written by the district commissioner of North Nyanza, 9 October 1935.
87. KNA:PC/NZA/4/5/2. Intelligence Reports of the provincial commissioner, Nyanza.
88. KNA:PC/NZA/4/5/6. North Kavirondo District Intelligence Reports, September 1936.
89. KNA:PC/NZA/4/5/6. North Kavirondo District Intelligence Reports, 1938.
90. KNA:DC/NN/1/21. *North Kavirondo District Annual Report, 1939.*

Chapter 10

ORIGINS AND DEVELOPMENT

T H E R E are several versions depicting the actual circumstances of Dini ya Msambwa's origins and several claims by founding members to be the 'real' founder. Elijah Masinde is generally assumed to be the founder. Samson Wafula, one of the original members and Msambwa's secretary, provided this account of Dini ya Msambwa's emergence:

> The reason why we left Friends [Quakers] is that the missionaries forbade us to marry many wives. They said that by doing this we broke the rule of God. Then God called Elijah in a vision at night . . . to go to the top of Mt. Elgon to a lake known as Zion. God informed him that "everyone in this world belongs to me, even the polygynist belongs to me and all others are my people. So I'm telling you to go and start a *dini* that allows all my children—mothers, girls, young people, and polygynists—to become members because they are all my creatures."[1]

Another founding member, the vice-president, Benjamin Wekuke claimed on the other hand, that it was he whom God had told in 1937 to start Msambwa and that it was he who had asked Masinde for help, rather than the other way round:

> I was called by God. God told me to leave Friends and to follow the religion of my ancestors. The missions were teaching foreign and not traditional beliefs and God wanted us to follow the old ways. . . . This happened on March 16, 1937. . . . By 1938 God told me to bring Masinde from the Tribunal Court to help me with this work. . . . God told me that I have changed my face, and I will lead you from the darkness. Tell the *wazungus* to go to their former home. Their time is over. Then they will leave all the riches of your country and you will carry on with your life. I'll send my holy spirit to be with you all the time. . . . At that time I called Elijah and explained the whole thing to him. . . . He left his job and joined me. Now we were two. In 1939 we went up Mt. Elgon to pray to God because we were not safe down here. We were aware that the government would not allow us to hold meetings so we went up the mountain to a

cave under a big rock, so we could be free. . . . We didn't have many members. . . . We continued this way until we found Joasch Walumoli in 1943. He was a vital member and then we found Israel Khaoya. We now began to preach the word of God strongly. Almost everyone in the location knew about us.[2]

Whether Masinde or Wekuke was the actual instigator will be hard to ascertain. Both were in Msambwa from the beginning. The movement, however, definitely bears the mark of Masinde's rather than Wekuke's personality. But what is more significant, Msambwa was started by ex-mission converts who rejected particular mission teachings, especially monogamy, and claimed a mandate from God. (The original members, Elijah Masinde, Benjamin Wekuke, Samson Wafula, Joasch Walumoli and Israel Khaoya, were still the leaders in 1965.)

Masinde was said to have first called it Dini ya Israel or the African Church of Israel and he allegedly tried to unite with Bishop Kivuli's African Israel sect. This sect, also known as Dini ya Israel, is an independent church eschewing politics. Under Bishop Kivuli's leadership it has been one of the most durable of the independent churches. Pascal Nabwana, a peer of Masinde's and a major figure in Bukusu politics, described the events leading up to the founding of Dini ya Msambwa:

> Masinde joined Kivuli's African Israel. He was made a branch leader but he wouldn't take the church collection to Kakamega [the headquarters]. He didn't want to be bossed but to boss. He didn't rhyme with Kivuli so he left. He came back here and said, "I'm starting my own *dini*, that's all. If you want to come with me let us follow our ancestors' way of life."[3]

('Rhyme' is a local way of saying 'to get along with someone'. Similarly 'collide' means 'to disagree' or 'clash with someone'.) The fact that two groups of dissidents which later broke away from Msambwa to form their own sects each has Israel in its name supports the story of the short-lived Kivuli-Masinde union.

Masinde first tried the name Dini ya Umoja or 'togetherness', but it was dropped when seen to have no particular significance for the Bukusu. His next choice, Dini ya Msambwa, proved to be more popular and appealed particularly to the elders worried about the destruction of tribal customs. 'This is the *dini* [religion] of your ancestors', Masinde reportedly told the Bukusu. 'You should join. It is the true *dini* of this tribe . . . the real national *dini* of long ago.'[4]

125

The core members met secretly for five or six years before the movement appeared in the open around 1943 and began its anti-colonial crusade. There were assaults on government employees, refusals to accept labour summons, the burning down of government buildings, settlers' farm buildings, mission churches and several African houses and grain stores. Settlers were harassed, chiefs and other Africans employed by the administration openly defied, and the government's land reform programme thwarted in a number of ways. (This campaign will be discussed in Chapters 11 and 13, and a chronology of events in Dini ya Msambwa's career listed in Appendix G. Here we will concentrate on Msambwa's development and the authorities' response.) These incidents brought a recommendation from the district commissioner in January 1945 that more tribal police, up to ten, be recruited for Kimilili.[5] In the end, the addition of three policemen proved sufficient. This lawlessness culminated in Masinde's arrest in 1945 on charges of assault. With the establishment of a police post at Kimilili and Masinde's subsequent commitment to Mathari Mental Hospital, Msambwa's political activities died down though secret meetings continued. In October 1946 there was unrest, strikes on settlers' farms, rumours of riots and a general strike, in the Trans Nzoia District of the White Highlands in the area that bordered the Bukusu reserve. The Bukusu were said to be ready to take land they had been claiming as theirs by force. The Governor doubled the strength of the Kiminini police force by adding nine men and put the police reserves on the alert. A mobile police unit patrolled the border.[6]

Masinde's release was strongly opposed by the district and provincial commissioners. Provincial commissioner K. L. Hunter wrote in June 1946 to the medical officer at Mathari, 'I was shocked to learn that he may be released from detention shortly, and I ask that you should not act precipitiously in this case in a desire to create accommodation, for I feel strongly that his return to his home will be accompanied by fresh outbreaks of his disciples.'[7] Masinde's subsequent release in 1947 coincided with more militancy, the demonstration at the Kibabii Mission in February 1948 and the Malakisi Riot a few days later. The administration took these events as ominous signs. Only two months before, members of a similar movement, the Dini ya Jesus Kristo in Central Province, had ambushed and killed assistant inspector T. D. Mortimer and two African constables at Gatundu.[8] The British feared that the spread of 'fanatical' cults would lead to full scale rebellion. Consequently police work on Msambwa was strengthened. There was intensive patrolling and dozens of suspects were rounded up.

Prior to the riot, Masinde had been hiding out from the police, as a warrant had been issued for his arrest. Evading the authorities, he had travelled about the district surreptitiously propagating his gospel. A week after the Malakisi Riot he was caught and Dini ya Msambwa proscribed. With Masinde's removal, the militancy again diminished. Ninety-four convicted members were released from prison in the latter part of 1948.[9]

Still towards the end of the year there was evidence that Msambwa was invading the white settlers' area of the Trans Nzoia and Uasin Gishu and the Mbale District of Uganda. The intelligence system was further strengthened. In November 1948, the administration wrote the settlers asking them to report any information they had on strangers or unusual meetings in their area and warning them about Msambwa.

Government officials visited the missions to acquire information. The mission stations along the Kenya-Uganda border were losing members to Msambwa. The missionaries organized themselves into thirteen teams with each team visiting four or five villages in an effort at counter propaganda.

In 1949 and 1950 arson broke out in the Trans Nzoia District. Violence in the reserves was one thing but violence against the settlers was tantamount to open revolt. The administration mobilized even more force. A district officer was seconded to Kitale along with the Kenya Riot Squad, the regular police force was strengthened, and the Kenya Police Reserve was ordered to stand by. Severe sentences were handed out to those convicted of arson. Francisco Tiete, one of the arsonists, was sentenced to six years with hard labour.[10] Joas Kibayo, an African who assaulted a settler, was sentenced to life imprisonment for attempted murder.[11] Native pass rules were instituted for the Bukusu and Bugishu in the Trans Nzoia and Uasin Gishu that restricted their movement within and between the districts and the reserve. A curfew was imposed from 7 p.m. to 6 a.m.[12]

Despite vigorous repression, reports of secret meetings continued. Gatherings were small yet frequent. By the end of 1949 evidence indicated that Msambwa's activities were even increasing in the Trans Nzoia. The administration arrested suspects, enforced the pass rules, and repatriated suspects from the Highlands to the reserves. For instance, during the month of September 1949, 186 were repatriated, of which 121 were Bukusu and the rest were mainly from other Luhya sub-tribes.[13]

A district officer was posted to the Bukusu reserve with an assistant superintendent of police who concentrated entirely on anti-Msambwa work. Ten additional tribal policemen were allocated to each of the locations of Malakisi, Kimilili, South Bukusu and Elgon. *Barazas* were called to inform Africans about the dangers of Msambwa and to warn them that if more police were needed the expense would be born by them.[14] More arrests were made. By the end of June 1949, 125 convictions had been obtained under the pass rules. Suspects were ordered to appear before a *baraza* where they were identified as members and required to report weekly to the sub-headman. The administration, aware that tribal authority was breaking down, made efforts to strengthen the authority of the chiefs and elders.[15]

From a meeting the provincial commissioner had with his European officers and African representatives came the idea that Dini ya Msambwa was 'largely actuated by a desire to break away from many of the Christian mission teachings and prohibitions.' As a result of this meeting and because the reserve was 'settling down', the provincial commissioner decided to hold large *barazas* on 20 and 21 October in the Bukusu locations, where he announced that the government did not wish to interfere in any way with the ancient practice of Msambwa as a family sacrificial rite, and that it did not impose any restrictions on the freedom of worship provided that such worship was conducted in an orderly manner and did not indulge in violence or politics. The pass rules were withdrawn on 1 November.[16]

A clash between several hundred Pokot tribesmen, who were members of a branch of Msambwa and a government party, occurred at Kolloa in the Baringo District in 1950. With the Kolloa Affray, Msambwa took on an even more foreboding quality. The tribe was severely punished. The sanctions were so effective that Dini ya Msambwa never again made any progress among the Pokot.

The usual areas of activity in the Kimilili-Elgon area were quiet during 1950. In the first half of the year, many meetings were held and sixty-two convictions made for membership in an illegal society. By this time all leaders of any importance had either been jailed or deported to an isolated area. The government introduced the policy of giving lighter sentences to the followers while reserving the heavier for the leaders. Close police scrutiny caused meetings to be held across the border in Uganda where, because Msambwa never posed much of a threat, police supervision was less intense. There was a marked reduction in the surveillance during the latter part of 1951, with no resulting increase in militancy.

1952 brought the declaration of the state of Emergency. With the outbreak of Mau Mau, the administration, afraid of an alliance between the two movements and of an even more massive revolt, increased its vigilance. The local district officer stated that 'anti-Dini ya Msambwa work is No. 1 priority with the police and takes precedence over anything but the most serious crime.'[17] The missionaries called together their local clergy in order to plan how to cope with Dini ya Msambwa. They asked the chiefs to assemble their clans so that they could speak to the members. In discussions with the Bukusu and Bugishu, the missionaries emphasized the benefits Christianity had brought them.[18]

The feared alliance did not occur and North Nyanza and the Trans Nzoia remained relatively quiet. Sporadic arrests were made. In June 1952, thirty-one suspects were arrested in the Mount Elgon area. In the same year, the district officer at Bungoma prosecuted twenty-eight Africans for Msambwa activity, giving each three years with hard labour. Many hardcore members were released during the year after long terms of imprisonment but were back in jail by the year's end for resuming membership in Msambwa.

Dini ya Msambwa activity gradually diminished from 1953 to 1956. Police raids in 1954 on suspected premises revealed nothing. Many Bukusu practised the religious rites, which they were permitted to do, in private.[19] Still the government was wary. District commissioner C. J. Denton in his 'Handing Over Report' to E. H. Risley warned him that 'The *Dini ya Msambwa sect is a greater potential threat to law and order than Mau Mau* owing to the fact that a large percentage of the labour force in the district comes from North Nyanza Reserve.'[20] (Italics mine.) Msambwa still attracted considerable support in 1955 and there were rumours of numerous meetings.[21] During the latter part of the year, Msambwa activity increased throughout the Trans Nzoia. More vigorous police patrolling was instituted and there was the suggestion of opening a police post.[22] In 1956, though the threat of Msambwa activity remained below the surface, there were fewer incidents than the previous year and the security was generally satisfactory. This was due in part to the creation of the District of Elgon-Nyanza in which the Bukusu formed the majority. In this way a closer watch could be kept over the Bukusu than if they had remained in the old North Nyanza District. The emergency regulations which had been applied to the district, notably the curfew, were rescinded on 22 December.[23]

Many followers were released in 1960 and 1961 on condition that they desist from any further Msambwa activity. Masinde himself was released in May of 1961. But even as the British prepared to turn the government over to Africans, arrests were made. For example in April 1962, sixty-seven were arrested, in August, seven, and in October, eight. It would appear that the British were sceptical about what Msambwa might do despite the all but formal granting of independence.

The early and successful repression of Dini ya Msambwa, particularly the arrest of its leaders, stifled the movement. Proscribed and persecuted, it was made ineffectual. After 1950, while secret meetings and sporadic violence occurred, Msambwa was finished as a serious subversive force.

With Masinde's release and the lifting of the ban on Dini ya Msambwa the post-colonial phase began. It was not long before Msambwa was in trouble with the African authorities over a number of relatively minor issues. Finally, the government, tired of Msambwa's disruptions, proscribed it in 1968. At present (1975) Masinde is in jail and the movement, as far as we can ascertain, is inactive.

Notes

1. Interview with Samson Wafula, 13 March 1965.
2. Interview with Benjamin Wekuke, 9 November 1965.
3. Interview with Pascal Nabwana, 5 November 1965.
4. *Ibid.*
5. KNA:DC/NN10/1/5. Letter from district commissioner F. D. Hislop to the provincial commissioner of Nyanza, 8 January 1945.
6. KNA:DC/NN10/1/2. Report on Alleged Unrest in Kitosh Reserve, by G. M. Taylor, assistant superintendent of police, Eldoret, to the superintendent of police, Rift Valley, Nakuru, November 1946.
7. KNA:DC/NN10/1/5. Letter from provincial commissioner K. L. Hunter to the medical officer-in-charge, Mathari Mental Hospital, 11 June, 1946.

8. Rosberg and Nottingham, *Myth of 'Mau Mau'*, p. 327.
9. KNA:DC/NN10/1/2. Letter from A. C. Griffiths, assistant superintendent of police, Nyanza, to the district commissioner, Kakamega, 18 August 1948.
10. *East African Standard*, 29 August 1949.
11. See below, pp. 339–40.
12. *East African Standard*, 3 June 1949.
13. KNA:DC/NN10/1/5. Letter from the district commissioner, Kitale to the district commissioner, Kakamega, 8 September 1949.
14. KNA:DC/NN10/1/5. Letter from provincial commissioner K. L. Hunter of Nyanza to the honourable chief native commissioner, 6 June 1949.
15. KNA:DC/NN10/1/5. Letter from provincial commissioner K. L. Hunter to the honourable member for native affairs, 26 May 1949.
16. KNA:DC/NN10/1/5. Letter from provincial commissioner K. L. Hunter of Nyanza to the honourable member for law and order, Nairobi, 7 October 1949.
17. KNA:DC/NN.2/6. Handing Over Report and Notes, R. S. Winser to L. C. Mortimer, August 1952.
18. *East African Standard*, 3 October 1952.
19. KNA:DC/NN10/1/5. Acting chief native commissioner, C. M. Deverall to the provincial commissioner, Kisumu, 17 October 1949.
20. KNA:TN/2. Handing Over Report, C. J. Denton to E. H. Risley, May 1955.
21. *Nyanza Province Annual Report, 1955*.
22. *Trans Nzoia District Annual Report, 1955*.
23. *Trans Nzoia District Annual Report, 1956*.

Chapter 11

BELIEFS AND ACTIVITIES

THIS section on 'Beliefs and Activities' really comprises four separate chapters. (1) Dini ya Msambwa's message, (2) tales about Elijah Masinde, (3) the anti-colonial campaign, and (4) some deviant practices. We have kept them together in order to underline the different dimensions of Msambwa's beliefs and practices. Viewpoints which are too narrow have tended to obscure the movement's complexity.

In the absence of documents (no declarations of aims, creeds, pamphlets lambasting the imperialists, prayer or hymn books), statements from the leaders and followers about Msambwa's goals, beliefs and rituals, folk tales, legends, prophecies, songs and prayers will be examined. In the post-colonial period, in order to comply with government regulations, Msambwa submitted a constitution to the registrar-general of societies but it was of little help in understanding the movement.

We will examine not only Msambwa's beliefs but the actions taken to further its goals, or put another way, the kind of movement in which these beliefs were incorporated. These two dimensions are important for the same beliefs can be associated with movements of withdrawal into isolation, militant nationalism or religious revolt.

Many studies have focussed on the writings of the most sophisticated ideologists, giving scant attention to the rank-and-file's interpretation of the movement. While this is hardly a problem in a movement of peasants led by peasants, (there is not likely to be much of a discrepancy in terms of the leaders' and followers' intellectual understanding), where there is no intelligentsia between the mass base and the ideology, major attention will still be paid to the beliefs as perceived and understood by the rank-and-file. For, as

Smelser has stressed, in order to have collective action, grievances, dissatisfactions and strains must be made meaningful to the potential participants.[1]

It should be noted that there are two distinct periods in Msambwa's career, the colonial and post-colonial. The main analysis pertains to the former, as it is by far the more important. The latter will be treated separately at the end.

Msambwa's Message
Msambwa's message exhibits a complex blending of the old and the new, of religious and political concerns. First, we will sketch in some aspects of traditional religion and leadership in order to compare them with what Dini ya Msambwa presented as the traditional religion. Secondly, we will examine Msambwa's nativistic element, thirdly, its Christian and millenarian, and fourthly, attempt to answer the question, does it practise the traditional religion.[2] The reader will notice that the separation of nativistic from Christian beliefs is not too successful since a fusion between them has occurred in a number of instances that prevents any sharp categorization.

Some Aspects of Luhya Religion and Leadership
Luhya religion despite sub-tribal variations centres upon three different kinds of supernatural beings, ancestor spirits, the creator-spirit or supreme being, and other spirits.

The pivot of the religion, and by far the most important element in people's lives, according to La Fontaine, are the ancestor spirits. The *basambwa* are spirits of people who have died and are still concerned with the wellbeing of their descendants on earth. ('Ba' is a Bantu prefix that denotes persons.) Ancestor spirits are considered active members of the society. They are prayed to and cared for by agnatic kinsmen. This is important in understanding the difference between the traditional religion and Dini ya Msambwa. Not all people who die become ancestor spirits or, to be more specific, have the power to influence their descendents. Young children, uncircumcised men, and women who have died without bearing children, in other words, people who have not achieved a full social life, do not have this power. Sacrifices are not offered to them. The ancestors are believed to act as intermediaries between man and other supernatural forces. Their cooperation is required if prayers directed to other spirits are to be successful.

133

Since the ancestors are an integral part of tribal life, exercising control over men's lives, they require constant attention. If angered they can bring misfortune or even disaster upon the culprits by causing cattle to die, women to be barren, and crops to wither. They are always remembered at important ceremonies — circumcision, puberty and marriage — that mark the life cycle. On these occasions oblations are performed in order to ward off misfortune. In crises, for which the ancestor spirits might be responsible, they are called upon to intervene in order that the social order may return to normality. *Gumusambwa* denotes the whole complex of sacrifices and religious practices that relate to both ancestral and non-ancestral spirits. These rites vary in detail from clan to clan and even within clans.

Shrines are built to the ancestor spirits in the home compounds of prestigious men or in a special grove connected with the circumcision ceremony. There are usually two shrines, one for male ancestors called *namwina* which occupies a conspicuous place in front of the main door, and another for women, called *wetiri*, which is built under the eaves of the house. These shrines are constructed in the shape of small huts and covered with grass. Branches from two trees, the African fig and the *lusoola*, are commonly used in the ritual and may be stuck through the roof of the shrine so that a fork projects above. Offerings of meat are hung there for the spirits.

The Luhya have no definite idea as to where departed spirits go. The spirits are believed to remain in the vicinity of their earthly homes. If a person happens to die far from his home, his spirit will return there. Only under exceptional circumstances, such as when very angry, do spirits enter the body of any living thing. Then it is the body of a large snake. People kill the snake and perform rites to appease the spirits within.

A second supernatural force is the creator-spirit or high god known as *Wele*, *Were*, or *Nyasaye*,[3] believed to live in the sky, and to be the guiding and controlling principle in the world— hence the ultimate arbiter in people's lives. He is the chief spirit, the *musambwa*. *Wele* is omnipresent although invisible 'like the wind'. In his manifestations to man, *Wele* assumed different forms according to his activities, *Wele Xakaba*, the creator-spirit, and his two assistants, *Wele Muxove*, the provider, and *Wele Murumwa*, the light. *Wele* bestows life, is the source of prosperity and health, and is the protector of all people. He is viewed as having the power to alter the social order and prayers are offered to him to 'let things take their normal course and to bring peace to mankind'.

There is disagreement about the actual role *Wele* plays in the lives of men. Gunter Wagner maintains that sacrifices are often made to him and that he is looked upon as a benevolent father who will punish his children should they do wrong. Jean La Fontaine argues, on the other hand, that he is a vague and distant force hardly involved in the lives of men, and that consequently, sacrifices are not made directly to him. The Bukusu, she states, admit he is the ultimate recipient of all sacrifices though 'far away'. Father Joseph Orther supports this view. The Bukusu do not sacrifice to *Wele*, according to him, but to the ancestor spirits.[4]

The natural order does not embrace the disruptive, evil forces of nature which cause unhappiness and disturb the normal course of events. Misfortune, illness, and death are not part of the natural order. They are believed to be caused by forces that oppose that order. Among the Bukusu all evil things in life are attributed to the 'black god', the opposite of the creator-spirit, but an independent though weaker force. None of the other Luhya sub-tribes share such an explicit belief in a force parallel though opposite to the creator-spirit. They have, rather, a belief in a dichotomy between good and evil forces. There are malevolent spirits, some of them nature spirits, whose actions run counter to the welfare of mankind. *Welutsi* and *Wimbi*, spirits of the river and field, respectively, bring illness and misfortune. Another important spirit, *Lufundu*, whose sign is the rainbow, causes infertility, miscarriages and the death of children. These malevolent spirits must also be placated with sacrifices.

The Luhya have ritual specialists, the dream prophet, the diviner, and the rain magician, who possess secret knowledge and positive magical powers thought to have been acquired from *Wele* or the ancestors. Since *Wele* delegated these powers to them, they, in turn, ask him for his help. The dream prophet wields wide powers that enable him to enact laws, innovate practices, and to influence people's actions. These experts, with the exception of a family of rainmakers in Bunyole, enjoy local prestige only. The Bunyore rainmakers, in contrast, were so famous that delegations came from afar to offer them tribute.[5] Yet even though they enjoyed wide prestige, like the others, it is limited to their area of expertise. The expert's skill does not entitle him to political power or to partake in priestly functions, in short, to any special privileges. It is assumed that secret knowledge has to be acquired legitimately, that is, through the prescribed rules. In contrast, the more common crafts such as basket-weaving, pottery and leatherwork do not involve the idea of secret knowledge and are open to anyone.

Luhya religion is practised by local groups each praying to its own ancestors. Clans are divided into sub-clans which are further divided into the descendants of a common grandfather or great-grandfather. Only on rare occasions does an entire clan participate in a ceremony together. Then an elder in each group performs the sacrifices. Age and lineal seniority are the criteria used in determining who performs the ritual. No man with a living father can build a shrine on his compound or sacrifice to the ancestors. His father must do it for him. In a society where the elders hold positions of power and authority, a man can ill afford to anger them.

Authority is dispersed through a wide arrangement of religious, social, economic, and kinship institutions and lies generally with the elders. Old age is accompanied by a gradual elevation in status and influence as the principle of seniority operates in all relationships. The elders, because they are enmeshed in a network of kinship and group affiliations are particularly well situated to keep peace among the clans and to look out for wider tribal interests. The qualities looked for in the leading elders are persuasiveness, wisdom, gentleness, and the ability to judge quarrels dispassionately. One of their major tasks is to settle witchcraft accusations.

Success in battle brought not only wealth but considerable prestige. Former clan heads were usually remembered for their prowess in battle. Courage, physical strength and the ability to convince others to join an attack were admired. Since several clans might unite in a raid, leadership in fighting, more than other qualities, tended to establish prestige that cut across clan divisions and brought its possessor superior status.

Wealth confers power and if properly used gains its possessor prestige. It enables a man to entertain generously and this makes it possible for his homestead to become a centre where important people meet. Wealth also permits a man to help others, who are then supposed to praise their benefactor. If the debtor cannot repay the loan, he might become his creditor's retainer. Thus, riches permit an individual to build up a network of relations that in turn increases his power and influence.

Luhya genealogy has been traced back to around 1550.[6] The first ancestor noted was *Wele*. Whether the Luhya thought of the creator-spirit as their originating ancestor, or whether he was merely a person named after the creator-spirit, a common practice and the more likely of the two, is debatable.[7] *Wele* begot a boy, *Mwambu*, and a girl, *Seera* or *Sela*. (Here is another example of the 'r' and 'l' interchange.) Some narrators point to a third child, *Mukhobe*. *Mwambu* married his sister *Seera* and they are regarded as the tribal father and mother. This brother-sister marriage would not be surprising since they were supposedly living in Egypt where pharaohs also married their sisters.[8]

Nativistic Beliefs

Turning now to Dini ya Msambwa, its main edict 'Europeans get out!' was supported by nativistic beliefs and rituals.[9] The members were admonished to return to the ways of their forefathers. An extreme version rejected not only the government and the missions, but hospitals, maternity centres (where women were said to be given medicine that would prevent them from bearing children), western education, clothes, and cooking utensils, and even salt and sugar.

In one breath, Masinde rejected 'all things European' and, in the next, he promised his followers all the Europeans' riches after they had been expelled from Kenya. For his part, Masinde did not reject a gift of a landrover. Because of the inconsistency with which the edict was followed, the vice-president, Benjamin Wekuke, was asked what was actually meant by it. He replied:

> No, it doesn't mean to reject all European things because God sent Europeans to bring civilization to Africans. Whenever a group goes naked and completely returns to the old ways they are a *dini* without fruits and should be done away with. Some of the old ways are not as good as the ways the Europeans brought. What God really wanted was for *wazungus* to come and give Africans knowledge. Now they have done that. We know about clothes, we know about cars, about good houses and health and so it is now time for them to go. We can carry on by ourselves.[10]

Msambwa's members like those of the Mumbo cult admired western technology and had no intention of rejecting it for traditional ways. This distinction was also made in the Ghost Dance of the North American Indians. Although it laid great stress on reviving certain aspects of traditional Indian culture, in particular games and ceremonies, it permitted the followers to continue to use cloth, guns, kettles and other European manufactured utensils that were obviously superior to their own.[11]

The Kimilili market where people gathered once or twice weekly was a favourite place to spread Msambwa's message. Wekuke reminisced about an appearance he had made there. 'I stood on an ant hill [ant hills are sometimes as tall as a person] and I started to shout to the people telling them that God had opened the way to African independence. "All of you follow me and go back to our own traditional ways. Then the provincial commissioner, the district commissioner and the administrative ranks will be taken by Africans."'

Msambwa's nativism focussed on the old Luhya religion. People were admonished to forsake the Christian religion and to return to the religion of their ancestors. The intermeshing of political and religious themes was evident in hymns and prayers. The creator-spirit as well as important ancestors were called upon for their help.

> *Wele* our Father, help us;
> *Wazungus* should go back to their homes
> Maina of Lugali, Wachiye of Wanaumbwa,
> Mutonyi Bukerembe help us.[12]

Wele was the creator spirit. Maina was one of the earliest ancestors of both the Bukusu and Gusii. 'Lugali' may be a misspelling for Lugulu, the site of the Bukusu-British battle. The phrase, Maina wa Lugali, may mean Maina of Lugulu (the place) or Maina of the Lugulu clan. Wachiye was a famous nineteenth century magician who according to legend performed many miracles. Naumbwa was the father of Wachiye so this would be a reference to Maina, literally 'of the people of Naumbwa' or Maina of the Naumbwa clan. Mutonyi Bukerembe, usually referred to simply as Mutonyi, was the prophet who predicted the arrival of the British.

Other prayers went as follows, 'Our Father Mwambu and Mother Seera we beseech you to bring back our old rule. Let the foreigners depart from our land,[13] and

> Oh God the Father forgive us and feel pity for us.
> The foreigners brought the new missions which made us
> leave our traditional customs which are now lost.
> We are asking you to bless and give us freedom.

Massive Mount Elgon, an extinct volcano lying on the Kenya-Uganda border, became the holy mountain of the Msambwa people.

It was believed to be the home of the ancestor spirits, especially their prophets. Supernatural signs and portents were sought there and the members faced it for prayers and hymns. The mountain and a small, beautiful glacial lake, that nestled just below the towering peak, Wagagai, were Msambwa's most sacred shrines.[14] The lake called Zion (the members' pronunciation is 'Sayuni') was the place of divine revelation. There God 'spoke' to Masinde who, like the Biblical Moses, climbed the mountain to receive His instructions. Masinde allegedly scooped up water from the lake, touched his lips to it, and gave thanks to *Wele*.[15] On Zion's shores the members sacrificed to the ancestor spirits and communicated with God in a special cave. Wafula described such an encounter, 'When you reach there you hear a voice speaking from the house and from the lake itself. The whole place is filled by the voice. It is a deep male voice. You don't see anything just the lake and you hear the voice.'[16]

Pilgrimages to the lake were undertaken whenever God indicated through a dream that he desired one.[17] A leader explained why they made the long, arduous climb:

The main reason we go up there is that it is a wonderful place. Our ancestors went there yearly for prayers. They did this because the lake [with its towering peaks] is like a church. As you know, it is cold and the climb difficult and tiring. People made this climb in order to show God what they would do for him. . . . If you had sinned badly you wouldn't reach the lake for it is especially difficult for sinners. There is a fragrant white flower. If a sinner smells it his body grows weak and he becomes so cold that he cannot travel any farther. We demonstrated to God by this climb that we were devoting our lives to him. We took a ram or a sheep like our ancestors did and sacrificed it. We prayed and sprinkled the ram's blood on the lake and on the shores. We slept up there. God told us in a dream that he had accepted our sacrifice and that Africans would obtain their rights.[18]

Donisio Nakimayu recalled that he had made three pilgrimages to the lake, once with thirteen people, another time with about thirty-five, and on still another occasion with sixty-five. He described his first trip. He was sitting near the lake when he and others saw a figure, twelve feet tall, walking on the water robed in a *kanzu* with parallel red stripes. In his right hand was a staff and in his left a 'shiny godlike object'. The figure approached them from the lake, climbed onto a perpendicular stone, and looked at them. The followers began to pray and it disappeared. On their descent from the lake, they encountered many buffalo. Some members were afraid. Donisio said, 'Let us pray', and the buffalo disappeared. Next they met a large elephant and the same thing happened. Finally, they reached the bottom safely. Donisio thought that the figure in the vision might have been either *Wele* or one of the great Biblical prophets like Moses or Abraham because of the type of garment worn, and that he had been sent to look after them.[19] The similarities between the figure in their vision and Jesus Christ walking on the sea also come to mind, as well as Jesus Christ in John the Baptist's vision at Patmos. He was 'clothed with a garment down to the feet' and 'he had in his right hand seven stars'. (Mathew 14:25 and Revelations 1:9–18, respectively.)

There is little in the literature to indicate that Mount Elgon played an important role in the traditional religion. It is important in Bukusu history but it is not clear whether it had particular religious significance. The Bukusu are said to be descendants of Mundu who supposedly came out of a hole in the ground at the top of the mountain and was the first man to live on the mountain. (According to another tradition, Mundu came from the north.) It was also alleged that the Bukusu formerly lived on the summit and gradually spread to the lower regions when their numbers increased or when the volcanic mountain erupted and forced them to move. Wagner, still the authority on Luhya religion, expressed surprise that 'the broad massif of Mount Elgon, which extends over the northern horizon and is seen from every point in the district', had not evoked any myths or stories nor did it figure in any rites or ceremonies.[20]

In opposition to this view, several informants maintained that Mount Elgon as well as Lake Zion were traditionally sacred to the Bukusu.[21] Each year, according to them, before planting began, two prominent elders were selected from each of the Bukusu clans to sacrifice an animal, sometimes a bull, to *Wele* on the mountain. Planting could not begin before the pilgrims had returned. If they are correct then Masinde was following an old custom, a custom that may have been reinforced by Christian ritual, since there are many references in the Bible to animal sacrifices and to the prophets, and indeed to Jesus Christ himself, praying in the hills. On the other hand, until more evidence is available, it is best not to dismiss altogether the idea that Dini ya Msambwa might have instituted a new practice but called it old.

The rocks and caves that surround Lake Zion provided overnight shelter for the pilgrims. They bathed in the lake's icy waters to cleanse themselves of sin and to wash away the pollution caused by contact with Europeans. Some water was taken back home for purification rites.[22] These practices may have come from the traditional belief in the purifying action of flowing water. Formerly, warriors cleansed their bloodstained spears in a swiftly running stream and evil magic was thrown into a stream because flowing water was believed to carry evil things away.

The use of water as a means of purification is part of many traditional African religions. Water rituals were widespread among the Yoruba. Christian baptism symbolizing spiritual cleansing may have reinforced traditional beliefs. Certainly these rites appeared in many of the independent churches. Turner comments upon the purification aspects of baptism in the Aladura Movement of West Africa and Sundkler observed this practice among the independent churches of South Africa.[23]

Another practice honouring the ancestors, particularly the warriors, was the growing of flowers about the leaders' homes. The profusion of brilliant flowers in neat rows around simple mud and thatch huts was unusual as peasants in that area were not in the habit of planting flowers. 'Our ancestors loved flowers, especially their perfume so should our ancestors' spirits come to visit our home at night with angels [an interesting bit of syncretism] to bring us special messages . . . the spirits smell the flowers and are very pleased if we have many flowers growing around our homes', Wafula said.[24] Before battle, the warriors were said to have climbed to Lake Zion where they decorated themselves with the flowers that grew around the lake in order to ensure success.

The planting of flowers probably reflects mission and settler influence. There were mission stations in that area with spacious green lawns and neat flower beds. Kimilili, too, the movement's stronghold, is only thirty miles from Kitale in the White Highlands and labourers employed on the settlers' farms moved back and forth.

Traditional ceremonies to propitiate the ancestor spirits and to confer the status of elder were stressed.[25] These ceremonies extolled truth, peace and wisdom, respect for parents, ancestors, and all forms of life. God was asked for his blessing and to keep evil spirits away. Murder and adultery were forbidden.

An old prophecy by Mutonyi was resurrected. It went as follows:

There will come to our country people who travel in a small thing like a granary and they will be able to fly like birds. They will bring a thing like

141

a snake that will travel on iron and it will swallow and vomit up people. They will possess spears that your shields will not be able to stop. Their spears will reach you from afar while yours cannot reach them. You'll try to fight them but you won't do them any harm. They'll conquer you. You will stay together in peace for some years and then they'll leave in peace without fighting. After they have stayed for several years *there will come something from Mount Elgon which will chase them away to their own country. That small thing is the voice of God that talked to Masinde on Mount Elgon.* (Italics mine.)[26]

Thus the Bukusu's spiritual leaders foretold the coming of the white man with his automobile and deadly weapons, the opening up of the country by railroad and airplane as well as Masinde's prophetic mission. Whether this prophecy was actually voiced or whether it was an after-the-fact creation of an inventive imagination can only be guessed at. Interestingly, such a prophesy has also appeared among the Gusii, Maasai and Kamba.[27] This way of communicating messages—the voice of God talking to Masinde on a mountain—is reminiscent of similar occasions in the Old and New Testaments where God spoke to his prophets and disciples. For instance 'a still small voice' spoke to Elijah at 'Horeb the mount of God' (1 Kings 19:9–18). God spoke to Peter, James and John on a mountain (Mathew 17:5; Mark 9:7) and to John the Baptist in 'a great voice, as of a trumpet' (Revelation 1:10).

The Bukusu's militant tradition was resuscitated. In September 1947, about five thousand Dini ya Msambwa members dressed in warriors' garb and led by Masinde made a pilgrimage to the remains of the old fort at Lugulu, the site of the 1895 battle against the British. There, Masinde paid homage to the warriors killed in that battle, evoked the ancestors' blessings, declared war on the British, and pledged those assembled to the struggle for independence.

More specifically, since the warriors had been left unburied, their spirits were believed to be crying out for a proper burial. Masinde killed a black ram and buried its head, signifying the warriors' burial. Then the sacrificial meat was roasted and distributed to the followers to eat. (A practice with similarities to the Christian Holy Communion where bread symbolizing the flesh of Christ is eaten.) Masinde addressed the crowd. 'This is the place where our forefathers were killed. I make this sacrifice to commemorate the truce between the whites and the Bukusu at the end of the war.' So saying, he took a bottle containing a piece of paper symbolizing the agreement and buried it. Later, he dug the bottle up, poured ram's blood on it, burned the paper and broke the bottle, saying' 'I'm making a sacrifice that breaks the agreement between the Bukusu and the British. It no longer exists. The *wazungus' power is finished!* They won't stay any longer. We shall have our own *dini*, our own government and *be masters of our own destiny!*'[28] (Italics mine.) By their presence, the pilgrims had publicly dedicated themselves to further Msambwa's goals. This dramatic event thus became enshrined in the movement's 'collective memory'.

Msambwa displayed an elaborate symbolism composed of natural materials — woods, creepers, plants, birds and fowl — common to that part of the country and appropriate for a rural people.[29] Traditional ideas combined with Christian and many traditional symbols had taken on new, militant meanings.

This was the symbolism of an insurrectionary movement where secrecy and danger are prime elements and magical protection sought, rather than that of a Christian religious group open to all and concerned with a doctrine of social ethics. There is no emphasis here on meakness, forgiveness, and loving one's enemy, but rather military virtues, courage, determination, and commitment to a cause, were extolled. Hopes were expressed for safety from arrest, the destruction of their enemies, and the movement's success.

Msambwa had its seers and prophets. Next to Masinde, there was Joasch Walumoli, the *omwisanyi*, who provided the dreams and prophecies. He was described with admiration as a 'great prophet' and a 'real prophet'.[30] Israel Khaoya, from the same clan as Walumoli, was also believed to have spiritual power, though not as powerful as Walumoli's. Zebedayo Walukau was another seer through whose mediumship heavenly signs were received and passed on to the members. Most of his dreams had a Biblical theme.[31]

According to Max Weber, the absence of women in important leadership positions would indicate Dini ya Msambwa's essentially masculine and martial nature since political and military type prophecy is directed exclusively to men.[32] It is probably more accurate to say that it reflected the masculine nature of institutionalized leadership in Luhya society, that while certain rituals could be performed by women, the important ritual specialists and leaders were predominantly men.

Contrary to much writing on these movements, nativism was not a sign of an atavistic movement. By returning to the religion of their ancestors, the members believed they would secure the

143

favour of the creator-spirit, their great prophets and important ancestors and this would help them banish the Europeans. Conversion to Christianity had apparently angered the ancestors who retaliated by permitting the colonialists to defeat them.

The stress upon tradition was also expedient in that it defied western values. What else could a subjugated people take pride in? Certainly not in their conquered state. Other people in such circumstances have likewise turned to the past in order to preserve, in part, their cultural heritage. Msambwa, like Mumbo, used the prestige of important ancestors to legitimize its aims and to acquire support. It anchored its revolutionary ideas in tradition, thereby stressing the continuity of the past with the present and uniting people around symbols they understood and revered. Nor have modern African political parties ignored the advantages of using tradition to legitimize modern ideologies, as noted by David Apter and other political scientists.[33]

Christian and Millenarian Beliefs

Msambwa was permeated with Christian symbols, stories and practices. Its leaders quoted liberally from the Bible, especially the Old Testament.[34] The cross was much in evidence. At services the members would line up in the shape of a cross. On their uniform there was a cross which stood for Jesus Christ and under it a V which represented the shafts of light that fell on either side of Masinde when he talked to God at Lake Zion.[35] Even the leaders' names, Elijah, Joshua, Samson and Benjamin, were Old Testament names and, most ironic of all, Msambwa's sacred shrine was named Zion.

But Msambwa's identification with Christian values, like its nativism, was *selective*. The members rejected monogamy for polygyny. Monogamy was said to be merely a European custom and not one of God's commandments since some Old Testament patriarchs had had more than one wife. The selective process was eclectic, ranging through different denominations and even different religions and cultures. Prayer and hymn books came from the Quakers and the Anglicans, the wearing of beards, turbans and the *kanzu* from Islamic culture, and the drum from their own culture, although its specific use in church services may have been encouraged by Salvation Army practices.

Some members carried nine foot staffs like Moses, split into three prongs at the tip and said to represent the Trinity. The Luhya's three forms of the creator-spirit were interpreted as evidence of the Christian Trinity. On earth Masinde represented *Wele Xakaba*, Wekuke, *Wele Muxove*, and another follower, *Wele Murumwa*.[36] The members claimed the missionaries had taught them nothing they had not already known about the Trinity.

Msambwa, by returning to the old religion and by emphasizing the creator-spirit and ancestor spirits, as well as by incorporating the Christian God and the Old Testament prophets, was faced with a plethora of gods, prophets, angels and ancestors. So what did it do? It simply made them all equal. Mount Elgon became the dwelling place of not only the Luhya but the Biblical prophets. All prophets, Christian and indigenous, were regarded as ancestor spirits and were prayed to interchangeably; *Wele* was equated with the Christian God; Seera and Mwambu, the tribal mother and father, were seen as Mary and Joseph; and ancestor spirits and angels were treated as similar ethereal creatures.[37]

Certain stories from the Old Testament were particularly popular with the members. For instance, Jonah and the whale, Jacob and his sons, Moses and the Ten Commandments. Stories were selected from the Old Testament that were similar to their own beliefs or were in some other way meaningful. According to a member, 'The people mix Christian and old beliefs. The ones that rhyme.'

The Jews' exodus from Egypt fitted in with a Luhya belief that long ago they had fled from a country in the north. The followers 'discovered' that their ancestors were the Israelites. Their origin's myth went as follows: When Moses led the chosen people from Egypt, some including the Bukusu, remained behind. Later when they found themselves hated by the Egyptians they too fled. Coming to the sea they were stopped until a frog swallowed them and spewed them out on the other side—another version of the Red Sea story and/or Jonah and the whale.[38] They journeyed to East Africa, drove out the original inhabitants, and settled there. Now Masinde, a modern-day Moses, has come to lead Africans in their struggle against colonial bondage. According to Osogo and Were, many Luhya clans, including the Bukusu, claim to have come from Egypt (Misra) through the Sudan and Ethiopia to Mbale, Uganda, where they settled for a time before continuing their journey to their present home.[39]

145

The Bible, with its stories of an oppressed people led by a prophet to a Promised Land, provided a framework within which to reinterpret their own history, especially their position in relation to Europeans. From the Congo to the Cape separatist movements like the Bakongo cults of Simon Kimbangu and André Matswa have preached the coming doom of the white man and the ultimate triumph of a Black Messiah and his chosen people.[40]

The triumph of blacks was associated with a millennium wherein Masinde, the messiah, would rule the world. There were many versions of this millennium. Like Mumbo's followers, the faithful were assured that once the foreigners were evicted they would inherit all their riches. According to one story, the foreigners were to be diiven out by former chief Maina. In another, they were to be wiped out by an avalanche of blood from the sky. A plentiful supply of everything the followers wanted would be theirs for the taking on Mount Elgon. Large herds of cattle would roam the mountain, clothes and blankets would hang from trees, and stores of food would be found near Lake Zion.[41] Millennial fantasies were probably abetted by mission teachings about the blissful afterlife of the faithful.

The zealotry of a few followers helped to promote an image of Msambwa as composed of fanatics. Christian teachings about the afterlife were apparently so attractive to a few that they decided to speed up its attainment. One overly curious adherent sought to explore Dini ya Msambwa's future by climbing a high tree and proclaiming he was going to fly to heaven. His wings unfortunately failed to arrive in time and he fell to earth, breaking his neck fatally.[42]

In 1965, newspapers bore the headlines, 'Crucified Man Dies after Two Weeks', and 'Death of Man on Cross'. Apparently a follower, Daniel Waswa, had died from injuries received from having himself crucified.[43] An investigation revealed that the newspaper accounts were inaccurate and that the man had not been crucified but that he had driven a spike into his head and had subsequently died from the untreated wounds. Although his family refused to discuss it, neighbours and others in the area said that for several years he had been acting strangely. He had told them about speaking with God and about dying for the sins of all Kenyans. His suicidal act was variously interpreted. Some said it was a great event for Msambwa, others merely commented that 'something was wrong with his head'. Elijah Masinde, perhaps not wanting to share the spotlight with any other claimant of divine communication, rejected Waswa's action as contrary to Dini ya Msambwa's true beliefs, because, he explained, Jesus was crucified by the Jews and did not crucify himself.[44]

On another occasion a member claiming to be Jesus Christ went to a police station, lay down on the ground, arms outstretched, and ordered the officer in charge to crucify him. When the officer prepared to drive a spike into his head, he suddenly changed his mind and jumped up. He was given six months in jail to think over his would-be martyrdom.[45]

The African capacity to accommodate and assimilate diverse cultural elements has been noted by a number of scholars. Wagner wrote that if an exceptional situation arose in one clan for which the ritual had repeatedly and conspicuously failed to achieve the desired results, some procedure from another clan's ritual would be used which, if successful, would then be incorporated into the ritual. This ability to assimilate foreign elements is, in fact, the essence of the revitalization process. Fernandez states that, given the turmoil, extensive migrations, dominations and subordinations in African tribal history, assimilation has occurred quite frequently in the past.[46] Hence, Msambwa's capacity for assimilation was not a new but rather a traditional response.

Does Dini ya Msambwa Practise the Traditional Religion?

In comparing Msambwa's beliefs with the traditional, it is evident without a detailed comparison that while there are strong similarities, the members as a whole did not strictly practise the old religion. Traditional rites were practised by some but, by and large, Msambwa revitalized only certain aspects of the old religion, gave old symbols new meanings, innovated new practices but called them old, and combined these with certain Christian practices and beliefs.

The ancestral cult was a small scale religion that brought members of the same family together in the performance of common rites. With Msambwa the criteria designating the congregation changed from a group of agnatic kinsmen to all those who shared Msambwa's beliefs regardless of kinship ties. Thus the movement extended the limits of membership from family, clan and kinsfolk to a community of people who shared common beliefs. It moved from membership by ascription to achievement, that is, instead of being born into a family that automatically guaranteed one's participation, one

147

could choose or not choose to join Dini ya Msambwa. Since a steady membership was no longer guaranteed, and since Msambwa's aim was to grow larger, proselytizing followed, at least in its early years.

Masinde and his disciples did not fulfil the main criterion of leadership, old age. In the 1940s they were young men. Masinde had little wealth, was harsh, impetuous and autocratic. If certain traditional criteria were used—age, wealth, and qualities of character such as wisdom and gentleness—Masinde would have been debarred from the office of priest as would most of his assistants. And what was even more damning, on numerous occasions, Msambwa's leaders showed contempt for traditional authority, such as Masinde's assault on the head of the traditional council of elders. Another time, he refused to permit the clan elders to confer the status of elder on Wekuke, insisting that he would do it himself. Msambwa opposed tithes, a traditional chiefly prerogative, although it could be argued that chiefs no longer represented traditional authority. We suggest that Msambwa's leaders represented rebellion against, and the breakdown of, traditional authority. Indeed, any view of Msambwa as traditionally-oriented must account for its rejection of traditional authority.

Masinde clearly did not possess the traits expected of a clan elder. But did he qualify on other grounds? Masinde's role was not totally divorced from traditional leadership. His claims to have special powers and a mandate from God were consistent with the claims of such ritual specialists as the dream prophet, the rain magician and the diviner. His use of his position to introduce new and revolutionary ideas was not out of keeping with the leeway to innovate given the dream prophet.

But in the traditional religion, the roles of priest and prophet were separate and distinct. A prophet was recognized for his ability to prophesy and his gift did not empower him to act as a priest in either an ancestral cult or in spirit worship. Prophets occupied essentially secular roles divorced from religious ceremonies. Only if an individual qualified on other grounds, such as being an elder, could he unite in his person the two roles. Masinde, for his part, merged the two roles. He communicated with God, prayed to the ancestor spirits, prophesied and used dreams as vehicles of supernatural communication.[47]

Msambwa displayed the same paradox as the cult of Mumbo. It eulogized the traditional yet in certain respects was strongly anti-traditional. At the time Msambwa originated, Masinde and his assistants were young ex-mission converts, marginal to both the traditional and colonial systems. Although Dini ya Msambwa opposed traditional authority, there were still a number of aspects about Masinde's leadership that were derived from the past.

Wele became the central element in Msambwa's religion, as witnessed by its name Dini ya Musambwa or Dini ya Msambwa meaning, religion of the creator-spirit or supreme being. (*Musambwa* is the Luhya singular for spirit, *msambwa* the Swahili-ized singular, and *misambwa* the Luhya plural). Had Msambwa stressed ancestral spirits, as many writers have contended, then the plural, *basambwa*, meaning spirits of people or ancestor spirits, would have been used. Or, if it had stressed spirits in general (which would have included ancestral and free spirits as well as the creator-spirit) then the plural for spirits, *misambwa*, would undoubtedly have been used.[48] But this was not the case. Both terms used to designate its name, *musambwa* and *msambwa* are singular forms. Hence it would appear that Msambwa did not emphasize spirits in general or the ancestor spirits in particular, but rather the supreme spirit, *Wele*. However, one hesitates to push this interpretation too far because, though it holds logically, there is no rigid rule and a singular form may well indicate a plural (like the word multitude). 'Musambwa' to many members may simply mean 'ancestor spirits'.

What Dini ya Msambwa seems to have done, contrary to a number of interpretations, is to have modified, by emphasizing and de-emphasizing, certain elements in the traditional religion so that it paralleled Christianity more closely. Just as Christians sing and pray to God, so do Msambwa members to *Wele*. Just as the Christian God sent his son Jesus Christ to lead the Jews, so has *Wele* sent Elijah Masinde to lead the Africans. Ancestor spirits were still important as intermediaries between man and God, but instead of being the most important element in people's religion, they have given ground to *Wele* and Masinde.

And while a main plank in Msambwa gospel rejected Christianity, we find many Christian elements in its beliefs. That there should be is not surprising in one way since its leaders were former mission converts. But why did Msambwa not follow its own edict and return to the old religion completely banishing any traces of Christianity? Why, as we shall see in the next section, were so many of Masinde's powers similar to, even greater than Christly powers, and why did

149

so many of his feats have a Christian flavour about them? We suggest that these are tactics of emulation. The white man and his religion had made too much of an impact to simply be ignored. They had somehow to be taken into account and here was another mechanism—we previously discussed Mumboism's reversal theme—for doing it.[49]

In sum, Msambwa, in revitalizing the traditional religion, enlarged its scale so that anyone professing to believe in its creed could join, changed the qualifications of leadership, elevated the concept of creator-spirit to a central position in the belief system, and adopted innumerable Christian symbols, ritual, and beliefs.

The argument that Msambwa did not practise the old religion is correct.[50] Its beliefs were a synthesis of foreign, traditional and new ideas. In its attempt to return to the old religion, it took much liberty in changing practices. Whether this was done haphazardly because the old rites were inaccurately remembered, or whether it was done deliberately, is difficult to say. Probably, there was more of the former than the latter. The leaders themselves did not argue otherwise. Samson Wafula, though he may sound illogical, explained their form of worship, 'We do it the same [as traditionally] but we modernize it.'

However, to dismiss Msambwa as not the old religion, or as a debased version of Christianity, or as simply a mixture of the old and new, is to overlook two important dimensions, *intent and belief*. Masinde and his assistants intended to go back to the old religion. The fact that they modified it somewhat, that some of them may not have understood it very well, or even that Masinde used it in order to win support for Msambwa, overlooks the important fact that Msambwa aimed to revitalize the ancestors' religion and beliefs in the ancestors, even if it meant innovating some new practices to commemorate them. Besides, there is considerable evidence that Masinde broke with tradition whenever he so desired.[51]

Members were questioned on why they joined Dini ya Msambwa and their answers revealed that, regardless of how superficially or calculatedly some leaders believed in Msambwa's gospel, many members believed they were practising the religion of their ancestors.

A middle-aged woman spoke with my assistant, Charles Onyango, at Kimilili Market:

> I tell you that our *dini* is your *dini*. *A dini of black skin, the black skin, the real black skin as this yours is*. [She stood very close to Charles, talked intently and pushed her finger into Charles' skin, shaking her head as she spoke.] Don't follow those whites for they will take you to hell. They *bring their own ancestors' rules pretending they are God's rules and they make Africans leave their ancestors' ways and follow the wazungus' ancestors' ways which is very bad*. I tell you my boy, this is a secret . . . the missions are taking you to hell. They make you live their way of life and you forget your own. So I warn you, be careful, be careful. *Don't forget your own traditional ways, the black skin*, an African.[52] (Italics mine.)

An old man expressed similar feelings to Charles:

> I've been a member of Dini ya Msambwa since 1945. The reason we follow this *dini* is that *it is our ancestors' dini, so we can't leave it behind*. . . . You see, the *wazungus* bring the missionaries with their different *dinis*. These *dinis* practise according to their ancestors' ways of worshipping. And this is what they are trying to introduce to Africans. Everyone has his own way of worshipping God. There's no point in one group copying another. Let the *wazungus* keep their religion in their own country and not bring it here. This is beyond their territory. We should remain as we are and worship our old gods like our ancestors and our elders did. Why do we forget our own behaviour? This is very silly of you boys who are followers of the missions. [Charles, incidentally, was a mission convert.] Tell the *wazungus* not to play with you. Tell them to take their *dini* back to their own country and practise it there. And let us continue with ours here. Then we shall see.[53] (Italics mine.)

A young woman explained:

> *I like the dini of an African better than a dini of a mzungu*. Our ancestors prayed and they knew God quite well. But when the missionaries came here they said they knew God better than the Africans so they started to lead Africans astray in the word of God. We were really lost when we followed the *wazungus' dini*. Everyone should stay in his own country with his own traditional rules and customs and should leave other people's customs alone.
>
> And so I'm telling you that *we prefer our dini more than any other because it is our ancestors' dini. It's a dini which was there long before the missionaries came*. Our ancestors prayed on the mountains and the hills, the same way as we are doing now. But the other *dinis* [meaning missions] do not pray on the mountains. Praying on the mountains is not a bad thing because even Moses received the Ten Commandments on the mountain. So I'm telling you that *our dini is the best dini. It is the dini of an African, a black skin*. It is a *dini of the customs of our ancestors* because our ancestors they too knew the Bible as we do now, even before the Bible came. [Probably means that Africans knew the word of God even before the missionaries brought the Bible.] This is the *dini* which God gave to Africans. There is no need to follow the *wazungus*.[54] (Italics mine.)

My main goal here has been to ascertain whether religion was an essential aspect of the movement and, if so, was it the traditional? Evidence shows that the movement did advocate a return to the old religion and that this aspect attracted much support. While purists may dismiss Dini ya Msambwa as not the old religion, this misses the crucial point, *what Dini ya Msambwa meant to the followers.* Colonialism involved not only political but cultural subordination.

E. J. Hobsbawm, who studied nineteenth and twentieth century peasant movements in Spain, Southern Italy and Sicily, wrote:

> All the phenomena studied in this book belong to the world of people who neither write nor read many books—often because they are illiterate—who are rarely known by name to anybody except their friends, and then often only by nickname, *who are normally inarticulate, and rarely understood even when they express themselves.* Moreover, they are a pre-political people who have not yet found, or only begun to find, a specific language in which to express their aspirations about the world.[55] (Italics mine.)

In regard to the underlined phrase, we found just the opposite. Although many Kenyan peasants were also illiterate, not only could they express themselves and make their meaning clear to me, an outsider, but they tended to use colourful similes that vividly portrayed the situation and their feelings. The followers, as well as the leaders, may not have had a 'specific language' but even without it they adequately explained reasons, expressed aspirations, and defended viewpoints. They may not have read many books, but they often spoke several languages and as for political astuteness, there were a number of chiefs and other political figures quite the match for any administrator.

Elijah Masinde—a Folk Hero

Few in Kenya have aroused more controversy than Elijah Masinde, stories of whose feats have circulated far and wide, and who, in the course of his enigmatic career, has been called a 'dedicated nationalist', a 'strident demagogue', a 'religious maniac', and a 'great leader'. This debate has continued for more than a quarter of a century on questions of whether he is a politician or priest, a madman or messiah. The fact that his repute extended much farther than his own locale, that people all over Nyanza and even in distant parts of the country had heard of him, attests to his appeal. Many tales are undoubtedly fabricated or, at least, enlarged upon, but others appear to have a considerable base in facts. The separation of fact from fiction, however, is not our main concern here, but rather, what do the stories tell us about the kind of leader the people wanted, and, in turn, what does this say about the society? An important dimension of Msambwa's message, in terms of the psychological needs it fills, is apparent from these tales. Having already briefly discussed Masinde's role as a priest-prophet, we will now explore the role he played in the community at large, one probably best designated as a 'folk hero'.

The kinds of heroes a society creates provide insights into its values, ideals, strains and conflicts. In the classical era, mythical gods were enthroned as heroes. The Middle Ages produced saints; the Renaissance idealized the cultivated man; nineteenth century America paid homage to the 'self-made' man; while the twentieth century western world, in contrast, proclaims the 'anti-hero'. What can be said about the heroes of colonial societies?[56] First, I will relate some myths about Masinde; second, inquire into the role he filled; and third, examine some of his personal characteristics.

The Masinde Mystique

To his followers, Masinde was as powerful as any leader the world had ever seen. He was the African counterpart of the Jews' Moses, the white mans' Jesus, the Muslims' Mohammed, and the Indians' Gandhi. In trying to describe just how powerful Masinde was, Wafula explained, 'I've been as a witness to Masinde. I've been with him almost all the time since he started this *dini*. This man is as powerful as Moses . . . . There is no difference. All that Moses did he can do. That is why he has many followers. He was given this power by God.' A member, when asked who was the greater, Masinde or Jesus Christ, without hesitation, replied, 'Why Elijah. He's next to God. Jesus was just a child who was born in Jerusalem. But Elijah came right from heaven and he dropped onto Mount Elgon. He can talk to God. He can sit down with God and discuss matters. But Jesus couldn't. You can't compare Masinde with Jesus.'

God supposedly sent the same dream to three men, Masinde, an Asian, and a European. The dream indicated that the key to heaven's gates and a notebook were to be found on Mount Elgon. The first person to obtain these would lead the others to everlasting life. Masinde woke up very early the morning after the dream,

153

climbed Mount Elgon and obtained the key and notebook. On his way down, he met the European and the Asian on the same quest. But both men were too late and Masinde reached home safely.[57] God, in this way, showed that he had singled out Africans for his blessing, and had chosen Masinde to lead them as well as the Asians and Europeans to spiritual salvation. This story bears some similarity to the New Testament story of Jesus entrusting the 'keys of the kingdom of heaven' to Peter who consequently opened the door of Christian service to the Jews and to the Gentiles. (Mathew 16:19; Acts 2:38-42 and 10:34-46. In Biblical times, a key was a badge of power and authority.)

It was never quite clear whether Masinde was considered a prophet who acted as an intermediary between man and God or whether he was the 'Black Messiah' himself. Some followers indicated the former, others, the latter. Of those holding the latter belief, some maintained that one day Masinde would rule over all black people. However, regardless of the various beliefs about his powers, his followers generally believed that he was sent by God expressly for Africans and that his powers equalled or were greater than Jesus Christ's.

Stories circulated that 'proved' he was God's anointed. It was said that God had given him a small book, no longer than a matchbox, which was so heavy that it could not be removed from a table. Masinde supposedly could banish the Europeans whenever he so desired. An old man confidently stated, 'Just you wait and see. Masinde will blow his whistle which was presented to him by God and every *mzungu* will be on his toes running.' Another tale related how Masinde escaped from jail in order to return to the beautiful house which God had built for him on Mount Elgon. The story went as follows:

Elijah disappeared again. This time he went to his beautiful house on Mount Elgon built by God. God built that modern house in a night, completely furnished with beds, chairs and tables. Everything was ready. . . . No one can enter except Masinde and a few of his trusted followers. If a *mzungu* tries to enter this house disappears. An African can see the house but a *mzungu* can't. Once lucky *mzungu* managed to see the house and he entered. In the house he saw a huge snake coiled up and there was an opening in the roof so that the head could stick out and enter any of the rooms of the house. When the *mzungu* saw the snake he was frightened and he shouted. Then he found himself under a rock. The house had turned into a rock with grass growing around it. This was Masinde's hiding place. The *mzungu* walked down the mountain and told the police and other government leaders such as the district officer and the district commissioner that they shouldn't persecute Elijah Masinde any more because he was a person of God.[58]

The 'beautiful house' it should be noted, was furnished with European comforts and the event convinced a European of Masinde's holiness.

Three other reasons were given for knowing that Masinde was a real prophet:

1) He was persecuted by the alien British just as Jesus Christ was persecuted by the alien Romans.

2) His prophecies have all come true. For instance, a member related, 'Yes, all he has prophesied has come true. When he was put in jail some were against him. He told them that "When I come out of jail I'll find you alive; some of you will be dead and some of you who have high government jobs will lose your jobs. I'll be taken out of jail by the *wazungus*. It won't be long before they will go away to their own country." We have seen all these things happen'.[59]

3) Several members said that they had been informed through dreams that Masinde was their true leader. For instance Donisio Nakimayu had a dream in 1942 in which the sky lit up and Jesus Christ appeared with two Africans, one of whom had several medals pinned to his shirt.[60] He was at a loss to know what this meant and consulted Father Paullard at Kibabii Mission. The father told him that it was a good sign and that he should follow in the footsteps of Christ. Consequently Donisio gave up his employment and devoted himself to full time preaching. When Donisio first met Elijah in 1947 he recognized him immediately as the African with the medals that had appeared in his dream. (Masinde won medals for playing football.) He thought the second African was Joasch Walumoli.[61]

Though little detail is given, this dream brings to mind the transfiguration scene where Jesus, after having taken the disciples,

Peter, James and John up a mountain to pray, appears in a vision talking to Elijah and Moses. 'A bright cloud overshadowed them: and behold a voice out of the cloud, which said, This is my beloved Son, in whom I am well pleased; hear ye him.' (See Mathew 17:1–8; Luke 9:28–36; Mark 9:2–8.)

Some of the specific powers attributed to Masinde were that he could:

1) predict the sex of unborn children,
2) heal the sick, cure madness and make barren women conceive,
3) make himself invisible or transform himself into a white man,
4) leave a jail though locked in.

One hesitates to draw too many parallels between Masinde's feats and Biblical stories though the similarities are there. For instance, Peter was sleeping, chained between two guards when the angel of the Lord appeared and guided him out of prison—the iron gates opened of their own accord. (Acts 12:6-10). Or when the apostles were put in prison, (Acts 5:18-20) 'the angel of the Lord by night opened the prison doors, and brought them forth . . .'

5) 'smell-out', that is, discover, Europeans. 'Smelling-out' is a term used in witch-finding and means to detect the presence of witches. Witch-finders declare that they can smell the thoughts and designs of the evil-minded. It is interesting to note that Europeans are here equated with witches.[62]

All kinds of miraculous feats were attributed to Masinde. A member of Friends Africa Mission had been with Masinde at Kimilili market where they had parted company. The young man travelled directly to Masinde's only to be greeted upon his arrival by Masinde:

> When we reached his home he came out of his house to meet us. Everyone wondered how he had reached his home because when he left us he was facing Misikhu [the location of a nearby market and mission]. Now when we returned to his place we find him there and the car is not there. From that day I feared Masinde. He is a wonderful man. I think it must have been a miracle. After leaving us at Kimilili maybe he flew like a bird to his home. He's a very powerful man. Masinde can talk to God. He can disappear in his home when you are with him. Sometimes he can be with you but you don't know it. Maybe he is with us now. He can heal the sick by touching them or through prayers.

This ability to travel rapidly from place to place regardless of distance bears a striking resemblance to a similar ability attributed to Pierre Mulele, a leader of the 1964–67 Kwilu rebellion in the Congo. Mulele supposedly could move long distances through government lines by making himself invisible, by flying like a bird, or by using a small airplane no bigger than the palm of his hand.[63]

Masinde's followers were allegedly protected from their enemies. One of Masinde's prison-mates recounted how Masinde foiled a British plan to dispose of Msambwa members:

> Another thing he did was when we were jailed at Kisumu. In the 1940s there were many crocodiles in the lake. Each day the prisoners were taken to the lake to work. They were made to work in the water as a trick to kill the prisoners. The crocodiles used to catch two or three men daily. When it came to our turn, the prison authorities suggested that all the followers should go to work in the lake—there were 160 of us. When Elijah Masinde heard this . . . he prayed very hard and God told him that he need not worry as He would save us. "No crocodile will catch any of your people and all the crocodiles in the lake will be friendly." Elijah told us not to be afraid so we started to work in the lake. We worked there for nine months and not one crocodile touched any of us. We all came out safely. That is one of the wonderful things he did that made us trust him. I was there in person—no one told me this—I saw it myself.[64]

Another protective device was the belief that the members of Dini ya Msambwa were invulnerable to bullets which, upon touching them, would turn into water. The bullets-to-water magic apparently indicated a desire to nullify the Europeans' most lethal weapon and suggests destroying colonial power. At the same time, it would be a supreme test of Masinde's power. It would be interesting to know whether the shooting of Africans at Malakisi disconfirmed the belief or whether, like as in *When Prophecy Fails*, the members become more fervent than ever.

A further dimension in this concern with power were stories relating how Masinde had discovered the secret formula whereby Europeans had emasculated Africans. In one episode, Masinde led two thousand people to some survey beacons on the hills of Kimilili where he said the British had planted a powerful medicine. (Surveyors sometimes put their findings in bottles and planted them under their bearings.) Masinde gave instructions on where to dig and, much to everyone's surprise, they found a bottle with a piece of paper inside.[65] In discovering the Europeans' secret weapon Masinde had ended African subservience. This was one version of the idea that God had sent Europeans to bring civilization to Africans but that they had cheated Africans and had hid the powerful

157

civilization-bringing medicine. The idea of acquiring secret knowledge was probably linked to the secret knowledge and magical powers of such indigenous specialists as the prophet or diviner.

The commemorative service at Lugulu is another event which illustrates the same theme. Masinde supposedly discovered the heads of important Bukusu ancestors, Maina, Wachiye and others, killed by British bullets. By finding their bullet-riddled heads, he had discovered the key to European domination and he would use this power to banish them.[66]

The bullets-to-water and secret knowledge beliefs are found in one form or another among many traditional peoples engaged in a struggle against a much more powerful enemy. The American Indians of the Ghost Dance movement believed that the white man's bullets had no effect against their sacred 'ghost shirts'.[67] In the Maji Maji rebellion that swept southern Tanzania in 1904–5 it was believed that a person secured immunity from mishaps, in particular bullets, by drinking or being sprinkled with a 'protective water'. The name of the rebellion, Maji Maji, means 'water, water'.[68] The followers of the Talking Serpent cult of 1932 in the Belgian Congo were likewise convinced that they had acquired invincible power by drinking a magic potion from special cups.[69] The Congo leader, Pierre Mulele, was thought to be invulnerable to bullets, demonstrated when he fired blanks at himself. The battle cry of the Simba (Swahili for 'lion', here the name of the insurgents) was *Mulele-mai* or 'water of Mulele'. The Simba believed not only in their leader's invulnerability, but in his ability to give them similar protection.[70] Max Gluckman reports that the bullets-to-water belief was used in the Zulu Bambada rebellion of 1906.[71] Based on my research, the belief in secret knowledge is equally important.

This mythology takes care of great discrepancies in power. How were men, meagrely armed and otherwise poorly equipped compared to the British, and aware of the devastation inflicted by modern firearms, to mobilize themselves? Africans turned to supernatural aid of several kinds, here, magical protection that would be used to counter overwhelming power and to assure victory.

What other dominant traits were imputed to Masinde? Stories about his defiance of, and aggressiveness towards, the establishment —how he beat up a chief or a tribal policeman and castigated a judge or a district commissioner—were particularly relished. Pride was taken in Masinde the 'tough guy' who made it difficult for the foreigners.

In 1937, Masinde took a job as a Native Tribunal process server. His task was to give summons out to people but, according to an informant, he told the president of the Tribunal, 'I'm sent by the government from Nairobi. I need not take summons around. You can find someone else.' The uniform, a pair of shorts and a short-sleeved shirt, he threw to the ground, and said to the district commissioner, 'I can't put on this childish dress. I'm returning your uniform. I'm your servant no longer.' He stalked out without even signing the papers of resignation.[72]

After a clash with the unpopular agricultural officer, Masinde openly boasted that he would cause the officer to leave the area. A few weeks later the officer's house burned down.[73]

A former follower evaluated him in these words, 'Masinde has been a rebel leader. He has given the colonial government a really hard time. The police have continually hunted him. . . . I'm amazed that he is not afraid of the police. Even his followers are not afraid of the police. They don't even protest about being taken to jail.'[74] An Anglican convert said, 'He is a very tough person. He is difficult to handle. He has even defeated the government. . . . Masinde himself has been fighting for his rights as God sent him to do. He has brought us freedom and has done many wonderful things.[75]

Masinde walked the countryside organizing meetings and expounding his message. The following account, related by a villager, provides insight into his tactics and the impact he must have had upon the community:

One day he came with hundreds of his followers to the town of Kimilili. It was a market day. He was in a car surrounded by his followers who were drumming and singing. The car was driven slowly and Masinde was smiling broadly and laughing. When he reached the middle of the town, he silenced his followers. Many people gathered around him. He climbed onto the roof of the car and began to tell everyone that they should leave what they were doing and come to listen to him. Many people came until the whole area was jammed. When he saw the crowd, he was very pleased and ordered his followers to sing and drum again. After a while he stopped them and began to speak. "This is a very important day. I've come to talk to the Bukusu and I want all of you to lend me your ears and to listen carefully to what I have to say. It is time the white people left. God told me this. The whites' stay in our country is over. If they remain any longer they are committing a sin before God. They should depart and never return. And when they go they will have to leave all their possessions here. They will

159

leave with their families and only the clothes they are wearing because everything they own, they acquired here. They will have to leave all their possessions here for the people of this country. And the Asians had better listen to me for when I tell them to go they will have to pack off."

He said so many things I can't remember them all. Then he stepped down from the roof of the car and went into an Asian shop to buy cigarettes. He bought 80 cents [about 11 cents, U.S.] worth of cigarettes. The Asian shopkeeper gave him cigarettes worth 1/- [14 cents, U.S.]. He told the shopkeeper that he didn't want a shilling's worth of cigarettes. "I want my rights. I gave you 80 cents and I want only 80 cents worth of cigarettes. No more, no less. After all, this isn't your country. You came in order to trade and now your time is up. So my friend, give me 80 cents worth of cigarettes, please." His voice was cruel and his eyes were bloodshot. The shopkeeper started to tremble. He was really afraid and so was everyone around him. They couldn't say a thing, not even move or cough.

Masinde returned to his car smoking and saying, "I know you will go." He was enjoying himself. He told his followers to tell the crowd to escort him to the market. So they all marched to the market drumming and singing. Masinde's car led the procession like the president's car. The people were happy. They sang and clapped their hands to the beat of the drums. Just before they reached the market, they met a *mzungu* driving towards the town. When they met, the *mzungu* honked so the crowd would let him pass. When Masinde heard this he stopped everyone and got out of the car quickly in a temper. He went to the *mzungu*, banged the front of his car with his fist: "Who are you? And what do you want here? Can you tell me who has given you permission to honk your horn on this road? Is this your country? Don't you know that we can drink your blood now?" The *mzungu* didn't say a thing. He was afraid and rolled up the window. Masinde ordered him to drive his car off the road into the bush and park there until his people had passed. The *mzungu* obeyed him. Then Masinde said to his people, "Okay, you can carry on now." He took the lead and they continued on to the market.[76]

Masinde's message became progressively more radical. In July 1947 he addressed a crowd of four hundred at Kimaliwa, announcing that the Europeans would have to go, whereupon an African king, governor and administration would be appointed. The next month, the message was even stronger. He exhorted the Bukusu to make guns and drive the Europeans out. The crowd at the Malakisi Riot, five months later, sang, 'Europeans have troubled us. We now have our own God. Let us go forward. We are not going to be stopped by these people. They are nothing. The Europeans are troubling us. It is better if we kill them.'[77] He sent his followers about the country proclaiming, 'Our God has come. All *wazungus* must go. All of you being troubled by *wazungus* join us and we will expel the *wazungus*. Our God has come.[78]

No doubt Masinde's daring and belligerant spirit brought back memories of past heroes who had aggressively withstood the foreigners. But part of his appeal lay in his weakness *vis-à-vis* the powerful foreigners. He personified the fighting spirit of the underdog who gamely struggles on, using his wits against ridiculous odds. (There are obvious incongruities in the myths. One set emphasizes his great power while another emphasizes his courage in the face of powerlessness.)

When a warrant was out for his arrest, Masinde supposedly sent a message to the police telling them he would meet them at the Kisumu Hotel at a specific time. Masinde arrived, so the story goes, as a white man and being unrecognized left a chit telling them who he was.

A young boy who attended the Friends Africa Mission Sunday School related this tale:

> I have heard many things about their leader, who is Mr. Elijah Masinde. I've asked my elders about him. They say that he is a great man. . . . They say that sometimes he can have supper with you at the same table but you don't know it. For example, when he was in jail for thirteen years he never ate the food that was prepared for the prisoners. He ate with the prison superintendent [a Britisher] every evening, but the superintendent didn't know it.[79]

What Masinde lacked in power, he compensated for in style. It was not merely what he did but the way he did it that was important. Even though engaged in contests with serious consequences for himself should he lose, he played with a devil-may-care air. Not content to let well enough alone, he sought out opponents far superior in size and strength and impudently tweaked the tail of the British lion.

There was a persistent strain of light-hearted humour running through many anecdotes and people recounted them in that fashion. (They didn't believe them all, nor did they expect me to, but they were fun to relate.) The British were presented not so much as tyrants or ogres, but more as annoying overseers whose self-importance should be shaken up a little. Masinde was cast into the role of a gamesman who was having fun baiting the 'upperdogs' by irritating and embarrassing them. He was giving the British as hard a time as the agricultural officer gave Africans in demanding that they bend their backs in the hot sun to uproot weeds. The colonial official was punished to be sure, but the punishment was more in terms of one-upmanship, of failing to give the 'proper' respect and of causing him to 'lose face' rather than in exacting some cruel revenge.

These tales about Masinde outwitting the authorities are reminiscent of the legendary Robin Hood who was forever escaping the Sheriff of Nottingham or of Sir Percy, the Scarlett Pimpernel, who outwitted a whole army. There is an emphasis on one man against the system, the idea that one man can make a difference. They show the underling unexpectedly defeating a formidable opponent, much to everyone's amusement and satisfaction. Here, a lowly peasant takes on the powerful colonialists who have made the peasants' lives more difficult with their myriads of rules and regulations. This David and Goliath theme, evident in anti-establishment stories, is part of the folklore of the underdog everywhere. As Marya Mannes writes of the American hero, he is still 'the private who shows up the general, the boy who fools his professors, the hoodlum who tricks the police.'[80]

But closer to home there are the 'trickster tales' that treat African roguery in the way sixteenth century picturesque romance stories did. There can be human, deity, and animal tricksters but they are all 'intelligent, selfish, vindictive, cruel, vicious, and morally unrestrained',[81] a description that in some ways fits Masinde. Although trickster tales vary from place to place, the effect is gained by having a character as small as a tortoise in a contest with an elephant and the former winning by outmanoeuvring the latter. Thus there is a cultural base for the tales pitting Masinde against the powerful British.

Wonderful stories circulated about Masinde's considerable athletic ability. In one, he kicked a football so high that it disappeared. Everyone waited for the ball to descend but it never did. Masinde supposedly remarked to the players, 'You can rest now because the ball has gone to heaven.' Masinde's football ability was probably taken as yet another sign of his beating the foreigners at their own game.

The administration, well aware of his growing idolization, tried to prevent the spread of stories. When Masinde received publicity for playing football at Lamu where he had been deported to, the district commissioner wrote to the provincial commissioner:

I told you over the telephone that the district officer, Kavujai, had reported that the Chiefs in the Kitosh area had taken exception to an article which appeared in *Baraza* on the subject of Elijah Masinde playing football at Lamu. I have traced the article which appeared in the issue of Saturday 18 June. . . The article in question is even worse than I had thought and must have given great encouragement to the followers of Elijah Masinde. I do not suggest that it is possible to prevent him playing football, but I do consider that his exploits either on the football field or in any other sphere should not be glorified in the press.[82]

Officials were instructed to see that in the future Masinde was not praised in any way.

Later when Masinde was moved from Lamu to Marsabit, the administration again expressed concern that this move would be used to 'verify' one of Masinde's prophecies. An intelligence report stated:

There has been no consultation with officers of this province and I am seeking information as to the reason for this move as it appears that it will lend considerable colour to the local supporters of the *dini*, because Elijah Masinde boasted before he left Kisumu that he would not remain long at Lamu. It is true that he indicated that he would return to Kitosh but the change in his place of detention from Lamu to a destination rather close to Kitosh will be accepted at best as a partial fulfillment of his boast.[83]

However, despite the administrators' efforts, an extravagant personality cult did develop.

The Role of Folk Hero

It is doubtful whether Masinde himself (since he was in prison most of the time between 1945 and 1961) organized much protest. He was absent when settlers' property was destroyed and he was not present at the Kibabii Riot. Dini ya Msambwa's impact was achieved through the efforts of individuals with central direction being minimal. Masinde's accomplishments, in one sense, were distinctly limited. Why then was he revered? Why did he emerge at that time and what is significant about the figure the community in part created?

The times were propitious for the emergence of folk heroes and other kinds of charismatic leaders. The legitimacy of the traditional system had, to a large extent, been exhausted and the colonial system never was legitimate in the eyes of the masses. Charismatic leaders emerged outside both the traditional and the colonial systems and their appearance signalled the approaching end of the colonial era.

163

Colonial systems subject the indigenous people to particular kinds of stresses, which in turn, create particular needs among them. Colonialism in Kenya meant that the native people were conquered, subjugated, and placed in the lowest stratum of a caste-like system. The foreigners both deliberately as well as unconsciously showed contempt for their customs. Alien institutions were imposed and indigenous political and judicial systems abolished. (Customary law did operate in some areas.) Fears were aroused by the alienation of land and resentments generated by government policies. Thus colonialism brought anxiety, frustration, and anger.

The people needed a hero with whom they could identify, a person who would personify certain ideals. They viewed Masinde as their protector and liberator from the injustices of the colonial order. His enemies were their enemies — the foreigners — who had introduced such burdens as taxes, compulsory labour, and agricultural regulations. Despite his failings, Masinde defied the colonialists, a hazardous and thus highly regarded pastime. He did what others longed to, but dared not do. While they hesitated, he acted in a forthright manner. Even though some people did not like him, they spoke admiringly of his courage. The idolization of Masinde is reminiscent of other peasants who openly defied the social order, like Pancho Villa and Emiliano Zapata of Mexico who fought the rich on behalf of the poor.

Despite Masinde being the messiah to many followers, and despite there being parallels between the Bible's and Msambwa's symbolism, between Masinde's powers and those of Jesus Christ and God, neither Masinde's image nor personal traits fit those of the gentle, loving, forgiving Jesus Christ. When his mystique is examined, the qualities for which he was admired—power, physical strength, arrogance, style and cunning—turn out to be hardly saintly qualities and he emerges, not as an African saint, but as a symbol of resistance to the alien invaders.

In contrast to Christianity that looked for regeneration of the world in terms of individual moral redemption, Masinde preached about a new order that would come into being with the destruction the foreigners. Instead of focussing upon individual morality and responsibility, as the missionaries had, Masinde focussed upon changing the system, and he encouraged what they discouraged, rebellion against the status quo. The missionary language of love and peace, and the Christian virtues of humility and patient suffering were cast aside and in their place, defiance, toughness and revenge were extolled.

By rejecting the doctrine of white superiority, the politics of compromise and cooptation, Masinde brought new self-respect and pride to rural Africans and helped ease bitter memories of defeat. His bearing and example, an affirmation of blackness, provided a different image of the African, just as Malcolm X has more recently done for Afro-Americans. The folk hero mythology helped 'neutralize' the inequities of the African-European positions and made the African the equal of, if not superior to, the white man. A reversal of black-white positions was envisaged whereby the underdog emerged on top.[84]

Masinde aroused a political climate essential to revolt. His exploits stimulated widespread undercurrents of opposition to the regime, for many responded to his message, if not in overt action, at least in their hearts. Impelled by his fierce rhetoric, some members struck out boldly. He stirred the peasantry by bringing up questions of their rights and dues. Inchoate sentiments were awaiting a leader to give them some form. Masinde resuscitated memories of past warriors: his assertion of the primacy of traditional values awakened in Africans a powerful dream of a new era where they would order their own lives, be free from the ills that plagued them, and enjoy bountiful riches. His leadership united people across clan, location and ethnic boundaries into a new community resolved to banish the foreigners. No longer were Africans willing to accept the status quo or to confine their efforts to constitutional methods. In the final assessment, Masinde may best be remembered for advocating and mobilizing support for militant action and thus opening up a new line of attack.

Masinde the Man

Even though Masinde was created by a public in need of a hero, we should not overlook his own personal contribution. While this aspect is not as important for my purpose as the legendary Masinde, it enables a more accurate separation of fact from fiction and points to some qualities that prevented him from changing in the post-colonial era. It also highlights some personality characteristics often found in folk heroes. Additionally, public figures are often assumed to have a private in contrast to a public self. Bearing this in mind, what was Masinde 'really' like? What do we know about his personal life? Let me recount a few events in his life that provided fodder for the tales, as well as some of my own impressions.

Masinde was born around 1908 or 1909 into the Bichachi clan of the Bukusu sub-tribe.[85] His grandfather on his mother's side was an important prophet. His family did not own much land. Masinde attended several mission schools, Kamusinga Friends School and the Church of God at Kima from 1925 to 1931. Not a particularly good student, he refused to study subjects he disliked. His family were Quakers and he, following in their steps, became a member of Friends Africa Mission until obliged to leave when he took a second wife. His first wife bore six children and his second, two.

Masinde was good at track and field and an excellent football player and coach. His teams, the Wasio and Simba, defeated the Luo and Maragoli, in those days the strongest in Nyanza. Masinde captained the Bukusu Union football team and was a member of the all-star Kenya team that played Uganda at the Gossage Games in 1930. His athletic ability brought him acclaim, not only because Africans admired athletes, but because he associated with the British. Stories were told about how a European would pick Masinde up and drive him to a game. Later the administration gave him a job first as a physical education instructor and then as a Native Tribunal process server, the latter abruptly terminated by him. Still, the foreigners had shown an interest in him and he had repudiated them, not a bad move for his repute in the eyes of the people.

Masinde was committed to Mathari Mental Hospital in 1945 and released in 1947. But when his presence correlated with an outbreak of unrest, a warrant was issued for his re-arrest. He eluded the police and from October 1947 to February 1948 was on-the-run. At one point the trackers thought they had him cornered in a cave on Mount Elgon. They were sure he was inside but when they entered he was not to be seen. A member of the party recounted, 'We noticed what appeared to be a pyramid that for some strange reason rose up from the floor of the cave. And when we scaled it we saw that Elijah could reach a hole in the cave's roof which we had not noticed before and haul himself up and escape into the bush, into the back country, which is exactly what he had done!'[86]

Masinde lives on his farm, when he is not in jail, like any other subsistence farmer in the Kimilili area. He has eight cows and many of his possessions are gifts from his followers. Prior to his latest arrest, he lived a boisterous life, entertaining at large feasts (when he could afford to), where a cow was slaughtered and large quantities of liquor consumed. Although criticized by mission converts, taught frugality and sobriety, this trait appeals to many and enhances his reputation. For after all, a mark of a chief or other important person is generosity and the means to entertain lavishly.[87]

Dressed in baggy trousers, a vivid yellow shirt to which were pinned his football medals, and sporting a maroon fez, Masinde cut a striking figure when I met him in 1965. Although he was well into his fifties, his appearance was youthful. Masinde gave considerable attention to his ceremonial garb, choosing vari-coloured flowing robes. On one occasion, he changed no less than three times to enable me to photograph him.

Two qualities more than any others—defiance of authority and extremism of many kinds—have facilitated Masinde's folk hero role. His actions from the time he was a small boy displayed a perpetual flaunting of authority, whether it be that of his parents, schoolteachers, church leaders or government. From the accounts of local people, he was a headstrong, 'cheeky' boy who refused to obey his parents. He would not tend the cattle or sheep. If he returned home and his meal was not ready, he would fly into a tantrum and smash the dishes. When caned by his parents, he ran away. At school he disturbed the other children.

Paulo Loyana, once a local Msambwa leader, remembered Masinde as always complaining about government regulations. 'He didn't like anything the government did.' Nor did he like the local people to give the chiefs a tribute of beef and beer. He chided the chiefs, 'You're robbing poor people.' Later in post-colonial Kenya, Masinde was still seen by his supporters as fighting for the rights of his people against an unjust African government, impervious to the consequences for himself.

Masinde's career over the years reveals him to be a free spirit, a man indifferent to the opinions of others. Like any zealot, he appeared completely convinced of his own rightness and saw the world in 'black and white' terms. Impatient at compromise and half-way measures, he had no use for people who did not share his views. Among his peers, he 'could only rhyme with a boy who follows him', as one lifelong associate put it. A former member jailed with Masinde recalled his disdain for conciliatory measures:

In jail I used to tell Masinde that he should not be against the government, but Masinde kept telling me that the *wazungus* should go to their own country. Then I told him that, "Remember that this is a *dini*. It is politics when you oppose the *wazungus*. God does not oppose anyone and you were told by God to come and introduce his word. Still you oppose the *wazungus*. Why are you doing this?" . . . Then Masinde told me I should not speak nonsense. . . . This country is not the *wazungus*' and that if I'm a coward I should go home and stay with the women. The *wazungus* can't come and cheat the people. Secondly, this is not their homeland. They shouldn't come and reign over people. And so I told Masinde, "The way you are trying to organize this *dini* is not right, so please change your mind and let's go to the government and apologize for causing it so much trouble." Then Masinde told me that "If you say that go away. You're not a man. You are too cowardly. I don't want you to be with me in this jail for I must perform my duty which God told me."

I stayed in jail for six months and then I appealed and apologized to the government and was let out. They left Masinde in because he was very rude to them.[88]

Even his enemies admitted that he was the Bukusu's first radical nationalist and he held this stand regardless of the counsel of close associates, who agreed with the goal but differed on the means.

We can only speculate about Masinde's mental stability. His volatility and violent temperement lent a vividness to the tales, while at the same time they impeded the movement's attempts to carry out meaningful action. E. R. N. Cooke, the medical officer-in-charge at Mathari Hospital, wrote in June 1946, 'I do not expect that he will ever recover his sanity and be discharged.'[89] A year later at the time of his release, J. C. Carothers, another medical officer, evaluated him as follows:

> The above mentioned inmate of this hospital is likely to retain a generally persecutionary attitude and peculiar religious ideas for the rest of his life. But he has been of excellent behaviour here for a long time, and is the sort of case that might be looked after at home satisfactorily by his relations, provided the latter were responsible persons and recognized that he was mentally abnormal.[90]

Psychological diagnoses, at best, are subject to doubt and even more so when the diagnostician is from a different culture. By way of comment, it was not at all surprising that Masinde was paranoid, for much of the world he was dealing with was hostile towards him.

According to a local resident, Masinde had for years acted strangely. One day in court he ordered the judge to call the Archbishop of Canterbury or he wouldn't talk. 'He ordered the judge to have

King Georgie come because he said to the judge, "You are a child. I can't talk in front of you." He completely refused to talk. For that reason I don't think his head is working properly.' The general opinion among the community, and many of these people had known him for years, was that he was mentally disturbed. (These opinions were gathered in the post-colonial period when the community had begun to define Masinde's activities as 'trouble-making'.) My own opinion of Masinde, based on a few meetings and of limited use because of my different background, coincides with the community's evaluation. One occasion that demonstrates his volatility occurred when after considerable planning he had assembled his assistants and elders so that they could give me Dini ya Msambwa's 'full history'. On the spur of the moment, he changed his mind, saying he could not tell me until I returned with the 'President of Canada'! We all had to sit down while he dictated a letter to the 'President'.[91] The discussion, to my great disappointment and to the consternation of the others he had assembled, never took place.

Whether Masinde was a self-seeking leader who manipulated others for his own ends, as the negative stereotype suggests, is another question. If he tried, he was certainly a failure, since he has spent more time in prison than any follower. The evidence suggests rather that he did exactly as he pleased and people could follow him or not as they pleased.

Masinde possesses that curious amalgam of traits called colour. A dominant personality, heady invective and extravagant behaviour made him unforgettable. Wherever he went, he commanded attention and controversy—unfailingly providing people with something to talk about. His adventures—narrow escapes from the police, deportations, jail, carousals and football championships – are the stuff of legends. With his violent passions, he was well qualified to become an object of veneration or of vilification, but never of indifference. Thus the Masinde magic, compounded of a bold style, dashing escapades, and a stark, audacious dream, in a situation crying out for a hero, was all that was needed. A few twists and turns in stories with a romantic cast and he emerged a figure larger than life.

The Anti-Colonial Campaign[92]

Unlike Mumboism, which told the Europeans to get out and waited for a millennium to accomplish the task, Msambwa backed up its demands with action. Its targets were the foreigners who had first imposed their rule and then tried to impose their values and ways, and others identified with them or as supporters of the regime—settlers, missionaries, Asians, mission converts, chiefs and tribal police.

In outlining Msambwa's anti-colonial activities, we will try to ascertain their relevance for the community at large. We will argue that Msambwa's protest stemmed from the larger context of grievances that had been developing over the years among the people of North Nyanza, and the labourers and squatters in the White Highlands, and that it expressed grievances felt by ordinary peasants and articulated by other groups.

The administration found it difficult on a number of occasions to decide whether Msambwa or the Bukusu Union were responsible for particular incidents. A number of administrators felt that the Union was Msambwa in a different guise, that the names were used interchangeably, or that the Union was a branch of the Kenya African Union, the main Kikuyu political organization at that time. Formed by Pascal Nabwana in 1940, the Union's ostensible goals were those of a mutual aid society: to promote better farming practices, cooperatives, a trade union, secular as opposed to religious education, as well as to assist widows and orphans. Although the Union collected some money for schools and scholarships, its accomplishments in those areas were few but it, like Msambwa, expressed popular grievances and took action to back up its demands. Since there is some confusion about what each did, issues they articulated in common will be discussed together. Next, Msambwa's relations with the Bukusu Union, the Kenya African Union and Mau Mau will be briefly discussed, since its failure to form political alliances had serious consequences for its effectiveness.

Trans Nzoia Settlement Scheme

At the same time as Msambwa was announcing that the colonialists' time was up and demanding that they get out of the country, the government was encouraging European immigration. After World War II, it decided to put land in the northwest section of the White Highlands up for sale for a settlement scheme for British ex-soldiers. The aim was to cultivate a strong settler community that would expand the country's commercial agriculture.

To abet this policy, Major F. W. Cavendish-Bentinck was appointed to the important post of Member of Agriculture, Animal Husbandry and Natural Resources, and made responsible for the million and a half pound scheme.[93] Africans viewed Cavendish-Bentinck's appointment with foreboding, as he was a leading exponent of white settlement and a former secretary of the settlers' organization, The Convention of Associations.

This development had particular implications for the Bukusu, since it involved land around Kamakoiya on the boundary of the reserve and the White Highlands, that they had been using for farming and grazing and had long claimed as theirs. As far back as 1932 they had petitioned the Kenya Land Commission and they had continued to petition year after year in spite of repeated refusals. If Bukusu claims had been granted, the boundary of the reserve would have been extended some twenty miles east. When they heard that the land was up for sale, they redoubled their efforts to get possession of it before the settlers.[94] At a *baraza* attended by the Governor in June 1946, the Bukusu Union claimed a number of border farms as tribal land.[95] Their efforts, however, proved futile. Settlers began to arrive and occupy the land. Needless to say, their presence was bitterly resented.

The new arrivals were harassed by both Msambwa and the Union. Msambwa members erected a wooden cross on a European's farm with the warning that he should abandon his farm. Nabwana, president of the Union, urged Africans to claim land around Kamakoiya and to settle there. He reportedly ordered the members:

We want to know that, *whenever any European comes into this country, he must be troubled,* and no one must identify the person who annoyed the European. . . . *If any European comes into the country he must be punished by the inhabitants* and if a man or men gives information to the European it will be considered a crime.[96] (Italics mine.)

The settlers' grazing lands were burned, cattle poisoned, and squatters settled back onto the farms. In fact the settlers were 'troubled' to such an extent that they requested a police outpost.[97]

In October 1946 there was a strike on the farm of a long time settler, Commander Carter. His farm was situated in Kamakoiya. Strikes on a small scale had occurred on nearby farms and the Commander felt that a general strike was in the offing timed to coincide with harvesting maize. Rumours of riots, violence, and the forcible extension of the border some twenty miles east (taking in the Commander's farm) caused him to evacuate his farm, alert the authorities and take off to personally see the Governor. At one point, he had even decided to sell out.[98]

Boundary markers between the settlers' area and the reserve were broken or removed, probably indicating that Africans considered the land to be rightfully theirs. A Msambwa flag to which two letters were attached was planted on a road built by conscript labour between Kimilili and Kamakoiya. The letters, written in Bukusu, were signed by Eriya, a Msambwa member. They demonstrate a peasant's attempt to express himself in an unfamiliar medium:

> I write this. I greet everyone on the plains and on the mountains and all races. Grass, birds, locusts, flies, water and fish. . . . I greet everyone thrice. Black child, do not take away this letter. Let others take it. Also everyone, conscripts refuse to work. Also chief Amutalla don't beat people like this. Don't. Leave them alone. Also Olugongo [a sub-chief] don't arrest people to lock them up. Don't. I have started a war with Europeans. It will last five months and then it will finish. I will pay 30/- salary to *Mulango's* [chief's] *askaris*. I will spend Christmas at Kitale.

When arrested, Eriya, an ex-Anglican convert, said he had joined Msambwa because the Europeans had been ruling over them for fifty years and had not improved their lot. A man could earn only 9/- or 10/- a month working on a European's farm and that was insufficient to feed and clothe his family.[99]

Msambwa advised farm labourers to stop working altogether for Europeans and to return to the reserve. Those who could not afford to stop working were urged to 'go slow', to absent themselves from work, and not to cooperate in any way with the farmers. At the same time they were to demand higher wages and shorter working hours.[100]

The influx of settlers involved removing squatters from the land the settlers had purchased and repatriating them to the reserve. At first, the Bukusu Union, afraid of overcrowding and overstocking in the reserve, fought their return. Then, when it became obvious that their return could not be stopped, it asked that only Bukusu, and not members of other sub-tribes be allowed to settle there.[101] The settlers' treatment of the squatters aroused the Union's indignation as documented from notes taken by an informer at a 1946 Union meeting. 'Their relatives who are working as squatters in the Trans Nzoia District are so badly being troubled by the farmers, that some of them are driven from farms to Enyembe, Suku and back to the Kitosh Reserve.'[102]

In 1955 a settler, whose land bordered the Kamakoiya River, received threatening letters. An investigation revealed that there had been several Msambwa meetings at which killing him, as an example to other Europeans and in the hope of forcing them out, had been discussed.[103]

Despite the settlers' occupation of the Kamakoiya land, the Bukusu continued to petition. The Governor, Sir Philip Mitchell, refused their petition in 1949; the Acting Governor, J. D. Rankin, did so in 1950; and the Secretary of State for the Colonies, Mr. Lennox Boyd did so yet again in 1952. District commissioner Campbell commented in 1952, 'The African-European land question is voiced more loudly here [Kimilili location] especially as the Kitosh have always laid claim to part of the Kamukuywa-Kimilili area.'[104] The issue was still going strong on the eve of independence with their member of parliament, Masinde Muliro (no relation to Elijah Masinde) claiming most of the Trans Nzoia, including Kitale, for the Bukusu.[105]

In 1949 and 1950, there were oubreaks of arson in the Trans Nzoia. In Chapter 13 we will explore why this area became the scene of radical protest.

Agricultural Reform

The administration, in keeping with its policy of white settlement, largely ignored African agricultural production and concentrated upon developing the European sector.[106] But by the end of World War II soil erosion had become critical over wide areas of the countryside and, coupled with increasing population pressures, the government was faced with drastically expanding food production if disaster was to be averted. Since a world shortage of agricultural products meant that Kenya could sell everything it produced, there was an additional incentive to improve and promote cash crops and animal husbandry in the African sector.

In getting its programme underway, the government brought in veterinarians, agricultural and medical officers and increased the administrative staff to coordinate their activities. The presence of more Europeans in the rural areas and the building schemes that were undertaken to house them aroused African fears of permanent European settlement and land alienation. Regulations

173

concerning the innoculation of cattle, contour ploughing and the uprooting of noxious weeds, came into effect. Destocking, terracing, the planting of grass, and the building up of river banks were instituted to combat soil erosion. For purposes of experimentation, areas were fenced off for pilot schemes—another project that aroused fears of land alienation.

Masinde, who was against cooperating with the government in any way, was soon embroiled in obstructing this programme. When the veterinarian came to inject his cattle, he chased him away. His first run-in with the Agricultural Department occurred over the uprooting of Mexican marigold, a weed that takes nutrients from the soil. An agricultural instructor was showing local people how to uproot this weed when Masinde and Wekuke appeared and threatened him with assault. Masinde queried, 'Why do we have to uproot a plant sent by God?' An onlooker intervened and conducted the instructor safely out of the area. Other instructors received similar treatment.

When questioned as to why he had refused to eradicate Mexican marigold, Wekuke replied:

> These weeds were not growing only in our *shambas*. They grow everywhere. . . . *This is extra work*. Maybe you live alone with your wife. Weeds really don't harm crops you know. The *wazungus* came here for riches. . . . This was perhaps a way to get rich. They [the administration] knew that uprooting weeds was extra work and that people would fail to do it. Then you are fined 50/-. If you don't have 50/-, they can take your cattle which are worth even more. They may take four or five cows which are worth 300/- each.

To the suggestion that this money was for the government and not for individual Europeans, Wekuke reasoned:

> They are all British. *When they took our money they used it for themselves*. We Africans weren't in the government. We didn't know whether they were putting our money into their own pockets. *We didn't have any representative. If we had we could have found out* what they were doing with our money.[107] (Italics mine.)

In explaining African resistance to colonialism, there is a tendency to ennoble motives by interpreting them all in the framework of the struggle for freedom and equality. A more objective examination reveals some quite commonplace motives.[108] For example, pulling up Mexican marigold involved 'extra work' and Africans were not convinced that they benefitted. This held for other agricultural reforms that the authorities were trying to introduce. Wekuke's statement illustrates the problems a distrusted government has in trying to change everyday habits.

Several weeks after Masinde's arrest on charges of assault having to do with another incident, the home of Mr. Bickford, an agricultural officer widely disliked for his authoritarian manner and for forcing people to uproot Mexican marigold, burned down and the investigation showed that it had deliberately been set on fire. The administration strongly suspected Msambwa. The provincial commissioner, in discussing the case, wrote:

> The outstanding fact which astonished me in this matter is that the Kitosh made no complaint at any time of harsh treatment, despite the fact that just about a year ago I had personally held a *baraza* and informed them that *they would not be prosecuted for failing to uproot Mexican marigold* and this communication was made in the presence of Mr. Bickford's successor. Unfortunately this information was not passed on to him. The point, however, is that it is very unlike the African to suffer punishment without demur, in a matter which they have specifically been advised will not be punished. . . . Mr. Bickford was obviously a hard task master. . . . The whole enquiry points to the fact that there was a *general public resentment of his methods* and it seems highly probable that the man Elijah, being aware of this fact, and having a personal grudge against Mr. Bickford for reporting the incident when he and others forcibly resisted a conscript labour summons, gave expression, through his agent to *the oft repeated threat that Mr. Bickford's house should be burnt*.[109] (Italics mine.)

The Department of Agriculture was continually harassed and the authorities believed Msambwa to be responsible. Annoyances such as letting the Department's cattle loose at night were not a serious impediment to its work, but taken altogether suggest strong resentment.

Nor was Msambwa alone in its opposition. In North Nyanza, hostility and suspicion greeted most measures the government tried to introduce. District officer N. F. Kennaway commented:

> It is certain that the general population of Kimilili location resent many of the Agricultural Department activities in the area. Apart from unpopularity of soil conservation works, the compulsory uprooting of Mexican marigold has raised the resentment of the people—which in view of the fact that no such compulsion is used in European areas, would not seem unreasonable.[110]

The Veterinary Department also came under fire, especially over its rabies control campaign, when local dogs were rounded up and killed. The following letter stuck to a farm gate expresses one peasant's feelings. Written in Swahili by someone barely literate, it stated:

"From N. K. Bukusu,
"Namawanga,
"Lukongo Jelote
"May 10, 1948

"To the DC, Kitale Station

"I had one word to speak. Why you Europeans are killing native dogs, you want to finish them. What does the dog done which make you to finish native dogs. You Europeans want to do wrong things. When you come to this country from Europe you find us with dogs in this country and now you start killing them all.

"Some years ago Jesus Christ told us not to pay any poll tax. You Europeans came here to give us trouble in Africa. What made you to leave your country. Ghost made you to leave your own country and came here and made us to be your wives [probably, in our terminology, workers or servants]. You will see me."[111]

The Bukusu Union, like Msambwa, opposed many of the government's efforts. For instance, when the district commissioner suggested communal farming in order to allow land to lie fallow, Nabwana told Africans that it was a government trick to get them to leave their farms which would then be taken over by Europeans.[112] The government introduced compulsory destocking of cattle in the locations of Kimilili, Malakisi and Elgon because over-grazing was eroding the soil, already a serious problem. Again Nabwana at a Union meeting warned that three hundred police were about to raid the reserve to seize their cattle and that they had better be ready to prevent this from happening.[113] Having been employed in the Agricultural Department (1943–46), Nabwana was viewed as an expert and listened to by the local people.[114]

A notebook of an arrested Msambwa member, Mayafu, suspected of having removed a boundary marker, contained the following:

Why *wazungus* force people to carry *kipande*,[115]
Why *wazungus* force people to do compulsory labour,
We Bukusu people of three locations viz. South Kitosh, Malakisi and Kimilili *we do not like our cattle to be taken during active service*.[116]
(Italics mine.)

176

Unfortunately for the government the advantages of destocking for the Kenya Meat Commission (to whom the cattle were sold) were more apparent to Africans than for themselves as cattle owners.

The government at first tried to carry out soil conservation measures through persuasion, but when this failed, it forced people to work six days every three months on conservation schemes. Policemen stood behind agricultural instructors overseeing the terracing of hillsides.[117] One can well imagine the hostility such coercion evoked and it would help to explain Msambwa's strong dislike of chiefs and policemen.

This programme, conceived in haste after years of neglecting African agriculture, suffered a number of failures. Projects were launched for which inadequate experimentation had been undertaken. Peasants, a group which can ill afford to take risks, were asked not only to take risks, but to expend extra work when there was little assurance of gains. Lonsdale describes some of the problems involved.

> Peasants encouraged to grow coffee—long forbidden fruits—were required to adhere to planting restrictions more appropriate to the experimental laboratory. Dams built at vast expense and often with the aid of unpaid communal labour remained empty of water for several seasons, thus vitiating attempts at controlled grazing in areas cleared of tsetse fly bush—also by communal labour. Cattle especially innoculated by the veterinary department continued to die in these same areas. Sisal prices dropped catastrophically in the very year that peasants were encouraged to invest in mechanical decorticators. Bench terraces for soil conservation collapsed after a few years because they were too narrowly based. . . . There was indeed impressive progress but disaster is more likely to attract notice.[118]

Humphrey, in examining why North Nyanzan peasants had not adopted in their own farming, techniques exhibited by the model farm at the Bukuru Agricultural Training Centre, though many had visited it and had seemed impressed, concluded, 'Various reasons for this are given when inquiries are made, but these are evasive or superficial, though one can generally detect in them the underlying belief that here is an alien system which does not fit in at all with the social life of the people.'[119]

Once protest began to be voiced it swiftly gathered momentum. An atmosphere of tension and suspicion was created that meant minor incidents often became full-blown issues which were used as emotional pegs upon which to hang deep-rooted frustrations and fears. Regardless of how many government regulations were carried out for the direct benefit of Africans, they were constantly interpreted in terms of exploitation. Luhya nationalism extended its justifiable objection to European rule into distrust of everything European. The Bukusu Union and Msambwa constantly used these suspicions to sabotage the government's agrarian programme, intensify issues, and build up hatred against Europeans.

Government efforts to enforce rural change have sparked more than one protest movement in East Africa. The earliest was probably the Maji Maji rebellion that swept southern Tanzania in 1904–5. Eight thousand rebels took part in the largest single action and about seventy-five thousand Africans died, mostly from famine and disease. Iliffe contends that a major determinant of this rebellion was the government's attempts to institute the large scale growing of cotton on a communal basis. Each person was required to contribute a number of work days to a communal plot—the exact figure is unknown, although twenty-eight days a year to two days a month are frequently mentioned.[120]

From the early 1930s, but particularly from 1946 to 1957, the government of Tanzania imposed rules concerning farming practices aimed at soil conservation and improved cultivation methods. These practices were deeply resented and gave rise to protest so great that by 1958 the administration admitted defeat and ceased its attempts to change indigenous modes of cultivation.[121]

And in the south of Kenya's Rift Valley Province in the 1950s, an attempted settlement scheme at Olenguruone, designed to give long-time squatters some land of their own, broke down when the squatters moved onto the land only to find that they had to farm according to a set of rules. A strict agricultural officer tried to force them to dig erosion ditches and to divide their land into areas for crops and for stock. The situation became so bad that the agricultural officer had to leave and police were brought in to supervise the settlement. Finally the scheme was abandoned altogether after a sitdown strike outside the district commissioner's office, the imprisonment of one group of squatters and the return of another to the reserve.[122]

The Missions

Dini ya Msambwa denounced Christianity as the religion of the imperialists and castigated the missionaries for being an arm of foreign domination and for having taken African riches and land instead of helping Africans as God had commanded them. The gist of the accusations was that the missionaries took money from their converts, built themselves comfortable homes and drove about in large cars, yet the African church elders had nothing. Allegations of land grabbing do not seem to be borne out by the facts, at least in North Nyanza. Mission stations were settled on sufficient land to build schools, churches and medical dispensaries, but few received large grants. Only two obtained more than a hundred acres: the Quakers were granted 951 acres of freehold, 146 acres of leasehold in several scattered plots in North Nyanza, and 1,685 acres of leasehold in several scattered plots in North Nyanza, and 1,685 acres of leasehold in Kericho; and the South African Compound and Interior Mission purchased 2,913 acres at Bunyore.[123]

The missionaries, according to Msambwa, perverted Christian teachings by straying from such Biblical practices as animal sacrifice, circumcision, polygyny and praying in the hills. In addition, the missionaries had presented Jesus as white and the devil as black, thus leading Africans to equate white with goodness and black with evil. Interestingly, it may not have been mission teachings which introduced this idea, but the traditional religion which held that all evil in life was ultimately the work of the 'black god', the opposite of *Wele*, the 'white god'. In prayers, the 'white god' was implored to drive away the 'black god'. For example:

> *Wele*, you made us walk in your country,
> You made the cattle and the things which are in it,
> You may spit the medicine on your person,
> He may recover and walk well,
> He may plant his gardens.
> Drive away the black god,
> He may leave your person,
> He may move into the snake,
> And into the abandoned homestead;
> He may leave our house.

Wagner noted that these beliefs were recorded in a situation 'very unlikely' to have been influenced by Christian teaching.[124]

Members' views about the importance of following their own indigenous religion have already been presented. The following exemplify some other common criticisms.

179

An old man, a member for more than twenty years, expressed his feelings to my assistant:

I like this *dini* the most and I would advise you not to follow the missions because they came to trade [make money] with their *dini*. God said you shouldn't buy his things but these people they print Bibles and take them to the bookshops to be sold. Then they say, 'Alright you are now a person of God because you have bought a Bible. Try to give us some more money and then we'll give you a name' which they call baptism. Why should I be named twice? I was named by my mother when I was still young and then when I grew old the *wazungus* wanted to name me again. They call this baptism but this is not baptism. It is simply their own native names. Do you think this is bad?

Charles: 'Does it mean that you don't like the missions?'

That's right. They just read about our country in the Bible and they came because they read in the Bible that Africa is a land of milk and honey. They came here and told us that there is a person known as Jesus. That our *Wele* is not a real God and that we should leave him and follow this God. But we didn't want this. They came to seduce us with beads and sweets but their main aim was to get this rich land of ours. So now that they have eaten their fill I think that they should go and let us remain as *Wele* created us.

You know, boy, these *wazungus*, they are like jiggers [a flee that burrows into the skin]. They suck our blood just exactly like jiggers do. And when you find that there are jiggers in your foot, what do you do? You get a safety pin and remove them from your foot. That is what Masinde is going to do to the *wazungus*. *They will be forced to leave and all their possessions which they are so proud of will be ours.* And we are going to be the bosses just like they have been.[125] (Italics mine.)

Another elderly man answered the question, 'Are you a member of Msambwa?' as follows:

Yes, I've been a member of Dini ya Msambwa since it began in 1947. Before that I was a Roman Catholic. I left the Roman Catholics because it was a mission and I like our *dini* because it is the true *dini* of Africans. The Roman Catholics tried to mislead me. They wanted me to pray all day and all night. They wanted me to join a religious order, become a priest and never marry. Why shouldn't I get married? How shall we build the Kenya of tomorrow? What do they think by telling me not to get married. That's very silly of them. If the *wazungus* want to do it, then let them. But they should not bother Africans to join them in such a silly undertaking. We Africans are used to our old way of life. We are used to marrying women. You can even marry sixty if you feel like it. And according to our old beliefs no one was considered a rich man unless he had many wives and many cattle. Now why should we leave this practice and follow the *wazungus*' monogamy. A man with one wife is no different from a man with

.. one eye. It is a very precarious situation. If you lose the one eye you won't have another to replace it. You will be blind. And so it is with one wife. I don't agree with the missionaries.[126]

A young woman gave her view of the missions:

I don't like the missionaries because they have misled our country. Not only have they cheated us about God's teachings but they take our riches. And God did not say the people should use his teachings to make money.

Secondly, God did not say that people should not practise polygyny, drink or smoke. Just because the missionaries don't drink, they don't want us to. They don't want us to marry many wives. And because the missionaries have misled us in God's teachings, God has revealed himself to an African so that he will lead us in the way God wants.[127]

Missionaries were harassed and several mission churches and schools burned down. Approximately eight hundred Msambwa followers invaded the Roman Catholic Mission at Kibabii. They told the occupants to abandon it as they did not want Europeans in their country and threatened to burn it down. A mission father ordered the crowd off mission property and when it did not depart he fired several shots into the air. Gradually the demonstrators left without doing any damage. When the district commissioner heard of the incident he went immediately to the mission with a force of police arriving at 8 p.m. By that time all was quiet. He left an assistant inspector and fourteen policemen to guard the mission.[128]

There were two cases of arson at the Seventh-day Adventist school at Malakisi and the windows of the Roman Catholic mission at Lugulu were broken in 1947. Two years later churches and schools were set on fire in and around Kitale in the White Highlands.

The 1940s and 1950s witnessed increasing disenchantment with the missionaries among certain segments of the population. Mission education was criticized. 'There appears to be a growing feeling among the intelligentsia [the educated young men], almost amounting to hostility, against the mission bodies,' wrote the district commissioner of North Nyanza in 1951. 'The feeling which is probably only widespread among the vocal few seems to stem partially from a spirit of rising nationalism allied to a sense of disillusionment . . . and partially from a genuine feeling of frustration and disappointment with the educational work undertaken by the missions'.

181

Dislike of the missionaries expressed by Msambwa leaders seemed to be shared by many followers and some local people. The missionaries were bitterly criticized, among other things, for having shown contempt for African culture and for not practising all that they preached. However, without systematically sampling various populations, it is not possible to gauge how widespread or localized these attitudes were.

The Asians

In North Nyanza the Asians were the owners of small shops, as used to be the case throughout East Africa. Since these were family run businesses Africans with no training and no capital were employed only in the lowest jobs. They had long resented the Asian monopoly of business and commerce and had felt that they were exploited by high prices and low wages.

Wekuke organized a campaign to raise wages and better working conditions. Five or six members visited Asian shopkeepers in Kimilili and Broderick Falls and laid down conditions regarding hours of work, housing and perquisites, such as cups of tea during working hours. They demanded that Asians give invoices for all goods purchased and threatened to withhold supplies of milk, eggs and fuel unless these conditions were met. African tailors threatened to strike.[129] It was also reported that Africans went into Indian shops in two places and took goods for which they did not pay and were 'very abusive and truculent' to the shopkeepers.[130] The Asians reported Wekuke to the labour officer, who told the two groups to negotiate. Africans consequently gained a number of concessions: tailors' wages were doubled, they could report one hour later for work (8 a.m. like all government employees, instead of 7 a.m.), and food was to be supplied for workers who came from afar.[131] Here we have the beginnings of labour protest and the threat of a strike used as a bargaining tactic.

There is little else to record about Msambwa's anti-Asian activities. Masinde threatened the Asians, as he did the missionaries, that they had better leave the country. But in Msambwa's overall campaign, the Asians are of minor significance.

Chiefs and Tribal Police

Dini ya Msambwa's *bête noire* were the chiefs and tribal police. The former called 'dogs of Kiminani' or 'Kinoholi', terms for gorilla or wolf-like creatures that supposedly ate human beings[132] were especially disliked by members for cooperating in the practice of conscript labour. On a number of occasions, Msambwa members not only refused to accept a labour summons but assaulted chiefs and others serving the summons. For instance, Masinde and Wekuke assaulted a chief who was serving a labour summons and were taken before a location *baraza* where they refused to obey chief Amutalla's order to sit down and be quiet. They made what the district officer described as 'subversive statements' and later, when their case was being tried in court, the judge said they were 'truculent'.

Another time Masinde, Wekuke and nine followers ambushed and attacked the *liguru* (head of the traditional council of elders) and two of his men, who were on their way to serve a labour summons. The affair developed into a riot with their supporters cheering them on. Arrested for assault, Masinde, on his way through Kimilili under police escort, shouted to the Asian shopkeepers, 'I go now—but I shall return. You and all non-natives will go soon and permanently.'[133]

Once Masinde armed himself with a whip and blocked the road to forty men who had been conscripted for a labour camp. 'If people have to work on the roads they must be paid,' he insisted. 'These men have paid their poll tax and must not be forced to work.'[134]

Since Msambwa's stand on this practice was particularly adamant, Wekuke was asked to explain their position:

> Chief Amutalla had been offered money, I think, to come and take people by force to the settlers' farms. Working on settlers' farms is very hard. We refused to do it. The workers were paid 8/- a month, given a piece of sack to sleep on, and a rough blanket. The settlers gave the provincial commissioner a lot of money, some of which he gave to the district commissioner, who in turn gave some to the chiefs. *The chiefs forced many people to work. This is a form of slavery.* They came with big lorries and loaded them with people. These people had to work six months and then they were exchanged for others. *If you ran away, you could be arrested and forced to return.* We opposed this practice by speaking out against it. The *askaris* came and started to assault us but we fought back.[135] (Italics mine.)

It is true that workers who left places of employment were often forced by the intervention of headmen, district and labour officers to return.[136]

Msambwa's most serious clash with the police occurred in February 1948, when a thousand followers decided to go to the police station at Malakisi to rescue three members detained by the police. According to Nabwana, Masinde, who was then in hiding, was the instigator, 'He sent his followers to attack a police station at Malakisi and to burn down the houses of the *askaris*. "You go and attack the police station. Our God has said that the *wazungus* must go." '[137] Simiyu Mutoro addressed those gathered and said that they would have to fight any Europeans that were with the African police. He further assured them that they need not worry about any bullets fired at them because they would not harm them.[138]

J. H. Walker, assistant superintendent of police, who had served in Kenya for twenty-five years, supported by a small force of tribal police, remonstrated with the threatening crowd, many of whom were waving sticks. Walker ordered the crowd to disperse. One man rushed forward and tried to grab his revolver, while another hit him on the head. Walker shot the man who was trying to take his revolver. This quietened the crowd for a brief time. Then it reformed and members threw clods of earth at the police. There was drumming and shouting. A man ran forward, seized the muzzle of Walker's revolver and tried to wrest it from him. Another hit him again on the head, penetrating the crown of his cap and knocking him to the ground. As he fell, Walker gave the order to fire to the tribal police. Eleven Africans were killed and sixteen wounded.[139] The Colonial Medal for Gallantry was later conferred upon Walker and Sergeant Kamitu Waita for the 'great courage' they displayed.[140] (This account by an army officer may well be subject to the commonplace distortions found in the reporting of such events by agents of social control.)

Msambwa's secretary kept a notebook in which their version of what had happened was recorded:

> The first time twelve followers were killed at Malakisi. They were shot when they were passing the Malakisi Police Station on their way to hold a meeting. When they were near the police station they were stopped by the police and told not to go to the meeting. They asked why they were forbidden to go to a meeting and instead of replying the police started shooting. Seven men were killed and five women, one of whom was pregnant.[141]

This is a somewhat different version from the government's. In this and other ways, beliefs to mobilize opposition to the regime were developed.

Fights over chieftainships and the methods employed by chiefs have characterized Luhya protest for the period under study. By the 1940s, inter-clan rivalry had become so factionalized that any chief tended to face strong opposition.

In some tribes tithes were traditionally paid by the subjects to their chiefs. When government-appointed chiefs claimed these perquisites they met opposition from Msambwa. 'At that time any poor person when he slaughtered a cow for visitors had to give the ribs and the hind leg to the chief as a present,' said Wekuke. 'They gave the chiefs presents such as eggs, chickens and many other things. Our *dini* refused to. . . . When we heard that someone was taking the chief a present we told him: "You are very poor; why are you giving your supplies to the chief? You should keep them for yourself. You need them. There is no need to give things away free of charge." '[142]

Members of clans other than the chiefs' had long felt that chiefly clans benefitted disproportionately from colonial rule. Under colonialism, a chief's position, in one sense, became more secure as it no longer depended on popular consensus but rather on government approval. Moreover, with the development of a cash economy and western education, new opportunities opened up for the long-term consolidation of chiefly power. A chief's association with the administration, technical experts and local courts gave him a number of advantages—information, contacts, and patronage—that he could exploit for personal gain. His discretion decided whether to inform superiors on the failures of his staff. Since he had a major voice in vetting candidates, he could often secure the appointments he wished. Some chiefs like Murungu nominated their own protégés to posts because they were more controllable than the Bukusu.[143] Thus, the office of chief gave scope for a wide range of behaviour and chiefs tended to be controversial figures and to some people particularly irritating symbols of the entrenched system of colonial privileges.

Chiefs were accused of acting harshly and autocratically. So dictatorial were some chiefs that district commissioners sometimes had to override their decisions. For instance, district commissioner Campbell wrote to his district officer:

> I understand that Chief Amutallah (Mr. Vishinsky) has said "no" to the meetings of the Kimilili Farmers Co-operative Marketing Society. This is extremely unwise of him and is on a par with his general veto of everything.

Will you please tell Amutallah that he will allow meetings of this particular Society and is at liberty to go himself to the meetings or send a representative. In fact, the officers of the Society themselves have, or are inviting him to attend their meetings.[144]

In a letter to the honourable chief native commissioner on the subject of chief Jonathan Baraza, Jason Matete voiced a number of common complaints about chiefs:

When this person was elected some people thought that he was going to be a good man particularly a few government officials and his kith and kinsmen. But now he has begun to show very bad signs which prove that in future he is going to be a sort of dictator. These are some of the bad signs:
1) He gives trading licenses to only kinsmen and his friends (this can be proved).
2) He despises the educated boys, thinking that they will compete with him about the Chieftainship.
3) He rules only parts of the location, this same fault was committed by a previous ruler who belonged to the same family.
4) He hates many people privately.
5) He causes enmity between clans.[145]

With the stabilizing of district and reserve boundaries, clans were denied their traditional weapon for coping with an overbearing chief—secession from his territory.[146]

In areas where there were pronounced church-and-chief alliances, members of non-chiefly clans felt they had few opportunities for advancement.[147] Ambitious young men lacking advantageous lineage connections turned to the voluntary associations and the independent churches as avenues of mobility. This power struggle was exacerbated by inter-generational conflict—less educated, older chiefs against more educated, younger men.

Nabwana of the Bukusu Union challenged the chieftainship of Amutalla. District officer Kennaway commented on this clash, 'For some time Chief Amutallah and Pascal Nabwana have been at loggerheads. Chief Amutallah regards Pascal as a young upstart (not even of Kimilili origin) who is intriguing to oust Amutallah and to become chief himself. Pascal regards Chief Amutallah as a retrograde ignoramous who is inimical to progress.'[148] Nabwana's supporters charged Amutalla with having enriched himself by taking bribes but after a three day hearing the magistrate concluded that no complaints had been substantiated.[149] The chiefs, for their part, harassed the Union.

Five years later the struggle was still going on. The chiefs advocated a hard line towards the Union while the administration wanted a softer approach. The district officer, after meeting with the chiefs at Kimilili in 1949, reported:

> All were unanimous in stating that the Union was a 'bad thing' . . . Chiefs Sudi, Amutalla and Mulipi said that they refused permission for the Union to hold meetings and wished to refuse. We pointed out that it might be better to allow the Union to come out into the open and let it hold meetings, if it produced proper books, agenda, minutes, etc., and obtains permission. The "old school" won the day (Amutalla, Sudi, Mulipi, etc.) and wanted the Union prohibited. Jonathan Baraza and two others only agreed with the suggestion. We did not press the point. . . . It [the Bukusu Union] undoubtedly passed some seditious resolutions and stirred up a lot of trouble. I think the best thing to do is to let sleeping dogs lie. There will be much opposition and disgust from the chiefs of the old school if we try to force them to allow meetings but I doubt if requests for meetings will be made.[150]

The government, alarmed at the growing militancy among the young, wanted their support, preferring that they express their views publicly through recognized channels rather than privately through secret meetings and agitation. It realized that failure to acquire their support would almost certainly result in radical opposition that could be difficult to control. It also realized that its efforts at reform were being thwarted because the chiefs who introduced them were disliked. But the government's attempts to acquire the young men's confidence were impeded by prior commitments to the chiefs with whom its own authority was linked and whose support it needed.

Msambwa's and the Union's dislike of pro-establishment Africans included sub-chiefs, headmen and, in particular, tribal police who had the day-to-day task of seeing that colonial regulations were met, the unpopular job of assisting in the capture of labour deserters, and who, on occasion, employed force against their own people. The Union objected to the very presence of police in the reserves and threatened, if the district commissioner couldn't provide an adequate explanation, to find the 'best ways of destroying the police.'[151] Nabwana expressed the feelings of other Bukusu when he told the district officer, 'I suppose one in a thousand Kitosh would look on a policeman as his friend. I am most anxious to see a change of heart on the people's part. The quickest way to bring this about would be by instructing the police not to beat and ill-use us.'[152]

This period witnessed a challenge by a group of mission-educated men, in the main, school teachers, ex-servicemen, heads of co-operatives, leaders of independent churches and voluntary associations who were trying to divest members of the old guard of their privileged positions. Nabwana and Masinde were allied, if for no other reason than that they were both anti-establishment young men working to unseat chiefs and other pro-establishment Africans.

The Bukusu Union and Dini ya Msambwa as Alternate Responses

The Bukusu Union, like Msambwa, advocated a return to 'their old laws, rules and regulations as before the Europeans arrived.'[153] But this, together with its opposition to agricultural reform, did not necessarily indicate that the Union was a regressive movement and that its modern goals—schools, cooperatives, trade unions— were only a guise to hide its true concerns. Again, as in Mumbo and Msambwa, nativistic elements were used for symbolic purposes. But even more important, the Bukusu wanted to retain certain aspects of their indigenous way of life. Nabwana was one of the most 'progressive' men in the location. In all likelihood, he and other members genuinely wanted schools, trade unions, and co-operatives, but they wanted them to be African institutions based on African values. This, we suggest, is a better explanation of the Union's refusal to cooperate with various government measures than atavism.

On the relationship between Msambwa and the Bukusu Union there has been much speculation. Both originated about the same time among the same people and their membership, in part, over-lapped. Wafula, Msambwa's secretary, was vice-president of the Union; Wekuke, Msambwa's vice-president, referred to Nabwana as 'father', and though not related by blood, their clans were on special terms. Masinde played football for the Union's team.[154] Nabwana was suspected of being the organizing force behind Msambwa, since Masinde was believed to be too disorganized to cope with any concerted campaign and Nabwana was obviously talented.[155] For one thing, he was an experienced organizer.

Nabwana publicly defended Masinde. 'I don't see that Elijah has committed any fault. In England there are many religions and many fights over religious questions.' His aggressive criticism of the administration, while less extreme than Masinde's, made him in the eyes of some administrators the greater danger. He obstructed the chiefs' attempts to persuade the people to hand over Masinde when he was in hiding. In December 1946, he was fired from the Soil Conservation Service for being a 'troublemaker'. However, despite reprimands from the administration, he continued to protest. He ordered people not to volunteer for communal labour.[156] He was arrested along with Masinde and Wekuke for allegedly instigating the Malakisi Riot, and the Bukusu Union was proscribed at the same time as Msambwa. Subsequently Nabwana was released due to lack of evidence.

The administration possessed a fairly effective intelligence system and in spite of Nabwana's present protestations that he never associated with Msambwa or advocated violence, considerable evidence links him to both. Reports of Bukusu Union meetings show that he was not as opposed to violence then as he now maintains he was. Furthermore, his membership in the North Kavirondo Central Association, his chairmanship of the North Nzoia branch of the Kenya African Union, and his association with Koinange and Kenyatta, suggest that he shared many of their aspirations. In answer to a question about Msambwa's leadership and why he was so suspect, he replied forthrightly, 'They [the administration] felt I was leading the Bukusu because I was more intelligent than Elijah.'[157]

The issue of the chieftainship provides a further clue to Nabwana's character and position. Nabwana wanted to be chief. On the other hand, he was allegedly involved in activities designed to overthrow the colonial system. Among his compatriots there are some who feel that had he succeeded in replacing Amutalla, his anti-colonial stand would have vanished. For what it is worth, he told the district commissioner, 'I am not fool enough to suppose that we could wield power alone if the British left. A lot of nonsense is talked in this respect by ignorant people, who, if the Europeans left tomorrow and started pulling out the railway to Mombasa, would be the first to clamour to be allowed to go with them and not be left without protection.'[158]

Administrators tended to see Nabwana as opportunistic. District officer Simpson commented, 'Pascal Nabwana is a sly chap and I get the impression he is waiting to see which way the cat will jump.'[159] A former provincial commissioner, K. L. Hunter, said essentially the same thing, 'He was a thorn in my side until I gave

189

him a good job and then he would eat out of my hand.'[160] Nabwana
appeared to equivocate on whether he was for or against the colonial
system while Masinde launched an unequivocal attack. An evaluation
of the kind of commitment Nabwana had to independence and
Bukusu nationalism is obviously speculative, but the evidence does
suggest that he, more than anything else, wanted a good position,
whether the system was run by Africans or Europeans.

Though Nabwana's links with Dini ya Msambwa will likely
remain a subject of speculation, he deserves a passing note since he
has played an important role in local politics. Born in 1898, Nabwana
early in his life became interested in western education, and as far
back as 1928 had opened two unlicensed schools, for which he
was arrested and sentenced to six months imprisonment.[161] He
founded and was president of the short-lived Bukusu Education
Society, begun in 1935 and closed down by the government in 1939,
because it opened unlicensed schools. He was inspector of village
schools from 1939 to 1942, a member of the African District Council
from 1935 to 1955, its deputy vice-chairman from 1956 to 1959,
the first African chairman (unofficial, instead of the district commissioner) in 1959, and vice-president of the District Appeal Court
at Kakamega. He served on the Finance and General Purpose
Committee and the Location Advisory Council.[162] Towards the
end of the colonial era, he received the Order of the British Empire
for his contribution to community affairs. Nabwana owns about
100 acres of land and several small shops, a butchery, a mill, and
a tavern. He has five wives, thirty children, and more than seventy
grandchildren. Many of his children are educated and four were
abroad on scholarships in 1969.[163]

Our investigation has revealed a number of parallels between
the Bukusu Union and Dini ya Msambwa. They protested many of
the same grievances, were not all that different in their tactics, and
were led by men from the same generation and background with a
few men participating in both, but the Union had a better grasp
of the realities of national politics and of the importance of a
widely based nationalistic movement. Msambwa, repelled by some
Mau Mau tactics that confirmed longstanding anti-Kikuyu feelings,
doggedly pursued its own way relatively oblivious to the national
scene.

The Bukusu Union and Dini ya Msambwa were alternate
responses to the same grievances. The Union was more in line

with modern political associations, while Msambwa maintained stronger links with traditional symbols. Nabwana himself acknowledged that the Union lost many members to Msambwa because Masinde preached that he had been told by the great Bukusu prophets to start Msambwa and he promised people free land and cattle when the foreigners were driven out. In this transition period between old and new forms, Msambwa's message had a special appeal to the uneducated.

What were the Bukusu Union's relations with the Kenya African Union (KAU)? Nabwana was the Union's representative among the Bukusu. According to him, 'I was asked by KAU to be the leader here. I was trying to convert people to join the Bukusu branch of KAU. . . . I was in touch with Kenyatta and Koinange. Kenyatta made trips here. I was also helping him campaign. I was in it from 1943 to 1952 when KAU was closed down.'[164] The Bukusu Union sent students to the Githunguri Teachers' College, an independent school organized by the Kikuyu of which Kenyatta was the principal. When the Bukusu Union was proscribed, many of its members joined KAU.[165]

KAU gained some popularity with the Bukusu because it supported their claims to land in the Trans Nzoia. Nabwana explained, 'When KAU came . . . they started telling us that it was no use asking for a piece of land, we should ask for the whole country. We said, "alright, but first we want our piece." ' This suggests that members of the Bukusu Union at that stage were thinking more in tribal terms than members of the KAU, who were thinking in erms of the country as a whole.

A few joint meetings took place between the Bukusu Union and KAU. One such meeting held in February 1947 was attended by Nabwana, Hudson Sanja, secretary of KAU, and William Kibulo, chairman of the Kimilili branch of KAU. Those present were asked to contribute money to send delegates to Nairobi and to England to plead their common grievances before representatives of the Home Government. (Aside, it is interesting to note the faith in the Home Government that Africans displayed. Up to the time of independence, many Africans felt that if only they could plead their own case in England they would receive fair treatment. They looked to the British government as a kind of just father, removed from petty Kenyan politics, who would understand and handle their problems fairly. And, as it turned out, their faith was justified.

191

The Home Government, despite strong opposition from the settlers, ultimately decided the issue of independence in favour of them.)

Political tensions increased rapidly in the years immediately prior to the outbreak of Mau Mau. KAU accelerated its activities outside Central Province in an effort to arouse anti-colonial sentiments and to enlarge its base of support. District reports from 1947 to 1952 when KAU was proscribed, note its efforts to make inroads into North Nyanza, but it appears to have met with little success. Two or three meetings were organized in Kakamega and various KAU officials came from Nairobi. Attendance was limited, however, to several hundred people.[166] In 1948 a branch of KAU was formed under the chairmanship of ex-chief Mulama. Just as the British before them had courted Wanga support through Mumia, so did KAU through Mulama.[167]

In 1951 and 1952 the political tempo in North Nyanza quickened. The administration blamed KAU. Frequent meetings varying in size and success were held throughout the district. Towards the end of 1951, Jomo Kenyatta, president of KAU, held meetings at Mbale Market and Chwele. The district commissioner concluded, 'It is a fair summary of the situation to say that considerable local support for KAU was obtained but that there was no district-wide enthusiasm; financial contributions must have proved disappointing to the sponsors.'[168] District officers complained that after these meetings location chiefs and other administrative officers found their work more difficult.[169] As a result of a disorderly meeting at Nyeri, Central Province in 1952, where some twenty-five thousand Kikuyu effectively demonstrated the power of the militants, KAU was banned.[170] Nabwana and other local Union leaders were given stern warnings to sever all ties with KAU. The district commissioner of North Nyanza noted that from then onwards political tensions decreased and his district 'settled down'.[171]

With the advent of the Mau Mau insurrection all contacts between the Luhya and the Kikuyu were severed. Government documents as well as testimonies from leaders of the Bukusu Union and Msambwa support the view that there were no connections between their organizations and the Kikuyu. Even though the followers admitted that both they and the Kikuyu were fighting for independence, they did not hesitate to point out that they would never commit the atrocities the Mau Mau fighters had. The vice-president, the secretary, and various local leaders condemned Mau

Mau's tactics. They clashed with our customs, was the gist of the replies. Nabwana explained:

> The Bukusu completely rejected Mau Mau. A Kuke [Kikuyu] kills another Kuke, a brother murders his brothers and sisters. Our people don't like that. Our tradition from the beginning was not to fight other Bukusu or Gisu [the other part of the tribe separated by the Kenya-Uganda boundary]. *There is an ancient law that forbids this*. (Italics mine.)

Would Masinde, had he been free, joined up with Mau Mau?

> Masinde wouldn't do that. Our laws forbid us to kill young children and women. In war they are taken prisoners. We kill only mature men. The Kukes were murdering women and children. The people of Msambwa couldn't do that. In our tradition, if you do such you would be cursed or the people of the location would kill you. To this day Masinde is against Mau Mau. He is still cursing Mau Mau because it killed people. During the circumcision ceremony our young men are given orders *forbidding the killing of women and children. This was our ancestors' custom right from the beginning*. . . . Mau Mau is completely different from Msambwa. Even now the Kukes don't like the Bukusu because the Bukusu don't like the way they behave. We say the Kukes used to give people medicine that turned them into rogues. We heard that they killed pregnant women, little children, they slaughtered any helpless person.[172] (Italics mine.)

Wekuke put it this way:

> The Kukes tried to talk people into joining them but we couldn't reach an agreement with them. We said we have our *dini* . . . we carried on here and they in their country. We didn't make any contact . . . It is not easy to run two things at once. . . . We supported them in praying to God but *they went beyond the order of God and began to slash out at everything with pangas* [large knives]. (Italics mine.)

Would your *dini* have joined the Mau Mau struggle?

> If they hadn't murdered people we could have united with them. But they started fighting and we don't like that. If they had used their tongues politically we would have joined them. We had intended to get rid of the British politically by following God's orders. We would have a meeting and send our petition to the government.[173]

Joasch Walumoli, the prophet, also vouched that Msambwa wanted peace and, unlike Mau Mau, did not kill people. Even Donisio Nakimayu, an admitted arsonist, maintained that Msambwa's tactics had emphasized prayer and forbade killing. In fact, so convinced were some members in the power of prayer that they took credit for achieving independence, arguing that it was their prayers rather than the Mau Mau insurrection that really brought it.

It should be noted that these statements were made after the Mau Mau rebellion had been suppressed and independence achieved. Whether such strong statements would have been forthcoming at that time is questionable. Besides, by the time Mau Mau broke out, the British had all but stifled Msambwa. So there may well be some rationalizing in these statements.

This stand may sound strange in light of Msambwa's own involvement in violence, but one needs to carefully distinguish between different kinds of violence. Msambwa used violence primarily against foreign property, state property, mission property, and the settlers' personal property. It threatened violence against the missionaries and settlers but there is little to record there. Its members attacked chiefs with their fists, spontaneously and openly, in contrast to Mau Mau's planned, secretive and murderous attacks.

This raises the question of how widespread the belief in non-violence was? Did those who opted for it also believe in a millennium and rely heavily upon supernatural means? There is evidence in the stories of Masinde's exploits that magical solutions had a wide appeal. Jean La Fontaine noted that the members believed 'their sacrifices and ceremonies would be enough to wipe out Europeans and the troubles of their country with a flow of supernatural blood falling from the sky.'[174]

It could be, that in the early stages, prayers alone were thought to be sufficient and that only later after their ineffectiveness had been demonstrated did members turn to militancy. Masinde was said to have at first believed that Europeans would go when Africans returned to their old customs, thus showing them that they were no longer wanted. Later, he advocated more aggressive tactics. He assaulted some people, threatened others, and there were suggestions, though unproved, that he would go even further. As early as 1949, the provincial commissioner wrote:

> An unconfirmed report has reached me from an African source to the effect that at these meetings they are discussing the futility of carrying out their earlier policy of violence and overt acts and that they are considering whether they should not conduct their *dini* in the true spirit of religion and endeavour to attain their ends through prayer.

Msambwa's tactics may have shifted throughout its career from non-violence to violence, then to non-violence again.

Our analysis suggests that Msambwa had strong links with the Bukusu Union, embryonic links with KAU, but no links with Mau

Mau. Msambwa's connections with organizations protesting similar issues lend weight to the contention that its goals were mainly political and that its protest fitted in with the increasing radicalization of Luhya and Kikuyu protest.

Though Msambwa's links with outside organizations were tenuous and ineffective in terms of forming a united opposition, they were important for other reasons. They drew the members into the wider stream of radical ideas. A dent was made in the armour of tribal parochialism. The Luhya began to realize that the allocation of national resources was going to the most effectively organized group, the settlers, and that they shared problems with other tribes, the solution of which might better be realized through cooperative effort. These initial attempts of a tribally fragmented people to come together were the first steps in the building of inter-tribal unity. Had independence been delayed, they might well have been of major significance in the development of territorial nationalism.

The contrast between the Kikuyu and the Luhya in terms of utilizing modern techniques and of developing a national consciousness is striking. The Kikuyu had sent delegates to England to plead their cause in the early 1920s, but only in the 1940s were the Luhya attempting to do the same. By the early 1930s the Kikuyu had established independent schools, whereas the Luhya were only beginning to do so in the mid-1940s. By the 1950s the Kikuyu were able to unite their many clans in opposition to the British, while the Luhya, still clan-centred and fragmented, were in the early stages of building a wider unity. The different pace at which tribal opposition to colonialism developed, stemmed, in part, from the uneven impact of European settlement. The Luhya suffered little land alienation in comparison to the Kikuyu, therefore they lacked that strong impetus to action.

In the decade prior to the Mau Mau emergency, there was a heightening of tensions as the situation fast approached a crisis. In Smelser's terminology, the conditions were structurally conducive to radical protest. But it did not occur everywhere. In Chapter 13, we will explore the additional conditions that may explain why protest surfaced in some places and not in others.

Some Deviant Practices
From a number of reports there were Msambwa stalwarts who drank to a degree termed 'excessive' by local standards. The members

freely admitted that they smoked tobacco and many allegedly smoked bhang.[175] On several occasions the members were referred to as 'great opium smokers', although the extent to which opium was smoked is not easily ascertained. Knowing neither moderation nor discretion in living habits, Masinde took the lead in these undertakings. His close associates stated that he smoked opium and bhang and drank heavily.[176]

The evidence is sketchy as to whether the smoking of bhang and opium were regarded as deviant. Certainly the use of bhang was long entrenched (note Hobley's reference to the Bukusu in the 1895 battle having primed themselves on bhang and beer),[177] but on questions of whether it was commonly smoked, by whom, and under what conditions, data are lacking. Among the Gusii the smoking of bhang appeared to be accepted, particularly among the old people, and since they were related to the Luhya it may have been the same with them. Nevertheless, as practised by members of Dini ya Msambwa in the post-colonial period, the smoking of bhang and opium was strongly condemned by the local people.

A district commissioner of North Nyanza reported that on 8 February 1948, acting on information received, he had gone with a force of police to Sangola and there he found about five hundred men, women and children, followers of Msambwa 'stripped and trembling . . . rolling in a frenzy on the ground.'[178] There were accounts of Msambwa 'orgies' in caves, especially among the West Pokot, whose initiation rites were said to consist of copulation, often incestuous.[179] Since the Pokot movement was autonomous it could be that these practices occurred in one place and not in another. Besides, the line between religious and sexual ecstasy can be hard to draw. Like some sects, the members may have practised free love among themselves and even engaged in communal ceremonies for reasons sanctioned by the movement. Certainly the episode where Masinde chastised a member's wife by making her kneel naked beside him and pray suggests he may have cultivated such activity as part of Msambwa's ritual.[180] Just how widespread such practices were is hard to tell. It could be that only a few members were involved and that others were even ignorant of their existence.

Did these practices break indigenous norms? Sexual liaisons outside of monogamous or polygamous unions were not permitted in Bukusu society. A wife's adultery was regarded as an infringement of the husband's rights and the guilty party was usually fined a cow which was paid to the husband. Likewise, sexual offences against an unmarried girl were regarded as a serious transgression of the father's rights and were generally handled in the same way.[181] Since single women, except for a few widows and divorcees, were rare, there was a short supply of women with whom men could have sexual liaisons outside of marriage without breaking norms.

The community condemned not so much occasional lapses as a pattern of activities that could be called hedonistic. Msambwa encouraged activities strongly condemned by the missionaries, elevating hedonism over the more sober virtues. It inversed the 'Protestant Ethic' values substituting carousing for hard work, extravagant living for frugality, taking drugs for sobriety and 'free love' for Christian love. Just how common this pattern was is not known, but it may have become more common in the post-colonial period when Msambwa's anti-colonial campaign was finished.[182]

Were these activities indulged in to deliberately profane the way of life Christians, and particularly African converts, held sacred? What better way to reject mission teachings than holding the occasional Dionysian revel? Whether these counter-norms were cultivated in direct opposition to the missions, or whether some members simply engaged in what appealed to them, is debatable. Probably it was some or both. When members were asked why they joined, a number said it was because Msambwa permitted activities condemned by other *dinis*. The idea of engaging in forbidden pastimes had an obvious appeal to some adherents described as rebellious, contentious and non-conformist.[183]

It might be more accurate to say that Msambwa strained to the limit certain norms and that it emphasized certain subterranean values. In any society there are deviant and even antithetical values which, though officially condemned, are to some extent privately lauded and even practised by particular groups. For instance, there was a norm that important people should entertain lavishly. Did Masinde's boisterous parties conform to, or deviate from, the hospitality norm? How far can one go before the norm is considered broken? And even if Masinde's parties were generally considered too boisterous, they still brought him kudos, at least from some people.

To sum up the evidence that suggests these practices:

1) Local people suggested their presence but refused to elaborate on any details.

2) Government records, though not particularly trustworthy on such matters, noted particular instances.

3) People said Masinde engaged in these activities and he dominated Msambwa.

4) These activities supported each other. They fitted in with a core value—defiance of Europeans—and later when millenarianism became more prominent they likewise fitted into this configuration.[184]

Interpretation and Conclusions

Jean La Fontaine argues that while Dini ya Msambwa did not practise the traditional religion but a modified version, it was essentially a religious group.[185] If we accept the La Fontaine view, then what do we do with its anti-colonial campaign? What do we do with much ritual that was concerned with what are usually considered political as opposed to religious concerns? How do we explain the many tales about Masinde that had little to do with religion, but much to do with the foreign oppression?

J. D. Welime, on the other hand, contends that 'Dini ya Msambwa was really a political party couched in religious terms.' He maintains that Msambwa's religious beliefs were used to conceal its political motives and notes its connection with the Kenya African Union.[186] Again, if we accept Welime's position, what about the leaders and members who joined because they wished to continue their forefathers' religion? What do we do with the ancestor cult that for many members was an integral part of Msambwa? One can, of course, always impugn the motives of others. But the members had no reason to hide their motives, especially in the post-colonial period when it would have been to their credit to emphasize Msambwa's opposition to colonialism. How do we explain the later attempt, described in Chapter 16, by members to form a purely religious group?

Jan de Wolf calls Dini ya Msambwa a millenarian movement and emphasizes its expressive content.[187] Totally absent is any appreciation of its pragmatic efforts to banish the foreigners or of the active components of millenarianism, that while millenarian beliefs may have deterred some, they encouraged others to engage in militant action as did magically acquired 'protection'. By studying a movement at only one point in time (the post-colonial) and that a period of decline, de Wolf has made generalizations about a total movement that at best hold for only a limited period.

We have argued, as opposed to all of these positions, each one being partially correct, that Dini ya Msambwa's religious and political beliefs were inextricably linked. Next we will look at Msambwa among the Pokot, a tribe geographically and culturally quite distinct from the Luhya. It was among these people that Msambwa's most violent episode occurred.

Notes

1. Smelser, *Theory of Collective Behavior*, p. 16.
2. This description is based mainly on accounts by Wagner, 'The Abaluyia of Kavirondo', pp. 27–54 and J. S. La Fontaine, 'Notes on Ancestor Worship among the Babukusu and its Difference from Dini ya Msambwa', (typescript copy, Kampala, Uganda).
   There is disagreement by the above authors on various aspects of the traditional religion. This may be due to local and clan variation. As La Fontaine noted, traditional beliefs varied from clan to clan and even within clans. Besides, no comprehensive study has yet been made of Bukusu religion. When these data were collected many of the traditional practices were no longer being performed. And as always when one is dependent upon oral tradition, the chance of variation through forgetfulness and individual recollection is great. For these reasons there is likely to be considerable variation among different analyses.
3. The Bukusu are the only Luhya sub-tribe that spell his name *Wele*, according to Osogo. Since 'r' and 'l' are largely interchangeable, it probably, at the most, represents a slight difference in dialect. The term *Were* is common among the other northern tribes in the district, while the term, *Nyasaye*, according to Wagner, prevails among the southern tribes.
4. Father J. Orther, 'An Account of the Political and Religious Tenets of the 'Watu wa Misambwa',' a typescript copy from the Archives of the Catholic Mission, Kibabii, 28 May 1948.
5. Wagner, 'The Abaluyia of Kavirondo', pp. 37–9.
6. Osogo, *A History*, pp. 78–9.
7. *Ibid.*, p. 16.
8. *Ibid.*, p. 79.
9. See above, p. 8 for definition of a nativistic movement.
10. Interview with Wekuke, 9 November 1965.
11. Linton, 'Nativistic Movements', p. 231.
12. KNA:DC/NN 10/1/5. Letter from district commissioner J. H. Lewis of Kitale to the provincial commissioner of the Rift Valley, September 1949. The text was translated from
   Were Babu yetu tusside
   Wazungu waende kwao
   Maina wa Lugali
   Wachie wa Wanaumbwa
   Mutonyi Bukerembe wasaide
13. *East African Standard*, 3 October 1952.
14. I accompanied the district officer when he made his rounds of the Elgon area. We travelled a considerable distance up Mount Elgon by landrover and then hiked to the summit. Lake Zion is surrounded by many interesting

rock formations and caves excellent for hiding in. During our visit the sun shone brightly but it was so cold at the summit that my fingers had difficulty in pressing the shutter of my camera. As for bathing in the lake as some Msambwa members reputedly did, that would have been a severe penance.

15. Interview with Paulo Loyana, 3 November 1969.
16. Interview with Wafula, 13 March 1965.
17. Interviews with Loyana and Donisio Nakimayu, 3 November 1969.
18. Interview with Wekuke, 8 November 1965.
19. Interview with Nakimayu, 3 November 1969.
20. Wagner, *The Abaluyia of Kavirondo*, pp. 33-34. The belief about the Bukusu living on the summit of Mount Elgon was reported by La Fontaine *The Gisu of Uganda*, (International African Institute, London, 1959), p. 11.
21. Wekuke, Nabwana, Walumoli and Loyana in interviews on 1 and 2 November 1969.
22. Interview with Wafula, 3 November 1969. J. D. W. Welime, in Dini ya Msambwa, suggested the second reason for bathing in the lake.
23. H. W. Turner, *African Independent Church: The Life and Faith of the Church of the Lord Aladura*, Volume II, (Clarendon Press, Oxford, 1967), p. 194; Bengt G. M. Sundkler, *Bantu Prophets in South Africa*, pp. 201–12.
24. Interview with Wafula, 6 November 1965. Wekuke told a rather fanciful story about ancestors and angels that illustrates the way the two were linked in their thinking. 'Ancestor spirits, most are good people. When they died they joined company with angels. So wherever they go the angels come with them. This is very important. Each time an angel stands at the top of your head and the shadow of an ancestor stands in front of you. The words pass from the angel to the ancestor and then the ancestor's shadow tells you. So the next morning you recall how a particular ancestor talked with you but it really was an angel sent by God with the ancestor to bring you a message.'
25. For the sake of readers not interested in ceremonial detail, descriptions of these ceremonies have been relegated to Appendix C.
26. Compiled from accounts by Wafula and Nabwana.
27. Lonsdale, A Political History, p. 80, mentions the Gusii prophecy. Kennell Jackson told me about the Kamba prophesy.
28. This account was given by Nabwana, 14 March 1965. Reports of the march differ in detail. Nakimayu said that more than fifteen thousand people participated and that a red ram was sacrificed. He, too, said that Masinde prophesied that the foreigners would soon return to their own country. Interview on 3 November 1969.

   Nabwana proudly told me that his father, Wakoli Mukisu, led the attack against Hobley and Grant in 1895. 'The Arabs sold three guns to Wakoli. When they returned they told Hobley that the guns had been stolen so Hobley came to our home and found the guns. My father tried to explain but it was no good. A battle started.' This roughly jibes with the historical account of how and why the battle started.
29. See Appendix C for details of symbolic materials.
30. I visited Walumoli at his home about twelve miles from Kimilili. It was spacious by Bukusu standards with a lovely garden of poinsettia trees. We sat in a sparsely furnished house, typical of Bukusu dwellings. Walumoli, with his youngest son, a boy of two or three on his knee, began to tell a long and rambling story about the prophets and origins of the Bukusu. Walumoli is known as a healer of the sick. He carefully stressed that his power came from God and that when a person is cured it is God's will. He did not realise that he possessed the power to heal and to prophesy until he had reached maturity. Before he was detained by the British he prophesied that Kenya would gain independence and that Dini ya Msambwa would be 'disturbed' by the government. Both have taken place. My meeting with Walumoli, in addition to what I had heard about him,

convinced me that here was another man like Wekuke with strong religious interests.

31. Intelligence Reports, 1961, District Office, Kimilili.
32. Max Weber, *The Sociology of Religion*, p. 104.
33. David E. Apter, 'Political Religion in the New Nations', Clifford Geertz (ed.), *Old Societies and New States*, (The Free Press, New York, 1967), p. 83.
34. See Appendix D for excerpts from one of Masinde's sermons.
35. Conversation with Wafula, 14 March 1965.
36. There is some disagreement, mainly spelling variations, due probably to differences in pronunciation over the names of the three aspects of the Trinity. The discussions of Msambwa religion by Father Orther and the article entitled, 'Exposition of Chief Articles of Dini ya Misambwa', write of *Wele Webumbi, Wele Mukhobe,* and *Wele Khakaba.* Osogo also writes of *Mukhobe* and *Khakaba* but simply of *Wele* rather than *Wele Webumbi.* Since these are all brief discussions, the names used here are taken from Wagner's authoritative study. See Father Orther, 'An Account', pp. 233–235; Osogo, *A History*, p. 79; and, 'Exposition of Chief Articles of Dini ya Misambwa', 6 April 1948, the Vicariat of Kisumu. I am indebted to de Wolf for a copy of the Vicariat Exposition.
37. Interview with Wafula, 6 November 1965.
38. Farson, *Last Chance in Africa*, (Victor Gollancz, London, 1951), p. 235. This is a journalistic and not a scholarly account.
39. Osogo, *A History*, pp. 12, 21 and 79; Were, *Western Kenya Historical Texts*, p. 68. This claim, however, is subject to considerable debate.
40. Georges Balandier, Messianism and Nationalism in Black Africa, P. L. van den Berghe (ed.), *Africa: Social Problems of Change and Conflict*, (Chandler Publishing Co., San Francisco, 1965), pp. 443–60; Balandier, 'Contribution a l'étude des nationalismes en Afrique noire', *Zaire*, VIII, 4, April 1954, 379–89; René Lemarchand, 'The bases of nationalism among the Bakongo', *Africa*, XXXI, 4, October 1961, 344–54; Lemarchand, *Political Awakening in the Belgian Congo*, (University of California Press, Berkeley, 1964); N. O. Biebuyck, 'La societe kumu face au Kitawala', *Zaire*, XI, 1, January 1957, pp. 7–40; Fox, deCraemer, Ribeaucort, The Second Independence; George Shepperson and Thomas Price, *Independent African*; George Shepperson, The Politics of African Church Separatist Movements, pp. 233–46.
41. de Wolf, Religious Innovation, pp. 140–41.
42. *Nyanza Province Annual Report 1961.* A sister at Kibabii Roman Catholic Mission also told me this story.
43. *East African Standard*, 29 October 1965 and the *Uganda Argus*, 30 October 1965.
44. *Uganda Argus*, 31 October 1965.
45. From a conversation with a police officer, 18 March 1965.
46. James W. Fernandez, 'African Religious Movements—Types and Dynamics', *The Journal of Modern African Studies*, II, 4, 1964, p. 533.
47. La Fontaine, 'Ancestor Worship'.
48. For examples of these kinds of interpretations see Usher-Wilson, 'Bishop's Study of 'Dini ya Misambwa',' *East Africa and Rhodesia*, 15 and 29 November 1951; La Fontaine, 'Ancestor Worship'; Osogo, *A History*, p. 135; and Father Orther, 'An Account'.
49. See above, pp. 44–5 and below, pp. 153–63.
50. La Fontaine, 'Ancestor Worship'.
51. An instance of Masinde defying tradition occurred on 16 March 1965. Wekuke's clan had gathered to confer upon him the status of elder. The elders, as the traditional ceremony required, were to present Wekuke with a cloak of monkey skins. Masinde said that he would make the presentation. Wekuke replied, 'No, for one thing you are younger than me and for another this is always placed by the clan elders, not you.'

Masinde shouted, 'No, No, No! I'm the one to put this cloak on you!' Wekuke and his clan were very annoyed and moved away from Masinde and started to hold their own meeting. Wekuke refused to attend Masinde's meeting until Masinde went himself for him.

52. Interview with a middle-aged woman at Kimilili Market, 11 March 1965.
53. Interview with an old man, 11 November 1965.
54. Interview with a young woman, 15 March 1965.
55. Hobsbawm, *Primitive Rebels*, p. 2.
56. For a discussion of major social types in American society see Orrin E. Klapp, *Heroes, Villains, and Fools*, (Prentice-Hall, Englewood Cliffs, 1962); Hobsbawm, *Primitive Rebels*, Chapter 2, The Social Bandit, discusses a hero type in Europe similar to the colonial folk hero.
57. Charles Onyango told me that an elder had told him this story. Onyango, who is a Luo, lived in Kisumu, about eighty miles from Dini ya Msambwa's headquarters.
58. Interview with Wafula, 13 March 1965. The old man's statement immediately before Wafula's came from an interview on 11 November 1965.
59. Interview with Wafula, 13 March 1965.
60. Dreams were traditionally used to convey messages to individuals. See La Fontaine, *The Gisu of Uganda*, p. 58.
61. KNA:DC/NN10/1/5. Notes on Dini ya Msambwa, dated 25 July 1949.
62. See Lucy Mair, *Witchcraft*, (World Universal Library, London, 1949), pp. 70–1, for an account of 'smelling-out'.
63. Fox, de Craemer and Ribeaucort, 'The Second Independence', pp. 20–21; James Bertsche, 'The Congo Rebellion', *Practical Anthropology*, XII, September–October, 1965, p. 218.
64. Interview with Wafula, 13 March 1965.
65. Farson, *Last Chance in Africa*, pp. 233–34.
66. KNA:DC/NN/10/5. This information is based on a report of an informer sent to spy on Dini ya Msambwa. He wrote in barely intelligible English of his conversation with Zakayo Wopicho who said among other things, 'Elijah has discovered many things concerning Europeans and had found them out by just smelling. He's also discovered the heads of Bukusu celebrated people of dead bodies such as Maina and Wachie, etc., and in those heads bullets were found which the Europeans kept in! I asked again, but he said that he would never tell all Bukusu secrets, for he had been warned never to tell such things. At last I said, "What was his decision about it?" He answered, "Elijah has taken off a spell of Europeans on which they were leaning and now they would soon trickle or slide along as water".'
67. James Mooney, *The Ghost-Dance Religion*, p. 181.
68. John Iliffe, 'The Organization of the Maji Maji Rebellion', EASSC Paper, December 1966, p. 12.
69. Fox, de Craemer and Ribeaucort, 'The Second Independence', p. 85.
70. *Ibid.*, pp. 98–9; and Crawford Young, 'Rebellion and the Congo'; Robert I. Rotberg and Ali A. Mazrui (eds.), *Protest and Power in Black Africa*, pp. 987–89.
71. Max Gluckman, The Magic of Despair, *The Listener*, 29 April 1954, p. 725.
72. Interview with Nabwana, 14 March 1965.
73. DC/NN10/1/5. Letter from provincial commissioner K. L. Hunter to the honourable chief native secretary, Nairobi, 26 January 1945.
74. Interview with a follower of a breakaway from Dini ya Msambwa, Judah Israel, 10 March 1965.
75. Interview with an Anglican convert, 11 November 1965.
76. Interview with a member of Friends Africa Mission, 11 November 1965.
77. *East African Standard*, 8 March 1948.
78. Interview with Pascal Nabwana, 14 March 1965.

79. Interview with a schoolboy, 11 November 1965.
80. Marya Mannes, *More in Anger*, (J. B. Lippencott, Philadelphia, 1958), p. 21.
81. Taban Lo Liyong, Traditional African Literature, *The Last Word*, (East African Publishing House, Nairobi, 1969), p. 76.
82. KNA:DC/NN10/1/5. Letter from the district commissioner, North Nyanza to provincial commissioner K. L. Hunter, 9 December 1949.
83. KNA:DC/NN10/1/5. Special Intelligence Report, North Nyanza, on Dini ya Msambwa, 6 December 1949.
84. See above, pp. 44–5.
85. Much of the information on Masinde comes from conversations with Nabwana and Wekuke. There were some inconsistencies in the date of birth, number of children, etc., but there was general agreement on his traits, style of life, and activities.
86. Farson, *Last Chance in Africa*, p. 236.
87. Wagner, The Political Organization, pp. 231–32. Also, La Fontaine, *The Gisu of Uganda*, p. 32.
88. Interview with the owner of Elgon Star Hotel, Kimilili, 16 March 1965.
89. KNA:DC/NN10/1/5. Letter from E.R.N. Cooke, Mathari Mental Hospital to the provincial commissioner of Nyanza, 17 June 1946.
90. KNA:DC/NN10/1/5. Letter from J. C. Carothers, Mathari Mental Hospital to the provincial commissioner of Nyanza, 6 December 1946.
91. See Appendix E for a copy of this letter.
92. We cannot discuss in the text all Msambwa's activities. A more detailed account is presented in Appendix G in order to provide some gauge of the intensity as well as the direction of Msambwa's anti-colonial thrust. Episodes discussed here will be re-listed in order to further this aim.
93. Rosberg and Nottingham, *Myth of 'Mau Mau'*, p. 201.
94. KNA:DC/NN10/1/2. Letter from the assistant superintendent of police, G. M. Taylor to the superintendent of police, Nakuru, 6 November 1946.
95. KNA:DC/NN10/1/2. Letter from the provincial commissioner to the chief secretary, 4 November 1946. Quoted in de Wolf, 'Religious Innovation', p. 138.
96. KNA:DC/NN10/1/2. Excerpt from a letter by the provincial commissioner, Nyanza, 8 November 1946 to the honourable chief secretary, Nairobi.
97. KNA:DC/NN10/1/2. Letter to the labour commissioner, 23 January 1948. Signature not distinguishable.
98. KNA:DC/NN10/1/2. Letter from the assistant superintendent of police, G. M. Taylor to the superintendent of police, Rift Valley, 6 November 1946.
99. KNA:DC/NN10/1/5. Kitosh Intelligence Reports, 15 November, 2, 6 December 1949. For brevity, excerpts from several letters have been combined.
100. KNA:DC/NN10/1/2. Letter from the assistant superintendent of police, D. C. Connor to the superintendent of police, 16 February 1948.
101. KNA:DC/NN10/1/5. Letter from the assistant superintendent of police, Rift Valley Province on 5 November 1946. See de Wolf, Religious Innovation, p. 34, for a similar statement.
102. KNA:DC/NN10/1/2. A Special Intelligence Report on the Bukusu Union.
103. *Trans Nzoia District Annual Report 1955.*
104. KNA:EN/15. Kavujai Handing Over Notes by Mr. C. Campbell to Mr. J. S. S. Rowlands, July 1950.
105. de Wolf, 'Religious Innovation', p. 156.
106. See above, pp. 103–110.
107. Interview with Wekuke, 9 November 1965.
108. Jamani Vincent brought this point to my attention.

109.   KNA:DC/NN10/1/5. Provincial commissioner of Nyanza, K. L. Hunter's report on the burning down of Mr. Bickford's house sent to the honour able chief secretary, 26 January 1945.

110.   KNA:DC/NN10/1/5. Letter from district officer N. F. Kennaway to the district commissioner of North Nyanza, 11 December 1944.

111.   KNA:DC/NN10/1/5. Twenty-five years later this is still a sensitive issue in Western Province as seen by the remarks of an Assistant Minister for Agriculture, Mr. Wanjigi, who said that the order permitting the killing of stray dogs in a 'rabies area was not designed to prevent people from keeping dogs and cats but they must have them vaccinated. The order could be lifted sooner if people would respond more positively to the Veterinary Department's annual vaccinations'. *East African Standard*, 16 November 1973.

112.   KNA:DC/NN10/1/2. Letter from the district commissioner, North Nyanza to the provincial commissioner of Nyanza, 4 March 1947.

113.   KNA:DC/NN10/1/2. A Special Intelligence Report on the Bukusu Union from the office of the assistant superintendent of police, Eldoret, 5 November 1946.

114.   When working for the Agricultural Department at Kitale, Nabwana was described by the district commissioner as 'the leading light of the soil conservation service.' He was credited with efforts to improve water supplies and construct dams. His opposition to the government may have stemmed from his being fired, though from notes of administrators, his opposition seemed to have been the main reason for his firing.

115.   See above, pp. 104–105.

116.   KNA:DC/NN10/1/5. Safari Report of I. Okwirry, North Nyanza to the district commissioner, North Nyanza, 16 December 1949.

117.   R. M. A. van Zwanenberg, The Land Question in Kenya from the Nineteenth Century to the Present Day, p. 22.

118.   See 'Political Associations', in Rotberg and Mazrui (eds.), *Protest and Power in Black Africa*, pp. 635–38. Though Lonsdale's criticism pertains to the problems raised among the Luo, it is applicable to the Luhya since they were involved in basically the same programme.

119.   Norman Humphrey, *The Liguru and the Land*, (Government Printer, Nairobi, 1947), p. iii.

120.   Iliffe, 'The Organization of the Maji Maji Rebellion'.

121.   Lionel Cliffe, 'The Effect of Opposition to Enforced Agricultural Improvement in Tanganyika During the Colonial Period', EASSC Paper, Kampala, December, 1964.

122.   Wambaa and King, 'The Political Economy of the Rift Valley', pp. 12–13; Rosberg and Nottingham, *The Myth of 'Mau Mau'*, pp. 243–44, 252–59.

123.   Sorrenson, *Origins of European Settlement*, p. 260.

124.   Wagner, *The Abaluyia of Kavirondo*, pp. 43–4.

125.   Interview on 11 November 1965.

126.   Interview on 12 November 1965.

127.   Interview on 15 March 1965.

128.   *East African Standard*, 8 May 1948 and *Inquiry Into the Affray at Kolloa, Baringo*, p. 2.

129.   Interview with Benjamin Wekuke, 9 November 1965. Wekuke's version was somewhat different from that of the superintendent of police who reported that Wekuke and three Dini ya Msambwa members patrolled the township demanding that prices be reduced and that invoices be produced for all goods purchased. The Asians were willing to comply with the latter but the superintendent said that calling for lower prices was 'ridiculous' since most of the goods already were under priced.

130.   KNA:DC/NN10/1/2. Intelligence Report, December 1946.

131.   *Ibid*.

132.   L. C. Usher-Wilson, 'Bishop's Study of 'Dini ya Misambwa',' *East Africa and Rhodesia*, 15 November 1951, p. 282.

133. KNA:DC/NN10/1/5. Letter from district officer N. F. Kennaway of North Kavirondo entitled, Report of Burning of Assistant Agricultural Officer's House at Kimilili, to the district commissioner, North Kavirondo, 11 December 1944.
134. Oginga Odinga, *Not Yet Uhuru*, (Heinemann, Nairobi, 1967), p. 71.
135. Interview with Wekuke, 9 November 1965.
136. van Zwanenberg discusses the ways in which labourers were controlled. 'When a man arrived at work, if he did not like either the work or the conditions, and had the courage and presence of mind to ask for changes, his employer could refuse and there was nothing the employee could do but desert, i.e. leave the employment. Desertion, as this practice was called, was a simple form of industrial action; but to the employer it could not be tolerated if his own bargaining position was to be made as absolute as possible. Between 1920 and 1925 desertion was made a criminal offence, and an employer did not even have to charge a man to have him brought back. After 1925 desertion was made into a civil offence, but in practice this change seems to have made little difference as long as District and Labour Officers were sympathetic to the employer. A practice grew up whereby a headman was informed of a desertion in his district and was asked to have the man returned.' R. M. A. van Zwanenberg, 'The Economic Response of Kenya Africans to European Settlement: 1903–1939', Bethwell A. Ogot (ed.), *Politics and Nationalism in Colonial Kenya*, pp. 213–14. Also see above pp. 104–105.
137. Interview with Wekuke, 9 November 1965.
138. Interview with Nabwana, 1 November 1969.
139. *Report of the Commission of Inquiry into the Affray at Kolloa, Baringo*, (Government Printer, Nairobi, 1951).
140. Foran, *The Kenya Police*, p. 147.
141. Interview with Wafula, 13 March 1965.
142. Interview with Wekuke, 9 November 1965.
143. de Wolf, 'Religious Innovation', pp. 88–9.
144. KNA:DC/NN10/1/5. Letter from the district commissioner, North Nyanza to the district officer, Kavujai, 5 July 1949.
145. KNA:DC/NN10/1/2. Letter from Jason Matete to the honourable chief native commissioner, 21 May 1947. Ochieng discusses both the positive and negative aspects of chiefs. He points out that to some of their subjects, particularly to the 'newly and half-educated mission boys,' chiefs were symbols of oppression, exploitation and alien rule. William R. Ochieng, 'Colonial African Chiefs—Were they primarily Self-Seeking Scoundrels?' in Bethwell A. Ogot (ed.), *Politics and Nationalism in Colonial Kenya*, pp. 46–70, in particular, p. 53.
146. Lonsdale, Political Associations, p. 591.
147. See above, p. 102–103.
148. KNA:DC/NN10/1/5. Letter from district officer N. F. Kennaway to the district commissioner, North Nyanza, 11 December 1944.
149. KNA:DC/NN10/1/2. Letter from the district commissioner of North Nyanza to the honourable chief secretary, Nairobi, 8 November 1946.
150. KNA:DC/NN10/1/5. Letter to the district officer, Kavujai to the district commissioner, Kakamega, 30 June 1949.
151. KNA:DC/NN10/1/2. A Special Intelligence Report on the Bukusu Union.
152. KNA:DC/NN10/1/5. Report from the district officer, Kavujai to the district commissioner, Kakamega, 2 July 1949.
153. KNA:DC/NN10/1/2. A Special Intelligence Report on the Bukusu Union.
154. Information from Wekuke, Wafula and Banda, 2 and 3 November 1969.
155. A number of letters and reports indicate this belief. See the following: KNA:DC/NN10/1/5. Letter from district officer John Simpson, Kavujai, to the district commissioner, Kakamega, 1 June 1949. KNA:DC/NN10/1/2.

2. Letter from the assistant superintendent of police, D. C. Connor, to the superintendent of police, Nakuru, 4 December 1947. KNA:DC/NN10/1/5. Intelligence Report from the District Officer's Files, Kimilili, 15 May 1961. In the last file mentioned, the district officer, Kavujai wrote to the district commissioner, Kakamega on 2 July 1949, 'I am personally slightly suspicious of Pascal Nabwana although I have nothing against him, unless it be that he makes himself out to be rather too perfect. However, it would be unwise to ignore him. He is paid considerable respect by the common people and evidently has great influence. It would be better to have him as a friend than an enemy.'

156. KNA:DC/NN10/1/5. Letter from the provincial commissioner to the honourable chief secretary, 4 July 1949.
157. Interview with Nabwana, 14 March 1965.
158. KNA:DC/NN10/1/5. Letter from the district officer, Kavujai to the district commissioner, Kakamega, 2 July 1949.
159. KNA:DC/NN10/1/5. Letter from district officer Simpson, Kavujai to the district commissioner, Kakamega, 30 June 1949.

Nabwana reiterated his non-involvement with Dini ya Msambwa, when I spoke with him in 1966. He claimed that the chiefs who didn't like him had reported that he was the leader. To the question, why did the British think the Bukusu Union was mixed up with Msambwa, he replied, 'They thought so because I was a leader in the educational field. The government thought Msambwa was being organized secretly by the Bukusu Union and that it had connections with KAU. I could take my students to the Kenya Teacher's College which was run by Kenyatta and Koinange.'

I am inclined to put more reliance on data collected by the administration in the pre-independence period than I am on Nabwana's explanation in the post-colonial period. There were reasons why Nabwana, a respected elder of the Roman Catholic Church would not want me, a European, to know of his previous involvement with Dini ya Msambwa. Nabwana had every reason at that point in his career to associate himself with the forces of law and order and to dissociate himself from Masinde who in the post-colonial period had little support. (The above quotations are from interviews with Nabwana on 14 March and 3 November 1965.)

In 1969, I revisited Kimilili shortly after the government had banned the opposition party, the Kenya People's Union, led by Oginga Odinga. Odinga and the main leaders had been arrested and it was feared that local level leadership would be next. The Kenya People's Union was strong in the Mount Elgon area with Nabwana the district leader. I arrived at Nabwana's home just behind a messenger informing him that he was slated to be arrested. (This did not lessen his welcome, nor did I learn until later that he had received such a message.) Within the next day or two, he visited the district commissioner and made amends. A veteran politician, Nabwana in independent Kenya was still working his way through the hazardous game of politics.

160. Interview on 23 October 1969.
161. de Wolf, 'Religious Innovation', p. 130.
162. KNA:DC/NN10/1/5. Letter from district commissioner Colin Campbell of North Nyanza to the provincial commissioner, 22 June 1949.
163. Interviews with Moses Banda, 3 November 1969 and Nabwana, 2 November 1969.
164. Interview with Nabwana, 3 November 1965.
165. *Ibid.*
166. KNA:DC/NN1/29. *North Kavirondo District Annual Report, 1947.*
167. Lonsdale, Some Origins of Nationalism, footnote 91.
168. KNA:DC/NN1/1/33. *North Nyanza District Annual Report, 1951.*
169. KNA:DC/NN1/1/34. *North Nyanza District Annual Report, 1952.*
170. Rosberg and Nottingham, *Myth of 'Mau Mau'*, p. 275.

171.   KNA:DC/NN1/1/34. *North Nyanza District Annual Report 1952*.
172.   Quotations from two interviews with Nabwana on 14 March and 3 November 1965 have been combined.
173.   Quotations from two interviews with Wekuke on 9 and 13 November 1965 have been combined.
174.   La Fontaine, 'Notes on Ancestor Worship'.
175.   My data and de Wolf's 'Religious Innovations', p. 141 agree on the smoking of bhang. Wolf's assistant claimed that he did not know a single member who did not smoke it.
176.   A former Dini ya Msambwa member spoke of a visit with Masinde who was smoking bhang and drinking. 'After drinking he brought *bhangi* and a pipe and he started to smoke it. He offered me the pipe and I smoked. When he was smoking I heard him calling the ancestors' names, "so-and-so, you are a very good prophet, I smoke in thy name." He called several names saying, "so-and-so, you are a great warrior. You fought until you won. We Bukusu shall not forget." He carried on smoking and calling to the different ancestors . . . until he was very high.'
177.   See above, pp. 52, 70, 94.
178.   DC/NN10/1/5 and *Inquiry into the Affray at Kolloa, Baringo*, p. 2.
179.   *The West Suk District Annual Report 1949*, states, 'The teachers of DyM have . . . little idea of what they were teaching and their habit of getting small girls to attend the meetings and then having illicit carnal knowledge of them has been proved.' (KNA:WP/4).

   In 1950, an Intelligence Report for West Suk stated, 'On 17–18 March a successful raid in the Tarter area was carried out by the Tribal Police under the DC and the Assistant Agricultural Officer. Alleged members of DyM were found in a cave in varying states of nudity at 23.30 hours on a chilly night.' (KNA:WP/4).

   According to a government report of January 1955, eleven Pokot men and women were arrested who had taken part in a ceremony in Karita location. Songs were sung followed by 'universal and incestuous copulation on a command of the teacher.' (KNA:TN/Z).

   The West Suk District Annual Report 1955 mentions the 'sexual and often incestuous initiation rite' of Dini ya Yomot. (KNA:WP/4).
180.   See below, p. 273.
181.   La Fontaine, *The Gisu of Uganda*, pp. 34–5.
182.   See below pp. 270–75.
183.   See below, pp. 281–85.
184.   See below, p. 286.
185.   La Fontaine, 'Notes on Ancestor Worship'.
186.   Welime, 'Dini ya Msambwa'.
187.   de Wolf, 'Religious Innovation', pp. 146–47.

Chapter 12

DINI YA MSAMBWA AMONG THE POKOT

T H E administration's belief that it had by 1949 effectively controlled Msambwa was shattered by a clash of several hundred Pokot tribesmen with a government party at Kolloa in 1950. The Kolloa Affray, as it came to be known, was an event that deeply shook the administration as much for its unexpectedness as for its violence. Until that incident, the administration was confident that all was well in that peaceful, little-policed area.[1] It was totally unaware that the members of this tribe who had always paid their taxes regularly and had appeared at *barazas* proudly garbed in ostrich plumed headdresses and carrying long spears harboured any anti-British feelings.

The Pokot, also known as Suk, along with the Nandi, Sabaot, Tugen, Kipsigis and Marakwet (the main groups) form a larger ethnic grouping called Kalenjin. The Pokot live northeast of Mount Elgon in the West Pokot and Baringo Districts. The West Pokot District covers an area of 3,000 square miles and its inhabitants at that time numbered 42,777, of which roughly 60 per cent were pastoralists and 40 per cent agriculturalists. Kitale and the European settled area lay to the south. To the north stretched Turkana country, a sandy desert peopled by the remote Turkana tribe, and to the west, Uganda. The East Pokot, who were involved in the clash, occupy the northern half of the Baringo District, an area a little larger in size than West Pokot. They numbered about seven thousand and lived a nomadic life roaming the plains in search of water and grazing for their herds. Left relatively undisturbed by the colonial regime, they had continued their traditional style of life. They were attacked over the years by more aggressive tribes like the Turkana and they had even welcomed government protection. The pastoralists looked with disdain upon the other section of the tribe, the agriculturalists, some of whom worked on settlers' farms in the Trans Nzoia. Long thought to be the most backward and tradition-oriented people in that region, they had in the 1940s begun to show an interest in education and had even subscribed money for a school.

Among the Pokot, the movement was known as Dini ya Msango, their pronunciation of Msambwa. It will be referred to here as Msango in order to distinguish it from the main body. Still another name was Dini ya Yomot. In Pokot, *yomot* means 'hot-air', and could refer to the practice common among Nyanzan sects of 'getting the spirit'.

Dini ya Msambwa among the Pokot had only a slight connection with the main body. Supported by a different tribe and separated by more than fifty miles from its usual Kimilili-Kitale 'battleground', it is doubtful if the main leaders had any but the barest knowledge of its existence. Its self-appointed leader, Lukas Pkech, appears to have had no contact with the headquarters except for the time of his conversion. His claim to be the son of God would certainly have been rejected by Masinde and his cohorts, as two sons of God in one movement would have been rather overpowering.

Msambwa demonstrates a phenomenon common among African movements of autonomous groups bearing the same name but with few links to each other. Movements penetrate various tribes and become 'indigenized', that is, they are changed to fit the customs and beliefs of a particular tribe. Only nominally are they all part of the same movement.

Lukas Pkech was born in 1915 in West Pokot.[2] He entered the government school at Kapenguria in 1932 and while there was converted to Roman Catholicism. In 1934 he went to the government's Native Industrial Training Department near Nairobi, where he trained as a tailor for two years and as a blacksmith for another two years. He returned to the Kapenguria area in 1938 where he cultivated a *shamba* and worked as a blacksmith until 1946, when he went to Bukusu country.

There he met Masinde and joined Dini ya Msambwa. He returned to his home, began to proselytize and acquired a few converts. Twice he was up before the district commissioner who warned him about his Msango activities. Later he had an affair with the wife of a tribesman. The outraged husband informed the police about Msango, whereupon Pkech was arrested along with fifteen followers during a meeting. On 18 August 1948, he was convicted of being a member of an unlawful society and sentenced to thirty months imprisonment with hard labour. He had been in jail at Nakuru for about a year when he was transferred to a labour camp halfway between there and Gilgil. Twelve days later he escaped and returned to East Pokot in northern Baringo where he travelled from place to place telling people about Msango.

Pkech's message, although similar to Masinde's, had a slightly different accent. The followers were promised land, cattle, eternal life, and freedom from taxation. The blind would see, the sick would be cured, and barren women would bear children. Pkech told his followers that he would take them to a place called Karossi where there were great rocks and much smoke coming from the hills. He would clap his hands and a cave would open before them filled with all kinds of wonderful things they had never before seen.[3]

Pkech, like Masinde, exhorted a return to the old religion, but for him it meant a return to Pokot and not Bukusu beliefs. (Since the missions had made no impact upon the Pokot, it was not a return in the sense of leaving Christianity for indigenous beliefs. Pkech may have been trying to revitalize some indigenous beliefs or it may simply be that the reporting of what he was teaching has been inaccurate.) He also prophesied that the Europeans would soon be expelled from the country. 'You sing these songs and the Europeans will leave', he told his followers.[4] At one gathering he sang:

> Who is our enemy? Is it not the white people?
> They began by killing many of us. They teach
> us bad things. Don't listen to this white man
> [referring to Collins, a missionary]. He is our enemy.
> Haven't we got a god? We pray to you Jehova.
> Who is Jesus? The *wazungus* say he is god but
> how could he be if he died?

The followers replied, 'We will overcome by our strength.'[5]

Shaven heads and the wearing of cowrie shells by men (traditionally worn only by women) were their insignia. Everlasting life was ensured by making cuts on the stomach and backs of the hands into which some medicine was rubbed. Sacrifices were often made of a goat or an ox, probably derived from the Pokot custom of sacrificing an animal to assure fertility and to ward off disease.[6] Initiation rights, allegedly consisted of copulation, often incestuous, on the instructions of a teacher. The free love ritual was said to have great attraction for the women who were normally not permitted to take part in tribal ceremonies.[7]

Toward the end of January 1950, Pkech conducted a drive for converts among the East Pokot. The authorities first heard of his whereabouts from Thomas Collins, an African Inland Church missionary. Collins reported that several hundred Pokot had sung and danced all the night of 21 April and on into the next day. Many of those present, he said, were in a state of 'frenzy'. As it was the time of the year for circumcision, it was not unusual for young people to be highly excited. Collins and his wife walked among those gathered and were told by a young Pokot that they were practising their 'religion of long ago' and that it was a better religion than the missionaries taught. Anti-European songs were sung. (The Collins' had lived for several years in the area and had unsuccessfully tried to win converts.) Later during the trial, a convert recalled that Pkech had told them to rest and eat, for the next day they were going to Zion where they would receive everything they wanted.[8]

On 22 April the district commissioner of Baringo, A. D. Simpson, spoke with Collins. Simpson took a grave view of Collins' account, sent a letter to the assistant inspector of police at Eldama Ravine, and dispatched two tribal policemen to follow the pilgrims and, if possible, to arrest Pkech who was again spreading the 'seditious teaching' of the proscribed Msambwa. Later the two policemen reported that their attempts to arrest Pkech were countenanced by threats from his followers. Simpson then requested more reinforcements. (The specific events leading up to the skirmish will be dealt with in some detail in order to probe into motives and degree of planning involved.)

The next morning the assistant inspector of police, R. G. Cameron, arrived with fifteen African police at Nginyang where the district commissioner was encamped and reported that the assistant superintendent of police, G. M. Taylor of Nakuru, was on his way to join them with twenty more policemen. An airplane flew overhead and dropped a message from the headquarters in Nairobi giving various code signals. The ground party signalled, 'All's well. No further reinforcements needed.'

That night Simpson, Taylor and Cameron made their plans. The goal was to arrest Pkech and to disperse his followers. It seems clear from the evidence that this was to be accomplished, if at all possible, without bloodshed. District commissioner Simpson said later at the investigation, 'Our object was still the same, but that if we could not arrest Lukas without shedding Suk blood, with provocation from the Suk, we would have to let him escape and concentrate on dispersing the Suk peacefully if possible.'[9] Taylor's notes made the night before the attack read, 'Send envoys ahead to parley with leader unarmed. If party comes back armed to be told when they reach a certain distance to lay down their arms; if they were coming on armed then order fire.'[10] The provincial commissioner of the Rift Valley, D. L. Morgan and the senior superintendent of police, K. P. Hadingham, arrived, approved the plans, and returned to their base at Nakuru.

At dawn on 24 April, the force took to the road. It consisted of four Europeans, forty armed African police, two chiefs, five of their followers and two drivers — in all, fifty-three. The Police Emergency Company stood by. The party travelled northwest over rugged countryside and reached Kolloa on the border of Elgeyo Marakwet and Baringo Districts around mid-afternoon. It stopped when the beating of drums was heard. The Pokot were singing and dancing among some trees just off the road. The government party took up a position in a clearing facing the Pokot. Orders were given to load and fix bayonets. The chiefs, Lobon and Ngeleyo, advanced to speak with Pkech.

After some twenty minutes, the chiefs returned and reported that there were about five hundred armed men. (Another estimate was three hundred.) They brought a letter from Pkech which, though hard to understand, said that if the district commissioner's bullets could kill him, the district commissioner could come and take his followers but if he (Pkech) was able to withstand the bullets then he would keep them. Pkech added that if any fighting developed, it would not be his group who began it.[11] A follower also told a chief that they were not making war but travelling in peace to pray to God. He pointed to the west.

The district commissioner decided that they should call for another force to intercept Pkech, while they kept in touch with him from the rear.[12] In the meantime they would withdraw down the road for the night. He then sat down to draft a reply. He was translating it into Swahili when he heard a shout from the police line that the Pokot were advancing. Later he recalled:

I was sitting at a table behind the lorry, and did not see the actual first movement. I came out from behind the lorry and saw a party of Suk tribesmen moving towards us, but still in the bush. They were dancing and jumping up and down with their spears and were behaving in the same way as they always do behave when the DC arrives in camp, and they come to greet him. Mr. Taylor started to give an order to fire. As chiefs Lobon and Ngeleyo with two or three of their followers had, by then, got to the front of the Suk on the edge of the bush, I told Taylor not to fire, and rushed forward with the interpreter screaming at them in Swahili to put down their arms. The interpreter was also screaming at the Suk. The chiefs and myself seemed to be having some success when one man with a shield rushed forward. At the same time the edges of the group of spearsmen which I estimated at about two hundred and fifty to three hundred strong started fanning out. I turned around screaming to Mr. Taylor to fire and raced back behind the police line with Chepkurgat. The chiefs rushed away to the side to the south. It is possible Mr. Taylor gave the order to fire a second time and I told him not to but this is only to the best of my re-collection and I am not sure about this point. I did not see who the front man was. As far as I can remember, I ran between two policemen when I ran back. When I screamed at Taylor to fire, he opened fire as soon as I shouted. I got behind the police line and turned round and it seemed that the firing was good as Suk seemed to be dropping hard in front of us. . . .[13]

Kinyanjui, the driver, gave a similar account.[14]

Simpson heard cries for ammunition coming from the right of the line. He saw about fifteen Pokot coming towards him. A tribal policeman who had been in front of him turned and ran past. Simpson shouted to the man to stop but the order was ignored. The Pokot were then twenty-five to thirty-five yards away though two were much closer. Still no spears were thrown. Simpson looked to his right and could not see any police. He decided that he must run for it and did so as fast as possible until he fell into a dry river bed about a hundred yards from the lorries.

In the river bed three or four police were fighting several Pokot with their bayonets. Simpson climbing out on the far bank, ran a few yards, turned, and saw a Pokot about eight paces distant aiming a spear at him. He shot him. He then saw a Pokot and a policeman in a hand-to-hand fight and killed the Pokot. He and several policemen retreated about a hundred and fifty yards from the river bed, where they found sergeant Kipsoi trying to rally his men. They decided to work their way back to the lorries in order to secure more amunition. Another group set off to search for missing members of their party. The bodies of Cameron, Taylor, Stevens, and the police corporal, Kipkoge Kibirir, were found. Pkech and twenty-eight followers were killed and another fifty wounded.[15]

In the subsequent investigation the government and the Commission of Inquiry argued that the Pokot planned and carried out the attack. While this interpretation would support my thesis of Msambwa's militancy, the evidence hardly supports such an interpretation, or, it is at least debatable for the following reasons.

1) According to Collins, the Pokot were making unusual preparations. The preparations could have been for battle (as Collins thought) or for their pilgrimage to Mount Elgon. Collins noted an air of truculence about them but this was not unusual for Msambwa's members.

2) Considerable evidence points to lack of intent on the part of the Pokot. Even district commissioner Simpson in his report to the provincial commissioner noted:

> I consider that in converting the Suk to his religion he [Pkech] did not at first stress the European slaughter aspect. From information available at the moment it seems as if even on the fatal day of April 24 the Suk who attacked us may not have known that this was Lukas' intention when he brought them out of their camping place at Kolloa. I gave the following reasons for this:
>
> a. When Chief Ngeleyo was trying to instill reason into the Suk at Kolloa he reported that the sub-headman from Karossi who had joined the movement got up and said that he and the others *were not taking war anywhere but were going in peace to pray to God*.
>
> b. When the band of Suk warriors appeared beyond the edge of the bush, *it was not deployed for battle but was in a bunch with the Suk dancing and singing as they always do when there are many of them together*.
>
> c. Of the 30 odd spears collected from the field of battle the same evening *at least a third still had their leather blade guards on*.[16] (Italics mine.)

Surely if an attack had been planned the warriors would not have charged with the blade guards on their spears! A number of Pokot, including the leader, maintained right up until the encounter that they were engaged in a pilgrimage and not a battle. Simpson thought they were advancing to greet him and this may well have been their intention.

3) Inadequate communication between the government party and the Pokot led to confusion. The district commissioner had difficulty in understanding Pkech's note and the government party was undoubtedly getting nervous as the Pokot advanced.

4) In the inquiry that followed, since Europeans were investigating Europeans, and considering the serious losses sustained by the

government party after its elaborate preparations, it would have been highly embarrassing to argue other than that the Pokot attacked first.

The evidence is inconclusive as to which group was the aggressor. The district commissioner and Kinyanjui stated that their side fired first upon the advancing Pokot. If the actual aggressive act indicates the aggressor then the British must be chosen, though it should be remembered that in order to hurl a spear, one has to be within a certain range of the object. But neither the government nor the Pokot apparently planned to fight. The administration appeared genuinely interested in arresting Pkech without bloodshed. Pkech's group, which included women and children, were on a religious pilgrimage and probably did not expect to meet any opposition.[17] On the other hand, the Pokot might have felt it was unnecessary to make any preparations because they believed themselves immune to bullets. Pkech's note suggested that he felt himself to be immune and this belief may have been shared by his followers.

My interpretation would be that since both sides were undoubtedly nervous, it took only the appearance of aggression on the part of either to set off the skirmish, and who fired the first shot or hurled the first spear is not of utmost importance. With inadequate communication, jittery nerves, and armed men, some action, insignificant in itself, triggered off the outburst and before either side knew what was happening the battle was on.

The administration, shocked at this eruption, severely punished the Pokot. A hundred and twenty-three Pokot were prosecuted for being members of Msambwa. A levy force, consisting of an assistant superintendent of police, two European inspectors, and seventy African policemen, whose maintenance the tribe had to bear, was assigned to disarm them.[18] The young warriors resisted disarming and told the elders to mind their own business and let them deal with things. Some spears were handed in, but many were hidden.[19] A fine of five thousand head of cattle was imposed and compulsory labour exacted. The latter accomplished the building of many miles of roads, an airstrip, a dispensary and chief's offices. Twenty-two were convicted of murder, though in the end, through appeals, commuting to lighter sentences and acquittals, seven were eventually hanged.[20]

After six months of taking Pokot cattle, the assistant superintendent of police asked that the quota be considerably reduced. Evidence showed that the Pokot did not have as many cattle as assumed and by exacting the quota, their supply would have been depleted:

> We shall, surely be defeating our own ends by impoverishing the Suk to an extent when Mr. F. Brockway's [a Labour Member of Parliament in England who backed African causes] statement to the effect that the Suk are suffering from economic repression might begin to have the seeds of truth. . . . If we reach this stage I think we might expect trouble. . . . The only blessing that the East Suk have received from our vaunted civilization is a mediocre school at Nginyang and a poorly stocked and unsupervised dispensary at Tangulbwe.[21]

A year after the Affray, the district was considered quiet enough to remove the levy force. Four hundred Pokot gathered at a *baraza* to hear the provincial commissioner read a message from the Governor in which he commended them for all the work that had been accomplished through the use of forced labour.

Among the Pokot, small groups of Msango members continued to meet even after the Affray. During 1950 an additional 249 persons were prosecuted for being members of a proscribed society. During July the inhabitants of West Pokot turned over a Msango cell to the police. The provincial commissioner took this as evidence that the people had had enough of Msango and were no longer being fooled by its preachings.[22] In his Handing Over Report, district officer Simpson wrote, 'To the best of my knowledge the East Suk have "had" Dini ya Msambwa. The Kolloa murderers have either been hanged, jailed or released on account of their tender years.'[23] In December 1950, a party of twenty-one men and fifteen women were arrested at Mount Mtelo by the local people.

In 1954 and 1955, there were rumours of Msango activity in West Pokot and across the border in Uganda. Secret meetings of up to fifteen people were reported to be taking place in river beds far away from the participants' homes.[24] Suspects were arrested sporadically. Pkech's old lieutenants were said to have been active around Kapenguria, Riwa, Kipkome and Mutonyi.

In 1955-56 intelligence revealed that the movement was continuing underground throughout a large part of West Pokot. A wave of murders that looked like witch killings had occurred and were suspected of having Msango backing. The victims were either alleged witches or informers. There was also some opposition to a stock census. Twelve additional tribal police were recruited to

West Pokot and three hundred people convicted. The entire male population of some locations was conscripted for communal labour.[25] There were no disturbances, however, in East Pokot. In 1956, three hundred members, led by an old blind woman called Chepkucia, were arrested. . . . In jail she expressed a willingness to reform. Upon her release she preached the Christian doctrine and robbed the movement of even more support. In May 1960, the Governor, Sir Patrick Renison, said that if the Suk District remained peaceful, the few members of Dini ya Msango still in custody would soon be freed. After the 1950s little more was heard of Msango among the Pokot.

Interpretation and Conclusions

While both the administration and Kipkorir[26] maintain that Pkech intentionally misled the Pokot with promises of wealth and miraculous cures, the data suggest another possibility. Instead of exploiting the Pokot for his own ends, Pkech may have believed in his divine mission and even in his immunity to bullets. His note to the district commissioner and his behaviour immediately before the clash suggest this interpretation.

Secondly, the movement may well have had an economic base. For one thing, the Pokot strongly objected to the government's efforts to make them destock. Stock reduction not only threatened their economic interests as they saw them, but since cattle were the focus of so many of their daily interests, destocking undermined the basis of important activities and sentiments. In fact, due to their opposition the programme collapsed in 1950.[27]

Also, it should be noted, some prominent Pokot supported the movement. Several chiefs and their wives were members. (Chief Lobon was reported to have welcomed Pkech and his assistants into his area and to have fed them from the time of their arrival in January until the Affray in April. Chief Lomeri also supported it.[28]) Obviously, if the chiefs had opposed it or, at least, had informed the administration, the movement could not have made such headway. Additionally, the movement's ability to continue underground for some time after the Affray suggests some commitment on the part of members. Unfortunately, the data on Msango's support is inconclusive.

In conclusion, both Msambwa and Msango preached the abolition of alien rule but the former dealt with it far more realistically.

Among the Pokot, the wish-fulfilment aspects of the message were uppermost. While the millennium theme was also evident in Masinde's teachings, it was de-emphasized, or at least not permitted to dominate. The Pokot, in contrast, apparently preoccupied with expressive activities, undertook little practical action to oust the colonialists. Even the Affray appeared to be more accidental than planned.

The different orientations of Msambwa and Msango, though both had political and religious dimensions, and activities with expressive and instrumental significance for their members, may be due to the different levels of political sophistication to be found among the Bukusu and the Pokot. The Bukusu were much more politically advanced in terms of nationalistic aspirations and political tactics than the East Pokot, who lived a traditional life in an area not only geographically remote but ideologically removed from current political ideas.

This event, occurring among a tribe thought to be peaceful, and at a time when Kikuyu nationalism was becoming threatening, undoubtedly increased the apprehension of the British, as it suggested underlying ferment that might erupt at any time. Should this have occurred simultaneously in several areas it would have been exceedingly difficult to control without a much greater investment in resources.

Notes

1. I examined the *Baringo District Annual Reports* from 1940 to 1950 and found no mention of Dini ya Msambwa. In fact, the district commissioner in the 1950 Report stated: 'Until that Kolloa incident there was no evidence whatsoever that the society of Dini ya Msambwa had been active in the East Suk location.' The Pokot in Baringo District are also known as East Suk, in contrast to the West Suk who live in the West Pokot District.
2. This discussion is based on the following: *Report of the Commission of Inquiry into the Affray at Kolloa, Baringo*, administrative records; Foran, *The Kenya Police*, pp. 164–71; and accounts from the *East African Standard*.
3. *East African Standard*, 17 June 1950. Article entitled, 'Baringo Inquiry Resumed'.
4. *Ibid.*
5. *East African Standard*, 9 June 1950. Article entitled, 'The Baringo Fight Inquiry is On'.

6. KNA:TN/2. A Report on Dini ya Msambwa among the Pokot. No heading.
7. *Ibid.*
8. *East African Standard,* 17 June 1950.
9. *East African Standard,* 3 May 1950.
10. Quoted in Foran, *The Kenya Police,* p. 167.
11. *Ibid.,* p. 168.
12. *Ibid.*
13. From evidence given by Simpson at the *Inquiry into the Affray at Kolloa, Baringo.*
14. KNA:BAR/8. Based on unsworn statement by the driver, Kinyanjui, on 26 May 1950.
15. Official Government Press Office Handout No. 248, Nairobi, 12 September 1951.
16. KNA:BAR/8. Report of district commissioner Simpson to the provincial commissioner, Rift Valley, on the Suk disturbances, 6 May 1950.
17. My and Kipkorir's interpretation, written quite independently of each other, come to the same conclusion, namely that neither the British nor the Pokot planned to fight and that the first outright aggressive act came from the British. See Kipkorir, Colonial Response to Crisis. However, the main thrust of his article is just the opposite, that the Pokot challenged and defied British authority, 'The Pokot's defiance—the defiance by a self-proclaimed prophet and a band of three hundred followers—of all that the colonial system stood for: its concept of law and order, its concept of authority and its ontology.' p. 35.
18. *Baringo District Annual Report 1950.*
19. KNA:BAR/8. Letter from the assistant superintendent of police, Baringo Levy Force to the senior superintendent of police, Rift Valley, 10 May 1950.
20. Official Government Press Office Handout No. 248, Nairobi, 12 September 1951.
21. KNA:BAR/8. Letter from the assistant superintendent of police, Baringo Levy Force to the senior superintendent police, Rift Valley, 10 May 1950.
22. KNA:BAR/8. Letter from provincial commissioner D. Morgan, Rift Valley to the honourable chief native commissioner, 24 July 1950.
23. KNA:BAR/9. Handing Over Report of A. B. Simpson to J. A. Cumber, 19 April 1950.
24. KNA:TN/2. A report with no heading on Dini ya Msambwa among the Pokot.
25. KNA:TN/2. Minutes of a Security Meeting on the Suk held at the district commissioner's office, Kitale on 14 May 1955; KNA:WP/4. *West Suk District Annual Report 1955;* KNA:BAR/4. *Baringo District Annual Report 1956.*
26. See above, p. 14.
27. *Baringo District Annual Report, 1950.*
28. *Ibid.*

Chapter 13

BASIS OF SUPPORT

IN this chapter we will examine some factors involved in support for Dini ya Msambwa, the breadth of that support, and two areas that produced particularly strong support.

Ideology in itself is insufficient to explain why people joined. For instance, many said it was to practise the traditional religion, but this they could have done better by remaining at home and practising it with other members of their family as was actually done in the past. Instead, they chose to join Msambwa. We concur entirely with Lipset, Campbell and Pinard who argue that the ideology of a movement may have little meaning or interest for the followers. It may simply require the development of a shared belief which identifies the sources of strain in the system and envisages an overall cure.[1] For example, the colonial authorities and their policies were identified as evil and a new slate of African leaders was substituted who were believed to hold an all-encompassing solution to Africans' problems. Or put another way, beliefs and support do not necessarily correspond. Some members may have known little or even cared about Msambwa's religion. What they did care about was land. Hence their support for a movement that promised them land.

Msambwa's stronghold was in the northern locations, Malakisi, South Bukusu and Kimilili, and to a lesser extent, Elgon of the North Nyanza District. These locations lie south of Mount Elgon and north of the Nzoia River. From that area came its main leaders and numerical strength. Outside the reserve, Msambwa recruited labourers and squatters from the Trans Nzoia and Baringo Districts of the Rift Valley Province particularly from around Kitale, Cherangani, and Hoey's Bridge, all settler areas. The movement moved northward into Pokot country, being especially active among the

East Pokot and to a lesser extent among the West Pokot. On the west, it spread into Gisu country ranging along the western slopes of Mount Elgon on the Uganda-Kenya border. Branches were reported as far away as Mombasa on the coast (more than five hundred miles), and Bombo, just north of Kampala in Uganda. These were probably isolated groups or groupings as there does not seem to be any evidence of a chain of branches extending either eastward to the coast or westwards to Bombo.

Msambwa cut across tribal boundaries, recruiting Luhya, particularly from the Bukusu and Gishu sub-tribes, Nandi, Kipsigis, Pokot and a few Turkana. The Bukusu formed the majority of inhabitants in Kimilili, South Bukusu and Malakisi and they constituted the bulk of the labour force in the Trans Nzoia, though it was a mixed tribal area with four to five thousand Kikuyu.[2]

Msambwa's main leaders were Bukusu ex-mission converts with Masinde and other important leaders living in and around Kimilili. Masinde, Wekuke and Walumoli were former members of Friends Africa Mission who had been deprived of full membership when they took second wives. Donisio Nakimayu, a local leader, had been expelled from a Roman Catholic mission, others had been members of the Church Missionary Society. They had had several years of mission education. Some were employed in the lower echelons of the administration. Three leaders of the Malakisi Riot were employees of the Department of Agriculture. These men, who would be considered educated by local standards, tended to come from the more prosperous areas of the district.

Breadth of Support

Estimates of Dini ya Msambwa's strength vary widely. Wafula said fifty thousand for the main movement, though a newspaper account said fifty thousand for the movement among the Pokot alone. Since Msambwa did not keep a record, estimates are not likely to be accurate.

Administrators' estimates backed by intelligence are valuable in estimating Msambwa's strength. In January 1945, the district commissioner in North Nyanza reported that *most of the people in his vicinity were followers*. Pritchard of the Kenya Police reported in December 1947, 'I have seen men in his [Masinde's] uniform all over the reserve and the number of followers seems to have grown enormously.'[3] The chief native commissioner P. Wyn Harris in

1949 maintained that the young men were 'out of hand' and that there were 'very definite signs of large patches of Dini ya Msambwa in the area.'[5] In 1950, district commissioner C. Campbell explained that since the main tenet of the creed was 'violently anti-European' it was 'therefore *fundamentally attractive to the majority of the population.*'[6] (Italics mine.) And in 1955, district commissioner C. J. Denton concluded that 'there exists among the *Vugusu a considerable sympathy for the aims of Dini ya Msambwa* which were largely of anti-mission and anti-settler nature.'[7] (Italics mine.)

Reports from missions located in Msambwa territory provide first hand accounts of its impact on specific localities. A priest at the Kibabii Roman Catholic Mission wrote in 1948:

> These doctrines and practices get around the country like wildfire. Secret societies spread them by threats, and teachers especially favoured the historical part, teaching it therefore even in mission schools. . . . Teachers left mission schools, became priests in that religion, children joined, women came by crowds, and soon even the chiefs favoured it. The great following gave encouragement, and the prophecies got bolder.[8]

Msambwa's membership appeared largest around 1948-49 when it made serious inroads into mission congregations. An Anglican schoolboy from Bombo wrote:

> Great numbers of my people are believing in this new religion of Elijah. . . . Many Christians have left the church and been converted to this new religion, even school boys and girls. Chiefs are trying to prevent them, but it is rather impossible because the sub-chiefs are not trying to stop them. . . . On Sundays we are only about four or five people taking the service in the church.[9]

Some chiefs and sub-chiefs openly sympathized with Msambwa's goals though at least publicly they maintained that these should be achieved constitutionally, and like several Pokot chiefs did little to stamp it out, failing to inform higher authorities about its presence.

The use of fear and coercion, however, should not be under-estimated. Given Msambwa's warnings of what would happen to collaborators, as well as examples of burned down homes, people justifiably feared reprisals. District reports stress the fear the movement had raised and how local people began to leave their grain in places where it could be easily watched. Provincial commissioner K. L. Hunter, disturbed over the apprehensiveness in the countryside, reported that the people had 'expressed a hope that the camp hut, in which I was spending the night, would not be burnt over my head.'[10] One particularly threatened group were Christian Africans. The district commissioner wrote:

> Father John [pseudonym] . . . is a Luo Roman Catholic priest who has information about the *dini*. . . . It has been arranged with Bishop Hall that we should not contact Father John direct but that he, the Bishop, will pass on to us any information he can get for us. Incidentally, the Bishop considers the *dini* is widespread, is worried about it, and fears for Father John's safety.[11]

As late as 1964–65 people feared Masinde and would not risk openly disobeying him. My stay in the area aroused the hostility of some followers. On several occasions, members highly suspicious of my activities, warned me to 'get out'. Sources of information would suddenly evaporate as people had been ordered not to talk to me. Secret meetings had to be arranged with the 'moderates', as they were afraid to be seen with me.[12]

Since support in numerical terms cannot be ascertained and since in a subversive movement a small cadre of dedicated members can be effective disrupters, the more important question is, did Dini ya Msambwa have the sympathy of the local people? Even though people do not directly participate in subversive acts, their active and tacit cooperation in terms of supplies, succour, information, secure retreats, and weapons' caches is important to a movement's success. From our investigation in Chapter 11 of the issues Msambwa protested and from the stories collected about Masinde, it would appear that he was a popular figure not only in his own neighbourhood but farther afield. When he was being deported to Lamu, the people of Lumbwa turned out *en masse* to greet him.[13] In Mombasa about fifty people attended a meeting to raise funds for his family. Girison Anyaga, the organizer, said, 'He is the father and the mother of our religion, and we must never leave our religion until we die. It doesn't matter what the *wazungus* do to us, they can imprison us, deport all of us, but we must never desert our religion which was started by Elijah.'[14] The fact that Masinde remained hidden for months, yet moved about the countryside when a warrant was out for his arrest likewise suggests that the peasants were on his side. Nor was information given to the authorities about the instigators of particular incidents of arson or other unlawful acts. In a rural community where people knew much about each other's activities, many knew more than they revealed. From the amount of activity

223

and from the effort it took to suppress Msambwa, many apparently sympathized with its aims, gloried vicariously in Masinde's exploits, and were willing to support it when they could, at least, if the price was not too high. The core activists were probably few in number, but the movement apparently could tap, when need arose, a much wider base of ancillary support.

Why Radical Protest?

The two areas where Dini ya Msambwa was strongest and where the most radical protest occurred were first, the locations of Kimilili, Elgon, South Bukusu and Malakisi of the North Nyanza reserve and second, the Trans Nzoia District of the White Highlands. We will now consider the elements that led to a higher degree of protest in those places than in others. The following interpretation is provocative rather than definitive. It utilizes various data, some impressionistic, makes inferences and suggests a number of hypotheses about support for Msambwa and support for protest movements in general, that require further research.

Economic Fears and Inflation

First, we will examine the situation in the reserve. Was there any relationship between Dini ya Msambwa's centre of militant protest and impoverished conditions? Were Bukusu fears over the expropriation of their land justified in terms of an actual shortage of land? Studies of recruitment to radical movements suggest that poverty and/or economic precariousness are positively related to political radicalism. According to Worsley, millenarian movements are likely to occur among the poorest sectors of agrarian societies.[15]

Information on the economic conditions of people in the North Nyanza reserve is scarce. The Bukusu are mentioned in district reports as being among Kenya's wealthiest tribes, because of their cattle and land. In 1945, the district commissioner stated that they were 'the wealthiest tribe in North Kavirondo, and therefore probably the wealthiest tribe among the agricultural peoples in the whole of Kenya.'[16] The best study for my purpose is one by Norman Humphrey, a senior agricultural officer, who examined some agricultural problems in North Nyanza in 1945–46. The table on page 226 provides various indicators of economic conditions by location.[17] These conditions and the population density were essentially the same in 1948–49 at the peak of Msambwa's militancy.[18]

When the population figures of North Nyanza are compared, the four locations where Msambwa was strong turn out to be among the least crowded and the most prosperous. South Bukusu, with 85 people per square mile, had the lowest density of any location. Of the nineteen locations, only two were definitely lower than Malakisi, Kimilili, Elgon, and South Bukusu, and eleven were higher. And when compared with the average density of 200, the figures of 85, 122, and 130 are far below. Using the measure, 'Average utilizable acreage per family', the Msambwa locations were among those with the most land. Comparing them with the average acreage per family unit of roughly 14, holdings of 32.5, 22 and 21.5 acres place them well in front. In 1955, the Agricultural Department estimated that a minimum of 4 acres was required to support a family and provide a small cash surplus. By this measure, South Bukusu, Kimilili, Elgon and Malakisi were well off and far above the absolute minimum.[19] As for wealth measured by the number of cattle per family, again they led the other locations. They had twice as many cows per family, 6.5, 7.5 and 7.9, as against the average of 3.5 cows. In fact, these locations were wealthier than any others, with the exception of Kabras, with 6.7 cattle.

In contrast, it was the southern locations of Bunyore, Maragoli, Kisa and Tiriki that faced extreme overcrowding. Bunyore and Maragoli had a density per square mile of 766 persons in 1945 compared with an average density of 200 for the other locations. Those locations presented a Malthusian picture. The District Annual Report described the situation in 1955 as:

> a teeming population with a very high birth rate, trying to live on small-holdings whose size and fertility is fast dwindling through continual sub-divisions and overcropping. . . . The present pattern is one of increasing frustration, litigation and all the bitterness and delinquency resulting from detribalization and extreme land hunger.

(The contrast between European and African acreage is brought out by comparing land holdings. By 1952 some nine thousand settlers held exclusive rights to 16,700 square miles of land, which gives a density of one settler per 1.85 square miles.)

Hence an investigation of broad economic factors does not support the hypothesis that impoverished conditions produced

225

radical protest. If anything, just the opposite was found. Msambwa's main support tended to come not from the poorest but the most prosperous locations. This finding is in keeping with the conclusions of a number of studies on recruitment to millenarian, political and revolutionary movements by Cohn, Shepperson, Lipset, Brinton and others.[20]

Given this information, how can we account for these locations' support? Malakisi, South Bukusu and Elgon, all border Kimilili known as 'quite the worst area for political agitation of any sort.'[21]

The Locations of North Nyanza—1945

Location	Area in sq. miles	No. of families	Total population	Density per sq. mile	Average Utilizable acreage per family	Cattle population	Average no. of cattle per family
S. Bukusu	336	5,972	28,686	85	32–1/2	38,735	6.5
Kimilili ⎫ Elgon* ⎬	320	8,364	39,080	122	22	62,629	7.5
Malakisi	130	3,495	16,860	130	21–1/2	27,483	7.9
Kabras	200	3,743	17,963	90	31	25,147	6.7
Itesio	208	5,313	26,738	128	22–1/2	20,535	3.9
Bukhayo	46	4,458	21,444	147	19	17,897	4.0
Marach	121	4,311.	21,350	176	16	20,371	4.7
Buholo	34	2,148	11,573	340	9	10,113	4.7
Kakamega Township	—	130	806	—	—	—	—
Bunyore ⎫ Maragoli ⎬	122	7,888	38,697	766	3–1/2	11,816	1.5
		11,997	54,798			22,686	1.9
Tiriki	90	7,510	35,770	397	6–1/2	6,525	0.9
Kisa	50	4,234	21,065	421	6–1/2	5,634	1.3
Marama	120	5,065	28,025	234	13–1/2	11,058	2.2
Wanga	180	8,186	41,710	252	13–1/2	35,067	4.3
Isukha	141	5,900	28,900	205	13–1/2	8,297	1.4
Idakho	100	4,905	24,434	244	11–1/2	5,443	1.1
Butsotso	77	2,439	11,858	143	18	7,179	2.9
Kakalelwa	55	1,248	6,085	111	24–1/2	7,268	5.7
Average				200	14.4		3.5

*These locations are bracketed in Humphrey's table and one set of figures provided. He does the same with several figures for Maragoli and Bunyore.

Masinde, Wekuke, and other important leaders, as well as many Bukusu, lived there. Hence it is not surprising if its inhabitants were subjected to more intense proselytizing and were more politically conscious than inhabitants of other areas, and that the Bukusu were more favourable to movements begun by their own tribesmen than were members of other tribes. But such an explanation overlooks Msambwa's impact on areas geographically distant and the proposition that contented people pay little attention to agitators. So by itself it cannot account for the strong support, though it undoubtedly accounts for some of it.

It may be that all members were not equally well off and that pockets of poverty existed amid general affluence. This has proven to be a particularly explosive combination. Evidence suggests that this was indeed the case. Kimilili, which borders the Trans Nzoia, contained the largest number of ex-squatters of any of the North Nyanza locations[22] and those people, dispossessed of their land, were extremely bitter and militant as will be discussed in the following section.

Another possibility is that Msambwa members, in general, were among the reserve's poorest. Our data on membership in the colonial period is inconclusive. An enquiry into the economic situation of the leaders in the post-colonial period did not turn up any evidence to suggest that they were economically any different from other people.[23] Although the interim years may have made a difference to their economic situation, it would appear that *poverty was not a major cause of radical protest among the Luhya in the reserve, except for the ex-squatters.*

After World War II, the Bukusu experienced inflation. Considerable money was in circulation from the guaranteed prices for maize, war veterans' remittances, wage labour and compulsory cattle sales. At the same time, there was a scarcity of goods. Money was useless for acquiring the traditional symbol of wealth, cattle, because most of the cattle had been sold and what remained brought highly inflated prices. Severe restrictions on western imports meant that there were few manufactured goods to buy.[24] Thus inflation was a sharp blow to the reasonably well off who saw their buying power rapidly declining and with it their chances for the 'good life'.

Another explanation may be that fear of losing land, rather than actual loss of land, was crucial in causing discontent. The Luhya, to all intents and purposes, had lost no land to the settlers

227

except for the Kamakoiya area they claimed. Still the followers beliefs bore witness to fear of landlessness.[25] And while the followers came from the more prosperous locations, they did not have to look far for evidence of severe land hunger. The squatters in the Trans Nzoia amply demonstrated what happens when Africans are turned from owners into tenants, and within a few miles many of their own tribesmen were eking out a marginal existence in extremely overcrowded locations. The government's soil conservation programme in 1945 had roused rumours that the district commissioner was selecting the best land in the reserve for European settlement.[26] (This rumour was assisted by the fact that the Soil Conservation Unit had its headquarters in the settlers' town of Kitale and Africans were suspicious of the Kitale connection.) Africans could recall the alarm caused by the 1931 gold rush when white miners had staked out claims on African land.[27] In fact, as far back as 1920, Luhya chiefs had argued that emigration from the reserves to work on European farms would only encourage more white demands for land, since the settlers would say that African areas were underutilized.[28]

In a country where the possession of land was a man's best insurance of a livelihood and of independence, where it was tied up with his dearest possessions—crops and cattle—loss of land was equated with loss of a way of life. Hence *the threat of a future land shortage rather than an actual land shortage appears to have been a powerful source of unrest* and to have gained support for a movement that promised the eviction of the alien land-grabbers and the return of African land. Moreover, not all supporters had to feel personally threatened in order to protest. Simply the fear that more Africans in the future would lose their land may well have spurred some to protest against a system that produced such a situation.

In these locations, *economic fears* (land alienation) and a *short-term economic decline* (inflation—the situation had improved by 1954), together with the already discussed strains, in particular the government's compulsory cattle sales, appear to be important in accounting for support. Although people had more money, land and cattle than peasants in other locations, they were determined to hang onto them and consequently, protested when they felt them jeopardized. More generally our data suggest that a short-term deprivation (inflation) after relative prosperity is conducive to militant protest and that economic fears among the reasonably well off can be just as conducive to protest as economic deprivations.

Economic Adversity, Assault on Way of Life, and Mobilization
In Chapter 11 we discussed the Kamakoiya settlement scheme and Dini ya Msambwa's and the Bukusu Union's harassment of the incoming settlers. It was there in the Trans Nzoia in an area that extended from Kitale west to Kiminini, Kamakoiya and Lugari, all bordering the North Nyanza reserve, to Hoey's Bridge in the Uasin Gishu District, and to Cherangani in the east, that Msambwa's attacks on property reached their peak. In 1949 there ware sixteen cases involving the burning of churches, schools, farm buildings, police huts and grazing land. A European farmer was assaulted while investigating the arrival of strangers on his land. It was clearly established that these incidents were organized by Msambwa.[29] The unrest continued and the authorities, fearful of an even more serious outbreak, imposed pass rules and a dusk-to-dawn curfew.

While poverty does not appear to have been a major factor in support for Dini ya Msambwa in the locations of Malakisi, Elgon, South Bukusu and Kimilili, it may be related to support in other areas, in particular among the squatters and migrant labourers of the Trans Nzoia and among the unemployed. What was their economic situation? A series of strikes occurred on the Trans Nzoia farms in 1946. In one strike the labourers demanded an increase of 8/- ($1.12), raising wages from 10/- to 18/- ($2.56) a month.[30] From what can be learned about wages in the Trans Nzoia, 10/- *a month appeared to be about average for manual labour*. In addition, the labourer sometimes received a small portion of land to cultivate. A government report noted that there were several bad employers in that area who 'milked their labourers'.[31] Coupled with low wages there were complaints about poor working conditions. In seeking to compare these wages with those in other parts of the country, we find a paucity of data on wages and, like many colonial statistics, what exist are of such poor quality that the needed statistical comparisons cannot be made. Nevertheless, there is a telling consistency among the available figures. The normal wage for labourers in 1938 for thirty days' work was in the region of 12/- to 14/-. In 1948 a total of 385,000 African workers earned an average of $73 a year.[32] At 10/- a month, Trans Nzoia labourers earned roughly $17 a year. In 1949 the government paid 40/- a month for road construction. This was the official rate laid down by the 1948 Secretariat Circular No. 68. In a government report the average wage in 1952 for unskilled labour was estimated to be 25/- a month.[33] Just how low the 10/- Trans Nzoia wage was, is brought home by a report on wages during the depression. Sir Alan Pim noted that during the depression 'wages fell to 8 shillings a month or less', and that Africans were hardly able to pay their taxes.[34] Seeing that the period of our concern was more than a decade later and that it was a time of prosperity, the mere 2/- difference speaks for itself.

A consideration of a labourer's taxes underlines how little his wage really was:

> Most of a man's wage would be taken from him by direct annual taxes which were 12 shillings per head and 12 shillings per hut, which in practice meant that a man had to pay at least 24 shillings a year in tax, while some with numerous wives or responsibility for old mothers might easily have obligations of as much as 60 shillings a year. At 10 to 12 shillings for 30 days' work on an estate, the tax requirement made a minimum of 60 days from home a necessity, which might have been tolerable if attractive conditions of work had been offered. . . . Money wages rose, it is true, but they rose from a very low base (even 19th century textile factory workers in England received in a week the money wages 20th century agricultural workers in Kenya received for 30 days' work).[35]

There are even fewer statistics about squatters' wages, though they were generally lower than those of labourers.[36]

Though African wages were generally low, wages in the Trans Nzoia were inordinately low. Even if we allow for urban wages to be somewhat higher than rural, the wages in the Trans Nzoia were less than half and sometimes as little as a quarter of those paid elsewhere. The demand for an 8/- increase was quite reasonable, in fact even conservative. And to emphasize the seriousness of the problem, by the mid-1940s more than one-third of the Luhya men—some fifty thousand of 139,151 in North Nyanza—were wage labourers.[37] This means that economic distress was not confined to small pockets of impoverishment in an otherwise prosperous population, but that it was widespread. Labourers without land of their own must have been desperately poor.

But if poverty was the main cause of radical protest, why did it not occur among the very poor in the most overpopulated locations, Bunyore and Maragoli in the reserve? The plight of many of those people was every bit as bad, if not worse than that of the Trans

Nzoia labourers. It was Africans from those very locations who were migrating to the Trans Nzoia in search of economic betterment. KAU had singled out Maragoli and Bunyore for proselytizing on the assumption that hatred of the government and of Europeans could most easily be stirred up there.[38]

Long endured poverty, as many have suggested, to the extent that it does not involve changes in economic conditions, does not appear to be a factor in radical protest. Quite the opposite appears to be the case. It has often been observed to be a condition of stability. People have never known and do not expect anything else. It was Trotsky who wrote, 'In reality, the mere existence of privations is not enough to cause an insurrection; if it were, the masses would always be in revolt.'[39] Davies argued that revolutions do not occur when a society is generally impoverished, when, as de Tocqueville put it, evils that seem inevitable are patiently endured. Revolutions are most likely to occur when a prolonged period of objective economic and social development is followed by a short period of sharp reversal giving rise to blocked aspirations.[40] Hoffer noted, 'When people toil from sunrise to sunset for a bare living, they nurse no grievances and dream no dreams. . . . Misery does not automatically generate discontent, nor is the intensity directly proportional to the degree of misery. . . . It is usually those whose poverty is relatively recent, the "new poor," who throb with the ferment of frustration.'[41] The intensified struggle for existence, Ross wrote, 'is a static rather than a dynamic influence.'[42] And on radicalism and poverty, Bell concluded, 'It is not poverty *per se* that leads people to revolt; poverty most often induces fatalism and despair, and a reliance, embodied in ritual and superstitious practices, on supernatural help. *Social tensions are an expression of unfulfilled expectations.*'[43]

Thus the low degree of support for Msambwa in the most impoverished locations may be related to steady poverty or to hopelessness, apathy and alienation, or possibly to recruitment to a strictly religious movement of which there were a number in that area. Until further data is available, we can only speculate.

Once squatters had changed in the settler economy from being an important asset to a liability, their economic decline was imminent. Their situation, as noted in Chapter 9, began to deteriorate around 1922 when the settlers in conjunction with the government started to restrict their rights and to turn them from tenants into labourers. Their proletarization, begun in the 1920s, culminated in the 1940s with the implementation of the revised Resident Labourers' Ordinance.

It was after World War II when the settlers, in response to the post-war boom in primary products, tried to increase the productivity of their farms by evicting squatters—a situation with some parallels to manorial agriculture in thirteenth century England where the expansion of estate farming led to pressures on the labour force, the full exaction of labour services and the encroachment on the commonage—that the implications of this Ordinance were felt. The Ordinance stated that squatters were *no longer tenants* and had rights only as long as they were working for a farmer. European-run District Councils were given the power to further reduce the acreage squatters could cultivate, to eliminate their livestock, and to increase their work obligations from 180 to 240 or 270 days a year. Nor was there any compensating wage increase. New agreements had to be signed between the farmer and labourer, and any labourer who refused the new terms or was redundant could be evicted along with his family.[44] The Secretary of State for the Colonies refused, however, to permit the implementation of this Ordinance until other land had been found on which to settle the evicted squatters.[45] But the promise of land elsewhere did not allay their fears about leaving some of the best agricultural land in the country, land to which they had become attached, for land of unknown quality. Certainly much of Maasailand couldn't compare in quality to the land they were being forced to vacate.[46]

The regulations, for their part, meant that a man instead of working half a year on a settler's farm could be required to work up to three-quarters of a year and that he had less land to farm, less time to spend on it, and fewer or no livestock to provide for his family's needs. Squatters clearly depended not on their meagre wages but on the produce from their farms to feed their families, any surplus of which was bartered or sold for livestock or other commodities.

The effects of these regulations on Kikuyu squatters (all Trans Nzoia squatters whether Kikuyu or not would be equally affected) were the following:

> The Kikuyu squatter, who hitherto provided labour rent of 90 days per year [the discrepancy between this and the previous figure may be due to a difference in dates] having 5–6 acres of land with 25–30 sheep and goats,

in 1946 was forced to work from 240–270 days, while reduced to having $1\frac{1}{2}$ acres of land and limited to owning 5 sheep. The monthly wage of 8–9 shillings (while at work for the settler) was not raised so that the *drop in real income of squatters was anywhere from 30–40 per cent*.[47] (Italics mine).

The District Councils in their anxiety to control squatters continued to issue orders reducing acreage and stock. 'Orders follow each other at close intervals. . . . This lack of security is tending in certain areas to promote unrest among the natives concerned.'[48]

But more than economic adversity and precariousness was involved. *Here was a direct assault on a way of life.* Even though the lines distinguishing squatters from labourers had over the years become increasingly blurred, and even though the working conditions of labourers were often better than those of squatters, those squatters that had remained had tenaciously clung for over a quarter of a century to a lifestyle despite efforts to undermine it. (From 1920 to 1950, the ratio of squatters to wage labourers was drastically reduced as the large estates evicted squatters and the new settlers from overseas and the young Kenyan born generation wanted smaller, mixed farms that did not require squatter labour, but only a few full time labourers supplemented periodically with casual labour.[49]) The squatters as discussed in Chapter 9, were closely tied to the traditional culture. On many of the larger farms, the 'traditionalists' had councils of elders that arbitrated disputes according to customary law. Marriages and circumcision ceremonies adhered to custom. One reason they had migrated in the first place was because the reserves were becoming too crowded and undergoing too many changes. (In this respect the squatters were not unlike the *trekboers* who trekked from South Africa and settled on the nearby isolated Uasin Gishu plateau.) The Highlands, without schools, medical centres and missionaries had allowed them to live their old life. 'Now their old freedoms had been interfered with. They could no longer go on living scattered in their little settlements on the white farms, cultivating as much as they wanted. Now they had to settle down. Remember that originally many of them had come up in order to get access to land and not to get the money.'[50]

The situation was similar for the Kamakoiya squatters, many of whom had been born and raised on settlers' farms. Evicted from the only home they had ever known, they were encouraged by the Bukusu Union and others to settle in Kamakoiya. When this area was turned into a British settlement scheme, these people were again forced to move.

The squatters' economic pursuits ran counter to the main streams of economic development. They, more than other rural occupational groups, strongly opposed the major socio-economic trends. Hence Msambwa's advocacy of returning to the traditional life and of ridding the country of aliens who interfered in and eventually made impossible that way of life, struck in them a responsive chord.

In the 1940s the squatters' frustrations and anger reached a peak. For years they had been economically squeezed and deprived of rights. They felt that the settlers had cheated them and that they had a legitimate right to land in the Highlands. In the early colonial years they and the settlers had made an agreement whereby in return for their labour they were guaranteed ample land for their crops and livestock. Then the settlers began to renege on their promises. This breach of faith was made all the more bitter by the fact that the settlers' prosperity had been made possible by their labour. Besides, they had no land in the reserves to fall back on nor were they equipped for any other way of life. Many were illiterate and did not have the skills needed to migrate to the city. They had no alternate means of surviving. The *squatters were a 'doomed class', wanted neither in the reserves where they would increase the population density on the land nor on the settlers' farms.* It is hardly surprising then if they were in an ugly mood and supported Msambwa's and the Bukusu Union's attempts to prevent the settlers from taking 'their land'. The attack on settler property can be seen as a desperate effort by members of a dispossessed economic group to fight back at a system that no longer had any room for their way of life.

It was not until 1948 that there was any definite evidence of Msambwa's presence in the Trans Nzoia and this was just two days before it was proscribed. (It is difficult to say exactly when recruitment took place. There was evidence of unrest and intimidation of settlers from 1946 onwards, but the most serious militancy did not occur until the outbreak of arson in 1949.) This suggests that the squatters and migrant labourers were late joiners (the movement appeared openly in 1943) and that their recruitment was directly related to worsening economic conditions and for the squatters the possible loss of a way of life. Since both squatters and labourers were economically dependent upon the settlers they had little tactical power and stood to lose much if they protested. This may help explain why they were late joiners. It was not until their situation became so desperate and they figured they stood to lose anyway that they joined. Then they reacted strongly. First by 'troubling' the settlers, a 'go-slow' policy, absenteeism and strikes and when these failed to better their position, they destroyed settler and government property.

Further evidence supporting the proposition that economic strains contributed to radical protest in the Trans Nzoia came in 1954. During that year little was heard of Msambwa in the reserves. It apparently had fallen into disrepute, but a number of Msambwa incidents occurred in the Trans Nzoia. A Church Missionary school was burned down at Lugari and twenty-four high grade cattle poisoned in Kiminini. A subsequent investigation revealed a number of adherents in the Kiminini area. During 1955 Msambwa activity increased. There were reports of activity throughout the Trans Nzoia but mainly in the Kiminini-Lugari-Kamakoiya area.[51]

Why the difference between the Trans Nzoia and the reserve? 1954 was a year of prosperity for the Bukusu as they harvested a bumper crop of maize. Many invested their profits in improvements to their homes and holdings. A stable middle-class was emerging that had much to lose in the event of unrest and their influence contributed to the growth of public opinion against Msambwa.[52] Its presence in the Trans Nzoia could be attributed to the absence of this stabilizing influence. Or, put another way, despite general prosperity, the squatters' conditions had not improved and could be said to have deteriorated when compared with those of the settlers and of Africans in the reserve. Thus the strains on the squatters were greater than ever, while the strain of inflation in the reserve had been alleviated and people were again enjoying prosperity.

Jan de Wolf agrees that the abrogation of squatter rights in terms of the number of cattle, sheep and goats they could keep, and the mass eviction of squatters from the Highland estates and the area bordering the reserves, were major reasons for Dini ya Msambwa support, but he ranks them in second place behind massive inflation.[53] We are not told, however, how he arrives at this ranking. Since the data on support is not sufficiently refined to be able to measure which group felt the most resentment, nor are there any figures to tell us how much support each grievance garnered, would it not be more accurate to see different grievances attracting different groups. In the reserves, inflation hit the wealthier farmers who felt strongly about it and in the Highlands, loss of rights and possible eviction aroused strong resentment among the squatters. There is no doubt that the squatters were in a much more desperate position than the more prosperous farmers. However, since strength of strains is not the only determinant in protest, we cannot simply assume that it led to greater or more radical support.

Mass society theory provides some useful propositions in helping to explain Trans Nzoia radicalism. William Kornhauser argues that rural labourers concentrated in large numbers, especially those who live apart from the landowners in isolated villages, (isolated from the common life of the larger society), have historically shown strong inclinations to join mass movements and to engage in non-institutionalized protest. This proposition assumes that an individual is more likely to engage in new ventures when he receives support from close associates and that a member of even a small group is more accessible for mass agitation, than a completely detached person. Additionally, rural labourers weakened ties to the social, political and economic orders make them potential recruits to a movement, in particular one that promises economic betterment, a secure position and status, all of which they lack. By living in their own community, cut off from the larger society, they develop and reinforce shared grievances.[54]

Were the political attachments of Africans living in the Trans Nzoia to the colonial order weaker than those of Africans living in the reserves? During this period the administration was particularly distant from the ordinary African. In the reserves the growing complexity of government kept the district commissioner increasingly in his office. (Recognizing this problem, the chief native commissioner in 1950 had instructed district officers to increase their contacts with the rural people.)[55] In the Highlands the situation was even worse. There, there was almost no contact at all except for the odd *baraza* held on farms by labour officers. In 1947 the European district councils at a joint conference had agreed that the system of African advisory councils then being implemented in the towns would not be applied in the Highlands.[56] Thus the squatters and labourers in the Trans Nzoia had no political representation even in an advisory capacity. The lack of African courts in the Highlands meant that disputes had either to be settled informally or taken to the district commissioner. Since settlers and administrators tended to share the same general perspective, Africans had little chance of winning a fight against a settler. No doubt revenge lay behind some of the arson. If an African couldn't have his day in court, he could, at least, have his revenge.

Though many squatters had originally come to the Highlands to escape the arbitrary power of chiefs, they were to find themselves in a comparable, perhaps even worse position *vis-à-vis* the settlers. The settler had almost complete authority to deal as he wished with his labourers, the government placing few restrictions on his activities.[57] For instance, the squatter was obliged, if the settler so desired, to sell him his produce or manure even at below market rates. In the Trans Nzoia and Uasin Gishu, the squatters suffered from one of the worst aspects of 'Kaffir farming'—the landowner helping himself to his labourer's animals. Settlers sometimes enforced discipline by a system of fines and the labourer might find himself penalized for a small offence and there was nothing he could do about it. Physical punishment was common and accepted by labour officers as an ordinary practice.[58] Vast differences in power were made all the more galling for Africans by the doctrine of white superiority believed in by so many settlers.

Up until 1922 a labour shortage had served as an informal curb on the harsher behaviour of the settlers since it was common knowlege that employers with a reputation for cruelty would find themselves without labour. But once the settlers' labour needs were met, even this informal curb vanished. Thus Africans in the Trans Nzoia, with no political rights or representation and with no native authority structure, had even less contact than reserve Africans with the administration and considerably weaker attachments to the colonial order. (Rosberg and Nottingham note that mass oathing spread with greatest rapidity among the Kikuyu squatters who were the most isolated from the administration.)[59] District commissioner Campbell went so far as to state in 1949, 'Lack of direct administration and tribal authority in the Trans Nzoia is generally accepted as the cause of the recent arson troubles there.'[60] In an attempt to rectify this situation, *barazas* attended by the district commissioner and chiefs were instituted in 1949.[61] These *barazas* were apparently quite successful. Eight years later, the *Trans Nzoia District Annual Report 1957* stated, 'The Bugusu who comprise the majority of labour in the district have remained generally content. A large number of barazas held on farms has enabled any real or imaginary grievances to be dealt with as they arose and has thus helped to prevent the spread of discontent.'

Squatters' economic ties to the colonial order were weaker at this time than those of peasants living on their own farms, migrant labourers with land or Africans in the employ of the administration. A migrant labourer could always return to his land in the reserve where he had a place to live and food for his family. Africans employed by the administration had an economic stake in the colonial order. But eviction for the squatters meant extreme economic precariousness. The plight of the landless labourer was equally desperate.

The concentration of squatters and migrant labourers on specific farms, overcame one of the movement's perennial problems, that of communication. The spread of Msambwa's beliefs was facilitated by having people congregated together where grievances could be aired, resentments intensified, and a positive orientation acquired towards its goals and tactics.

Intelligence reports provide information on a number of fairly large gatherings on settlers' farms. For instance, 'there was a meeting on 13 February 1948 attended by a hundred Bukusu and sixty Nandi at Hoey's Bridge.'[62] On 15 February about a hundred Bukusu and a few Nandi were addressed by an unidentified Bukusu at a meeting on the Ganz Brothers' farm. The speaker led the assembly in prayers and hymns as they faced Mount Elgon. He then spoke in both Swahili and Bukusu telling those present to cast out all European things and replace them with things truly African, that European money was useless, that no taxes should be paid because all the money was being confiscated by the Europeans, and that some day Masinde would rule the world through his divine power. A few days later, about the same number met at Kitani Syndicate, both farms being located in the Kimanini area.[63] A week later there were meetings at Ziwa Ltd. in Hoey's Bridge and on Mrs. Fleming's farm at Kiminini.[64] About 165 squatters and labourers from different farms assembled on Nel's farm, Hoey's Bridge on 23 May.[65] Smaller meetings were held attended by headmen from settlers' farms who then spread Msambwa's message among their own workers.

Squatters, as noted, were not early recruits to Msambwa. Separated by distance and living arrangements from the reserve and Msambwa's headquarters, they were not easy to contact. Largely illiterate and ignorant of current political information, they were less sophisticated than mission-educated Africans in the reserves who participated in mission activities, political associations and mutual aid societies, and they lacked the leadership and skills required for routine 'pressure politics'. But once contacted and informed, given their severe economic deprivations, they became strong supporters.

Furthermore, living on settlers' farms, geographically and socially apart from the white landowners, tended to underline their common fate and the great gap in white and black standards of living—black poverty contrasted with white affluence—a gap that was being made all the more obvious by the increasing prosperity of the whites in the post-war years and the worsening conditions of the blacks.

Finally, squatters and labourers had the advantage of being well situated to attack settler property. The squatters had somewhat of an advantage in this regard since living spread out on settlers' farms but within communicating distance of each other meant they were harder to control than labourers who lived more compactly in rows.[66] If labourers had not lived on settlers' farms, they, like the unemployed, would have been more difficult to mobilize, regardless of the strength of their anti-colonial feelings.

In the Trans Nzoia four groups of Africans can be distinguished: the Kamakoiya squatters, other squatters, migrant labourers, and the unemployed. It might well be that one group provided far more support than another. Our data, unfortunately, are not specific enough to enable any exact assessment of their respective economic positions or support. Some administrators were particularly worried about the young, unemployed men turning to Dini ya Msambwa.[67] Even as late as 1960, Msambwa had a large following among the unemployed.[68] They may not only have been disproportionately represented but may have been among Msambwa's most radical members. It is to be hoped that future research will enable the specification of a number of these hypotheses. It would be valuable to examine more intensively than we have the separate effects of steady poverty, deteriorating economic conditions, abrupt adversity, and economic reversals, on support for radical protest.

Nevertheless, our analysis suggests that the squatters' socio-economic grievances were greater than those of other rural workers, that they were the most dissatisfied, and the best placed to attack settler property. Although all groups suffered hardship and insecurity, if the labourer had any land of his own, he was far better off than the squatter. And while the plight of the landless labourer was serious, his services, unlike those of the squatter, were still needed by the settlers. Additionally, landless labourers had experienced steady poverty which, as we have argued, is not particularly conducive to radical protest, whereas the squatters with the implementation of the Resident Labourers' Ordinance had suffered a sharp decline.

Squatters on previous occasions had shown their availability for recruitment into political movements. Their deteriorating living conditions in 1926–29 coincided with increased support for the Kikuyu Central Association, strikes and passive resistance.[69] Squatter resistance up to 1929 was but a first step in their attempt to defend their position. Throughout the 1930s they went on strikes, illegally occupied settler-owned land, and refused to accept many of the settlers' efforts to restrict their agricultural activities.[70] When KAU started to organize branches throughout the country in the late 1940s the squatters were among those easiest to organize.

Part of the difference in support for Dini ya Msambwa between Maragoli-Bunyore and the Trans Nzoia may be explained in terms of the colonial impact. Although economic destitution characterized those locations, it could only indirectly through the gazetting of reserve boundaries that interfered with migration, a traditional way of coping with a land shortage, be blamed on the settlers or the government. But the squatters and labourers could squarely blame settler greed and government policy for their plight. Having less contact with Europeans as distinct from those working in the Trans Nzoia, the North Nyanzans were spared the humiliating experiences which closer contact with the settlers' racist ideas would have brought. In comparison with the squatters and labourers, the 'colonial yoke' had been lightly worn. This factor, in addition to differences in political ties, economic strains, and ease of mobilizing, helps explain the contrasting levels of protest between the Trans Nzoia and Bunyore-Maragoli.

Mass Society Theory and Mobilization

Mass society theory argues that in a 'communal' society when powerful forces such as urbanization and industrialization begin to erode communal ties forcing segments of the population to leave their homes and migrate to new areas in search of work and a new way of life, these people, uprooted from their traditional moorings and having few ties to the larger society, in the sense of not being integrated into broad social groupings, are the most easily mobilized into mass movements.[71] This theory, too well known to require elaboration, generally emphasizes the restraining effects of these ties, though one of its proponents, William Kornhauser, does recognize their mobilizing effects among isolated workers.

This perspective provides a popular explanation of recruitment to new movements. For instance, Turner and Killian state that 'generally full integration into family, neighbourhood, community, and special interest groups mean the acceptance of obligations and the habituation to certain gratifications that will be deterrents to more than passive acquiescence in any new movement.'[72] Hoffer argues that 'the device of encouraging communal cohesion as a preventive of colonial unrest can also be used to prevent labour unrest in the industrialized colonizing countries. . . . A vivid feeling of solidarity whether racial, national or religious, is undoubtedly an effective means of preventing labour unrest. *Even when the type of solidarity is such that it cannot comprise the employer,* it nevertheless tends to promote labour contentment and efficiency.'[73]

Our hypotheses that Dini ya Msambwa's main support came from the more prosperous, northern locations rather than the southern, mpoverished locations (where land-hungry peasants were forced to migrate in search of work) and from squatters more than wage labourers (who moved to and fro between the Highlands and the reserves) raises questions about the theory's main proposition, the presumed restraining effects of these attachments and about the central role given to alienation, uprootedness and social atomization. (The latter group in each comparison is assumed to have more members with fewer attachments than the former group. Fewer attachments lead to more alienation, uprootedness and social atomization and hence more recruits to mass movements.) Our Kenyan data suggest, on the other hand, that support for Dini ya Msambwa was related far more to economic strains, both actual and anticipated, and to integration into communal and primary structures than to lack of integration.[74]

Even though squatters' economic and political ties to the colonial order were weaker than those of Africans in the reserves, racial barriers meant that Africans in general were cut off from participation in the larger colonial society or, at least, permitted only limited roles in it. In that sense, all Africans had weak ties to the colonial order—politically, economically and socially—and far stronger ties to the indigenous society. Indigenous structures exhibited a diffuse orientation of alienation *vis-à-vis* many features of colonial society. Dini ya Msambwa, the Bukusu Union and the earlier North Kavirondo Central Association appeared to have been supported by kinship and communal networks. There is some evidence that Dini ya Msambwa's leaders were likely to have participated in mission groups and in various associations, but our limited data preclude any but tentative propositions until there is more investigation into the relationships between recruitment and lineage, tribal, associational and other social networks.

In sum, our data suggest that instead of recruiting the uprooted and socially atomized, as mass theory proposes, *Dini ya Msambwa recruited individuals with strong primary and communal ties, people well integrated into indigenous structures and it was these people who were at the centre of non-institutionalized political action.* Thus in a communal society with a colonial superstructure, communal groupings may serve *to promote rather than to restrain non-institutionalized political behaviour.* This is especially likely to happen if these people feel that their grievances cannot be handled by the existing political channels or if they do not have access to any political channels.

These propositions are in keeping with Gusfield's critique of mass society and pluralist theory which he argues fails to distinguish between two types of segmentation, that of 'linked pluralism' and that of 'superimposed segmentation'. In the latter, while there may be many intermediary groups and associations and high rates of participation, membership in one group also implies membership in another. Hence since group memberships are drawn predominantly or exclusively from particular social strata, classes, or in the case of Kenya, caste like strata, each stratum or class may be highly participatory but bound together in mutually exclusive networks of intermediary groups. This situation, which characterized colonial Kenya, promotes rather than deters the rapid mobilization of classes or strata against each other. It is only in a structure of linked pluralism that cross pressures from multiple group membership serve to moderate conflict and prevent the development of strong, overlapping cleavages.[75]

Furedi's study of Kikuyu squatters supports the economic thesis and casts doubt on just how uprooted and socially atomized squatters really were. He shows that squatters had a proclivity to move to places where they had friends and relatives and that this pattern of movement led to the maintenance of clan solidarity. Squatters carried on their traditional way of life perhaps to an even greater extent than reserve Africans. They strongly supported the Kikuyu Central Association. Though it could not recruit openly, age groupings were used to spread its message and a network of personal relationships existed among the members.[76]

To strengthen the hypothesis that it was the more rather than the less integrated people who joined, data are needed on migrant labourers and support for protest movements. It may be that they conform more to mass theory's atomized and rootless and support these movements to an even greater extent than the squatters. Our findings do not suggest this hypothesis but it requires more rigorous testing.

The integration thesis is also supported by Furedi's work on squatter involvement in Mau Mau. He argues convincingly that grassroot leadership came from the most successful, enterprising and popular element among the squatters—the traders, artisans and farm teachers—who lived on the farms and were an integral part of squatter life. 'The movement on the farms was led by the most skilled and articulate section of the squatter community. These local leaders had commanded widespread respect from Africans on the farms as a result of their skills and position. This respect and influence was now used to mobilize support for the Mau Mau.'[77]

Barnett's study of Mau Mau lends more weight to the integration thesis. The Mau Mau movement's territorial criterion of recruitment, according to Barnett, fostered the emergence of groups comprised of people from the same villages or sub-locations and leaders whose position *vis-à-vis* their followers was reinforced by strong kin, friendship and neighbourhood ties and loyalties. The movement's cells which might contain anywhere from fifteen to three hundred members were based on the traditional *itura*, formerly a cluster of relatives, neighbours and tenants who, while living on their respective *shambas*, shared a common stream and behaved as a unit in times of crisis. Residence within such a neighbourhood of highly interacting and diversely related persons was an implicit *criterion of membership in the reserve cells*.[78] A similar organizational basis was utilized in Nairobi. It was a duty of every member to bring into the movement as many friends, relatives and acquaintances as he or she could.

The Maji Maji rebellion, likewise, used the fundamental loyalties of kin and tribe to mount an assault against the German regime bringing eight thousand rebels together at Mahenge in the largest, single action.[79]

As the above evidence indicates, it was not the socially atomized, rootless person who joined these movements, but just the opposite, the person well integrated into communal and primary groups, and these groups acted as important centres for mobilization. We would not deny, however, the restraining effects of primary and communal attachments, but would argue that it depends on whether a new movement's interests are seen to be in harmony with, or opposed to, indigenous interests. Thus these attachments can either mobilize or restrain. This argument leads to the proposition that in communal type colonial societies, protest movements will receive stronger backing in the rural areas if primary and communal attachments are strong, than in the urban areas if these attachments are weak, other conditions being equal.

Millenarian movements in the Middle Ages spread not in the farming areas as in Kenya but in the expanding cities among the poor rural and urban migrants uprooted from their traditional life. They did not take hold among the peasants, according to Cohn, because the peasants were integrated into a network of communal relationships which gave them security and a place in society which the urban migrants lacked:

> To an extent which can hardly be exaggerated, peasant life was shaped and sustained by custom and communal routine. . . . In the course of long struggles between conflicting interests each manor had developed its own laws which, once established by usage, prescribed the rights and obligations of each individual. To this "custom of the manor" the lord himself was subject; and the peasants were commonly most vigilant in ensuring that he did in fact abide by it. . . . And to most peasants it [custom] gave at least that basic security which springs from the hereditary and guaranteed tenancy of a piece of land.[80]

We would question the major emphasis Cohn gives to integration into a stable communal network because it, in itself, is insufficient to explain non-recruitment. Under other circumstances, as we have argued, integration can act to mobilize rather than to deter recruitment. Cohn's countryside was obviously a stable area with peasants living in steady poverty. Nothing had occurred to raise their hopes, to give them unfulfilled expectations.

Kenya, in contrast, had experienced the trauma of colonial occupation and the dislocation of indigenous cultures. Rapid social change introduced severe strains that impinged sharply on particular sectors. The rights of Kenya's squatters were not sanctioned by years of tradition nor were they inviolable. Kenya's settlers, unlike feudal lords, did not abide by the rules and Kenya's squatters and labourers soon lost the bargaining power that a labour shortage gave to feudal peasants. Hence the feudal peasant had far more security than the Kenyan squatter or labourer who suffered from some of the same strains as Cohn's urban migrants. Migrants to the medieval cities were miserably paid, had no guilds to protect them, were entirely at the mercy of the market, and had new wants but no ways to satisfy them. Kenya's squatters and labourers, likewise, were miserably paid, had no unions to protect them, were entirely at the mercy of the settlers and the government, and were experiencing a continual economic decline. Thus, both groups suffered from severe strains.

Mass theory provides a more limited model than Smelser's value-added model to explain protest dealing with only some of the conditions. In terms of Smelser's model, it deals mainly with three determinants, or at least some aspects of them, conduciveness, mobilization, and control. To be sure, several general strains are mentioned, industrialization, urbanization, wars and such, but they are seen as part of an overall set of forces leading to mass movements not because they produce various types of deprivations, but above all because they weaken the system of attachments of non-elites to elites. Strains are seen as only one type of factor among many others that bring about a mass society and it is this type of society which produces mass movements.

In our view, mass theory overemphasizes one particular type of conduciveness and underemphasizes the role of strains as independent determinants. Strains are not limited to providing the appropriate structural conditions but are determinants in their own right. The social structure of western Kenya was conducive to protest movements, as seen by their proliferation. But they did not occur everywhere. Further specification is required. Loss of rights, severe economic deprivations, and alien interference, are strains that gained Dini ya Msambwa recruits and are essential to explaining Trans Nzoia protest.

Conclusions

Taking into consideration some conclusions reached in Chapter 11 as well as in this chapter, Msambwa's support apparently cut across tribal boundaries, age groups and economic divisions. It attracted people for different and even opposing reasons. Old people who feared the eclipse of traditional ways and young people rebelling against both traditional and colonial authority, found in Masinde a kindred spirit. The prosperous joined because they feared economic deprivation, while the economically deprived were attracted by promises of land and wealth. Many joined not because they were 'non-achievers' (which they were in one sense), but because of intense frustration with a situation which provided few opportunities to achieve anything. If economic fears were important in gaining recruits, it points to a process whereby the same movement reaches the economically prosperous who perceive a threat to their prosperity as well as to the economically deprived. The economically deprived were not the founders of Msambwa or its core supporters. They apparently joined after the movement was underway and continued their support longer than those in the reserves where economic conditions had improved. The most militant group in terms of the actual destruction of settler property were the squatters, who had over the years experienced an erosion of their economic position and status–a gradual impoverishment. Their peak of protest came at the culmination of the process of proletarization, a process whereby the earlier relationships based on reciprocity and mutual advantage had gradually yielded to purely economic relationships between a foreign settler-owner class and an indigenous labouring class.

Our findings support the proposition that there is a weak relationship between radical protest and steady poverty or absolute level of deprivation. Situations which produce bitter frustrations, severe exasperations and dissatisfactions such as when aspirations are blocked or expectations unfulfilled, appear to be related much more to protest. Nor are intense feelings necessarily produced only by actual experience. Anticipated adversity (fear of land alienation or eviction) is sufficient, given other conditions, to trigger off protest. The potential for radical protest reaches its peak when long-term grievances (poverty, economic decline) are coupled with short-term grievances (inflation) or severe deprivations (loss of a way of life) in a situation conducive to mobilization. Mass theory incorrectly emphasizes only the restraining effects of primary and communal attachments as the socially isolated and rootless appear less inclined to join movements than the more integrated. Our most general findings support the well-known propositions that relative as opposed to absolute deprivation is more important and that changes, fluctuations and reverses in economic conditions appear to be particularly crucial in generating discontent. The assumption that no one particular strain can give rise to a protest movement but rather a combination of strains appears correct in the light of our analysis.

Karl Marx made a more sweeping generalization about the peasantry than mass theory, arguing that peasants are not mobilizable because, living and working dispersed on their individual holdings, they did not enter into cooperative relationships with each other and hence were incapable of representing their own interests and of becoming a revolutionary force.[81] The industrial proletariat, on the other hand, was capable of revolution because under capitalism the workers were brought together in large economic enterprises. Our study supports Marx's thesis only in part. Certainly the squatters and labourers living together on settlers' estates were among the most radical and best able, because of their proximity to each other, to organize. But our findings on Msambwa, those on the more broadly based Mau Mau and Maji Maji rebellions, and, going even farther afield, evidence from the great revolutionary movements that have erupted among the peasants in the past several decades, (especially in Asia) suggest that Marx's theory may need to be qualified. The data show that peasants under certain conditions can indeed be mobilized and that they are a potentially revolutionary force. Though Marx was undoubtedly correct in his emphasis upon the need for cooperative action, and that in general these movements have been led by non-peasants, our movements provide ample evidence of the mobilization of fairly large numbers of peasants by a peasant leadership.

Given the conflicting hypotheses about the mobilization of peasants, it appears that more research is needed on this dimension. The following discussion suggests areas which might be profitably investigated.

Some proselytizing tactics, Wekuke's speechmaking at the local market, Masinde's marches through a town interpersed with diatribes against foreigners and white rule, secret meetings on settlers' farms—have already been described. In what other ways was Dini ya Msambwa's message spread among people that usually walk, though sometimes ride bicycles or take a bus to far away places, but do not own cars, seldom read a daily newspaper, have no telephones, and may or may not own a transistor radio?

More than one observer has noted the rapidity and accuracy with which news travels in the rural areas. How were members living many miles apart brought together at short notice where there were no fixed dates for services or meetings? When Masinde was being deported under police escort, he passed through a small town and the people lined the street to greet him, though the authorities had taken precautions to keep his whereabouts secret. Just how does the 'bush telegraph' work? Of what do the local and more distant communication networks consist?

How was the membership recruited? What were the processes of involvement or the steps in conversion? What were the relationships between the degree of involvement and the particular rituals such as the Mau Mau oath-taking? Previous studies have shown that social networks are important in recruitment. Did recruitment occur on an individual, group, or mixed basis?

Students of peasant revolts have stressed that the peasant is an unreliable fighter, since he has to break off his protest to tend to the annual agricultural cycle.[82] However, not all peasant systems are manned by men, and in a system where the women do the bulk of the subsistence farming, freeing men to engage in cooperative ventures (as in Kenya and many other African countries), this dimension may be of less significance. Certainly the Mau Mau struggle demonstrated the availability of men for fighting while the women carried on as food producers. The role of women in protest movements bears more examination.

Though it would appear that Msambwa's organizational base was slight (it will be discussed briefly, as well as its tactics in Chapter 15), what were the relationships between leaders and followers, between guerrilla units, ordinary members, and the peasant masses? What were the necessary steps to becoming a leader? How was conflict within the movement handled? What was the system of ranking and authority? In Mau Mau, the warrior groups were originally subordinate to the local councils, but as the fighting progressed and the situation became more disorganized, the status system was reversed and the leaders of the militant bands became superordinate.[83] Does this have a more general applicability?

The above are a few ideas and dimensions that need more exploration before we can advance an adequate explanation of just how it is that rural people are brought together for collective action.

Notes

1. Maurice Pinard, *The Rise of a Third Party*, (Prentice-Hall, Englewood Cliffs, 1971), pp. 94–6; Angus Campbell, Philip E. Converse, Warren E. Miller and Donald E. Stokes, *The American Voter*, (Wiley, New York, 1960), p. 436; S. M. Lipset, *Agrarian Socialism: The Cooperative Commonwealth Federation in Saskatchewan*, (University of California Press, Berkeley, California, 1950), pp. 121ff., 151–52; also in 'Fascism—Left, Right and Center', in *Political Man*, Chapter 5.
2. *Trans Nzoia District Annual Reports 1952, 1957*.
3. KNA:DC/NN10/1/2. Pritchard of the Kenya Police in an Intelligence Report, 22 December 1947.
4. Later Governor of the Gambia and a member of the Devlin Commission on Nyasaland.
5. KNA:DC/NN10/1/5. Letter from the chief native commissioner P. Wyn Harris to the provincial commissioner of Nyanza, 19 May 1949.
6. KNA:EN/15. Kavujai Handing Over Notes by C. Campbell to J. S. S. Rowlands, July 1950.
7. KNA:TN/2. Handing Over Report of district commissioner C. J. Denton to Mr. E. H. Risleg, May 1945.
8. From a report entitled, 'Exposition of Chief Articles of Dini ya Misambwa', 6 April 1948, The Vicariat of Kisumu.
9. Usher-Wilson, 'Bishop's Study of 'Dini ya Misambwa',' 29 November 1951.
10. KNA:DC/NN10/1/5. Letter from provincial commissioner K. L. Hunter of Nyanza to the chief secretary, 9 May 1945.
11. KNA:DC/NN10/1/5.
12. For a fuller discussion of this problem see Appendix A.
13. KNA:DC/NN10/1/2. Assistant superintendent of police, L. Griffiths in an Intelligence Report to the superintendent of police, Special Branch, Nairobi, 7 September 1948.
14. KNA:DC/NN10/1/2. Letter from the assistant superintendent of police, L. Griffiths to the provincial commissioner of Nyanza, 7 September 1948.
15. Worsley, *The Trumpet Shall Sound*, pp. 238–39. Kornhauser argues that in mass society since the poor are more socially isolated and alienated than other sectors of the population, they are the most likely to be attracted to mass movements. Kornhauser, *The Politics of Mass Society*, (The Free Press, New York, 1959).
16. KNA:DC/NN10/1/5. Letter from district commissioner F. D. Hislop of North Kavirondo to the provincial commissioner of Nyanza, 18 January 1945.
17. Humphrey, *The Liguru and the Land*, p. 2. The headings on columns 6 and 8 have been corrected. They incorrectly read on the original 'Utilizable acreage/average family' and 'No. of cattle per average family' respectively.
18. KNA:DC/NN1/30. *North Kavirondo District Annual Report, 1948*.

19. KNA:DC/NN1/36. *North Nyanza District Annual Report, 1955.*
20. Cohn takes issue with Marxists who have interpreted the millenarianism of the Spirituals (a thirteenth to fourteenth century European movement) as protest of poor peasants against an exploitive church. He argues that the Spirituals were drawn mainly from the privileged orders and that far from belonging to the poor peasantry, many had, in fact, renounced great wealth in order to become poorer than any beggar. 'Medieval Millenarism: Its Bearing on the Comparative Study of Millenarian Movements', Sylvia L. Thrupp (ed.), *Millennial Dreams in Action,* (Mouton, The Hague, 1962), pp. 35–36. George Shepperson makes a similar criticism from data on other millenarian movements in 'The Comparative Study of Millenarian Movements', *Millennial Dreams in Action,* pp. 48–50.

    With regard to revolutionary movements, both Tilly and Brinton maintain that the destitute classes were substantially under-represented in the popular rebellions of eighteenth century France. Charles Tilly, 'Reflections on the Revolutions of Paris: An Essay on Recent Historical Writing', *Social Problems,* 12, 1964, pp. 111ff., 113; for other revolutions, see Crane Brinton, *The Anatomy of Revolution,* (Vintage Press, New York, 1957), pp. 102–105.

    In his study of the Canadian socialist Cooperative Commonwealth Federation (CCF) movement, Lipset notes that between 1934 and 1944, the 'extremely poor farmers' were under-represented. Lipset, *Agrarian Socialism: The Cooperative Commonwealth Federation in Saskatchewan,* pp. 163–165. Pinard hypothesizes that the poor, though they may come to form an important element in political movements, and even to be disproportionately represented in them, are not the first recruits. Pinard, *The Rise of a Third Party,* pp. 136–61.
21. KNA:DC/NN.2/6. Handing Over Report and Notes, R. S. Winser to L. C. Mortimer, August 1952.
22. KNA:EN/15. Handing Over Report and Notes, C. Campbell to J. S. S. Rowlands, July 1950.
23. See below, pp. 284–85. Jan de Wolf, in 'Religious Innovation', also makes this same observation, p. 150.
24. de Wolf, 'Religious Innovation', pp. 34, 146.
25. See Appendix C, Symbolic Materials.
26. KNA:DC/NN10/1/5. Letter from district commissioner F. D. Hislop of North Kavirondo to the provincial commissioner of Nyanza, 18 January 1945.
27. See above, pp. 112–14.
28. *Nyanza Province Annual Report 1920–21.*
29. *African Affairs Department Annual Report 1949.*
30. KNA:DC/NN10/1/2. Report from assistant superintendent of police, G. M. Taylor to the superintendent of police, Nakuru, 6 November 1946.
31. *Ibid.* Furedi also mentions 10/- a month as the wage of farm labourers. 'The Social Composition of the Mau Mau Movement in the White Highlands', a paper presented at Centre of International and Area Studies, University of London, 2 October 1973, p. 11.
32. The figure for 1938 comes from R. M. A. van Zwanenberg, 'The Economic Response of Kenyan Africans to European Settlement: 1903–1939', Bethwell A. Ogot (ed.), *Politics and Nationalism in Colonial Kenya,* p. 212. The 1948 figure comes from Barnett and Njama, *Mau Mau from Within,* p. 27.
33. Other information on rates of pay support this conclusion. In 1939 in Mombasa there were a number of wildcat strikes. A Commission of Inquiry investigated the working conditions of urban labourers. Fifty-two per cent of the total railway staff received 20/- a month and many of these people were not provided with housing or a housing allowance. Labourers building roads received 16/- monthly and were accommodated

in condemned quarters. Daily wage rates for unskilled labour had been cut in 1931 from 2/- to 1/50 a day due to an economic slump and had not increased since then. Rosberg and Nottingham, *The Myth of 'Mau Mau'*, pp. 183–184, 204.

34. Sir Alan Pim, *Report on Some Financial Questions*, (1936), quoted in E. S. Atieno-Odhiambo, 'The Colonial Government, the Settlers and the 'Trust' Principle in Kenya to 1939', *Transafrican Journal of History*, II, 2, 1972, p. 111.

35. van Zwanenberg, 'The Economic Response', pp. 212, 214. van Zwanenberg is discussing wages up to 1939. But since the Trans Nzoia wages ten years later were the same it is an appropriate comparison of the demands on wages and, if anything, somewhat conservative since taxes in the interim had probably risen.

36. *Ibid.*, p. 226. The only comparison I could find between squatters and labourers was vague as to the time period. Referring to the early period (probably the 1920s) it stated: 'He [the labourer] might be attracted to the idea that his money income was larger—he got 25/- a month compared with the squatters who would get only 8/-. Also he got a free house in the labour lines, and he also got *posho*.' Wambaa and King, 'The Political Economy of the Rift Valley', p. 6. A word of caution is in order when using the above figures. Discussions of wages often fail to clearly differentiate between wage labour and squatter labour. While I have tried to distinguish between the two types of labour the failure of many reports to do so has made an assessment of differences in remuneration difficult to make. Additionally, labourers were sometimes given small plots of land to farm for themselves. Whether there was any wage differential between them and labourers who were not given land, and how widespread this practice was, I do not know.

37. Humphrey, *The Liguru and the Land*, p. 6.

38. de Wolf, 'Religious Innovation', p. 147.

39. Quoted by Brinton, *The Anatomy of Revolution*, p. 34.

40. James C. Davies, 'Toward a Theory of Revolution', in Barry McLaughlin (ed.), *Studies in Social Movements*, (Free Press, New York, 1969), pp. 86–7.

41. Eric Hoffer, *The True Believer*, (Mentor Books, New York, 1951), pp. 25–7.

42. Edward A. Ross, *The Changing Chinese*, (The Century Co., New York, 1948), p. 92.

43. Daniel Bell, *The End of Ideology*, (Free Press, New York, 1962), p. 31. Italics in original. See also Hobsbawm's and Cohn's statements in the same vein on page 7 of this study.

44. Rosberg and Nottingham, *The Myth of 'Mau Mau'*, pp. 251–52.

45. Some 52,500 acres of land in various parts of Maasailand, including the area known as Olenguruone were made available for the settlement of ex-squatters. The failure of the Olenguruone scheme because the squatters found they *were expected to farm according to a set of regulations* enforced by an agricultural officer, has been discussed earlier in Chapter 11.

46. The Trans Nzoia District is relatively small, consisting of 953 square miles. 84 per cent of the total land is classified as high potential agricultural land receiving more than thirty inches of rain per year. As of 1975, it is one of the most important mixed farming areas in the country.

47. H. P. Wyn, *A Discussion of the Problem of the Squatter*, (Nairobi, 1946). Quoted in Furedi, 'The Social Composition of the Mau Mau Movement'.

48. *Ibid.*, original source, p 5.

49. Wambaa and King, 'The Political Economy of the Rift Valley', p. 6. This paper refers mainly to Kikuyu squatters but general motives for migrating were probably quite similar for members of different tribes.

50. *Ibid.*, p. 7.

51. *Trans Nzoia District Annual Report 1955.*
52. KNA:DC/NN.1/35.
53. J. de Wolf, Religious Innovation, pp. 34, 146.
54. Kornhauser, *The Politics of Mass Society*, pp. 93, 212–13.
55. See below, pp. 257–58.
56. Rosberg and Nottingham, *The Myth of 'Mau Mau'*, pp. 323–24.
57. Furedi, 'The Kikuyu Squatter', p. 5.
58. *Ibid.*, pp. 5–7, for a telling discussion of settler power. See above, pp. 172–73. The harsh treatment of the squatters aroused the concern of the Bukusu Union.
59. Rosberg and Nottingham, *The Myth of 'Mau Mau'*, p. 324.
60. KNA:DC/NN10/1/5. Letter from district commissioner C. Campbell of North Nyanza to the provincial commissioner, 30 May 1949.
61. KNA:DC/NN10/1/5. Letter from district officer John Simpson to the district commissioner, Kakamega, 1 June 1949. Also from the same file, the letter from the district commissioner of North Nyanza to provincial commissioner K. L. Hunter, 14 April 1949.
62. KNA:DC/NN10/1/2. Letter from assistant superintendent of police, D. C. Connor, Kitale to the superintendent of police, Nakuru, 16 February 1948.
63. *Ibid.* Letters dated 16 and 20 February 1948.
64. *Ibid.* Letters dated 24 February and 1 March 1948.
65. KNA:DC/NN10/1/2. Assistant superintendent of police, H. N. Instone, Eldoret in a Weekly Intelligence Report to the superintendent of police, Special Branch, Nairobi, 12 June 1948.
66. Furedi, 'The Kikuyu Squatter', p. 4. Furedi agrees that the squatters were one of the most militant groups in Dini ya Msambwa. Personal letter to the author from Furedi, 14 March 1974.
67. KNA:DC/NN10/1/5. Letters from district commissioner Campbell of North Nyanza to the provincial commissioner, 30 May 1949 and to district officer John Simpson.
68. KNA:TN/2. Minutes of a Liaison Meeting held in the district commissioner's office, Bungoma, 19 December 1960.
69. See above, pp. 106–107.
70. Furedi, The Social Composition of the Mau Mau Movement, p. 5.
71. We are relying mainly on the study of William Kornhauser, *The Politics of Mass Society*, (The Free Press, New York, 1959). See also Hannah Arendt, *The Origins of Totalitarianism*, (Harcourt and Brace, New York, 1954); Philip Selznick, *The Organizational Weapon*, (McGraw-Hill, New York, 1952); Erich Fromm, *Escape From Freedom*, (Rinehart, New York, 1945); and Robert Nisbet, *The Quest for Community*, (Oxford University Press, New York, 1953).
72. Turner and Killian, *Collective Behaviour*, p. 432.
73. Hoffer, *The True Believer*, pp. 43–4.
74. See Pinard, *The Rise of a Third Party*, for an excellent critique of mass theory in which he notes the mobilizing effects of intermediary groups; pp. 182–194.
75. Joseph Gusfield, 'Mass Society and Extremist Politics', *American Sociological Review*, 27, 1, 1962, p. 29.
76. Furedi, 'The Kikuyu Squatter', pp. 7–8, 10, and Wambaa and King, 'The Political Economy of the Rift Valley', p. 9.
77. Furedi, 'The Social Composition of the Mau Mau Movement', pp. 11–12.
78. Donald L. Barnett, 'Mau Mau: The Structural Integration and Disintegration of Aberdare Guerrilla Forces', unpublished Ph.D. thesis, University of California, Los Angeles, 1963, pp. 53–4.
79. Iliffe, 'The Organization of the Maji Maji Rebellion'.
80. Cohn, *The Pursuit of the Millennium*, p 25.

81. Karl Marx, *The 18th Brumaire of Louis Bonaparte*, (International Publishers, New York, 1973), pp. 123–24.
82. Wolf, *Peasant Wars*, p. 289.
83. Barnett and Njama, *Mau Mau From Within*, Chapter 9.

Chapter 14

ATTITUDES OF AGENTS OF SOCIAL CONTROL

OFFICIALS of the administration, police, churchmen, native
authorities and journalists held different views of Dini ya
Msambwa, some already discussed in the Introduction, and summarized by the negative stereotype, which influenced the ways in
which they dealt with it. (The government's tactics in handling
Msambwa were discussed in Chapter 10.) This section elaborates
several of the main perspectives, which lend further substance to
our contention that Dini ya Msambwa was negatively stereotyped,
and seeks to explain the purpose they served for the agents of social
control.

Since Dini ya Msambwa's militancy occurred at a time when
Kenya was becoming increasingly tense because of Kikuyu unrest,
some views may be more extreme than they would have been under
less stressful circumstances. However, they are basically not any
different from those held about Mumboism in the early decades of
the twentieth century, and appear, from my reading at least, to
reflect long held viewpoints.

Some of the more perceptive administrators recognized the movement for what it was, and while they knew that it could not be
eradicated, they hoped to effectively control and channel its
aspirations into 'constructive avenues'. By this they meant areas
which would not threaten the status quo. Campbell, the district
commissioner of North Nyanza when Msambwa was at its peak,
assessed it accordingly:

> Dini ya Msambwa is to simple people an attractive faith incorporating
> violent nationalism together with a certain amount of superstitious
> "mumbo-jumbo" . . . I do not think that anyone has been so rash as to
> maintain that the sect has been completely stamped out during the past
> year and I would say that the normal opinion was that trouble would

recur and continue recurring until the Kitosh have learned to express their nationalistic aspirations in a more constitutional fashion.[1]

Provincial commissioner K. L. Hunter made much the same evaluation:

We believe also that there is a very strong desire to give expression to nationalistic determination in the Kitosh area and that the *Dini* has provided a means of giving expression, albeit an undesirable means, and while all the native authorities are desirous of stamping out the overt acts of the *Dini* we believe that nevertheless, they have some considerable sympathy with the national spirit which is prevalent; and when we talk of giving concessions we must bear these facts in mind, for we feel we can in fact overcome the violent expressions as demonstrated by the sect, but cannot hope entirely to suppress the desire of national expression.[2]

Other administrators, not recognizing the various signs of burgeoning nationalism, attributed Dini ya Msambwa's protest to resentment over the missionaries' supercilious and intolerant attitudes towards certain aspects of their way of life, in particular, polygyny. Although the missionaries were resented, they were only one among other issues that generated dissatisfaction.

Convicted members were looked upon by some officials as not ordinary political prisoners but were treated as if their minds had been seized by some strange mania or hypnotic spell and hence were in need of psychological treatment. A programme, euphemistically called 'rehabilitation', was set up. Daily educational classes and religious services were conducted with the aim of restoring 'diseased minds'. Lectures were given about the evils of Msambwa and confession was stressed as a therapeutic device. (This attitude was later carried over to Mau Mau and the same 'rehabilitating' techniques used on the detainees.) When the word circulated that those who confessed were released sooner than the others, the number of repentants quickly soared.[3]

Lengthy sentences were justified not on the grounds of punishment but that this amount of time was needed to 'effect a change of mind'. 'There have been many cases,' wrote district officer R. S. Winser, 'where Dini ya Msambwa convicts imprisoned for three years, although unfortunately released on license at an earlier date have confessed their intention of continuing to follow Dini ya Msambwa. Most of these have been immediately re-convicted but it indicates the shortcomings of their re-education in prison.'[4] Community development officer L. G. Miller, reported in January 1957:

In conclusion, to my mind the year 1956 in the Dini ya Msambwa Works Camp at Kapenguria has been quite successful . . . that with patience, the physiological [sic] side of the bad types of Suk and Abaluhya prisoners and detainees do not appear too difficult to deal with especially and provided one has in the first instance
a) sense of humour
b) of tolerance and
c) of discipline.[5]

Elijah Masinde was regarded as the personification of the 'bad type'. The provincial commissioner, in writing to the medical officer in charge of Mathari Mental Hospital in 1946, expressed shock at the news that Masinde was to be released, 'This man is a very dangerous political character as he was obsessed with a religious mania which dictated him to undertake propaganda and in some cases action, to evacuate all non-natives from the area of his location.'[6] In light of the criticism that followed Masinde's release, Douglas M. McKean, chairman of the Mathari Committee, retorted, 'My committee took the view—which was undoubtedly the correct one—*that mental homes were provided for the treatment of disease and not for the "incarceration of political undesirables"*.'[7] (Italics mine.)

A tendency existed among officialdom to equate militant anti-colonialism with insanity. Confusing political for pathological symptoms, mental hospitals and therapy were recommended in the expectation that these would effect a cure.

While the psychologically oriented had hopes of rehabilitating the members' psyches, churchmen looked to religion to bring changes into their hearts. The Right Reverend L. C. Usher-Wilson, Bishop of the Upper Nile, after examining some of the already suggested causes, concluded:

It is evident that, human nature being what it is, the fundamental causes lie deep in the human heart. That is why this movement has expressed itself in religious form and will continue to do so until the hearts of those concerned are changed. . . . What is the Christian teaching in these matters? That God is the Father of all, that Christ died to save all, and that we must learn to live as a family, some elder, others younger. But time will show that some of the younger get on as well as the elder . . . . Judaism superceded paganism, and Christianity, Judaism, and animal sacrifices were discarded. . . . Is polygamy a fair custom? Does it make women inferior to men? Christianity teaches that in Christ there is no distinction in race, sex or status. In the long run then the cure must lie in religion—the Christian faith, not less but better demonstrated, showing itself to be true, more reasonable and more attractive than this neo-paganism.[8]

The 'idea of progress' is clearly evident in the bishop's diagnosis of the problem. At the top of this implicit scale of values are European-Christian-monogamous societies and at the bottom, African-pagan-polygenous societies. The African is the younger member who, as he matures, will take his place as an adult member of the family, provided, of course, he discards his customs for 'superior' European customs. Though no one religious leader speaks for all Christians, the bishop's views are known to have been widely shared by early missionaries.[9] The agents, in general, seemed to have no doubts whatsoever about the superiority of their own values and expressed wonderment at Africans' inability to see 'this fact'.

One way the agents tried to improve black-white relationships came from the belief that the solution lay in Africans and Europeans getting to understand each other better. Based in part upon a simplistic interpretation of the brotherhood of man and popular psychology, it totally disregarded relations of power. Bishop Usher-Wilson, after examining such causes of anti-British feeling as land hunger and monogamy, concluded that efforts must be made to improve inter-racial relationships:

> The best effort I have seen so far has been made by some Kitale farmers. . . . In collaboration with the Native Authorities they invited leading Africans to spend the day on their farms, showed them around, . . . and entertained them as guests. These guests departed with something more positive and constructive in their minds and gratitude in their hearts. Improvements of relationships like this will dispel suspicion on all sides. It is a long term policy and can be successful only through those who have faith in the Fatherhood of God and Brotherhood of Man.[10]

This suggestion as to how to remedy a situation of inequity brings to mind the oft-repeated adage: When the white man came to Africa he had the Bible and the African the land. Within a few years, the African had the Bible and the white man the land.

Yet another example of the agents' failure to grasp the essential issue were the instructions issued by chief native commissioner E. S. Davies, to field officers. When the countryside was seething with unrest and anti-European hostility, he stressed that they must increase their personal contacts with Africans:

> I consider it quite essential that at all times, and particularly in these difficult days when politics loom large, when inter-racial questions are constantly being brought to the forefront of the African's mind, and the human element in African administration is becoming increasingly difficult to cope with, personal contacts with Africans in their homes, shops,

in schools, in the field and the markets, in welfare centres, and indeed over a pot of beer, must be maintained. I believe that this can only be done if officers spend sufficient time out in the country with the African, walking wherever possible, and making as many contacts as they possibly can. *Much of the criticism now made by the African concerning government and much of the gross misrepresentation of government that is made to the African, will disappear if officers make these contacts and the ordinary African in the street gets a chance to hear the other side.*[11] (Italics mine.)

Inter-racial contacts are obviously important for the sharing of viewpoints, but the contacts suggested by the chief native commissioner were to be between people in antithetical status-power positions, and largely for the purposes of informing the low status-low power person of the viewpoint of the high status-high power person. (The former, for his part, had been trying unsuccessfully for decades to get his point of view across to the latter.) Social intercourse between people in equal status-power positions might well lead to a free exchange of ideas with each person having an equal opportunity to influence the other. But the situation the chief native commissioner envisaged lent itself to one-way communication rather than an exchange of ideas.

Both the chief native commissioner and the bishop cast what was essentially a power struggle into the idiom of personnel management. Instead of making any deep rooted changes in the system that would assure Africans land and equal rights, there would be a 'talking it out' and minor changes made within the present system.

Others advocated treating Africans with kindness and firmness as you would children. The advice of a provincial commissioner is illustrative:

> The line I have taken with them in recent *barazas* has been "you have been very naughty boys and it was necessary to punish you by imposing the pass rules and compulsory labour" . . . I believe that the proposals [punitive labour for Msambwa suspects] will be understood by the people, and in the end appreciated, as they provide prompt punishment of delinquents, resulting in development of their own area.[12]

From yet another perspective, already noted in the cult of Mumbo, the leaders were viewed as cunning and unscrupulous manipulators and fanatics who aroused, for their own benefit, simple peasants.[13] The *Native Affairs 1946–47 Report* stated, 'In Kimilili location of North Nyanza there was considerable trouble caused by a religious pervert called Elijah Masinde.' The following year the *Annual Report of the African Affairs Department* had this to say:

Its particular prophet, Elijah Masinde, had apparently found sufficient leisure during his period as a certified lunatic to frame political policy to fit his pronounced tendency to religious mania, and on his release in 1947 had immediately set about the task of stirring supporters into action under the guise of religious fervour. By the end of 1947 his followers numbered thousands who, though they had not had his excuse of a previous history of mental illness, showed themselves quite ready to adopt the principles devised in his aberrant brain.

The *East African Standard*, which probably reflected the views of a good portion of the settler community, editorialized as follows:

> He [Pkech] returned to a group of adherents among the Suk and spread his gospel of hatred with fanatical zeal. . . . He told the incredulous Suk that he had twice been killed and had returned to life. He died from a police bullet, leading to their death tribesmen *whose minds he had poisoned and distorted.*[14] (Italics mine.)

The Rift Valley Provincial Annual Report 1951 expressed the same perspective:

> The influence of the sect has ceased to be a factor in the lives of the East Suk, whose punishment for permitting themselves to become dupes of hysterical fanatics was formally terminated on 25 April by a baraza at Nginyang.

This perspective, satisfying as it may be for the agents because it finds a simple answer, overlooks an alternative proposition, namely, that an agitator is likely to have difficulty in arousing contented people. Those who adopted this perspective tended to advocate stronger punitive action believing that severer sanctions would deter people from joining.

The agents' paternalism led them to view Africans as children, or to put them into some equivalent category — primitives, psychologically maladjusted, extremely naive — that meant they were not fully responsible adults and that the agents knew best. Only the first perspective, discussed at the beginning of this chapter, acknowledged protest as stemming from legitimate grievances and aspirations. The others viewed it mainly as pathological or as derived from the antics of a few malcontents and other anti-social forces.

The agents' views were based in part on their experiences in circumstances where they feared a breakdown of law and order. If the adherents were unstable, psychologically disturbed people, then their protest could be dismissed as irrational and as not representative of the majority of Africans. It was comforting to believe that a 'rational administration' was being confronted by an 'irrational mob'.

Just as Msambwa's beliefs legitimized revolt, the agents through these perspectives reassured themselves that all would be well if only Dini ya Msambwa could be brought under control. Such thinking concentrated on changing the African and not the system. For years discontent had been evident. Instead of taking this protest as a sign of fissures in a system that required immediate and drastic change, the administration responded with half-way measures. Even at this time, it could not accept the depth and magnitude of African frustration. Masinde and his cohorts were rejected as spokesmen for the masses. But soon it would be apparent that Masinde was indeed a truer spokesman for the times than the more moderate leaders.

Notes

1. KNA:DC/NN/10/1/5. Letter from district commissioner Campbell of North Nyanza to the provincial commissioner, 30 May 1949.
2. KNA:DC/NN/10/1/5. Letter from provincial commissioner K. L. Hunter of Nyanza to the honourable chief native commissioner, 6 June 1949.
3. KNA:TN/2. Letter from community development officer L. G. Miller to the acting secretary, Ministry of Community Development, 6 January 1957.
4. KNA:DC/NN/2/6. Handing Over Report and Notes of Mr. R. S. Winser to Mr. L. C. Mortimer, August 1952.
5. KNA:TN2. Rehabilitation Report on Dini ya Msambwa prisoners and detainees Kapenguria Prison Works' Camp, November 1956.
6. DC/NN/10/1/5. Letter from provincial commissioner K. L. Hunter of Nyanza to the medical officer, Mathari Mental Hospital, 11 June 1946.
7. Letter from Douglas M. McKean to the editor of East Africa and Rhodesia, December 1951.
8. L. C. Usher-Wilson, 'Bishop's Study of 'Dini ya Misambwa',' p. 346.
9. David B. Barrett, Schism and Renewal in Africa, (Oxford University Press, Nairobi 1968), pp. 83–89; Kenyatta, Facing Mt. Kenya, pp. 269–271; Sundkler, Bantu Prophets, see especially pp. 32–37; Odinga, Not Yet Uhuru, Chapters 2 and 3. For a discussion of the racist, paternalistic and ethno-centric attitudes of the British Protestant missionaries in nineteenth century Madagascar, see Bonar A. Gow, 'The Attitude of the British Protestant Missionaries Towards the Malagasy Peoples, 1861–1895', Kenya Historical Review, III, 1, 1975, pp. 15–26. Their views are in keeping with the various dimensions of the negative stereotype, with the exception that there is no mention of the Malagasy rejecting the modern world and advocating a return to traditional life.
10. Usher-Wilson, 'Bishop's Study of 'Dini ya Misambwa'.'

11. KNA:WP14. Letter from E. S. Davies, chief native commissioner to all provincial commissioners, 26 July 1950.
12. KNA:DC/NN/1/1/5. Provincial commissioner K. L. Hunter.
13. KNA:BAR/8. Assistant superintendent of police D. Wright to the senior superintendent of police, 10 November 1950.

   Mr. Norman, the defence counsel for the Pokot on trial for the Kolloa murders, used this tactic. He summed up Dini ya Msambwa's attractions, 'I shall suggest that these people whom you see charged are nothing else but the innocent victims of a wicked and cunning man. I suggest to you that this man deliberately chose what is probably the most backward tribe of this Colony and the most undeveloped area of this colony for his activities.

   It is patent that these people live in a hard and ungrateful country. . . . It is perfectly clear that the life of these people is principally and primarily a struggle for existence. It is clear that infant mortality is high among them. It is clear that they suffer much from their eyes. To these people, living this hard life, there comes a prophet with healing in his wings; one who can promise them that they will never die; that their women will be pregnant and the children which these women will bear will never die; that sight will be restored to the blind; a man they can follow to a place where they will be rich and where they will see those who have died and meet them again.' *East African Standard*, 17 November 1950.

14. *East African Standard*, editorial entitled, 'The African Scene', 27 April 1950, quoted in Kipkorir, 'The Kolloa Affray 1950', p. 122. In another editorial the *Standard* stated that Masinde 'was once an adherent of a Christian European mission and what he taught his dupes to believe in his plea to return to the life of the old uncivilised Africa, was based upon his distortions and perversions of the Bible and abuse of the symbols of the Christian faith.'

Chapter 15

AN INTERPRETATION OF DINI YA MSAMBWA'S PROTEST IN THE COLONIAL PERIOD

THE negative stereotype suggests that Dini ya Msambwa's protest was a bizarre and irrational response to colonialism, that there were no real grievances but only agitators stirring up otherwise happy people with false promises. We would emphasize different dimensions.

Hostile outbursts often occurred on the spur of the moment, seemingly triggered by hatred of whites and their lackeys, the chiefs and tribal police. These events seemed to erupt from the boiling over of long smouldering anger, to be a kind of lashing out at the enemy. This spontaneity provided much of the movement's dynamism. The Malakisi Riot and the assaults on chiefs are examples. Of course, some of these incidents may not have been as unpremeditated as they appeared to be. Masinde, when in hiding, allegedly instructed his followers to attack the police station.

Coupled with spontaneity was an element of senselessness in terms of the consequences. Beating up a chief for issuing a labour summons was costly. It brought imprisonment. Much activity directed towards the missionaries and the chiefs was open defiance, a direct refusal to cooperate with the authorities regardless of the penalty. Under the colonial regime, acts of sheer defiance were clothed in an anti-colonial rhetoric. But in the post-colonial period they were to stand out for what they were.[1]

Msambwa engaged in direct action—its leader was that kind of a man. Not for him the slow-moving petition and pressure group. Msambwa meted out a kind of rough justice; a policeman who had harassed the members was beaten up, the bothersome agricultural officer had his house burned down. Although some reliance was placed upon magic, this was a minor element and appeared to be used as additional assurance that their objectives would be achieved.

262

The ancestors required oblations or else they might impede the attainment of goals.

Let us not be deceived, however, by the flamboyant character of the protest. Even though many events seemed to be spontaneous reactions they werre goal-directed. The followers did not beat up just anyone, but particular chiefs who had aroused their enmity. They did not roll boulders down a mountain upon anonymous individuals, but upon a police party. The same holds true of the other objects that were attacked, they were carefully not randomly selected.

Dini ya Msambwa helped shape and express peasant grievances, skillfully articulating a deep well of discontent, by focussing the blame on well chosen targets. Far from being isolated and aberrant, Msambwa's appeals were well attuned to people's dissatisfactions. The advocacy of returning to a world without persistent tax collectors, authoritarian agricultural officers, autocratic chiefs, harsh tribal police and patronizing missionaries was widely shared. Taxation, conscript labour, agricultural regulations and church collections were regarded as onerous and to be avoided when possible. As far as many peasants were concerned, the government, the chiefs, and the missionaries provided no useful or essential services, but instead were making new demands on them that ran counter to their welfare.

Nor did the movement vacillate from one goal to another. Stands were taken and maintained. Granted, its activity was sporadic—often of necessity, because of government vigilance—but examined over a decade there is evidence of sustained action towards consistent goals. We disagree in part with Wolf's assessment of peasant movements as 'unstable and shifting alignments of antagonistic and autonomous units, borne along only momentarily by a millennial dream. . . . and even if a millennial dream of justice persists among the peasantry, the short-term interest of the individual peasant inevitably takes precedence over any long-term ends.'[2] It seems to underemphasize the extraordinary difficulties peasants living on their separate land holdings have in mobilizing, and to overemphasize the instability of these movements, whereas instability characterizes social movements in general. (Besides, to leave the barricades in order to harvest this year's crop or to plant next year's crop, the absence of which means starvation, seems to me to be not only a legitimate but quite rational decision despite being merely a 'short-term interest'.)

Msambwa's protest was largely the work of autonomous, un-coordinated groups. Masinde's assistants proselytized and branches were established through local initiative. When leaders were arrested, members carried on alone. Individual initiative explains, in large part, the haphazard quality of the protest, and, in turn, its resilience. Individuals and small groups were effective disrupters, witness the atmosphere of uneasiness created by burning down a building once in a while or by leaving an occasional threatening letter.

Once the administration had arrested the leaders the movement had less direction than ever. The members simply followed their own dictates even if it meant going against some leader's instructions. In this way Dini ya Msambwa resembles Mau Mau, when, after important leaders were arrested, autonomous bands of forest fighters employed more violence than the top leadership would probably have permitted.

If the accusation that Msambwa was an irrational movement is based on the use of inappropriate means to achieve goals, let us examine its tactics. The British had demonstrated time and again that they could handle military confrontations, at least on the scale waged by Africans. But guerrilla warfare was a different matter. The mountainous terrain of Mount Elgon, full of rocks and caves with nearby rain forests, made detection difficult. The elaborate preparation the British made to track down Lukas Pkech and their rout at Kolloa demonstrates the considerable effort required. To maintain vigilance over a large area of restless people the government had to invest heavily in police, equipment, and personnel, none of which it had in abundance.

The peasants had only to cause an incident now and then to make the administration strengthen its surveillance. When the area was being closely watched, they could carry on with their ordinary lives. But when the government relaxed its vigilance, they could recommence their disruptive activities. While the cost to the government was high, the cost to the peasant was low — a few acts of sabotage could be included in a daily routine. It is not suggested that costs were not high to peasants, in terms of years in prison, harassment, and the suffering these brought to individual families. Nevertheless, one act of violence meant disproportionate effort on the part of the administration. In fact, the *1949 District Annual Report* stated that it was going to be impossible for the government to maintain its large police force and that a new approach had to be found to bring the area under law and order. In hitting upon guerrilla warfare, Msambwa effectively disrupted the system.

As for a go-slow policy, absenteeism and wildcat strikes, they were useful in bringing attention to the workers' plight, they made it difficult for the settler-farmers and when combined with arson made many of them question the wisdom of remaining. These tactics had a long history among the Bukusu. As far back as 1905, government buildings had been burned down and in the 1920s strikes and passive resistance had been used against the settlers.

While some would say that the riot is a primitive form of protest, it can be argued that it may be more effective than petitions and pressure, since it causes an administration to take immediate notice. Riots cannot be shrugged off as easily as petitions. And although riots and arson may not bring the goal the rioters wish, still they serve notice to an administration in a way a petition does not, that time is running out. Msambwa used selective violence. Violence against people was limited, but considerable foreign property was destroyed.

As for the use of extra-constitutional tactics, it must be remembered that legal channels had been tried for years and had failed to bring the sought after goals. In competition with a powerful settler lobby equipped with vastly superior tactical knowledge, as well as close personal ties with those in power in both Kenya and in Britain, Africans were bound to lose out. (Take, for example, Commander Carter going off to see the Governor when he feared a strike on his farm.) Africans were only becoming acquainted with the system of rules by which the Europeans played — hence the latter's tremendous advantage.

In an authoritarian system like Kenya where the different sectors of the population were marked by great disparities in power and wealth, where a tiny minority (the Europeans composed less than one per cent of the population) exercised inordinate power and influence which it was ever using to solidify its privileged position, what was the vast majority to do? It had limited means by which to express grievances and obtain redress. Since the authorities had long been indifferent to African demands for justice, Africans showed that they could be indifferent to the authorities' demands for order.

Msambwa's pattern of dissent directly challenged the administration and showed the populace that some people were not afraid to question, defy, and even fight their colonial masters. Dini ya Msambwa contributed to weakening British authority by weakening Luhya obedience to it. Its protest demonstrated a crude planning even though its activities lacked an overall strategy tailored to a programme. That was its great weakness. The movement possessed an overriding goal and grassroots activity but little in between.

Dini ya Msambwa bridged some clan rivalries and tribal differences to build a new basis of solidarity but it was unable to unite all the Luhya. It gave expression to strong anti-chief feelings that could not simply be equated with anti-colonialism, that is, the chiefs were not only disliked because they were agents of the imperialists but they were disliked in their own right because they represented the superior power of one clan over another. A policy of indirect rule where, in the early colonial period, clans had joined forces with the British to put down their traditional enemies, encouraged inter-clan factioning. Those clans that prospered under foreign rule were hated by the others, yet animosities separated the others as well. This fragmentation into clan-based groups meant that protest was tied to narrow units. Therefore, even though North Nyanza was the most politically conscious of the Nyanza districts, persistent parochialism plagued its politics and prevented the development of a united protest. The British had relatively few administrative and military personnel and if the dissenters had united, the dynamism of their combined efforts would have made it extremely difficult for the British to govern.

The Kikuyu saw the need for a common front and approached Msambwa, but were rejected. Msambwa, like many peasant movements, failed when it came to large scale mobilization and organization. Its leaders lacked the breadth of view and the ability to move from localized opposition to a mass movement on a territorial scale. Masinde, although capable of creating by his bold feats a revolutionary elan, was unable to weld this spirit into a nation-wide anti-British campaign. Yet, while Msambwa failed in its immediate objectives, it undoubtedly helped convince the British that the colony was becoming too costly to maintain.

Msambwa was a forerunner of a new era soon to emerge. Five years hence, the Kikuyu showed how increased guerrilla warfare, together with more strategy and effective leadership, could bring the system to a standstill and force the settlers, when the countryside was seething with rebellion, to call on the mother country to put it down. Mau Mau was a stronger, surer movement. Perhaps the basic reason was that the Kikuyu, united around the deeply felt issue of land, were able to fight the foreigners with a far larger backing than any other Kenyan tribe had hitherto been able to muster.

Notes

1. See below, pp. 271–74.
2. Eric R. Wolf, *Peasants*, p. 108.

down, Mau Mau was a stronger, surer movement. Perhaps the
basic reason was that the Kikuyu, united around the deeply felt
issue of land, were able to fight the foreigners with a far larger
backing than any other Kenyan tribe had hitherto been able to
muster.

Chapter 16

A LATER PHASE OF THE MOVEMENT

THE evolution of Msambwa in the post-colonial period[1]
provides further indications of its nature and basis of support.
These years witnessed Masinde's release, his impact upon the local
community, the drop in membership, the breakaway of Benjamin
Wekuke to form a separate religious group, and finally the government's proscription of Dini ya Msambwa and Masinde's imprisonment.

In the years immediately prior to independence, agitation began
for the release of Masinde and other Msambwa detainees. Daniel
arap Moi (Kenya's vice-president, 1975) and W. Wabuge petitioned
the government for their discharge. The Buluyia Political Union
in September 1960 demanded Masinde's immediate release.[2] A
member of the Legislative Council, Masinde Muliro issued a
statement which read, in part:

> Elijah Masinde and his two strong followers B. Wekuke and Joasch
> Walumoli as well as many others and West Suk people . . . have been
> under restriction for over ten years. These men never at any stage ordered
> anyone, but sought to worship in their own way. . . . The further restriction
> is completely unjust and devoid of human feelings. I call upon the
> Government to release these men to join their families without any further
> delay.[3]

Wisely, their pleas emphasized Msambwa's religious side.

The special place Masinde held in the hearts of the people was
demonstrated when he was freed in May 1961 after thirteen years
in detention. He returned to a hero's welcome. Gifts were given
him and a public collection sponsored by the Kenya African
Democratic Union (KADU) taken up towards building him a house.
The *East African Standard* newspaper reported the homecoming:

After a meeting at Chwele Market, Elgon-Nyanza, members of a crowd of about 10,000 were so anxious to see the founder of the proscribed Dini ya Msambwa, Mr. Elijah Masinde that they entered the bar into which he and Mr. M. Muliro had gone. Mr. Masinde left the bar and stood on top of Mr. Muliro's car for nearly 30 minutes before the crowd was satisfied.[4]

Such was his hour of triumph.

Clashes with the Authorities

The African government that came into being with independence told Dini ya Msambwa to register like any other organization if it wanted to resume its activities. The alternative was 'to disband and refrain from secret acts'. Even though not registered, Msambwa continued to hold meetings and arrests continued to be made.[5] On 12 April 1964, Prime Minister Jomo Kenyatta revoked the colonial order that had declared Dini ya Msambwa an illegal society. Those imprisoned nevertheless had to finish their sentences.[6]

In May of that year Dini ya Msambwa registered. Its constitution had five aims,[7]

    a)   To maintain our old way of believing in God.
    b)   To give respect to our Almighty God.
    c)   To respect our parents and neighbours.
    d)   To abide by the Law of the Land.
    e)   To be non-political.

The listing of Dini ya Msambwa's officials as president, vice-president, secretary, vice-secretary, treasurer and vice-treasurer, was simply copied from the sample application form the registrar-general circulates to organizations in order to help them write a constitution. The duties of the officers were similarly taken from the outline rather than what they actually did. Msambwa's officers, following the above order, were given as Elijah Masinde, Benjamin Wekuke, Samson Wafula, David Wanyonyi, Israel Khaoya, and Andrew Buluma. Its affairs were to be controlled by a committee made up of the office bearers together with fifty members elected at a general meeting. This body was to hold office for a period of three years. The funds were to be allocated for the following purposes:

    a)   For our visitors.
    b)   For orphans.
    c)   For the poor.

   d) For widows and widowers.
   e) For the upkeep of the landrover [a gift to Masinde]
       and maintenance of the society's property.
   f) For the building of our churches.
   g) For payments of staff employed by the Society.

Once the constitution was written, it is doubtful whether it was ever looked at again. As for being non-political and abiding by the law, it probably never occurred to Masinde what these entailed. Msambwa's officers held the same positions they had in the past and with minor variations were Masinde's assistants. He, as usual, made all the decisions. None of the staff except Masinde received any remuneration. He spent the funds as he saw fit. The money was apparently used to entertain guests (part of a leader's duties) and for personal expenses. Msambwa did not even pay the fines the assistant leaders incurred in pursuing its goals, nor is there any record of philanthropic undertakings. The schedule of meetings was not followed but took place irregularly as Masinde decreed. In short, the constitution was a piece of paper written to satisfy administrative requirements and not a guide for action.

A little more than six months after his release Masinde became embroiled in the crosscurrents of Kenyan politics. There were rumours that he would head a new political party called the Masaaba Nyanza Convention which would unite the Luhya-speaking peoples of Kenya and Uganda.[8] Masinde maintained that he did not support either KADU or the Kenya African National Union (KANU), but would work to unite them, 'I want to tell the political leaders to unite on every major national issue. I shall ask them why they are so much in dispute, delaying the country's independence.'[9]

Perhaps his biggest mistake, as far as alienating local people and important politicians, was his apparent support of KANU in an area strongly KADU. Introduced by the president of KANU, Jomo Kenyatta, as 'my greatest friend', he told a KANU rally in Kitale that he and Kenyatta were 'crucified in the cause of saving Kenya' and that God had revealed secrets to him while he was asleep.[10] KADU's deputy chairman, Masinde Muliro, who less than two years before had railed at the members of the Legislative Council for keeping Masinde in prison, and had promised that he would be responsible for Masinde's behaviour if they would only release him into his custody, was furious.[11] 'Mr. Masinde alleges that it has been revealed to him in his sleep that Mr. Kenyatta is a prophet.

Mr. Kenyatta should never be seduced by these hallucinations which are reducing him to a laughing-stock among intelligent Africans. KADU followers in the Trans Nzoia will not be moved by Mr. Masinde's claim that he was neither KADU nor KANU. . . . The sooner Mr. Masinde declares his identity with KANU and faces the consequences of a showdown among his own followers who support me, as KADU, fully, the better it will be for him.'[12] As far as KADU supporters were concerned, Masinde was an ungrateful turncoat.

With the removal of the British administrators and with the missionaries staying on at the request of an African government, Dini ya Msambwa, left without a major cause, engaged in a number of disruptive activities. Masinde and several followers would invade a mission and tell the missionaries that they had better leave the country as they were going to demolish the mission school and that it would soon be like the Congo. Several such incidents occurred during the 1964–65 Congo crisis. One occasioned the rushing of police reinforcements to Kimilili because it was feared that Msambwa members, out of their pro-Congolese sympathies, might resort to violence against the American missionaries in the vicinity.[13] Such carryings-on at a time when the mission schools were not only the best, but there was a scarcity of schools, raised the wrath of the community and Masinde began to be seen as an enemy of progress.

Msambwa's nightly ceremonies disturbed others. Chief Jeffrey Chebus issued an order forbidding members to beat drums at night and a year later the warning was repeated by the district commissioner.[14] Masinde led around five hundred members to Maitri Hill where they sacrificed a white goat. He condemned those who had purchased land saying they had wasted their money as the land actually belonged to them anyway and, furthermore, he would soon distribute it free to his followers. He castigated several policemen for spying on their meeting and caned two members because they had travelled to the meeting in the police landrover. Meanwhile the African who owned the land complained to chief Ntari that 'the people were spoiling his grass for his cow and were fouling his plot by making toilet on it and he feared they would steal his fencing posts and wire.'[15]

Msambwa's major project during the first years of independence was the opening of its own schools. This undertaking began when members returned from prison and did not have school fees for

271

their children. In characteristic Masinde fashion, schools were started despite having neither facilities nor teachers. The teachers, some little more than literate themselves, held classes outside under a tree or in private dwellings. Blackboards were frequently unavailable, so the ground was used. The manager of the schools, Samson Wafula, did not know how many teachers he had because he simply told any would-be teacher to start a school where he felt there was a need. Nor did he know the number of pupils enrolled. Some parents even withdrew their children from government schools and enrolled them in these schools because no fees were charged.

The district education officer repeatedly warned Masinde to either register his schools or close them down. Masinde paid no attention. Wafula replied to the question of whether they intended to follow the government's orders as follows:

> We won't close the schools because our children don't have the school fees they need to go to government schools. We also fought for freedom and if they close our schools by force we will fight the County Council. The government still hate us. We haven't wronged them. Our teachers haven't asked for a salary from the Education Department. They volunteered. . . . I don't see that we're doing any wrong to the government. Although I haven't heard anything from Kenyatta himself, just an order from the County Council. If they want to put us back in jail we'll accept that rather than close the schools.[16]

Years of opposition to a colonial government had taken their toll on Msambwa's amenability to any government authority. The government, however, had no intention of brooking any defiance on the part of Msambwa, and Masinde and Wafula were subsequently charged with opening illegal schools. Their case was heard at Bungoma in November 1965. The testimonies of Masinde's followers on his behalf were more damning than helpful. After swearing 'to tell the truth, the whole truth', they confused the issues, contradicted themselves and each other, until the judge, trying to operate within a framework of logic and rationality, could hardly contain his disgust. The outcome was fines or imprisonment for both Masinde and Wafula.

The school issue supports the view that Msambwa did not turn its back on the modern world and opt for the traditional life. Msambwa was against schools in the colonial period not because they represented modernity but because, sponsored by the missions, they represented colonialism. In fact, the little education that the

272

leaders had themselves was obtained from the missions. After independence the members defied their own government in order to open schools because they believed that education was the avenue to success for their children. 'I heard people saying how much they wanted education so I thought that it would be a good thing for our *dini* to open our own schools and organize them like those of the missionaries,' Wafula explained.[17]

Masinde took the law into his own hands again when he decided to punish Grace Nasimiyu, a former wife of a member, Japhet Werungu, for philandering. According to her court testimony, she had been married to Werungu for a short time in 1958 but he had deserted her. On 23 September 1968, Werungu and Masinde entered the *Sisi Kwa Sisi* bar in Kimilili where she worked as a barmaid. Masinde shouted, 'I don't want harlots in town. Grace is introducing prostitution and teaching other women. I don't need more harlots now.' They beat her with their fists and sticks and forced her to Werungu's home where Masinde ordered her to take off her clothes and kneel on the floor for a cleansing ceremony. He knelt opposite her and began to pray. Upon being released, Mrs. Nasimiyu immediately went to the police, whereupon Masinde and Werungu were arrested and later convicted of assault. Masinde was jailed for two years and Werungu for one year as he was a first offender.[18]

Masinde's confrontations with the authorities took on a characteristic pattern; they were held in public places, they were showy events, and while often of little significance in themselves, they were obviously important for each party concerned as a test of their power. Typical of these encounters is the following episode. Inspector Wilson Owuor, a prosecution witness, told how on 8 May 1972 around 1 p.m., he was driving along Kenyatta Avenue in Kitale with inspector Macharia Kabuthia. Suddenly he saw around five hundred people near Mwangaza Studio (a photographer's shop) with Masinde in the middle. Owuor stopped his car and heard Masinde tell the crowd, 'No vehicle will pass along this avenue until I finish addressing my people.' Owuor told Masinde that stopping vehicles was an offence but Masinde insisted he would talk to his followers. Masinde told his people that 'all Luos will go to Kisumu and eat fish and all the Kikuyu will go back to their home and eat potatoes [meaning they should clear out of Luhya territory].' Inspector Kabuthia tried to arrest Masinde but Owuor stopped him because he feared Masinde's followers would assault them. He then went to the Kitale police lines and sounded an alarm that brought twenty policemen, but Masinde had departed. Inspector Owuor testified that the insulting words Masinde used would have caused a riot.[19] (One should note the similarities between this episode and one described earlier on pages 159–60.)

Masinde's predilection for confrontations with the authorities came to be reciprocated on their part. The police, like any group charged with keeping the peace, had soon had enough of Masinde and were on the alert for any excuse to jail him. 'Masinde won't change,' said an inspector of the Kimilili police. 'Putting him in jail won't do any good but it keeps him out of the way. I hope he doesn't come back.'[20] Masinde was constantly being arrested on charges of 'conduct likely to cause a breach of the peace', 'incitement to defiance of lawful authority', 'obstructing a police officer in carrying out his duty', 'resisting arrest', 'being a member of an unlawful society' and 'holding an unlawful meeting'. In the late 1960s and early 1970s the charges, and his appeals against sentences, occurred so often that cases ran concurrently. (The chronology of events in Dini ya Msambwa's career, pages 336–46, catalogues their frequency.) Once it was for possession of Nubian gin.[21] Another time, he visited Uganda, though a prohibited immigrant, and was promptly arrested and imprisoned for six months.[22] (His presence was not welcome in countries with precarious political stability.) Three years later, he was in court again charged with three counts of inciting members of the Kenyan police force to mutiny if the government did not increase their pay.[23] Quite a turnabout for one whose arch enemy for years had been the police.

Some arrests were quite trivial. For example, constable Nyangweso Okumo told the court that on 24 April 1972, he and constable Kirome Muti saw a girl pushing an unlicensed bicycle followed by Masinde at Mabusi trading centre. When asked for the licence, Masinde held them by their shirts and then pushed them away with the order, 'Do not touch my bicycle or you will not go with it to the police station.' According to constable Okumo, Masinde pushed them a second time and as they tried to escape they were surrounded by a violent mob of fifty people. They raised an alarm by blowing a whistle and the mob dispersed.[24] This case, like several others against Masinde and his followers was dismissed for lack of evidence.[25]

Masinde complained of police harassment. He told a magistrate's court, a little more than a year after his release, that he wished the Kenyan government would order his re-detention 'Because I am tired of police threats. Twice I have been threatened with guns. Therefore, I prefer being deported and detained.'[26] On one occasion when two policemen appeared at a meeting he was conducting and began to take notes, Masinde caught hold of one policeman by the arm and said, 'What can I do to these fools. Police dogs, why are you following me wherever I go?' He then ordered them to be seated and not to take any notes. He was given thirty months sentence for assault and obstructing a policeman in the execution of his duty. Asked if he wanted to say anything before being sentenced, Masinde replied, 'Thank you for having given me [my] throne of kingdomship. I am going to inherit it. Prison is like my food. I wish you to care for my children.'[27] Fitz de Souza, an M.P., questioned this surveillance in the National Assembly. He asked the Assistant Minister in the President's Office whether he was aware that when police had invaded Masinde's religious meeting where they had started to take notes on the proceedings, that they had, in fact, provoked a breach of the peace, and that Masinde was perfectly entitled to throw them out.[28]

His followers not only complained of harassment but of being manhandled. Japhet Wafula, Masinde's uncle, testified that when they were arrested, police slapped and struck them with their guns.[29]

Disillusionment with Masinde

Masinde's mystique quickly faded under the impact of his presence. As he pursued his reckless ways, the image of the noble rebel became tarnished. Although admired for his refusal to compromise with the colonialists, his intolerance of views different from his own hardly endeared him to other Africans. Also when he returned from detention, an absence during which others had 'made the revolution' and continued to act 'the revolutionary', he made himself look foolish. True, he had cut a dashing figure in the colonial period, but now his outrageous shenanigans proved too taxing. ('Shenanigans' does describe the almost prankish quality of many of Masinde's escapades. His impetuous actions were costly to himself in terms of imprisonment and fines, and were much less dangerous than the carefully contrived Mau Mau plots. Masinde emerges as rather hapless, and a far less threatening figure than the Mau Mau fighters.)

The saying, 'distance builds the great man' was essentially true in Masinde's case. Legends were far more likely to flourish in his absence than in his presence. In the colonial period he performed an important function, the indomitable rebel, and this he performed better in jail than out. In the first place, arrest increased his stature and enhanced his authority. It was in prison that he began to loom large as a powerful prophet in more than his own locality. But once out of jail, his actions spoiled the myths. He annoyed and infuriated too many people.

Masinde's anti-Asian diatribes were now severely criticized. (There is evidence, see p. 160, that these went back as far as 1944). Masinde Muliro, after one such attack, publicly noted that he did not sound like a man of God for a God-loving person could not preach hatred among people of different races. 'I want to make it clear to the Asian community who are residents of Trans Nzoia where Mr. Masinde delivered his speech and all in Elgon-Nyanza, where he lives, that whatever he said does not represent the opinion of the people of Elgon-Nyanza or Trans Nzoia.'[30]

Masinde's shouting at a judge and excoriating a district commissioner now failed to win plaudists. Where in colonial times, his run-ins with the authorities had been taken as marks of distinction, that he, like Jesus Christ, was persecuted, now they were considered a disgrace. 'How can a holy man who talks to God be in jail every now and then?' a local person asked. 'The holy people we hear of are not put in jail for months and even years. This clearly shows us that he is not a real leader.'

Masinde differed from ordinary peasants in that he was a great hater and they were not, he loathed authority of any kind and they did not. The peasants grumbled and became angry with the government, but they did not hate with such intensity and they accepted what they believed was legitimate authority. Government regulations were viewed as onerous but part of the ordinary routine of life like tilling the fields and making oblations to the ancestor spirits. They were men and women of common sense and compromise who lacked fanatical passions to spur them on. Masinde's hatred and defiance, by contrast, were heroic as well as exhausting, but too much to be widely shared except under special circumstances.

The community had forgotten what it was like to 'live' with Masinde. Of his eighteen heroic years, fifteen had been spent incarcerated. Now the community was experiencing him daily. Weary of his confrontations with authority, the local people gave warning but Masinde, heedless as ever, failed to take note. Praise and adulation changed to condemnation and ridicule. Now he was viewed as an agitator instead of a nationalist, a trouble-maker instead of a defender of the oppressed. In fact, less than a year after his release (even before independence), the local residents denounced the movement and asked the government to deport him:

> Bukusu tribesmen want the founder of the banned Dini ya Msambwa, Mr. Elijah Masinde and his lieutenants deported from Elgon-Nyanza. About 1,500 Bukusu people at a meeting at Kimilili yesterday agreed that a deputation of tribal elders should seek an interview with the Governor, Sir Patrick Renison, and urge that this step should be taken. . . . A mass meeting of 73 chiefs and elders from the Bungoma district denounced the teachings of Elijah Masinde as 'misleading, wicked and dangerous' to the peaceful development of the district. The meeting was called by the Bungoma District Commissioner, Mr. R. F. Winser, and the Member for Elgon-Nyanza, Mr. M. Muliro. . . . The chiefs and elders called upon the government to impose restrictions and sanctions on Mr. Masinde and asked the community to reject his teaching.[31]

Later that year a KADU meeting of more than five thousand people condemned Msambwa.[32] Two years later, when Kenyatta revoked the order banning it, a KADU branch chairman strongly criticized the government. He said the movement was not a religion, but a political organization in disguise, affiliated to KANU.[33]

A member of the Friends Africa Mission expressed the community's hopes and later disillusionment with Masinde:

> He talks like someone who is causing the present government all kinds of trouble. We thought he might change for the new government is an African government but . . . he hasn't changed at all. It looks as if he might even overthrow the present government because his speeches and his feelings are strongly anti-government. Maybe he wants the leadership for himself. . . . He thinks the whole world is his and he is not prepared to ask anyone's permission when he wants to hold his meetings. He is quite ornery. When he is told not to hold meetings, he is more anxious than ever to hold meetings. When he is told not to start schools, that is the very reason he is building more schools than ever.[34]

A local storekeeper voiced a similar opinion. 'Masinde is not a good man. He is retarding the development of this location. We people are all tired of him. I just don't know why people follow him. All I can say is that that *dini* won't go for long if Masinde is the leader.'[35]

A one-time supporter said:

Elijah is no good . . . I don't rhyme with him. I don't want anything to do with him. He is an enemy of development. The Suk really honour him but we people who live near him know him for what he is. We hate him. The people of the location offered to help him when he got out of prison, to build his house. He was given a lot of money but he wasted it on drink and silly things so the house isn't built. The Bukusu of nine locations took up a collection because he had been in jail for a long time, 10,000/- or even more than that. They bought him iron sheets but he sold them to get more money. If his followers from Suk country comes he kills a bull for them, buys lots of liquor and they sit up all night feasting and drinking and sinning.[36]

A former member told how he had unmasked, to his own satisfaction, Masinde's claim to divine instructions:

I've known Elijah from his youth. When he started the *dini* he told us that God told him to organize us and to teach people the word of God. But I'm sure God has never spoken to Elijah since he was born. Elijah is a person who is filled up with devils.

He pretends he goes to Mount Elgon where God speaks to him. That is quite untrue. One day he told us that he was going to speak to God on Mount Elgon. I decided to follow him. I followed him secretly until he reached Lake Zion. I hid several hundred feet away behind a bush. I saw him kneel down in front of the lake, raise his arms to the heavens as if he were praying, and then he took some water and poured it on his head. He took his clothes off and ran naked around the lake. He came back where his clothes were and started to jump up and down. He flung his arms upward to the heavens and shouted. Then Elijah dressed and started to walk home.

The next day when I went to his church service I heard him saying that he had gone to the mountain yesterday and spoke to God. . . . God told him in a loud voice which filled up the whole place that he should tell his followers that they should take a black goat and sacrifice it at his home and then chase the *wazungus* away. But I knew in my heart that he didn't speak to God . . . I knew he was only cheating the people.[37]

Masinde's erratic moods and eccentricities were no longer admired or interpreted as signs of special powers. The opinion grew that he was demented. Remarks were made such as 'Something is wrong with his head'; 'Masinde talks rubbish. He has an empty head'; or 'He doesn't think logcially. He doesn't remember. He can ask the same question four times. You answer him and he asks you again.' Obviously Masinde had been that way for years but when serving a useful purpose no one noticed, or, at least, negatively commented upon these qualities. The distinction between being viewed as a messiah or a madman may well depend upon the function the person is serving and lie with the group making the assessment. Are they his supporters or critics?

The membership fell away. When Msambwa registered in 1964 it gave its membership as ten thousand. At the end of 1964 it was four thousand and from 1965 to 1967 it was over a thousand.[38] A government estimate of the three locations where Msambwa was strongest (Kimilili 336, Malakisi 84, and South Bukusu 211) placed it at 631, a much lower figure, and probably more accurate.[39] 'The followers are getting tired of paying their money for Elijah's fines,' an assistant explained. 'They say they use most of their money for Elijah but they need it for taxes. The followers have become very poor people just because of their leader. He hasn't helped them to prosper at all. . . . People are getting fed up. Some people are even saying to me, . . . leave this man alone. He's only depending on his stomach [meaning he wants food and gifts for himself only].'[40]

Masinde's response to this cooling of ardour did not help matters. Having already used up his quota of the community's goodwill, he compounded his offense and further weakened his authority by denouncing the government as one of 'usurpers' and predicting that Kenyatta would not reign long.[41] Kenyatta, the father of Kenya's nationhood, who had suffered for independence and had been democratically elected, was a far cry from a usurper and Masinde could no longer claim to be fighting foreign domination. In short, his message, without the legitimacy conferred by opposition to colonialism, lacked its former appeal.

The loyalty and patience of Masinde's assistants waned and opposition grew within the movement. Said to be befuddled by drinking excessively and smoking opium and bhang, Masinde was a constant source of confusion and worry, especially because he insisted upon being the sole decision-maker. When locked up he had been useful since this permitted the more organized to carry on. 'If Elijah would go away', a local resident said, 'the others could carry on and all would be well.'[42]

Israel Khaoya and a few 'old fighters' remained on Masinde's side, but the moderates, like Wafula, Wekuke and Walumoli, recognized that Msambwa was fast losing the people's sympathy and was isolating itself from the mainstream of Kenyan life. It was obvious to them that Masinde's leadership would soon return them to jail as the *African authorities were reacting in essentially the same way as the British*. In addition, they were suffering from 'battle fatigue'. Tired of all the commotion, fighting, fines and jailings, as well as Masinde's autocratic ways, they were ready to get on with the ordinary tasks and pleasures of life. They had paid dearly for their protest, many having spent more than a decade in jail. As far as they were concerned Msambwa should desist from politicking and concentrate on religion.

So serious had the division become that several left. In a letter dated 23 June 1968, Wekuke announced:

I have left Elijah Masinde because of his bad behaviour.
1) He is mixed up with government politics.
2) He does not want people to buy plots in the scheme. [Wekuke was trying to buy a plot in a government scheme so he could move away since his farm bordered Masinde's.]
3) He does not want children to learn at school.
4) He does not want the seventh day to be Sunday. [Probably he had come in contact with the Seventh-day Adventists.]
5) The money of the Musambwa people gets lost. He uses it for his purposes alone.[43]

Wekuke, tired of years of wrangling, moved to a settlement scheme some miles distant. In 1969, he and Walumoli formed their own religious group called Misango (Spiritual) African Mission.[44]

The talk of a change in leadership proved interesting. A member, following the constitution, maintained that Dini ya Msambwa's leaders held their position for three years only, whereupon others were chosen. Such action would certainly gain Masinde's wrath as it would deny his divine appointment. When asked how this would be done, given Masinde's claim to divinity which some still honoured, he replied:

God works on different people. God may work in you, then he may change and work through me or another person. We can't say he [Masinde] is a leader for life because one person could start spoiling things. God created human beings as his houses. He may dwell in one of his houses and when it starts to become dirty he leaves and goes to a clean house. Such are the changes that God makes.[45]

When belief in a leader's authority is questioned, it is already likely to be seriously eroded. The members' resourcefulness both in discarding a myth that had outlived its usefulness and in creating a new one is nicely demonstrated.

The central government came to regret that it had ever released Masinde. Attorney-General Charles Njonjo in December 1966 stated, 'The release in my opinion, was premature but I did it in good faith. I had been assured by some members who come from that area that Masinde was prepared to cooperate with the government.' He added that Msambwa was a bogus religion and that Masinde was only trying to line his own pockets. 'Masinde is an old man. I don't want to have the unpleasant task of having to prosecute him again and send him to prison. My appeal to the members . . . is that they should tell Mr. Masinde to keep off politics and to follow his own religion.'[46]

The government continued to keep Dini ya Msambwa under close surveillance.[47] Vice-President Daniel arap Moi, issued another warning in February 1968 that Msambwa might be banned 'if it continues with its political ideologies and destructive tendencies to disunite the people of Central Nyanza.'[48] He stated that Dini ya Msambwa had caused a lot of suffering in West Pokot and other places and had held up progress, a far different argument from his 1960 motion to the colonial government deploring its delay in releasing the remaining Msambwa adherents.[49] Finally, in October 1968, Attorney-General Njonjo proscribed Dini ya Msambwa as a 'society dangerous to the good government of Kenya'. He said it did not preach the word of God but sedition and revolt.[50]

Basis of Support

Members of the community were questioned about what kind of a group Dini ya Msambwa was, as distinct from Masinde himself, and about what kind of people joined it. An effort was made to acquire a representative, although casual sample, marked by differences in sex, age, occupation, socio-economic level and religion. Shopkeepers, government officials, mission converts, members of other religious groups, and the young and old were interviewed in the village of Kimilili and outside the village at the market place. Negative opinions were much in the majority.

An African who runs a small eating place replied heatedly when asked about Msambwa:

> Oh those awful people. Yes I know them very well. There are hundreds and hundreds of them around here. . . . I, myself, am a Muslim. And

I don't even want to hear about this group. They have caused a lot of trouble here. They are not good people. They drink too much and after they are drunk they come and shout at people, speaking nonsense. I really don't like them. This group is not a *dini*. Which *dini* permits liquor? Which *dini* permits smoking? Which *dini* permits talk about political affairs? Even you Christians, do you practise these things? Do you go about with your neighbours' wives? This is what these people do. Their leader is just this kind of person. I heard that one day he ordered some of his followers to bring him a beautiful girl. Now have any of your padres or bishops in your *dini* done that?[51]

A student at Kamusinga Secondary School gave this view of the followers:

The followers accept anything Masinde tells them. The followers are people who never spare even a single minute to think of whether something he said is wrong or not. They don't have time to think of that. They believe him so much and they have a strong faith in him. Because of that I'm sure no one can influence them or abuse their leader in their presence. They would do whatever the leader tells them. If they are told by the leader to kill someone, they do. If they are asked to bring presents they do. So their leader is someone you can't oppose in their presence or else you are killed.[52]

The point about killing was probably made for emphasis. To my knowledge, Masinde has never been charged with murder nor do such rumours even prevail.

A member of Friends Africa Mission was particularly incensed over the deification of Masinde:

These people are awful. They do things that Christians never do. And I think in the whole world there is no religion behaving like them. . . . These mad people keep on disturbing us, keep on disturbing the peace of our location. We are tired of these people. I wish Masinde had never come back from jail. In Dini ya Msambwa they are as free as rats are in a house where there is no cat. They don't have any commandments in Dini ya Msambwa and they don't have any rules. Anybody can do anything he likes. Do you think this is a *dini* really? A *dini* which never uses the Bible? They are pretending they are reading the Bible but they don't understand what is in the Bible. They mix it with ancestor spirits' beliefs. They mix it with a bit of politics. I can't believe in a *dini* that is mixed up with all these kinds of things. Their leaders keep on shouting in the streets of the village saying that the *wazungus* should go and all kinds of nonsensical words. They call Masinde their god, that he is the god of the Bukusu tribe. But I am sorry. I am a Bukusu but he's not my god. I know of one God who created the earth and heaven and His Son. But not Elijah Masinde. How can a human being who is married to women and having children like me become my god? Can you really believe that?[53]

From these and other opinions, Dini ya Msambwa was dismissed as a religious group because:

a) It was syncretic.

b) It preached politics instead of religion.

c) The members did not subscribe to local standards and the more general canons of Christian behaviour as preached in that area. They drank excessively, smoked bhang, committed adultery, and in other ways did not live up to standards.

d) The members engaged in idolatry since they regarded Masinde as their god.

According to local people, the following types appear well represented in Msambwa's post-colonial membership.

1) Diehard members who had supported the movement for years. Into this category fall the fanatics, members who would do anything the leader commanded or, in Hoffer's terminology, 'true believers'.[54]

2) The uneducated, followers of traditional ways.

3) The ignorant. They were described as 'uninformed', 'foolish', 'mad', 'superstitious', and 'people of little understanding'. This category often overlapped with number two.

4) The lazy and unprogressive. This designation is closely linked to number three.

5) Immoral people. People who were said to drink excessively, smoke opium, bhang, and commit adultery. Also people described as 'criminals', 'rogues', and regarded as dishonest and untrustworthy.

6) Emotional people. Those who engaged in spirit possession or other forms of religious ecstasy. Some of these people would also fall into category three.

7) Malcontents. People always at odds with the community, the chronic complainers and trouble-makers.

These categories are subjective designations by local people. It should be borne in mind that their opinions were collected at a time when Dini ya Msambwa had sorely tried people's tempers and hence their judgements were undoubtedly harsher than if Msambwa had been in better grace. Hence the above hypothesis requires more study. It would be useful if more objective data could be gathered on a sample of Msambwa's membership and compared with a sample drawn from the community at large. However, bearing in mind these defects, if this categorizing is at least partially correct, some members appear to be drawn from the most backward elements of the population, people unable to cope effectively with the world around them, and hence probably attracted by Masinde's utopian promises.

This view is supported, in part, by Welime's study. 'Dini ya Msambwa is composed mainly of illiterates most of whom do not know what is happening around them. They have failed to integrate in their sect the elites.'[55] Although his description is brief, it does suggest some of the same kind of people. Further weight is added to this interpretation by de Wolf. He describes the members as follows:

> But to others [Msambwa members] *expressive action was easier and more satisfying*. Marches and mass protests were believed to be immediately successful. *They were joined by people who were not very well aware of what Elijah was aiming at*. They would just join Msambwa marching along the roads, singing, hammering, and whistling, and walk for miles and in the end wonder what had been the purpose of it all, and what good it had done to them, as one perceptive Bukusu told me. . . . *Drug taking and disassociation were other symptoms of the basic rejection of the grid system* [an achievement orientation] and the differentiation through competition which it implied.[56] (Italics mine.)

According to de Wolf, the members tend to be gullible, unprogressive, and given to drug-taking and dissociation. (It is difficult to know exactly what is meant by 'dissociation' but from its context it probably refers to religious ecstasy or spirit possession.)

These data at first glance seem to support the negative stereotype, but if we consider both the colonial and post-colonial periods the data, instead of supporting the stereotype, provide evidence against it. The stereotype insists on Dini ya Msambwa's basic irrationality. The data support instead a major hypothesis of this study, namely that *during the colonial period Msambwa's protest was based on legitimate grievances and recruited sensible and intelligent people who later, weary of Msambwa's disturbances, withdrew their support. Far from being gullible, the evidence points to discriminating people who supported Dini ya Msambwa when its protest made sense and withdrew their support when it didn't.*

As to whether the members were among the poorest in the area, information on the leaders suggests that they, at least, were not. From visits to the homes of various leaders, they did not appear to be any different economically than other people. They, like the majority, were subsistence farmers with small cash incomes.[57] Jan de Wolf writes in the same vein, 'What I found out about the background of some important DyM leaders around Sirisia does not indicate at all that they were particularly poor. Their motives for joining the movement had been mixed.' He mentions polygyny, politics, and Bukusu traditions, and concludes that there was 'no indication that the poor only joined.'[58]

Eric Hoffer argues in *The True Believer* that deep-seated psychological motives propel people to join mass movements. Since these movements draw their adherents from the same type of people, it follows that their memberships are competitive and interchangeable.[59] If, as Hoffer proposes, individual psychological drives can explain Msambwa's recruitment rather than the relevance of its grievances, we should expect the membership to stay the same regardless of whether it is the colonial or post-colonial period. This our data suggest is not so. Furthermore, as for being psychologically maladjusted, there is little evidence that Dini ya Msambwa's membership in the colonial period contained any more maladjusted people than the population at large.

The Loyal Members' Reactions

How did those loyal to Masinde react to the community's hostility and to his imprisonment? The loyalists saw their leader as an innocent victim of police and government harassment.[60] They were appalled that an African government would arrest him and treat him like any ordinary person who broke the law. They were furious at President Kenyatta for not intervening. Their messiah, who had fought most of his life for independence, had been imprisoned longer than Kenyatta, and had even supported Kenyatta in his bid for power, deserved not only a place of honour but tangible rewards as well now that Kenya was free. If the members recognized the illegality of opening the schools, still they questioned the rightness of the law and the government's position in encouraging people to engage in self-help schemes. In their eyes, Masinde was being prosecuted for doing just what the government had encouraged.

An old man, well into his seventies, replied to the question of why Masinde was arrested as follows:

I don't know, I don't know. I thought you would know better than me because you still have bright eyes to read the newspapers. I have just come to listen with my own ears as to why they have arrested our great leader. If they convict him, as soon as he comes out of jail everyone in the government will come forward and kiss his feet and beg for his pardon. He's god. But these people don't know it. [He whispered this.] They think that if they severely punish him they will destroy his natural powers·

A man in his thirties expressed great indignation at Kenyatta's ingratitude to Masinde:[61]

> You know very well that Mr. Kenyatta was arrested for nine years but Masinde for thirteen years. And he, Kenyatta, knows Masinde very well. . . . Now when they are all out of jail Kenyatta puts Masinde back in jail again. [Said with great feeling.] How can you be in the same hole with your friend, come out of the hole, shake hands because you are out of your troubles, you are happy now, you are free and then you wait and when your friend has just turned his back you grab him by the neck and push him back into the hole. . . . Do you think it is clean before God and before other human beings to do such a thing?

Disappointment and bitterness gave rise to a new myth: Kenyatta's government was doomed because of the way it had treated Masinde. A new prophet (some said Masinde, others referred to an unnamed, shadowy figure) would appear, overthrow the present government and all of Masinde's enemies. Then Masinde would rule and his former persecutors would bow down and beg his forgiveness. A story circulated telling about the coming millennium:

> One day the world will come to an end. Masinde will whistle and then all the members will come from the four sides of the compass and they will march to heaven, drumming and singing on their way. Masinde will lead them because he has the key to heaven's gates. Now everyone else will be burnt to ash. Masinde has talked to God and God told him this.

Only a few years earlier, the idea of a millennium had been equated with independence. Now that that dream had been shattered, another millennium was in view.

Hostility also focussed upon long standing ethnic animosities. For instance, the inspector of police who jailed Masinde was a Kikuyu. The young inspector had not even been born when Masinde was already crusading for independence — a further insult.

Interpretation and Speculation

Masinde's stature as a true prophet who would lead his people to victory seemed fulfilled with the attainment of independence. Upon release from prison he was welcomed as a hero. Then, as he continued to clash with the authorities, disturb the location, and be jailed and fined frequently, that definition began to change. Resentment towards him grew as some members began to suspect that he was a 'false prophet' and an 'enemy of progress'. To others, however, he remained the all-powerful messiah. Thus, two sets of conflicting beliefs vied with each other. These beliefs evoked strong emotions from people who had paid a price—witness the years in prison and the hardship suffered by them and their families—for their adherence to them. In attempting to resolve the inconsistencies, members of each side tried to strengthen their argument and in doing so were probably led to more extreme positions than they would otherwise have taken.[62]

Some members resolved the discrepancy between Msambwa's beliefs and post-colonial evidence by rejecting Masinde's leadership. Those wanting to dissociate themselves from Dini ya Msambwa were helped because its major aim had been fulfilled and they could argue that since it had no new, worthwhile goals, it was simply dissipating people's energies. Yet in severing an allegience of many years that involved strongly held beliefs, there were, undoubtedly, feelings of guilt. In an effort to fend off accusations by the faithful that they were turncoats, the ex-members castigated them, in turn, for their stupidity in falsely perceiving the facts. Thus some of the harsh attacks on Masinde and on the faithful were aimed at stilling their own nagging doubts about Masinde's true stature as well as convincing others of the correctness of their new beliefs, thereby strengthening their cause by sheer numbers.

The plight of the still-committed followers was another matter. They reacted with anger and disbelief at the government's and some followers' treatment of Masinde. They rejected pressures to bring their perception of Masinde into line with the government's. The loyalists took the position that it was the government and not Masinde that was at fault and they came up with several rather ingenious arguments, already mentioned, about Masinde's innocence and a future millennium. Thus through a set of counter explanations and attacks, the loyalists discounted the evidence and held on to cherished beliefs. To discard those beliefs and/or to give up Dini ya Msambwa which was important in their lives, would have entailed relinquishing a view of themselves as loyal followers and admitting they had been taken in by a false prophet. Aiding the loyalists' position were Masinde's successful prophecies about the departure of the colonialists.

From the government's standpoint, what could it do with Masinde? His personality and rudimentary education did not fit him for a responsible position. His reluctance to eschew activities regarded by the authorities as political hardly made him an appropriate religious leader, not at least, in Kenya. From the viewpoint of the government, Masinde was an anachronism, his protest belonged to a past era. Now it wanted Africans to get on with other tasks.

At the crux of Masinde's inflexibility appears to be his attachment to a role that had, at that time at least, become obsolete. It is always difficult to leave the role of hero for that of an ordinary mortal, but another possible reason behind his inflexibility is that the role fitted him too well. His public image came close to his core personality. Or to put it another way, prior to independence the public had supported and confirmed the view he held of himself. Thus he was able to develop fully his potentialities as a rebel. Few could have done it better than he. His flamboyant personality and colourful antics attracted attention. In his fierce rhetoric, he voiced the gut-deep rage felt by some and awakened it in others. He played the role to the hilt and his performance was acclaimed. But unfortunately this was the 'real' Masinde. A career built on being a rebel—not just in relation to the British, but before them, parents, peers, teachers and employers—does not leave much room for the development of other talents.

In 1969, Wekuke submitted the constitution of the Misango African Mission to the registrar-general of societies requesting permission to start a new group. Its constitution set down religious, social welfare and economic goals and dissociated it from political activity. Misango's syncretism was broad, ranging through Christian, Muslim and traditional beliefs. One objective was:

> To preach and spread the Gospel of God with a reference from the whole Bible of God to sing the Songs which shall praise God, the Father, the Son, The Holy Ghost and other prophets sent by God to save the people on the Earth, like Mohamed, etc. But nevertheless shall not leave out or forget to do, our Natural and original Traditional Customs and activities originated from our ancestors or our forefathers.

The constitution listed a formidable set of goals—support for dispensaries, hospitals, nurseries, primary and secondary schools, the Red Cross, cripples, the blind, and orphans—for a group without funds. In addition, it proposed that land and commercial enterprises be purchased. Wekuke claimed a large membership though there was little evidence that anything had been done except to write a constitution. This inaction is explained, in part, because the government had not given it permission to organize.

The government has subsequently refused Misango permission to register which means that it cannot function legally. Since its main leaders, Wekuke as president and Walumoli as vice-president, had been key figures in Msambwa, it probably appeared to the government as an attempt to resurrect Dini ya Msambwa in a new guise. Provincial commissioner Simon Nyachae had issued a stern warning in 1969 about just that sort of thing, 'It is understood that some people are beginning to form Dini ya Msambwa under different names. These are known and will be dealt with according to the law.'[63] While he may not have been referring specifically to Misango, he clearly stated the government's position. The stand taken by an African government, like the British before them, underlines the fact that it too believes that Dini ya Msambwa is to be taken seriously and it highlights the problems a new government has in dealing with a movement that has for years been encouraged by unofficial norms to break the official.

Notes

1. Chronologically this is not exactly correct as events that occurred between 1960 and November 1963 are included. (Independence was obtained in December 1963.) However, it marks a dividing point in Dini ya Msambwa's career as significant changes took place at that time in its activities and a different attitude was taken by the government towards it. After the Lancaster House Constitutional Conference of 1960 it was obvious that the die had been cast and that it was merely a matter of time before Africans would dominate the legislature. The three years until independence witnessed British civil servants making way for an African takeover of power, and the generous release of Dini ya Msambwa members from imprisonment. That the movement itself was never given *carte blanche* reveals perhaps an understanding of its political thrust and anarchic tendencies.
2. *East African Standard*, 6 September 1960 and 26 October 1960.
3. Press release by Masinde Muliro, 21 October 1960.
4. *East African Standard*, 12 August 1961.
5. *East African Standard*, 13 August 1961. *Daily Nation*, 16, 27 April; 4, 27 October; 14 November 1962; 9, 21 March 1964; 1, 8, 11 April 1964; and 16, 24 January 1963.

6. *East African Standard*, 22 April 1964.
7. See Appendix F for full constitution.
8. *East African Standard*, 13 October 1962.
9. *East African Standard*, 3 January 1962.
10. *East African Standard*, 8 January 1962.
11. *East African Standard*, 12 May 1960.
12. *East African Standard*, 10 January 1962.
13. *Daily Nation*, 1 December 1964.
14. *Daily Nation*, 5 April 1965. See also *Daily Nation*, 1 May 1965.
15. From a report by chief Ntari Ndahi, 7 December 1964, District Officer's Files, Kimilili.
16. Interview with Samson Wafula, 5 November 1965.
17. *Ibid.*
18. *East African Standard*, 2, 9, 12 November 1968; *Daily Nation*, 4 November 1968.
19. *Daily Nation*, 6 June 1972.
20. Interview on 10 November 1965.
21. *East African Standard*, 19 May 1965.
22. *Daily Nation*, 23 May 1964; *East African Standard*, 5 June 1964.
23. *East African Standard*, 16, 17, 24 March 1967.
24. *Daily Nation*, 24 June 1972.
25. *East African Standard*, 14 November 1962, 26 November 1970, 2 October 1971; *Daily Nation*, July 1972.
26. *Daily Nation*, 27 October 1962. For another incident of alleged harassment see *Daily Nation*, 24 March 1972.
27. *Daily Nation*, 11 October 1965; *Sunday Nation*, 10 October 1965.
28. *East African Standard*, 22 October 1965.
29. *Daily Nation*, 16 May 1972.
30. *East African Standard*, 10 January 1962.
31. *East African Standard*, 18 and 15 January respectively, 1962.
32. *East African Standard*, 3 November 1962.
33. *East African Standard*, 2 May 1964.
34. Interview with a member of Friends Africa Mission, 9 November 1965.
35. Interview on 4 November 1965.
36. Interview on 14 March 1965.
37. Interview on 16 March 1965.
38. These figures were kindly supplied by the registrar-general of societies, Nairobi. The scale of registration fees (5/- for up to 25 members, 10/- for under 100, 25/- for under 1,000, and 50/- for 1,000 and more members) may help to keep figures on small groups accurate but does little for the larger groups claiming a thousand or more members.
39. From an Intelligence Report of 15 June 1961. The District Officer's Files, Kimilili.
40. Interview on 13 November 1965.
41. Interview on 3 November 1965.
42. *Ibid.*
43. Personal letter to the author from Wekuke, 23 June 1968.
44. See below, pp. 288–89.
45. Interview on 15 March 1965.
46. *East African Standard*, 1 December 1966.
47. *Ibid.*, 1 March 1968.
48. *Ibid.*, 23 February 1968.
49. See above, p. 268.
50. *East African Standard*, 25 October 1968.
51. Interview with a hotel owner, 11 November 1968.
52. Interview with a schoolboy who attends Kamusinga Secondary School, 11 November 1965.
53. Interview with an old man, 11 November 1965.

54. Eric Hoffer, who coined the expression the 'true believer', observes, 'It is the true believer's ability to 'shut his eyes and stop his ears' to the facts that do not deserve to be either seen or heard which is the source of his unequalled fortitude and constancy. He cannot be frightened by danger nor disheartened by obstacles nor baffled by contradition because he denies their existence. Strength by faith, as Bergson pointed out, manifests itself not in moving mountains but in not seeing mountains to move. And it is the certitude of his infallible doctrine that renders the true believers impervious to the uncertainties, surprises and the unpleasant realities of the world around him.' *The True Believer*, pp. 78–9.
55. Welime, 'Dini ya Msambwa', p. 4.
56. de Wolf, 'Religious Innovation', pp. 146–47.
57. Paulo Loyana had 21 acres, one wife, nine children, ten cows, and grew maize and millet for cash. Donisio Nakimayu had 4 acres (he claimed to have lost much land when he was in prison), two wives, eight children, and grew maize for cash. He also did some carpentry.
58. de Wolf, 'Religious Innovation', p. 150.
59. Hoffer, *The True Believer*.
60. An opportunity to question some loyalists came during Masinde's trial over the opening of schools. The followers packed the small courtroom and the remainder waited outside all day for a glimpse of their leader. I went into the courthouse to listen to the trial and Charles remained outside to talk to the followers. It was always difficult for me to talk to many of them since I was both an outsider and a white, and it would have been next to impossible at that time, since they were upset and angry. Charles presented himself as a new person to the area (which he was) and casually asked them what was going on. No doubt these people were among those most loyal as many had travelled considerable distances to reach Bungoma. The following replies were all given on 12 November 1965.
61. For a further discussion of some of these points and for speculation concerning the future of the movement, see the author's earlier paper, 'Elijah Masinde — A Folk Hero', Bethwell A. Ogot (ed.), *Hadith 3*, Proceedings of the 1969/70 Conference of the Historical Association of Kenya, pp. 157–91.
62. Leon Festinger, Henry W. Rieken and Stanley Schachter, *When Prophecy Fails*, (University of Minnesota Press, Minneapolis, 1956), pp. 25–30. Schachter, 'Deviation, Rejection and Communication', *Journal of Abnormal and Social Psychology*, 1951, pp. 190–207.
63. *East African Standard*, 21 January 1969.

Chapter 17

THE MAJOR DETERMINANTS OF DINI YA MSAMBWA—INTERPRETATION AND CONCLUSIONS

T H I S explanation is concerned with the appearance of a new movement in the colonial period and with emphasizing the determinants responsible for the development of an active millenarian in contrast to a passive millenarian movement. The determinants that are the same as those for the cult of Mumbo will be mentioned only, and the same stipulations apply for this interpretation as stated for that of Mumbo. (See Chapter 8.)

The Structurally Conducive Conditions

The Cultural Heritage

The conditions that made Gusii culture favourable to the development of the Mumbo movement were present among the Luhya. (The Luhya and the Gusii tribes are part of the much larger grouping known as Bantu-speaking peoples.) Their political institutions were likewise set within a sacred, cosmic order and the patterns and sanctions for political organization were thus derived from a religious cosmology. Luhya tribal structure, like the Gusii, was non-centralized. This favoured the growth of non-institutionalized leadership, but the absence of tribal solidarity put severe obstacles in the way of unified political action.

The Luhya also possessed ritual specialists with powers akin to the Biblical prophets and chiefly roles that in some ways resembled the missionaries' roles.[1] Role similarity facilitated the intepretation of the traditional into Christian forms and vice versa.

The Bukusu, like the Kitutu, had acquired a reputation as ruthless cattle raiders. Through struggles to survive they had developed their military expertise, and the qualities of resilience, flexibility

292

and a reliance upon practical solutions were to stand them in good stead in their opposition to colonialism.

The Colonial Experience

The Politics of Religion. Various missions arrived in North Nyanza at the same time as administration was being established and some even earlier. The Luhya, like the Gusii, were sufficiently settled on the land for mission teachings and western education to have an impact. Thus, new values began to seep into the tribal system in the early years of the twentieth century.

The inhabitants of North Nyanza experienced the consequences of the Anglo-Saxon tradition of denominational pluralism to an even greater extent than the South Nyanzans. Each mission preached its own interpretation of Christianity and competed with the others for converts. Their alliances with chiefly families established religion as an avenue for the pursuit of secular goals and reinforced the traditionally close association between religion and politics. Denominational conflict gave Africans experience in the politics of religion, made them skeptical of any one mission's claims to religious truth, and presented a pattern of religious schism that mission-educated men were soon to follow.

Absence of Adventists. In North Nyanza the dominant missions were the Quakers and the Mill Hill Brothers. Both emphasized a 'this-worldly' orientation—an activist solution to men's problems. Missing were the Seventh-day Adventists with their message of an imminent millennium. Although millennial ideas in all likelihood diffused from South Nyanza, the absence of on-the-spot proselytizing probably accounts for their weaker influence in Msambwa than in Mumbo.

A Challenge that can be Coped With. Early British encounters with the resisting Bukusu were harsh but there is no evidence that the Bukusu ever assessed the situation as one of total defeat, despaired of obtaining their goals through practical means, or suffered from feelings of inferiority. In fact, within a few years of the 1895 battle they had recuperated sufficiently to engage the British in several skirmishes and to fight the imposition of new and disliked regulations, as discussed in Chapter 9. This toughness was in keeping with their *history of successful responses to challenges, of adopting new, pragmatic means to cope collectively with problems.* Others faced with the same problems might have taken a more individualistic approach or have relied upon magic as did the Mumboites. The tactic of collectively dealing with problems led later to their involvement in Dini ya Msambwa and other political associations where practical solutions were again sought.

Loss of Status and Power. The Bukusu, like the Bogonko, were not only defeated by the British but the pain of defeat was enormously increased when their long-standing enemies—members of a clan they considered to be collaborators—were given chieftainships over their locations. This moved them again to oppose the government and, once embarked on that course, they continued with relative success. The struggle to regain their autonomy helped to ready the conditions for Dini ya Msambwa.

Increased Opportunities for Communication

The breadth of a movement depends in large part on the opportunities for disseminating ideas which, in turn, depend on the available media of communication. When communication is by word of mouth, literacy limited, and the main mode of transportation by foot, a movement will of necessity be confined to a much smaller area than when there is a literate public served by mass media and modern transportation.

By the 1940s, Kenya was connected from east to west by a railway and a network of roads. The missions were teaching a common language, literacy was increasing, and there were newspapers in English and in some tribal languages. Africans were developing tastes for western consumer goods as migrant labourers travelled to the farms in the White Highlands and to the cities in search of work. (It was a migrant labourer who carried Dini ya Msambwa's ideas to the Pokot.) Thus the consolidation of countrywide communication and trading patterns and a high rate of internal migration facilitated the exchange of ideas and experiences and laid the groundwork for a much more broadly based movement than the cult of Mumbo.

Absence of Legitimate Means to Rectify Grievances

An important factor in determining the kind of movement that developed was the political system that Msambwa confronted. Colonial Kenya's political structure virtually closed off the development of reform movements and fostered the development of militant protest, revolt and revolution as forms of collective action because

Africans were excluded from political participation or, at most, allowed only limited roles, unrelated to the important decision-making processes.

There were several government appointed representatives of African interests on the Legislative Council (usually ex-civil servants or missionaries) but in the eyes of Africans they were part of the white establishment and not their representatives. (Kenya was governed by a Governor, Executive and Legislative Councils. The first African, Eliud Mathu, was nominated to the Legislative Council in 1944.) Without a vote, Africans could not make major changes through the electoral system. They had sought a redress of their grievances from the authorities for years by pressure and petitions but had had little success. Finally, African political associations and activity, to all intents and purposes, were banned at the outbreak of World War II for its duration and during the Emergency in the next decade.

Multiple Strains
Some strains that garnered support for Msambwa were similar to those found in Mumbo, but alien intervention and economic hardship were far more severe.

Alien Attack on Traditional Values and Institutions
African sensitivity to cultural denigration was evident in the Masinde mythology. Deep resentment was voiced against the whites' attack on African customs, as discussed in Chapters 4, 8, and 11. The British saw themselves as superior and took next to nothing from African culture, while their agents attacked African customs they considered immoral, unhealthy, or primitive and encouraged and compelled Africans to change in particular ways.

Economic Strains
These strains were complex. They acted upon groups in different ways and various combinations produced support.
Discrepency Between Desires and Means to Satisfy Them. In traditional societies, where what little contact there was with outside communities was with people at basically the same level of development, any thought of a fundamental transformation in the society was inconceivable. As Cohn aptly put it, 'In an economy which was uniformly primitive, where nobody was very rich, there was nothing

295

to arouse new wants; certainly nothing which could stimulate men to grandiose fantasies of wealth and power.' This state of affairs abruptly ended with the advent of the white man. The lid on desires was suddenly removed and Africans' wants multiplied but without the means to satisfy them.

Land Alienation and Fear of Land Alienation. The findings of Chapter 13 suggest that the inhabitants of the locations from which Dini ya Msambwa's main support came were aware of the plight of dispossessed Africans and were uneasy about what might be in store for them. The Kamakoiya squatters lost the land they were living on when the settlement scheme for British ex-servicemen was implemented.

Inflation. Inflation hit the prosperous people hardest since they were involved in the market economy. It mattered relatively little to the traditional sector whose members were living at the subsistence level.

Economic Hardship, Decline, and Loss of a Way of Life. In the Trans Nzoia, the rural labourers and squatters received extremely low wages. The squatters, who had been in a situation of economic decline for years, faced the prospect of losing not only their livelihood but their way of life.

Loss of Traditional Rights

The encroachment on squatters' rights occurred when the squatters were already in difficult economic circumstances. It was the 'straw that broke the proverbial 'camel's back', gaining their active support for a movement that promised to oust the settlers.

Agricultural Reform

Msambwa gained in strength just after the government launched its programme of agricultural reform which affected all the peasants. Many regulations were not only a nuisance but required extra work. Destocking was particularly resented because cattle represented wealth and prestige. Among the Pokot, *cattle culling appeared to be the issue* that aroused the otherwise quiet pastoralists and secured their support.

Agricultural regulations, while irksome in themselves, might have been implemented had the government had more popular officials carrying out its policies. Instead of leaders the people trusted and respected, several men were strongly disliked and their presence might well have convinced some Africans that the British presence had become just too unbearable.

Agricultural reform, loss of rights, and loss of a way of life were probably the issues, more than any others, that aroused militant opposition. Missions, taxation, compulsory labour, chiefs and police had all been present for years and while disliked, were by then grudgingly accepted. But *efforts at rural reform, mass evictions and loss of rights were new.*[2] *They were 'gut' issues that aroused deeply-felt sentiments—fear rage, frustration and righteous indignation.*

Role Strains

Old people and others who resented the loss of their traditional ways joined because of Dini ya Msambwa's emphasis on the traditional. It appears to have recruited young, ambitious men from non-chiefly clans who felt they had little chance of advancement through the official system and resented the chiefly family's power and status.

Exacerbating Factors

Exacerbating factors obviously differs for various individuals and groups and throughout the course of a movement. The following dramatic events aroused particularly strong emotions and helped to crystallize support.

Masinde's Encounter with the Agricultural Officer (1944). Masinde's run-in with the agricultural officer who turned out to be wrong in forcing people to uproot Mexican marigold was important for its symbolic content. It provided a 'concrete enemy' towards which collective action could be directed. Additionally, this event in which an African defied a European and the African was right, gave substance to Dini ya Msambwa's complaints of administrative injustice. Taken more broadly, it could be seen as proof of the movement's basic premise — its rightness and the government's wrongness. Occurring at an early stage in Msambwa's development, this clash undoubtedly helped establish Masinde's reputation. He began to look like a man of extraordinary promise, a fearless and effective anti-colonial fighter.

The Burning Down of the Agricultural Officer's Home (1944). Masinde's threat followed by the actual burning down of the agricultural officer's home less than a month later may well have convinced people that here was a movement worth supporting.

By these defiant acts, Msambwa members showed that they were not afraid to tackle the colonialists and Masinde was shown to be a man of his word.

Masinde's Imprisonment (1945–1947). Masinde's arrest and subsequent imprisonment for assaulting an elder who was delivering a labour summons (Chapters 6 and 11) further established his credentials as a militant activist willing to suffer for the cause of independence.

The Appointment of Major Cavendish-Bentinck (1946). Cavendish-Bentinck's appointment to head a white settlement scheme (Chapter 13) increased Bukusu apprehension over their land claims and confirmed their worst fears as it signalled the government's commitment to white settlement. It served notice that time was running out if they were to regain their land, and gave impetus to more aggressive tactics. Bukusu anxieties were suddenly given a definite object to take action against, as shown by their harassment of the incoming settlers.

The Malakisi Riot (1948). The killing of Africans at the Malakisi Riot (Chapter 11) immeasurably sharpened the pro- and anti-colonial cleavages and put the police squarely among Dini ya Msambwa's enemies. This event, which added eleven martyrs to Msambwa's roster of heroes, came to symbolize the brutality and insidious character of the colonial regime, its corrupting effects on Africans who gunned down fellow Africans, and the sacrifice Africans must be willing to make for their cause.[3] It provided vivid 'proof' of the legitimacy of Msambwa's message, strengthened the militants who could now argue that violence must be countered with violence, and increased the membership.

Prophecies and Dreams. Around May 1949, when in prison, Masinde was moved from Lamu to Marsabit. This event may have been taken by some people as proof of his prophesy that he would not remain in prison for long.

   Members sometimes' mentioned that Masinde's appearance in a dream convinced them of his divinity and they then became active in Dini ya Msambwa.

General Beliefs

Msambwa revitalized the Bukusu's militant tradition, challenged the whites' evaluation of African culture, and called Africans back to their ancestors' ways. It rallied support around hated symbols of European dominance—the police station at Malakisi and the Roman Catholic mission at Kibabii—and revered symbols of the traditional life—Maina, the powerful chief, Mwambu and Seera, the tribal father and mother. At the remains of the Lugulu fort where the 1895 battle was fought, Masinde honoured the warriors killed in that battle and declared war on the British.

In reviving a militant spirit, the beliefs had to contend with previous disastrous confrontations. The members needed reassurance that they wouldn't be defeated again. The power of modern weapons was 'nullified' by magic that afforded protection and assured victory. The bullets-to-water belief was promoted, traditional rituals were practised to ensure the ancestors' blessings, old prophecies resurrected and new ones created that foretold the overthrow of foreign rule. Christian beliefs, in particular, the millennium and the struggle of the poor and oppressed against the rich and powerful, added significant strands of hope and confidence to the revolutionary rationale.

Msambwa presented a new dream in which not just the Bukusu, but all Kenyans would be free. Sometimes the entire African continent was indicated, other times it sounded as if the Luhya or the Bukusu would replace the colonialists, and at still others, that only the Msambwa elect would triumph. The dream was blurred. Msambwa was more explicit in what it was against than what it was for. But this was a time when ideas were being sorted and sifted in search of a new orientation and a doctrine to legitimize rebellion.

Masinde not only proclaimed a new order to supercede the old, but new loyalties to transcend old loyalties of kin and tribe. Membership was open to anyone who professed Dini ya Msambwa's beliefs regardless of race, tribe and colour. In practice, limitations were imposed by communication, transportation and ethnic conflict.

Msambwa's beliefs were an eclectic combination of western and indigenous, political and religious ideas. Msambwa exhorted a return to the religion of the forefathers but it combined a nostalgia for the old religion or, more broadly, the old way of life undisturbed by Europeans, with a desire for the European way of life, its comforts and wealth. It articulated grievances widely shared by

Africans, particularly those of a political and economic nature, seen as stemming from colonial rule.

Mobilization for Roles

Masinde, following in the steps of other great Bukusu warriors, was a 'liberating hero'. Unlike Muraa, the Gusii who counselled her people to abandon fighting for prayer, Masinde emphasized tough, aggressive action and eschewed half-way measures and faintheartedness.

Nothing in Dini ya Msambwa's millennial elements impelled militant action. In fact, just the opposite might be expected, the millenium would come through supernatural means if the members practised the correct rituals. But Masinde firmly grounded its coming on the members' practical actions. Msambwa members, unlike the Mumboites, used ritual to ensure success, while simultaneously attacking the colonialists. Nevertheless, it should not be assumed that the ritual versus action orientation was ever finally settled, but rather the two remained in an uneasy relationship shifting in importance with the circumstances.

Several other factors abetted this militant activism:

1) Although Masinde did not organize the protest activities himself, he had capable assistants who did;
2) The Bukusu who formed the mainstay of the movement had a history of innovative, pragmatic solutions to their problems;
3) A new generation of young men, with some familiarity with the colonialists' ways, perhaps from the early introduction of schools and voluntary associations or from working on settlers' farms, felt that militancy was needed.

It is significant that Dini ya Msambwa did not develop until half a century had elapsed from the 1895 fighting. Time permitted the Luhya to recuperate before they again mobilized their resources to aggressively tackle the foreigners. Msambwa's supporters were *two generations removed from the original fighters. Although they had heard stories of the encounter and had paid homage to its heroes, they did not have any firsthand experience with the horrors of battle.* Even then, they did not venture another head-on clash.

In contrast, the Mumbo cult originated among a demoralized people completely naive about the world of western man less than a decade after they had been twice defeated. The veterans of the earlier fights were not willing to risk all again. Hence their turning to magic and ritual. This generational difference probably accounts, in large part, for the different Gusii and Luhya responses.

Agents of Social Control

By imprisoning Masinde, the government helped turn him into an important rallying point for the forces of rural discontent. It performed a service for the movement, for Masinde was far more useful in jail as a hero-martyr than free as an organizer-strategist.

An intransigent government that fails to respond to grievances and even blocks change has been singled out as an important determinant in revolutionary change. The authorities at least in the North Nyanza District were not intransigent on all matters, if their response to complaints of Wanga suzerainty is any indication. Nor could the government be described as particularly harsh, corrupt, ineffective, or lacking confidence in its own goals, all common factors in inability to govern.[4] It was composed of earnest men attempting to give Africans good, if authoritarian rule. Many administrators made an effort to understand African customs and a number were amateur anthropologists who genuinely liked, and in turn were liked by Africans. They believed in their 'civilizing mission' and showed by the way in which they suppressed Msambwa, and later the Mau Mau rebellion, that they had the support of the military and could use force effectively.

But they had several strikes against them. They were foreigners who maintained their position by force rather than by the peoples' consent. As would-be innovators, they and their appointees were not considered legitimate leaders by the people concerned. It was not difficult for local leaders like Elijah Masinde, Benjamin Wekuke and Pascal Nabwana to sabotage their efforts. Hence we find a *government that tried to introduce change but did it badly*. It tried to reform an economy in dire need of reform but hasty efforts to which insufficient thought had been given caused their attempts at agricultural change to be rejected.

As long as the government had remained remote and had permitted the peasant to pursue his traditional round unhindered by new regulations, its presence was tolerable. Though not seen as particularly useful, it was not particularly obnoxious either. But when it began to *impinge in some direct way on the lives of the rural masses—to make new demands that interfered wtih their daily routine and to threaten their way of life*—it aroused strong antagonisms that Dini ya Msambwa effectively mobilized.

Notes

1. I could find little information on prophetic tradition among the Bukusu or Luhya, and whether they possessed a tradition of prophetic innovation and challenge to the status quo in the form of new cults like other East and Central African tribes is a moot question. Wagner and La Fontaine mention individual prophets but not prophetic movements. It would be in keeping with other East African peoples to find that cults arose in time of distress to help solve problems by innovating new solutions, and it would help to explain Dini ya Msambwa's origins.

2. The government had made earlier attempts, as related in Chapter 10, at agricultural reform. This strain was new in the sense that nothing had been done during the war years and only after the war did the government make another effort to change traditional farming methods.

3. Evidence suggests that the riot was a particularly important exacerbating factor. Donisio Nakimayu told me that the shooting of Africans had made him so angry that he set fire to police housing and settlers' homes. At a Dini ya Msambwa meeting five days after the riot, the Bukusu preacher said that those who had been shot had died for Masinde, that more would die but that they (Dini ya Msambwa members) were not afraid. (KNA:DC/NN10/1/2. Letter from assistant superintendent of police D. C. Connor, Kitale, to the superintendent of police, Rift Valley Province, 16 February 1948.) A common theme in Dini ya Msambwa's proselytizing was that Masinde would return and punish the police and the Europeans who had shot the Bukusu.

4. See Brinton, *Anatomy of Revolution*, and Chalmers Johnson, *Revolution and the Social System*, (Stanford University Press, Stanford, 1964), for discussions of the role of the political elite in revolutionary movements.

PART IV

Appendices

APPENDIX A

METHODOLOGY

The methodology has been discussed briefly in the previous chapters when it had a particular bearing upon the analysis. The data on which the Mumbo study is based came mainly from administrative records. Although I visited Kisii in June 1966 in the hope of speaking with some of the members I was not successful. I did interview several ex-chiefs who had been in charge of the district when Mumboism was at its peak, and spoke with local authorities and some local people. I have previously described my encounter with Marita who is said to be the sole survivor. The following discussion when it refers to interviews applies, in the main, to Dini ya Msambwa.

Research Design and Types of Data
To understand the broad conditions which gave rise to these move-ments and to learn about certain traditional institutions, various kinds of data were used.

Anthropological studies were available on the tribal life of both the Gusii and Luhya peoples. The East African Institute of Social Research at Makerere University has an excellent library that includes unpublished manuscripts, conference papers, and field notes of anthropologists that were useful in obtaining a general anthropological orientation. By reading widely, I came across unexpected information that enriched the analysis. For instance, I found a description of the attempt to abolish circumcision in the cult of Mumbo which provided further insight into its nature.

The early accounts of explorers, missionaries, administrators, settlers and the military provided data on the perspective of the agents of colonization. What did they see their mission to be? What kinds of relationships were established with particular chiefs

305

and clans? A knowledge of colonial policies and their implementation was necessary in order to understand Africans' reactions.

Several months were spent in the Kenya National Archives examining records. Annual reports at the district and provincial levels and Native Affairs reports were scanned for material on the movements' origins, development, activities and relations with the authorities. Since little was known about these movements, even the area they penetrated was only sketchily delineated, the records of districts outside the movements' stronghold were read to see whether they were mentioned.

New interpretations of events and issues are now appearing with the publication of native Kenyans' accounts of pre-colonial and colonial history. These help to correct biases in the European perspective. Gone is the ethnocentric view that tribal societies were unchanging over the centuries and that nothing really happened until the Europeans arrived. In its place is a much more complicated picture of tribal migrations, power struggles, the rise and fall of particular dynasties, innovations in, as well as the stability of, certain institutions. Although correcting certain biases, these studies introduce new biases, one being the tendency for researchers to magnify their own tribe's power in pre-colonial times.

Old editions of the *East African Standard* and *The Daily Nation*, Kenya's two daily newspapers, were reviewed. Both have catalogued back issues and these were of great help, especially for incidents like the Kolloa Affray and Masinde's clashes with the authorities.

All voluntary associations in Kenya must register with the government and file a yearly report. The Registrar-General of Societies' files provided information on Dini ya Msambwa's constitution, the names and addresses of its leaders and membership figures. This background information was useful as it suggested who should be approached first, helped to eliminate some routine questions, and provided useful leads to interviews, all of which helped to create rapport.

Outside of this information, both movements were without a literature of their own. Dini ya Msambwa's constitution, written to fulfil government regulations, followed the government's sample constitution and was of little help in understanding its beliefs and practices. Despite its deficiencies as 'inside dope', the constitution did provide guidelines for questions and probes.

Studies have presented these movements as vehicles of political protest and have hypothesized their disappearance when other avenues of political expression are available. Evidence that these groups have prospered since independence suggests that explanations of their emergence are more complex than previously believed. Thus a crucial dimension to be examined was the difference it made, if any, to Dini ya Msambwa to have African agents of social control instead of British. I talked with government officials, policemen, missionaries and indigenous church leaders in order to acquire the perspective of the agents of social control in the postcolonial period.

Another consideration to be borne in mind is that in studying social movements we are studying process through time. Since movements have different phases, an analysis of one phase does not necessarily hold for another. Hence it was important to examine Mumbo and Msambwa at different points in their career and to gather *data over as long a time as possible*. I was able to visit Kenya on three different occasions and have acquired data on Msambwa since its origin in the early 1940s until mid-August 1974, a period of more than thirty years. Kenya was on the eve of attaining independence when I first arrived late in 1963. By the time I returned in 1969, it had had an African government for five years, and my 1973–74 visit saw the celebration of its tenth anniversary.

Far more important for an understanding of these movements than the views of the agents of social control are the views of the members themselves. What did the movement mean to them? How did they interpret the colonial experience or a particular riot? The members, the agents, and the local people each had their own way of viewing 'reality'. Quotations are included to show these different perspectives.

Several well informed people in the community, in particular, Pascal Nabwana, gave freely of their time, patiently answering an outsider's many questions. Mr. Nabwana's knowledge of Dini ya Msambwa since its inception and his recollection of his father's stories about the 1895 punitive expedition were invaluable in providing background information.

I was able to interview four of Msambwa's five main leaders, Masinde, Wekuke, Wafula, and Walumoli, at least once, and Wafula and Wekuke on numerous occasions, and local leaders like Paulo Loyana, Donisio Nakimayu and Maloba Muliro.

307

Bearing in mind there might well be a discrepancy between the leaders' and the ordinary members' views of the movement and reasons for involvement, as well as the tendency among social scientists to gravitate towards the top leadership (perhaps because these people are more articulate and better informed or even for reasons of status and rapport), I paid particular attention to the rank-and-file. Who were they and why did they join? Since this question has raised so much speculation over motives and purpose and so many explanations in terms of demographic, political and social variables, I have quoted them extensively.

In colonial Kenya, Dini ya Msambwa apparently enjoyed wide support because it was expressing people's grievances. Hence it was important to question community opinion in the post-colonial period to see whether the movement could still claim this support.

Flexibility was stressed in interviewing. I often interviewed people in their homes or sat outside under the shade of a tree with any number of people listening in and with chickens, goats and babies every once in a while giving evidence of their presence. A 'listener' might interrupt the interview because he did not agree with what was said or even introduce a new topic, but as long as these interruptions did not occur too frequently they often clarified and provided new insights. Under such circumstances, however, it was best to cover the topics, but leave the exact wording and order loose in order to encourage the interviewee to speak freely. Considerable time was spent in training an interviewer and in informing him about the study so that he could use his own ingenuity to acquire information.

The length of the interview was determined, in part, by the interviewee's level of interest. If the interviewee seemed interested and time was not at a premium, more questions were added. If, on the other hand, the interviewee seemed disinterested, the interview was shortened. Interviews tended to be rather long, sometimes going on for several hours. A characteristic of those interviewed, especially older people, was not to give direct answers but to answer questions in a circuitious way by telling a story that supposedly illustrated the point. When I asked for clarification in order to be sure of the meaning, they tended to find my probes irritating. For my part, the time required to obtain information sometimes taxed my patience.

There were no set number of interviews. People were questioned on particular topics until we began to get information repeated, and when little new information was forthcoming the specific topic was dropped.

Participating in, and observing Msambwa's activities was limited. It was not a movement with a well-defined set of religious practices which an outsider could observe. During my stay there were few religious ceremonies, although I did attend a church service. On my first visit, the opening of schools engaged the members' energies. By the time of my second visit, the movement had been banned and membership in it was a criminal offence. As for information on meetings and ritual in the colonial period, I had to rely on informers' reports usually written by people barely literate in English. These provided glimpses rather than a comprehensive picture of activities.

I used informal situations whenever possible to observe the social world of the members and of the local people. Usually I was accompanied by an assistant, Charles Onyango, when driving in the reserves. If we came across some members walking we would stop and give them a ride or we might visit the local market where people met twice weekly to trade and to visit with friends. Conversations over tea and biscuits and plates of stew in a local restaurant or a member's home provided insights into the lives of these people, what troubled and amused them, and how they felt about Msambwa. Through these conversations I learned the folklore about Masinde.

I visited Dini ya Msambwa's most sacred shrines on Mount Elgon. A district officer who was making the rounds of his district invited me to accompany him on a trip up Mount Elgon where we climbed to Msambwa's sacred lake and explored the rocky crevices where the faithful went to worship and sometimes to hide out from the police.

Processing the Data

Administrators' records on the cult of Mumbo were microfilmed and later typed out in full. Msambwa data was scattered in too many different reports to microfilm so I copied pertinent sections from the records.

Extensive notes were taken during interviews. We usually translated from English to Luhya, sometimes Swahili, and back again and in the interim there was time for me to record almost verbatim what was said. Later I typed these interviews in paragraph form in

309

duplicate. One copy was then catalogued into a set of categories and cut up, enabling all items on particular topics to be kept together. A second copy of the interview was kept intact so that it could be read in its entirety.

The process of labelling and counting, while it has the strength of quantifying data, divorces items from their context and this has severe drawbacks. For example, a particular item that appeared highly critical of Masinde could have simply been catalogued along with similar items. However, on re-reading the entire interview several days later, I realized that even though this negative item appeared, the overall interview conveyed exactly the opposite view. Or new information and new insights lead to items hitherto overlooked taking on a different significance. These, in turn, affect the significance of other items. Additionally, subtle indications that appear in the course of an entire interview and which an interviewer may wish to check out later by pointed questions are lost. Instances such as these occur often and cast doubt on the accuracy of reports based entirely on piecemeal notes divorced from the setting and context. Actually interviews done in this way are subject to many of the same limitations and possible outright misinterpretations as analyses based on closed-ended questionnaires and structured data gathering techniques. In order not to lose the context I made a practice of periodically re-reading my notes intact to refresh my memory. After the entire analysis was completed, I again re-read my notes and was surprised to find evidence, hitherto overlooked, that strengthened and refined several arguments.

Since I was interested in general patterns and dominant themes, repetition of data was looked for. Careful re-reading of administrative records and interviews was useful in unearthing significant patterns. The study has not attempted to quantify patterns and themes but has tried to differentiate between the general and the specific. Activities that fit together and reinforce each other were considered to be of more significance than the isolated instance.

Although general patterns and themes were my main interest, deviance from the general was noted as I am unwilling to substitute one stereotype for another. For instance, although the colonial authorities tended to share a common view of Africans and of these movements, some men differed. Popham-Lobb severely questioned the rationale behind punitive expeditions, Archdeacon Owen strongly criticized, and encouraged Africans to challenge, administrators' policies; provincial commissioner Hunter clearly understood Africans' nationalistic aspirations; and Labour M.P. Fenner Brockway supported African causes before the Home Government. These men marched to the tune of a different drummer. They were highly critical of policies established by their own government and implemented by its agents. Furthermore, since some of them had power, their actions had more significance for the system than the actions of many powerless people. Hence, attention has been paid to non-conformity to patterns, especially when practised by people with power and influence.

Problems of Bias

Has an accurate picture of these movements been presented? What kinds of bias may have distorted the data? Two major sources of bias, the sampling of people in situations, and the nature of the information secured, regardless of the sample utilized, will be examined.

Social movements are among the more important as well as the more difficult social phenomena to study. They do not lend themselves to the orthodox methodological procedures for several reasons. Since they are often at odds with the established authorities, secrecy may surround their activities. Except for the hardcore, their membership tends to be nebulous and changing and since the movement itself changes, it needs to be observed for longer periods of time than more stable phenomena. These and other factors mean that social movements are particularly difficult to study for the lone researcher with limited resources. From a strictly methodological point of view, there are bound to be weaknesses which cannot be entirely eradicated. Nevertheless, phenomena characteristic of Kenya's and other countries' colonial period should be studied even if it entails making do with less then perfect research techniques. (The best way to obtain an 'inside' view of a conspiratorial movement is to join it. But since that option was not available, compromises had to be made from the outset.)

Representativeness of the Sampling. Are the views reflected in the study representative of the members of the movement, of the agents of social control, and of the local people? In order to have data that adequately reflects a cross-section of views, one needs representative samples drawn at the appropriate times.

In an unexplored population—all I had to start with were some views held by the agents—where the dimensions to be sampled are relatively obscure, it is impossible to know in advance what the composition of the sample should be. Should a sample be representative of age, tribe, sex and education or of years in prison, felt grievances and landlessness? Since the population of Dini ya Msambwa was unknown, the first task was to describe it. The main portion of the study concentrates on this description. Furthermore, even had I been present at the height of Msambwa's militancy and even had the membership criteria been known, to randomly sample a proscribed movement would have required remarkable ingenuity (unless, of course, all the members had been jailed which would have introduced another bias).

The above statement should be qualified in one respect. The main leaders were known and remained almost unchanged from the colonial to post-colonial period. As mentioned, almost the entire upper echelon leadership was contacted so that their views were adequately taken into account. They were relied upon for basic information about the movement, its history and activities and they introduced me to local leaders.

The ordinary members were harder to reach because Msambwa was not holding any regular meetings. During my first visit the members could sometimes be identified by the Msambwa insignia on their shirts or dresses. If we saw a member, my assistant would try to engage the person in conversation. On my second visit, since Msambwa had been proscribed, there was no way of identifying the members on sight. In addition, the country was in a state of unrest following the October 1969 Kisumu riot.[1] The political situation did not permit a white person to drive around the countryside casually asking the whereabouts of the followers.

As for the authorities, since they were few in number, sampling was not needed. I had access to the correspondence and written reports of the significant colonial civil servants. Administrative reports were unavailable for the post-colonial period but the strong consensus of opinion suggested that even had reports been available, they would have presented few different views.

Since there is information about the population of the community at large, sampling might have been worthwhile had the entire study concentrated on the views of the local people towards Dini ya Msambwa. However, since these views were only one facet of a many faceted study, it wasn't worth the costs that would have had to be expended to sample a community of peasants living scattered on their individual farms. Efforts were made, nevertheless, to acquire a diversified cross-section of people differentiated by major social categories. Old and young, men and women, elders and schoolboys, members of the mission and independent churches, shopkeepers, traders, and community leaders were interviewed.

A problem posed especially by subversive movements is their members' hostility to outsiders. Both Mumbo and Msambwa had been proscribed and suppressed. Hence their members were suspicious of, and hostile towards, outsiders, especially whites. Unlike visits with the members of other movements where I received the 'fatted calf' treatment, I was not welcomed. Even though I stayed at the home of an influential local leader who introduced me to Masinde, and even though Masinde had agreed to the study, the members generally suspected my motives. In addition, Masinde's mercurical temperment meant that my entrée might be closed off at any time.

The anti-Masinde faction, tired of his dominance, and perhaps desiring their contribution to be recorded, wanted to give me Msambwa's history. I had spoken with several members representing this viewpoint when word went out from a pro-Masinde group that no one was to talk with me. People who had previously agreed to be interviewed would be absent when I arrived at their homes. One leader disobeyed this order and agreed to meet me. For the sake of secrecy we met at the home of the inspector of police. A half-brother of Masinde's appeared and ordered him not to discuss Msambwa. If I pursued my work, he said, it would bring trouble,perhaps violence, to the area. He accused my informant as follows:

> You're helping this woman free of charge. She is going to get a lot of money out of what you are giving her. She is going to be a millionaire. She is going to take notes of money and spread them on her bed and sleep on them while you remain here poor, without food to eat. Secondly, she is going to tarnish our name. Instead of giving us a good name she is going to write 'Look at what these Africans are believing in. This is how they pray. They are primitive and illiterate. They're poor so they believe in bizarre things.' Instead of making Masinde's name great she is going to abuse him, belittle him and make him appear simple. But we respect him. We believe that he is a great man.[2]

The interview did not take place that day.

Another time when I arrived at the home of Joasch Walumoli for an interview to which he had agreed, angry followers surrounded my car and refused to permit the interview to take place. A story even spread that I had paid Wafula 10,000/- for the history of the movement and to have Masinde assassinated. That such a rumour did circulate was substantiated when I was questioned on two separate occasions about giving Wafula money. There was not the slightest truth to the allegation of paying interviewees since I never remunerate them financially.

This hostility might introduce a serious bias in that only the more accessible members who were not representative of the membership at large would be contacted. To guard against being 'captured' by any one group, efforts were made to seek out members from different factions as well as different types of members. Some of the most faithful were interviewed. (Those who had walked miles to Masinde's trial to catch a glimpse of him could be counted in this group.) Also, I did not depend solely on members for information but used other sources, namely informants, local people, and administrative records. But even though I made deliberate efforts to contact individuals from all the various groupings and social categories, there were undoubtedly groupings and categories unknown to me, and the views of some members may well be over-represented while those of others, under-represented. Without a survey of a random sample of members, I can only guess about areas of ignorance.

Part of the hostility towards me was overcome when I returned in 1969. Masinde was again in prison, Wekuke had decided to break away and form his own religious sect, and my first visit had proven not to have any harmful consequences for Msambwa members. Wekuke accompanied me on visits to members and, to my surprise, I was warmly received. Suspicions seemed to have vanished. I spoke to some of the activists like Donisio Nakimayu who explained why he had burned down government buildings.

Since the character of movements may change through time, the question arises, have we sampled at crucial points in Dini ya Msambwa's career? The members at the height of Msambwa's militancy, for instance, might well have differed on important social characteristics from the members in a period of decline when my fieldwork was carried out. To counter this type of bias, I did not calculate Msambwa's support in the colonial period from its support in the post-colonial period but used other measures based on data from the colonial period itself.

Reliability of Data. Another major source of bias stems from the data itself. How reliable were our observations and data? Did my presence mute the expression of feelings or simply rule out the voicing of certain views? Did the questions tap only certain responses and ignore other equally, or even more, significant responses? Did respondents provide erroneous information, calculatedly or not, through selective recall, exaggeration or lying? Here we will examine some ways the data might have been distorted through race, status, and cultural considerations, interpretor's errors and idiosyncratic perceptions.

Being white meant that certain topics such as race relations might not be freely discussed in my presence, especially by Africans who did not know me well. One way to handle this was to have my assistant go on his own when my presence might unduly influence respondents' replies. Since he was from another tribe, he could pass as a visiting schoolboy. He would spend time at the market or at the village casually talking with people or carrying on longer conversations over a cup of tea. When alone, he would take notes, and later we would discuss the conversations and I would transcribe them more fully.

Sometimes I would introduce the general topic but leave it to the interviewee to volunteer the information. If he indicated that it was a topic he preferred not to discuss, it was dropped. (In interviewing, one had to weigh the possible gains in information through probing against the risks of having all information cut off.) Or, to take another tack, especially if rapport had been established, I might bring the issue up and give my opinions. Bringing issues out in the open rather than hinting at them tended to clear the way for frank discussions.

Administrative records suggested that smoking bhang and opium, excessive drinking and illicit sex were practised by some members. Our attempt, however, to get information, failed. This was a sensitive area for a white outsider to probe into since local people felt such practices discredited their community and simply closed ranks against the outsider. The assistant leaders, whom I felt had been frank on other topics, tended to either deny the existence of

315

these activities, saying Msambwa members followed the Ten
Commandments or simply to cut off further enquiry with a dry
comment that those who indulged were 'backsliders'. Since the
topic was not crucial to the study, we concentrated on other areas.

The fact that a younger woman was asking an older man
questions, questions that he was not used to answering, at times
broke sex and age norms. It was important, I soon discovered, to
have an assistant who could handle social situations and was respectful of local norms. The proper introductions had to be made, the
right amount of deference given particular people, and questions
had to be phrased in ways that did not offend.

At the same time there were more positive aspects about my
position. Parents liked the idea of a history that would enable their
children to read about their and their ancestors' religion. Besides,
independence had been achieved, so there was no reason to fear a
white person. I travelled alone with a teenager and was completely
dependent upon people's willingness to talk to me. And since I
lived locally and ate at local places, they became used to seeing me.
Perhaps because I didn't fit into the usual categories of foreign
women—being a Canadian, and not being a district commissioner's
wife, a missionary or a schoolteacher—curiosity worked in my
favour. A category that some people were familiar with was that of
a research student. Once when an elder, tired of what he considered
were tedious and silly questions, complained to my sponsor, another
elder, my sponsor, asked him to be patient and help me out. 'She's
only a schoolgirl', he said.

It is hard to assess whether being a woman was advantageous or
disadvantageous. My impression is that the individual's approach
and personality are far more important than age, sex or ethnicity
in establishing rapport. I felt that people were generally relaxed
and talked freely in my presence.

Most interviews were carried out with the aid of an interpretor.
Any gross errors in translating would likely have been caught at the
time of the interview, since several people, one of whom understood
English fairly well, were usually present. And since assistants were
schoolboys and young men, older men did not hesitate to correct
them when they believed their translations to be inaccurate. It is
difficult to gauge how well my assistants performed on the more
subtle aspects of translating. For example, they seemed to
demonstrate considerable insight in explaining motivation and in

interpreting and helping me to understand the underlying social processes behind apparent ambiguities. Almost without exception, they showed a keen interest in the project (travelling to a place outside their home area and talking to all kinds of people was considered an adventure), and appeared to possess considerable social and intellectual skills.

Since part of my task was to chronicle the history of Dini ya Msambwa, I have used people's names extensively. If a particular event with the names of the people involved appeared in a newspaper there was no problem since it was already public knowledge. However, with interview data, I was more circumspect. First there was often the question of whether the translation was accurate. One way to see whether I had reported what had been said, or what the interviewee thought had been said, was to obtain their opinion of what I had written. On my second trip, since I had a draft finished, I read passages to people whom I had quoted extensively and asked whether these were indeed their views and whether they had any objection to begin quoted. Far from not wanting to be quoted, people wanted their names recorded. They wished their part in the movement to be recognized. Still, although I was given permission to use their names, in quoting critical statements I have refrained from doing so when I felt that to identify the source of a quote might evoke unpleasant consequences in the community.

All quotes were translated as accurately as possible. Preference, however, was given to a looser translation that preserved the original fluency than to a literal translation that would introduce an awkwardness of phraseology absent in the original. When these Africans attempted to write or to speak English, on the other hand, they obviously did not possess comparable skill. Hence, a discrepancy will be noted between passages which I and my assistant translated into English from Luhya or Swahili and passages written or spoken originally in English. The latter are often grammatically poor.

When examining an unknown universe, the first interviews need to be of an exploratory nature. A too narrow focus at the beginning of a study runs the risk of excluding the most relevant variables. Should I propose that Msambwa was composed of mainly expressive activities, it would not be difficult to find evidence — drumming, parades, visions and ecstasy — to support this hypothesis. Since I wanted the members rather than myself to define the important dimensions, informal but guided interviews with many open-ended questions were used. Later, when inconsistencies appeared in the data or when certain dimensions appeared interesting, the questions became more specific.

I talked to people singly and in groups. Both arrangements had their assets as well as their liabilities. By interviewing individuals alone the degree of consensus or diversity on particular subjects could be ascertained. Individual versions served as consistency checks on each other.

On a number of occasions, however, members insisted on meeting together in order to give me the 'official' version of the movement's history. The group interview allayed fears that one member would give a highly personal account that would misrepresent the 'true' history of the movement. Joasch Walumoli, Msambwa's prophet, refused to speak with me alone for the following reasons:

> We are a group. It is a well known rule that I should not say anything without the elders present so that they can witness what I say. For example, two brothers jointly own a cow. Now one of the brothers is on safari . . . and a stranger comes and tells you that you should give him the cow. You can't give it to him unless your brother knows about it because it is a cow you own together. If you give it away without your brother's consent he might be annoyed with you when he returns home. That's one reason why I can't give you our history without my elders.
>
> Another reason is that we have been persecuted so much by the government that if I give you the history without my elders' consent they will quarrel with me and tell me that perhaps I have reported our organization to the CID [Criminal Investigation Division]. So I must have my elders.[3]

The group interview ruled out idiosyncratic interpretations and individual fabrications. When arguments ensued among the interviewees, the researcher was acquainted with areas of ambiguity and conflict. On the other hand, group interviews did not rule out non-representative presentations in that only the views of a particular clique might be presented. They also tended to create a consensus of opinion where none may have existed.

The problem arose as to how much reliance to put on different kinds of data. Here questions of documentation, reputation of the author or respondent, and type of information came into play. One scholar's version of Gusii religion might differ in important aspects from another's and one version might be much better documented than another. One participant's explanation of the motives behind a punitive expedition might not jibe with another's. Accounts of past events were often plagued by problems of selective memory and discrepancies in dates, especially after a lapse of several years. Documents and *The Times London Index* were used, where possible, to corroborate dates and historical statements. We know that agents of social control tend to exaggerate the degree of unrest and subversive activity so this was borne in mind when assessing the data. The views of the present (African) authorities were compared with the colonial authorities. Internal checks on consistency of interview data were made by asking the same question in several different ways. The amount of crosschecking depended on the reliability of the original source and the importance of the event to the analysis.

Did any of the respondents intentionally mislead me? Among those interviewed, I was not aware of any such attempt. What about the miraculous tales and fanciful stories of Masinde's adventures and powers? These stories were related because I had indicated an interest in any stories about Msambwa. Although I could have probed to see whether people really believed them, I did not think it necessary or appropriate. To me, whether or not the stories were believed was not nearly as important as what they told about the people, their desires, dreams and the kinds of strains they were under. From what I could ascertain, some people believed the stories although the majority did not. Most accepted them much as we do folk tales about heroes or such wondrous events as discovered gold mines and rags-to-riches mobility.

Based on this research experience it seems to me that:

1) The successful undertaking of this kind of study is abetted by working through assistants who have roots in the local community, a level of sophistication higher than the ordinary person, and who are in some respects, marginal. Matters of dress, observance of social etiquette and local custom can turn out not to be trivial matters but can sometimes spell the difference between being able to obtain or being refused, information. (This is not to say that a person cannot work out a deviant role that breaks many of these norms and yet be accepted.) An assistant who has the researcher's best interests at heart can, by rewording a question that might otherwise be inappropriate or even offensive, save an interview from being broken off.

2) In the study of social movements as with other social phenomena, there are distinct advantages to be gained from combining fieldwork and survey research. Far from being mutually exclusive, both

methods have their strengths and weaknesses and research should profit from the 'deep, rich, insightful' data of participant observation and informal interviews as well as from the standardized, generalizable data of surveys. In fact, the special strengths of one technique may contribute substantially to the utilization of the other technique.

While the combination of survey and field techniques can take many forms, in the case of Msambwa, now that fieldwork has established its parameters, a survey could demonstrate the generality of particular observations and provide some quantitative evidence to support or dispute specific hypotheses. (The above assumes, of course, that the practical difficulties—the government ban on Dini ya Msambwa has been lifted and the members are willing to talk—have been overcome.) Far more precise information is needed, for instance, on the members. Data on socio-economic position, ownership of land, age, ethnicity, and measures of religiosity, political alienation, social integration, level of discontent, and attitudes towards social change, of a random sample of members would enable a more rigorous testing of hypotheses on recruitment. And, to further refine these hypotheses, a sample of members could be compared with non-members on the above variables.

3) It is important to discuss one's methodology so that others involved in similar studies can understand its strengths and weaknesses and can learn from its failures and successes. If this study had employed survey techniques there would be no objection, indeed it would be expected that one would describe the sample size, how it was drawn, and the kind of responses it received. Those using field-work and historical approaches should follow the same procedure as they have been far slower in recognizing the importance of making their methods explicit, and there has been far less work done in codifying these approaches than in survey techniques. Furthermore, since first hand studies of subversive movements are relatively rare and involve some problems in an acute form, it might be helpful for others to learn of particular experiences, good and bad, that are searcher has had with respondents, cliques, and agents of social control.

Notes

1. The Kisumu Riot occurred a few months after Tom Mboya, the Luo Minister of Economic Planning and Development, had been assassinated.

This event exacerbated tensions between the Luo and the Kikuyu. When President Kenyatta came to Kisumu, the capital of Luoland, to open a new hospital, youth wingers from the Kenya People's Union, (Oginga Odinga's opposition party), booed the presidential party and scuffles broke out which led to the security police firing point-blank into the bystanders. The official death toll was placed at eleven or twelve but unofficial counts placed it much higher. Odinga and other KPU party officials were arrested and the party banned. The Union had supporters among the Luhya and local leaders feared arrest.

2. Caleb Kakayi, 10 November 1965.
3. Interview on 15 March 1965.

APPENDIX B

APPENDIX B

PROFESSOR WERE'S QUOTATIONS

This quotation by Were was composed of sentences that appeared on pages 69 and 72 of *Under the African Sun*. Ansorge wrote:

Our leader [referring to a Britisher] kept a sharp look-out that the captured women and children were not carried off as slaves, but were handed over to his care. Amongst primitive tribes, war is simply a repetition of what one reads of in the Old Testament—*every adult male is put to death*, the women and children are captured and become slaves. Native women are often very callous, and readily accept as husband the murderer of their male relatives. (p. 69, Italics mine.)

Then, two pages later:

Though the enemy had comparatively few killed, the loss they suffered was a severe punishment to them; villages were burnt to the ground, a severe matter in a district where wood for rebuilding the huts had to be fetched from a considerable distance; standing crops destroyed; vast stores of corn found in the villages were used up by the invading army; and cattle, their most valuable possessions, were captured by the hundred. (p. 72, Italics mine.)

APPENDIX C

SOME MSAMBWA RITUALS AND SYMBOLS

Two Dini ya Msambwa ceremonies are presented. Benjamin Wekuke took me to the family shrine on his home compound where he reverently went through the ritual dressed in a brilliant blue robe on 8 November 1965. From what is written about traditional practices the following appear to approximate the old rites. Detailed descriptions of similar ceremonies, to my knowledge, are not available. It will be noted that Bible stories have been incorporated.

A Ceremony for Propitiating the Ancestor Spirits
At the heart of the traditional religion is the family shrine for male ancestors known as *namwina* built on the home compound where families worshipped together. Sacrifice was Dini ya Msambwa's basic ritual as it was in the traditional religion. Wekuke spoke as follows:

> You can go any time to the shrine and pray to God. I might go if one of my children was seriously sick or when something else bad happens. It might be once or twice a year. I might be told in a dream to slaughter some animal. The ancestor spirits come and talk to you. You see the particular faces of certain ancestors in your dreams. You slaughter the kind of animal you are told to by the spirit. No elders are needed this time.
>
> You put your cloak on top of the shrine before the sun comes up. You pray in front of the shrine with a knife in your hand. You choose someone close to you in age or someone born on the same day. You give them the knife to be used in the killing. You don't do it yourself because you need the blessing and if you killed the animal yourself its spirit might not feel comfortable with you. You choose a person from outside your family so its spirit [the animal's] won't affect him.
>
> The animal is slaughtered about nine or ten in the morning. Then you pour some of its blood on the two or three stones that are in front of the shrine. You do this so that the riches of your home will be solid like a stone.

Also the stone takes us back to the Bible when Moses was taking the children of Israel through the Red Sea. They passed through the Red Sea like a stone . . . (because water doesn't affect a stone). Pharoah's soldiers drowned. Also, when you read Moses you find that he took sheep's blood and smeared it on the front door of all the Israelites.

You pray to God [*Mungu*, Swahili for God] to bless your house. Then you put a piece of meat on the tallest stick. (The fly whisk may be there but it isn't a must in this ceremony. The cloak must stay there the whole day.) The first chamber of the cow's stomach is placed in front of the door of my first wife's house so that the ancestor spirits may come and dance on it and go inside.

When the sun is setting either myself or an elder comes with a knife and breaks the stomach into two pieces. The middle portion is given to the owner of the house—my wife—and the dung that remains on the outside two portions is removed. That is left there. At sundown the cloak is removed to the central pole inside my first wife's hut. [Wekuke showed me the cloak hanging on the pole. Under it was a cow bell worn by a special cow and an armlet carved in ivory that he wore on his upper left arm for the ceremony, and his spear.] The remaining meat is roasted for the feast and given to everyone who comes. Many people come for such a ceremony. Before the cloak is finally removed, I kneel and pray in front of the shrine. Then I take the cloak into the house and hang it on the middle pole that is the very centre of the hut and reaches the highest point of the roof.

An elder welcomes you. You are blessed by the elders in front of the shrine and an elder says, 'Now you must know that you are no longer a child. Leave alone childish matters and be a person who can keep peace inside and outside your home. Never shed a human being's blood. Your land is your home. Never commit adultery. Look after other people's property. Never misuse it or destroy it. Respect your mother and your father and every living creature. Even insects you should not step on them.' The elder puts the cloak on you as you stand and then you sit on the stool. [The cloak is made of monkey skins and trimmed with cowrie shells. It is worn by the head of the lineage.] His last words are, 'You are now blessed by us and you are a leader of every creature in this world.' The elders leave and I take my stool into the house.

The Ceremony for Conferring the Status of Elder

When the elders feel I should have my own shrine, *namwina*, some come to my home and they choose a place opposite the door of my house. It should be in front of the door so my ancestor spirits will take my prayers to the Creator . . . The ancestor spirits can go directly to my house and bless it. If the shrine is at the back of the house they might get lost.

After the elders have chosen the site they build it completely. It can be built by your father if he is alive. It signifies you are an elder. I can't touch a thing. It is a holy day for me. After the *namwina* is built and thatched by the elders . . . the *basambwa* [ancestor spirits] bring a dream and in the dream they tell you what kind of an animal should be slaughtered. It always used to be a male as the male is strongest.

The ceremony begins at the break of dawn, as the first red streaks of the sun come up over the horizon. I wake up early and put my spear and cloak on top of the shrine. The spear, according to our old traditions, symbolizes strength and truth. If you fought very hard and won in battle you bring honour and riches to yourself. If you were fighting over land and you win you will now be able to get food from the land. That is the riches. The spear is placed upright at the front side of the shrine and the blade stands for your tongue. May it speak the truth and may it speak clean words that you do not insult anyone. The fly whisk is also placed in the thatch of the roof. It is made of buffalo tail and it means you will have the strength of a buffalo in your heart. You put your spear and cloak on top of the shrine and wait until nine or ten o'clock when the elders come to slaughter the bull. When the elders slaughter the animal I'm sent away. I can't be near. After it is killed someone calls you from your hiding place and you come with a stick near the bull beating the ground and shouting, 'Who has killed the bull?' so that the dead bull won't be annoyed with you. Because if the bull's spirit was annoyed with you it might cause you to lose all your cattle. It could prevent you from having more cattle.

There are four different wooden sticks placed on the roof [of the *namwina*]. All different kinds of woods. The highest is known as *lukomosi*. It stops diseases from attacking your family, it increases your cattle and prevents danger and misfortune from coming to you. *Lukhenda* is a sign of good luck. It is from a tree used to clean gourds where milk is stored. *Lusunu* is to prevent you from being bewitched.

The elders bring a stool and place it near the *namwina* and I stand by the stool facing the shrine. The elders then cut some meat from the inside muscle of the bull and put a piece on the highest stick. You are given milk to pour on the bull. Then you are given some blood in a gourd to pour on the ground in front of the door of the shrine.

The meat is put there [on the sticks] for the ancestor spirits who come to the shrine. Your grandmother comes in a dream to tell you, 'My son I want a piece of meat.' You put the meat there. The spirits don't actually eat the meat—they smell it. They thank you for the food and bless your home. They come to tell you in another dream and thank you saying, 'We thank you for the food and we are pleased. You'll be blessed. You remain in peace in your house. Your cattle will increase and your children will never be sick.'

Symbolic Materials[1]

Kumwilima is a black hardwood which grows abundantly in the Bukusu reserve. It was taken by the authorities as a definite mark of Msambwa membership. At meetings this stick was placed next to the door and when not in actual use thrust into the thatch above the entrance. It served as a talisman for it was believed to blacken the hearts and blind the eyes of all Europeans, making it impossible for them to discover Dini ya Msambwa members. Traditionally, the stick was used in circumcision ceremonies and by herd boys who believed it protected the eyes of cattle from disease.

Lunyubti was a less common hardwood sometimes found at Msambwa meetings. It was customarily placed in the centre of the hut and signified that those present were stalwart believers in Msambwa, unafraid of the consequences of their beliefs. Traditionally, a diviner gave this stick to someone very ill who, upon recovery, performed a ceremony.

Lunsunu wood found only in the North Nyanza reserve symbolized the death of Europeans. Among the Bukusu, *lunsunu* signified integrity. They placed it in a hillock outside their huts in the belief that its presence would drive away dishonest people from their land.

Lukomosi, or the East African medlar, was a white hardwood that grows plentifully in the Bukusu reserve. Small twigs grow alternatively on a branch and resemble a cross. It was placed in the centre of a meeting and was believed to send the members' prayers to heaven. The hardness of the wood signified the members' resolve to stand firm in their beliefs and under no circumstances betray their religion. It was a badge of membership. Formerly it was used in circumcision ceremonies.

Lulwarakumba, a rare stick, was used by Msambwa to signify the death of their enemies or literally the disintegration of their enemies' bones. It was usually thrust into the thatch above the entrance to a house.

Lusilangokho was a small stick frequently used as a walking stick by Dini ya Msambwa's messengers. It was waved in the air to ensure a journey free from trouble.

Lulwabuala and *Lukhafwa* were creepers. After a meeting one or the other was thrown into a river to symbolize the spreading of Msambwa's beliefs throughout the land.

Ndari was a plant with bulbous roots commonly found in the vicinity of Mount Elgon. When it was removed from the ground Msambwa's secrets supposedly entered the hole from whence the roots came and were thus safely hidden from Europeans.

White fowl were commonly sacrificed in rites. After the bird had bled to death the stomach was examined for omens. If the examination revealed a white stomach, all was well. A red stomach signalled danger and the members were alerted to be on guard.

Sometimes the stomach was opened across a stream with the result that the contents fell onto either bank. This indicated the irreconcilable separation of Africans from Europeans. Usually the bird was burned in its feathers. The smoke was believed to carry the members' prayers to heaven.

Black fowl were also sacrificed as above, only the bird's entrails were thrown into a stream to symbolize the return of the European across the ocean to his own country. According to a Bukusu custom, black feathers were used to protect women in childbirth and to ensure a good harvest from a sick person's land.

Kisilili or *hawk wings* were highly esteemed by the members. The feathers were attached by grass to a stick or *lukomosi* and represented the legend of the dove that carried an olive branch to Noah.

Emande or *lourie* was a black and red bird. When the bird was killed at a meeting the leader retained the body but the feathers were distributed among those present. The members carried the feathers to show that they would never associate with Europeans. The feathers also served as an amulet to prevent Europeans from seizing African land. Any person found in possession of *emande* feathers was regarded as a prominent member by the authorities.

Khwenge was a small bird that lived in the bush close to rivers. Its cry was a short whistle. An old Bukusu legend tells of a bird that cried for its mother because smoke got into its eyes. Similarly, Africans' cries against Europeans went unheard.

Sacrificial blood was sprinkled on the ground both inside and outside the hut at meetings in the belief that it kept the inhabitants therein safe. Some leaders smeared blood on their forehead and chest to signify their rank within Msambwa instead of the usual practice of wearing a *kanzu*. In the North Nyanza reserve recruits allegedly took an oath of secrecy by drinking some of the sacrificial blood.

Note

1. The following information comes from KNA:EN/3. *Ethnology, Political Records 1957*. This information on Msambwa's symbolism is difficult to assess for its accuracy. The substances used and the acts performed are sufficiently similar to those used in Luhya ceremonies for

the document to have a compelling 'fitness'. In their descriptions of Luhya ritual, La Fontaine and Wagner mention the use of creepers, different woods and plants, the sprinkling of sacrificial blood over the homestead and sometimes on the participants, the significance of white and black fowl, and the searching of entrails for omens. There were no plants in their accounts the names of which coincided with the creepers and plants named in Dini ya Msambwa's symbolisms but both La Fontaine's and Wagner's descriptions are short and obviously incomplete. However Wekuke's account of the ceremony of conferring the status of elder (see immediately above) does mention two of the same woods, the *Lunsunu* and the *Lukomosi*. Wagner, *Abaluyia of Kavirondo*, pp. 50-2; La Fontaine, *Gisu of Uganda*, p. 52.

APPENDIX D

EXCERPTS FROM MASINDE'S SERMONS

I attended a church service on 14 March 1965. The theme of Masinde's sermon was love. He said in part:

This word that I want to tell you is love. . . . This is what God offered to man and the most important thing he offered was love. God said that everyone in this world should love, not hate, each other. Hatred is what God highly opposed. He gave man the ability to make weapons, bombs, guns, spears, bows and arrows and many others. But God did not say that these weapons should be used to fight and to kill. Men are misusing these weapons. They fight, they carry on wars which are very much against God's will. God said that love is his tool and that we should obey him. That means it is useless to disobey God. He didn't mean us to hate each other. I warn you that if you don't love each other God will leave you and you'll start to kill among yourselves with the strong weapons he has given you. Then God will destroy the world and make a new world where he will bring new generations. That's why I tell you—we should always keep peace in the whole world. God is hungry for love on earth. We learn this from the Book of Prayers [probably either the Anglican or the Quaker prayer book]. For that reason we should love each other as we love ourselves. We should love not only the people of Africa but even the people of France, Germany, Italy, India, Japan, America, the whole world. We are all brothers and sisters. . . . Another thing I must tell you is that if you beat or abuse someone, you have beaten and abused God because God made people in his own image. And people are his temple wherein he dwells.

Masinde concluded with a hymn. He took out his mouth-organ, gave a tune, and led the singing of an Anglican hymn. Then he continued:

Everybody had left the way of God and gone his own way. Why should we do this when our ancestors knew and loved God? I think that the most important thing for us to learn to do is to pray to God because if we pray to God, God will realise that we love him and have not forgotten him. God has forbidden theft. He doesn't want people to abuse each other and to glorify themselves. People are not God. You should be humble and always give God his kingdom in prayers.

After another hymn, an assistant led the group in prayer. Among other things, he said, 'God of heaven bless those who are in trouble. Bless those who are on long journeys such as our visitor here [the author] who will have to travel a long way from here. Lead her all the way home safely. God I pray thee help us all today and forever and ever. Amen.'

On another occasion, 16 March 1965, Masinde said in a sermon:

Another thing I would like to tell you is that today at this time I'm warning the Americans that they should not bring their bombs and destroy the creatures of God. This violates God's will. The same for the Russians because these bombs are very dangerous weapons and can destroy the whole world in a minute. And this is destroying God's property. I tell you boy [to Charles] to write this down. And I say this frankly that those who will go to the United States tell them not to fight the creatures of this world with their bomb. They will make God angry. This is very much against God's will and I say this freely and frankly. Everyone that has ears let him hear. Now let us sing.

This sermon may have been given for my benefit since the theme hardly fits Masinde's character, although, in one sense, it does, as he was erratic. It reveals the blending of African and Christian forms and provides insight into a peasant's interpretation of the power struggle between Russia and the United States.

APPENDIX E

COPY OF MASINDE'S LETTER

Kimilili Market,
Private Bag,
Kimilili,
March 16, 1965.

Dear Mr. Charbonneau,[1]

Thank you very much for sending this girl on a long safari, bringing her to me. But I didn't give her any history. What I to say is that you should come here together. Please don't leave her behind. I would like you to come with a notebook and I will tell you about the history of our home, Kenya. If you do that I will be quite ready to give you my full history. And I would like to emphasize—please don't leave this girl behind.

That is all Sir,

Yours,

The president, Mr. Elijah Masinde
The vice-president, Mr. Benjamin Wekuke
The secretary, Mr. Samson Wafula
The vice-secretary, Mr. David Wanyonyi
The treasurer, Mr. Israel Khaoya
The vice-treasuer, Mr. Andrew Buluma
Joseph Pascal Nabwana, O.B.E.[2]

Notes

1. I decided that if the letter was sent, better send it to Mr. Charbonneau, the supervisor of the Canada Council's Scholarship Programme which sponsored me. Anyway, by this time my nerves were becoming frayed. We had spent several hours following Masinde's orders and trying to cope with his whims. We didn't know from one minute to the next what would happen. He had during that time had a fight with our good friend, Wekuke. Charles informed me later that he had shared my apprehension and that when we arrived at Masinde's farm he had had me park the car headed for an exit in case we should have to make a fast exit.
2. Note the O.B.E. (Order of the British Empire) after Mr. Nabwana's name.

APPENDIX F

DINI YA MUSAMBWA CONSTITUTION AND RULES

1. Name: The name of the Society will be "Dini ya Musambwa".
2. Objects: The objects of the society are as follows:
   a) To maintain our old way of believing in God.
   b) To give respect to our Almighty God.
   c) To respect our parents and neighbours.
   d) To abide with the Law of the Land.
   e) To be non-political.
3. Membership: a) Membership is open to any who are interested. No entrance fee or subscription is payable but members may make voluntary contributions.

   b) Any member may be expelled from membership if the committee so recommends and if a general meeting of the society shall resolve by a 2/3 majority of the members present that such a member should be expelled [for] the reputation or dignity of the society, or that he has contravened any of the provisions of the constitution of the society. The committee shall have power to suspend a member from his membership until the next general meeting of the society, following such suspension a member whose expulsion is proposed shall have the right to address the general meeting at which his expulsion is to be considered.
4. Officials:
   a) The office-bearers of the society shall be
      (i) The Chairman
      (ii) The Vice-Chairman
      (iii) The Secretary
      (iv) The Assistant Secretary
      (v) The Treasurer
      (vi) The Assistant Treasurer
   all of whom shall be fully paid-up members of the society and

333

shall be elected at the annual general meeting to be held in each year.

b)   All office-bearers shall hold office from the date of election until the succeeding annual general meeting subject to the conditions contained in sub-paragraphs (c) and (d) of this rule but shall be eligible for re-election.

c)   Any office-bearer who ceases to be a member of the society shall automatically cease to be an office-bearer thereof.

5. Duties of Officials: The duties of the office-bearers will be as follows:

a)   The president is the head of the society.

b)   The secretary is to keep the records of the society.

c)   The treasurer is responsible for the safe-keeping of the society's money.

6. The Committee: The affairs of the society shall be controlled by a committee consisting of the office bearers together with 50 members who shall be elected at a general meeting of the Society and shall hold office for a period of 3 years. Meetings of the Committee shall be held every month. A quorum shall consist of 24 members.

7. General Meeting: General Meeting of members of the Society shall be held five times a year: on 8 February, 4 April, 15 August, 31 October and 31 December. A quorum shall consist of 700 members.

7a. Religious Meetings: Every branch shall hold a meeting of its members to worship God every Sunday.

8. Trustees: Property owned by the Society will be vested in two trustees appointed for the purpose by the members in a general meeting.

9. Use of Funds: The Society's funds can be used for the following purposes:

a)   For our visitors

b)   For orphans

c)   For the poor

d)   For widows and widowers

e)   For the upkeep of the landrover and maintenance of the Society's property.

f)   For the building of our churches

g)   For the payment of staff employed by the Society

h)   The officials shall be elected at a general meeting of the

Society and shall hold office for a period of 3 years from the date of their election.

THE CONSTITUTION OF MSAMBWA

Society and shall hold office for a period of 3 years from
the date of their election

APPENDIX G

CHRONOLOGY OF EVENTS IN DINI YA MSAMBWA'S CAREER[1]

1943–1944

1. 18 February 1943. The Native Tribunal buildings at Kamutiong were burned down and the investigation revealed that it was not accidental. The arson occurred after a request by people in Kimilili for the Native Tribunal to be built at Kimilili had been rejected by the district commissioner.

2. A portion of the assistant agricultural officer's residential plot and the site chosen by the agricultural officer for an implement store was ploughed up.

3. 9 June 1943. Cattle used by the Agricultural Department were deliberately let loose in the night.

4. October 1943. The Agricultural Department decided that only three trader's shops were desirable at Kimakungi and licenses were issued accordingly. Subsequently these shops were set on fire.

5. Masinde, Wekuke and Wemani, another member, assaulted a chief who was serving a conscript labour summons.

6. 17 April 1944. The above were brought before a *baraza* in connection with the assault. According to district officer N. K. Kennaway they 'made certain subversive statements in open baraza, and then refused to obey Chief Amutalla's order to sit down and be quiet.' This incident became the subject of subsequent court cases, first before the Native Tribunal and later the District Officer's Court where on both occasions their attitude was described as 'truculent'.

7. Masinde refused to let the veterinarian inject his cattle.

8. 24 October 1944. Masinde and Wekuke threatened to beat up an agricultural officer who was instructing the local people in the uprooting of Mexican marigold if he dared to come to that area again. Other agricultural officers received the same treatment.

9. 27 October 1944. A follower, Wekunda, refused to accept a conscript labour summons.

10. 30 October 1944. The head of the traditional council of elders and two of his men were assaulted and injured by Masinde and his men when serving a labour summons.

11. Masinde opposed recruitment of Africans to World War II.

12. Around mid-November, the cinema show sponsored by the administration's home news unit was forced to close down by people throwing rocks at the screen. While young boys threw the rocks they were said to have been egged on by young men.

13. 17 November 1944. Mr. Bickford's house burned down. The provincial commissioner, in addition to what has already been reported stated:

As I was DC of the North Kavirondo district for a period of approximately 18 months, immediately before taking up my present office, I can claim personal knowledge of the Kitosh [Bukusu], the people concerned in this matter. . . . I would describe the Kitosh as a sensitive and rather emotional people, ready to respond if handled with understanding but obstinate if driven. It is quite obvious to me that Mr. Bickford did not understand them nor seek their co-operation. He sought to carry out his appointment duty by force of rule, rather than by explanation and leadership and this attitude has caused resentment, culminating in the destruction of his house. . . . Mr. Bickford's nature appears to resent any form of direction.[2]

District commissioner F. D. Hislop concurred with the provincial commissioner. He wrote:

Mr. Bickford had no idea of how to conduct his work, apart from the purely agricultural side. If any officer senior to himself has in the past endeavoured to instruct him, it has apparently been without success. His one idea is to give an order and to see it was obeyed, just as if he were still in the Kings African Rifles, although be it noted he was like this before he went to the KAR and he is still like this at the time I am writing these lines, as I hear he is issuing entirely illegal orders to transport owners in connection with the bumper maize crop. While I hesitate to infringe on the affairs of another department in this case the Agricultural Department, nevertheless the latter is so closely bound up with the administration, more especially as its main activities have something to do with the most ticklish subject of land, that I feel compelled to submit the following.[3]

14. About the same time as the Bickford incident, a large Friends Africa Mission Church near Mr. Bickford's house was set on fires as well as several African houses and grain stores.

1945

15. 14 February. Masinde was convicted on two charges of assault. He was ordered to enter bond of 500|- to keep the peace for one year but he refused to sign the bond and was sent to prison for twelve months or until such time as he would sign. While serving his sentence he was certified insane.

16. 10 March. Masinde committed to Mathari Mental Hospital where he remained for two years.

17. When the district commissioner was demarcating a boundary between the Kimilili and Elgon locations, some Kimilili people who opposed the demarcation assaulted the son of the Elgon chief who was representing his father. About the same time, a peasant from Elgon location who had assisted in demarcating the boundary had his hut burned down. His wife, child, and another member of the family died in the blaze.

1946

18. 30 September. Assistant inspector Stewart of Eldoret with a party of police visited Kimilili market checking for stolen cattle. They were obstructed in their work by the local tribesmen to such an extent that it was considered wise for the police party to leave.[4]

19. October. A strike on Commander Carter's farm. Rumours of further unrest included a Bukusu movement to take land in the White Highlands they claimed as tribal land.

20. 30–31 October. The Governor of Kenya and the provincial commissioner of the Rift Valley confer with the district commissioner and the assistant superintendent of police, Eldoret, on Dini ya Msambwa.

1947

21. May. Masinde was released from Mathari Mental Hospital and recommenced his Msambwa activities. Many meetings were held.

22. A series of incidents occurred: two cases of arson at the Seventh-day Adventists' school at Malakisi and the breaking of windows at the Roman Catholic Mission at Lugulu.

23. 13 July. Masinde addressed a rally at Kimaliwa.

24. 14 July. Wekuke and other members started a campaign to raise wages and better working conditions of the Kimilili labourers.

25. August. Masinde addressed a gathering exhorting them to take

up arms against the Europeans. Wekuke also proselytized at Kimilili market.

26. 17 September. Masinde held a commemorative service at Luguru in honour of the 1895 warriors. Around five thousand attended.

27. Early October. Masinde was ordered to appear before the district commissioner at Kimilili. When he failed to, police were sent to his home but he had disappeared.

1948

28. 7 February. Dini ya Msambwa followers demonstrate at the Roman Catholic Mission, Kibabii.

29. 10 February. The Malakisi Riot.

30. 15 February. A secret meeting was held on the Ganz brothers' farm in the Trans Nzoia.

31. 16 February. Masinde was discovered hiding in a large hole dug in the ground near Chesamis over which potatoes had been planted as camouflage.[5] He was arrested and in late August deported along with Wekuke and Walumoli to Lamu.

32. 17 February. A notice in the Official Gazette declared Msambwa an illegal society. Meetings of the Bukusu Union were also proscribed.

1949

33. March. There was an outbreak of arson in the Trans Nzoia.

34. 9 April. A secret meeting was held on Mrs. Jackson's farm at Kitale. The farm manager, Michael Keane, heard that some strange Africans were on the farm so he went to investigate. As he opened the door of an African hut he was struck on the head with a *panga* which inflicted a four-and-a-half inch wound. Later, in court, the accused said he had not struck to kill or he would have used two hands. He explained that when he heard the '*Bwana* [title of respect for a man] was coming', he lost his head. Mr. Justice Thacker questioned the defendent, 'You know they [Dini ya Msambwa] have been destroying by fire the property of Europeans in this district?'

Defendant: Yes.

Judge: I put it to you that one of the objects of this Society is to destroy Europeans' property and also the Europeans themselves?

Defendant: Yes, that is so.

Judge: And in the pursuance of that policy you struck down this man?

Defendant: Yes. [It sounds as if the defendant may be confused as to the meaning of yes and no.]

In summing up the prosecution, Mr. Somerhough said, 'This case demonstrates that a society which is illegal and which has for its avowed object the arousing of hatred in people living in one part, and which up to now has not hesitated to practice violence against property, has now gone further and shown there is nothing they will stop at!'

In passing a sentence of life imprisonment, Mr. Justice Thacker said there was no doubt that the accused had attempted, without provocation, murder.[6]

35. July. Lukas Pkiech escaped from Nakuru jail.

36. November. A boundary marker separating the reserve from the White Highlands was removed. A Dini ya Msambwa flag and two threatening letters were left on the Kimilili-Kamakoiya road.

37. Late November. Masinde was moved from Lamu to Marsabit.

38. December. Another boundary marker that demarcated the White Highlands from the reserve was broken.

1950–1959

39. 1950. More arson in the Trans Nzoia District brought a dusk-to-dawn curfew.

40. Msambwa members erected a cross and left a threatening note telling a settler to abandon his farm.

41. 24 April 1950. The Kolloa Affray.

42. June 1952. Members of Msambwa rolled a large boulder down the mountainside at a police party which had just arrested one of its members. As it hurtled down the mountain the police scattered. Only one policeman was slightly injured.[7]

43. June 1952. On receipt of information that a big Dini ya Msambwa meeting was taking place in the foothills of Mount Elgon, a thirty man patrol of Uganda police was sent out. Thirty-one suspected Msambwa members were arrested but despite a five hour night march the police failed to find the main body. They continued to patrol the Uganda side of Mount Elgon but there were reports that the main body had either withdrawn into the depths of the rain forest or crossed the Kenya border.[8]

44. July 1952. Administrative and police officers from Kenya and Uganda hold a conference to discuss ways of cooperating in the suppression of Msambwa.[9]

45. 12 November 1952. A Dini ya Msambwa meeting in the hut of Elichuma Masufu was broken up by four policemen. Israel Khaoya, one of Masinde's assistants, was arrested and later prosecuted for being a member of an unlawful society.

46. September 1954. Cattle poisoned on a settler's farm at Kiminini. Church Missionary Society school burned down at Lugari.

47. October 1955. Two mission schools in Kimilili were burned to the ground.

48. October 1955. A settler in the Kamakoiya area received threatening letters.

1960–1961

49. 12 May 1960. Masinde Muliro demanded the release of Jomo Kenyatta and Elijah Masinde in the Legislative Council.

50. 13 September 1960. Benjamin Wekuke and two other Msambwa members, restricted to Lamu Island for their participation in Msambwa, were released on condition they did not revert to illegal and subversive activities.

51. May 1961. Masinde released from prison.

1962

52. 2 January. Masinde announced that he was seeking to reactivate Dini ya Msambwa and that he hoped to have an interview with the Governor, Sir Patrick Renison at which he would raise the question of its proscription.

53. 7 January. Masinde spoke at a KANU rally at Kitale.

54. 9 January. KADU's Deputy Leader, Masinde Muliro, strongly criticized Masinde for his alleged KANU affiliation.

55. January. About fifteen hundred Bukusu at a meeting in Kimilili asked the tribal elders to seek an interview with Sir Patrick Renison and urged the deportation of Masinde and his assistants from Elgon-Nyanza. At another meeting in Bungoma about seventy chiefs and elders denounced Dini ya Msambwa.

56. 16 April. Forty Luhya were arrested and charged with being members of Msambwa. They were discharged later in the month on condition that they did not commit any offenses for the next twelve months.

57. 13 August. Seven Bukusu were arrested at Kiminini and charged with being members of Msambwa.

58. 4 October. Eight people were arrested at Kakamega and charged with being members of Dini ya Msambwa.

59. 24 October. Masinde and four followers were arrested and charged with holding an unlawful meeting at Kaptalaj village, attended by four hundred people, and of creating a disturbance in the police station at Malakisi.

60. 30 October. Masinde told a Magistrate's Court in Bungoma that he wished the government would order his redetention 'because I'm tired of police threats'. Case adjourned.

61. November. A KADU meeting of five thousand persons at Kamakoiya market condemned Dini ya Msambwa.

1963

62. 15 January. Masinde and four others were arrested for being members of an unlawful society.

63. 24 January. Masinde and the four members appeared in court on a charge of taking part in an unlawful meeting. They pleaded 'not guilty', and were released on bail.

64. 18 March. Masinde appeared in a Kisumu magistrate's court charged with taking part in an unlawful assembly on 24 October 1962.

1964

65. 21 April. Prime Minister Kenyatta revoked the order declaring Dini ya Msambwa a prohibited society.

66. 15 May. Dini ya Msambwa granted official registration as a society.

67. 23 May. Masinde pleads 'not guilty' in a Kampala court to being in Uganda unlawfully.

68. 5 June. Masinde sent to prison at Mbale for six months for being unlawfully in Uganda.

69. 1 December. A Kenya police patrol was rushed to Kimilili for fear that followers of Msambwa might resort to violence against American missionaries in the area.

1965

70. 9 March. Police arrived with a search warrant at Masinde's home. Two bottles of Nubian gin were found at the edge of his bed.

71. 1 May. The district commissioner of the Trans Nzoia urged followers of Msambwa to desist from unlawful acts.

72. 19 May. Masinde was fined £15 or forty-five days in default, after being found 'guilty' of the illegal possession of Nubian gin.

73. 25 July. District commissioner Riyamy of Kakamega reported that members of Msambwa were harassing people and discouraging them from working hard.

74. 11 October. Masinde, charged on three accounts of offensive conduct and assaulting and obstructing a police constable in the execution of his duty at Kamakoiya, was sentenced to 30 months imprisonment.

75. 21 October. The M.P. for Elgon East, M. Barasa, asked in the National Assembly whether President Kenyatta would consider a pardon for Masinde.

76. 12. November. Masinde, Wafula, and two other members appeared in court at Bungoma on the charge of organizing illegal schools.

77. December 1965. A police party sent to arrest Manuel Kamoti, accused of participating in Dini ya Msambwa, clashed with him and his men, armed with spears, clubs and stones, in Bugisu District, Eastern Uganda. Two constables were injured and Kamoti and another man admitted to hospital.

1966

78. 9 June. On the order of President Kenyatta, Masinde was released from prison.

79. 24 November. Masinde allegedly told members of the Kenya police and administration police at a public meeting in Bukholi that they should go on strike if the government did not increase their salaries.

80. 1 December. The Attorney-General, Mr. Charles Njonjo, said that Masinde was not cooperating with the government and that he regretted the action he had taken in obtaining his release.

1967

81. 22 February. Masinde arrested and charged with incitement to defiance of lawful authority.

82. 16 March. Masinde went on trial charged with three accounts of stirring members of the police force to mutiny. (see above, 79)

83. 23 March. Masinde jailed for nine months for the above offence.

343

84. 25 August. Masinde appealed his nine month sentence to the Kenya High Court.

85. 2 October. Masinde's appeal is dismissed by the High Court.

1968

86. February. Vice-President Daniel arap Moi warned Msambwa that it may have to be banned 'if it continues its political ideologies and destructive activities to disunite the people of Central Nyanza.

87. 1 March. Vice-President Moi told the National Assembly that Msambwa's activities were constantly under government scrutiny in answer to an M.P.'s question, 'Since the former colonial government banned this sect, is it not high time that the present government banned this sect which has become a political organization rather than a religious one?'

88. 2 October. Members of Dini ya Msambwa were attacked by a group of Walago tribesmen. Nineteen people were injured.

89. 24 October. Attorney-General Njonjo proscribed Dini ya Msambwa.

90. 12 November. Masinde and Japhat Werungu, charged with assault and wrongful confinement of Grace Nasimiyu in Kimilili on 23 September, were found guilty. Masinde given two years imprisonment and Werungu, one year.

1969

91. 20 January. The provincial commissioner for the Rift Valley, Mr. Simon Nyachae, warned people in the Trans Nzoia not to try to revive Dini ya Msambwa under a different name.

92. 23 July. Eight followers were fined 50/- each with four months imprisonment in default for belonging to an illegal society.

93. 23 July. M.P. from Bungoma East, M. Barasa, asked the government to lift the ban on Dini ya Msambwa. The Attorney-General refused saying the organization was violent.

1970

94. 10 September. Six Pokot tribesmen were convicted of being members of Msambwa. Three who had had previous convictions were given four years each, and placed under police supervision for another four years after their release. The other three were given three years each.

95. 3 November. Twenty-three people, led by Cosmo Makakha,

a son of Masinde, were arrested on their way to Mount Elgon for a prayer and healing service and charged with being members of an unlawful society.

96. 21 November. The president of the Abaluhya Association Richard Kisaka, appealed to President Kenyatta to release Masinde.

97. 25 November. The case against the above '23', (see above, 95), was dismissed as Kakamega magistrate, P. N. Tank, ruled' that the prosecution had failed to prove its case against them.

1971

98. 20 January. Eight people suspected of being Msambwa followers were arrested.

99. 22 June. The M.P. for West Pokot, Francis Pollis Loile Lotodo, reported that Dini ya Msambwa was taking root in two locations in West Pokot and called for more police reinforcements to eradicate it.

100. 29 August. Masinde and eleven followers were arrested at Endebess for allegedly attending a Msambwa ceremony.

101. 1 October. Masinde and a follower were acquitted by a Kitale magistrate after the prosecution had withdrawn charges of their being members of an unlawful society.

102. 29 October. Masinde and eleven followers appeared before a magistrate and pleaded 'not guilty' to charges mentioned in 98 above.

103. 23 December. Above case adjourned until January as Masinde was ill.

1972

104. 27 January. The Endebess court case opened. It continued until 28 March then adjourned until 8 May.

105. 24 April. Masinde charged with resisting arrest and creating a disturbance at Mabusi trading centre when he prevented the arrest of a person pushing an unlicenced bicycle.

106. 5 May. Masinde appeared before Kakamega acting senior resident magistrate J. S. Patel, on above charge and released on 3,000/- bond.

107. 8 May. Masinde arrested and charged with conduct likely to cause breach of peace at Kitale.

108. 8 May. The Endebess case reopens.

109. 5 June. Hearing of Kitale charge (see above, 105) against Masinde opened.

110. 9 June. Masinde given a six year jail sentence in the Endebess case for being a member of an unlawful society and for attending a Msambwa meeting. The eleven charged with him were given sentences ranging from six months and a fine of £50 to twelve months and a fine of £100. Additionally, they had to pay £25 each towards the cost of the case which was termed 'long and expensive for the Republic.'

111. 3 July. Masinde acquitted of the Mabusi incident (see above, 103), because according to the magistrate the prosecution failed to bring sufficient evidence.

1973

112. 16 July. Masinde's appeal against the six year sentence opened and was adjourned.

113. 19 July. The appeal against the conviction and jailing of eleven members was placed before the Chief Justice, Sir James Wicks and Mr. Justice Simpson.

114. 27 July. Masinde's appeal dismissed but sentence reduced to five years because the six year sentence was deemed to be in excess of that permitted a resident magistrate without special powers to impose.

Notes

1. This chronology of events is compiled mainly from administrative records (KNA:DC/NN10/1/5 and DC/NN10/1/2) and *The Commission of Inquiry into the Affray at Kolloa, Baringo*, for the 1940s and the early 1950s, and from newspaper accounts in the *East African Standard* and the *Daily Nation* in the 1960s and 1970s. In these accounts where the exact date of the event could not be ascertained, the date of the article's appearance is given instead. Citations already noted in the text will not be footnoted again. A whole range of activities—many meetings and other proselytizing endeavours, sometimes mentioned tersely in administrators' reports in words to the effect 'growing contemptuousness on part of young men'—go unrecorded.

   During the 1940s and early 1950s, there was much unrest in the North Nyanza District, especially around Dini ya Msambwa's headquarters in Kimilili. Though the administration strongly suspected Msambwa was behind much of it and listed such episodes under its activities, evidence linking them to Msambwa was often lacking. Once Msambwa acquired an anti-British repute, it was probably unduly credited with activities carried out by others. For instance, the burning down of a particular peasant's dwelling and food stores may actually have been a private vendetta over land. Be that as it may, members openly defied the authorities, and while Msambwa may not have been responsible for all of these acts, it was responsible for a fair number of them. These activities are significant in themselves as they provide evidence of strong anti-British feelings and of a growing resistance.

Though this chronology is essentially a listing of events, several times commentary, additional to that given in the text, is included.

2. KNA:DC/NN10/1/5. Report of provincial commissioner Hunter of Nyanza on the burning down of Mr. Bickford's house sent to the honourable chief native secretary, 26 January 1945.
3. KNA:DC/NN10/1/5. A letter from district commissioner F. D. Hislop, 18 January 1945.
4. KNA:DC/NN10/1/5.
5. *Nyanza Province Annual Report 1948*.
6. *East African Standard*, 16 May 1945.
7. *Ibid.*, 24 June 1952.
8. *Ibid.*, 21 June 1952.
9. *Ibid.*, 15 July 1952.

Bibliography

Aberle, D. F.: *The Peyote Religion Among the Navaho*, (Aldine Publishing Co., Chicago, 1966).

Almond, G. A. and Coleman, J. S.: *The Politics of Developing Areas*, (Princeton University Press, Princeton, 1960).

Andersson, E.: *Messianic Popular Movements in the Lower Congo*, (Kegan Paul, London, 1958).

Ansorge, W. J.: *Under the African Sun*, (London, 1929).

Apter, D. E.: *Ghana in Transition*, (Atheneum, New York, 1963).

——: (ed.): *Ideology and Discontent*, (The Free Press, Glencoe, 1964).

——: 'Political Religion in the New Nations', *Old Societies and New*, Clifford Geertz, (ed.), (The Free Press, New York, 1967).

——: 'The Role of Traditionalism in the Political Modernization of Ghana and Uganda', *The World Politics*, XIII, 1, October, 1960, pp. 45–68.

Baëta, C. G.: *Prophetism in Ghana, A Study of some "Spiritual" Churches*, (SCM Press Ltd., London, 1962).

Balandier, G.: 'Contribution à l'étude des Nationalismes en Afrique Norie', *Zaire*, VII, 4, April, 1954, pp. 379–389.

——: 'Messianismes et Nationalismes en Afrique Noire', *Cahiers Internationaux de Sociologie*, XIV, 1953, pp. 41–65.

——: *Sociologie Actuelle de l'Afrique Noire*, (Presses Universitaires de France, Paris, 1955), pp. 417–504.

Barber, B.: 'A Socio-Cultural Interpretation of the Peyote Cult', *American Anthropologist*, XLIII, 1941, pp. 673–675.

——: 'Acculturation and Messianic Movements', *American Sociological Review*, VI, 6, 1941, pp. 663–669.

Barnett, D.: *Mau Mau from Within*, (MacGibbon and Kee, London, 1966).

Barrett, D. B.: 'Two Hundred Independent Church Movements in East Africa: A Survey, Analysis and Prediction', Paper read at University of East Africa Social Science Conference, Makerere University, Kampala, Uganda, December, 1966.

Bastide, R.: 'Messianism and Social and Economic Development', *Social Change: the Colonial Situation*, Immanuel Wallerstein, (ed.), (John Wiley, New York, 1966).

Bennett, G.: *Kenya, A Political History*, (Oxford University Press, London, 1963).

Bertsche, James: 'The Congo Rebellion', *Practical Anthropology*, XII, September—October, 1965.

Biebuyck, N. O.: 'La societé kumu face au Kitawala', *Zaire*, XI, 1, January, 1957, pp. 7–40.

Brazier, F. S.: 'The Nyabingi Cult: Religion and Political Scale in Kigezi 1900–1930', Paper read at University of East Africa Social Science Conference, University College, Dar es Salaam, Tanzania, January, 1968.

Brett, E.: 'Economic Policy in Kenya Colony: A study in Politics of Resource Allocation', Paper read at the East African Institute of Social Research, Makerere University, Kampala, Uganda, January, 1965.

Brinton, Crane: *The Anatomy of Revolution*, (Vintage, New York, 1957).

Burridge, K. O. L.: *Mambu, A Melanesian Millennium*, (Methuen, London, 1960).

Campbell, Angus; Converse, Philip E; Miller, Warren, E. and Stokes, Donald, E.: *The American Voter*, (John Wiley and Sons, New York, 1960).

Chilver, E. M.: 'Native Administration and Political Change in North Nyanza District', (typescript copy) East African Institute of Social Research Library, Makerere University, Kampala, Uganda.

Cliffe, L.: 'Nationalism and the Reaction to Enforced Agricultural Improvement in Tanganyika during the Colonial Period', Paper read at East African Institute of Social Research, Makerere University, Kampala, Uganda, January, 1965.

Cohn, Norman: 'Medieval Millenarism: its Bearing on the Comparative Study of Millenarian Movements', *Millennial Dreams in Action*, Sylvia L. Thrupp, (ed.), (Mouton, The Hague, 1962), pp. 31–43.

——: *The Pursuit of the Millennium*, (Harper and Row, New York, 1961).

Coleman, J. S.: *Nigeria: Background to Nationalism*, (University of California Press, Berkeley, 1958).

Colson, Elizabeth and Gluckman, Max, (eds.): *Seven Tribes of British Central Africa*, (Manchester University Press, Manchester, 1959).

349

Cranworth, L.: *Kenya Chronicles*, (Macmillan, London, 1939).

de Wolf, Jan Jacob: 'Religious Innovation and Social Change Among the Bukusu', Unpublished Ph.D. thesis, University of London, 1971.

Donovan, V. J.: 'The Protestant-Catholic Scandal in Africa', *African Ecclesiastical Review*, I, 3, July, 1959, pp. 169–177.

Eisenstadt, S. N.: *Modernization: Protest and Change*, (Prentice-Hall, Englewood Cliffs, 1966).

Evans-Pritchard, E. E.: *The Theories of Primitive Religion*, (Oxford University Press, London, 1965).

Farson, N.: *Last Chance in Africa*, (Victor Gollancz, London, 1951).

Fearn, Hugh: *An African Economy*, (Oxford University Press, London, 1961).

Fernandez, J. W.: 'African Religious Movements—Types and Dynamics', *Journal of Modern African Studies*, 11, 4, 1964, pp. 531–549.

——: 'Symbolic Consensus in a Fang Reformative Cult', *American Anthropologist*, LXVII, 4, August, 1965, pp. 902–929.

——: 'The Idea and Symbol of the Saviour in a Gabon Syncretist Cult', *International Review of Missions*, LIII, 1964, pp. 281–289.

Festinger, L.; Riecken, W. and Schachter, S.: *When Prophecy Fails*, (University of Minnesota Press, Minneapolis, 1956).

Feuer, Lewis S.: *The Conflict of Generations*, (Basic Books, New York, 1969).

Field, M. J.: 'Witchcraft as a Primitive Interpretation of Mental Disorder', *The Journal of Mental Science*, CI, pp. 425, 437–533.

Foran, W. R.: *A Cuckoo in Kenya: The Reminiscences of a Pioneer Police Officer in British East Africa*, (Hutchinson, London, 1936).

——: *The Kenya Police, 1887–1960*, (R. Hale, London, 1962).

Forde, D. (ed.): *African Worlds*, (Oxford University Press, London, 1954).

Fortes, M. and Evans-Pritchard, E. E., (eds.): *African Political Systems*, (Oxford University Press, London, 1940).

Fox, Renée C.: 'The Case of Congo-Kinshasa', Paper presented at the African Studies Association Annual Meeting, 3 November 1967.

——: De Craemer, Willy and Ribeaucourt, Jean-Marie: 'The Second Independence: A Case Study of the Kwilu Rebellion in the Congo', *Comparative Studies in Society and History*, VIII, 1 October 1965, pp. 78–109.

Freed, S. and Freed, R. S.: 'Spirit Possession as Illness in a North Indian Village', *Ethnology*, III, 2 April 1964, pp. 152–171.

Gluckman, M.: 'The Magic of Despair', *The Listener*, 29 April 1954.

Goldsmith, F. H.: *John Ainsworth: Pioneer Kenya Administrator, 1864–1946*, (Macmillan, London, 1955).

Goldthorpe, J. E. and Wilson, F. B.: *Tribal Maps of East Africa and Zanzibar*, (King and Jarrett, London, 1960).

Groves, C. P.: *The Planting of Christianity in Africa*, Vol. XIV, (Lutterworth Press, London, 1958).

Hagen, Everett, E.: *On the Theory of Social Change*, (Dorsey Press, Homewood, Illinois, 1962).

Harris, A.: 'Possession Hysteria in a Kenya Tribe', *The American Anthropologist*, LIX, 6, December, 1957, pp. 1046–1066.

Hayward, V. E. W. (ed.): *African Independent Church Movements*, (Edinburgh House Press, London, 1963).

Herberle, R.: *Social Movements*, (Appleton-Century-Crofts, New York, 1951).

Henderson, I.: 'White Populism in Southern Rhodesia', Paper read at University of East Africa Social Science Conference, University College, Dar es Salaam, Tanzania, January, 1968.

Hobley, C. W.: *Kenya: From Chartered Company to Crown Colony*, (Whitherby, London, 1929).

Hobsbawm, E. J.: *Primitive Rebels*, (W. W. Norton and Company, New York, 1959).

Hodgkin, T.: *Nationalism in Colonial Africa*, (New York University Press, New York, 1957).

Hoffer, E.: *The True Believer*, (Mentor Books, New York, 1958).

Humphrey, Norman: *The Liguru and the Land*, (Government Printer, Nairobi, 1947).

Iliffe, John: 'Organization of the Maji-Maji Rebellion', Paper read at University of East Africa Social Science Conference, Dar es Salaam, Tanzania, December, 1966.

Jackson, F.: *Early Days in East Africa*, (Edward Arnold, London, 1930).

Jarvie, I. C.: 'Theories of Cargo Cults: A Critical Analysis', *Oceania*, XXXIV, 1, September, 1963, pp. 1–31.

Jellicoe, M.: 'The Turu Rebellion of 1908', Paper read at University of East Africa Social Science Conference, University College, Dar es Salaam, Tanzania, January 1968.

Johnson, Chalmers: *Revolution and the Social System*, (Stanford University Press, Stanford, 1964).

Kenyatta, J.: *Facing Mount Kenya*, (Martin Secker & Warburg, London, 1953).

Klapp, O. E.: *Heroes, Villains and Fools*, (Prentice Hall, Englewood Cliffs, 1962).

Kopytoff, I.: 'Classifications of Religious Movements: Analytical and Synthetic', Symposium on New Approaches to the Study of Religion, *Proceedings, American Ethnological Society*, 1964, pp. 77–90.

LaFontaine, J. S.: 'Notes on Ancestor Worship Among the Babukusu and its Difference from Dini ya Misambwa' (typescript copy), East Africa Institute of Social Research Library, Makerere University, Kampala.

——: *The Gisu of Uganda*, (International African Institute, London, 1959).

Lang, Kurt and Lang, Gladys Engel: *Collective Dynamics*, (Thomas Y. Crowell, New York, 1961).

Lanternari, V.: *The Religions of the Oppressed*, (Mentor Books, Toronto, 1963).

Le Bon, Gustave: *The Crowd*, (The Viking Press, New York, 1960).

Lemarchand, Rene: *Political Awakening in the Belgian Congo*, (University of California Press, Berkeley, 1964).

——: 'The Bases of Nationalism Among the Bakongo', *Africa*, XXXI, 4, October, 1961, pp. 344–354.

LeVine, R. A.: 'An Attempt to Change the Gusii Initiation Cycle' *Man*, 179, July, 1959, pp. 117–120.

——: 'Gusii Sex Offences: A Study in Social Control', *American Anthropologist*, LXI, 1959, pp. 965–990.

——: 'The Internationalization of Political Values in Stateless Societies', *Human Organization*, XIX, 2, 1960, pp. 51–58.

—— and LeVine, B. B.: *Nyansongo: A Gusii Community in Kenya*, (John Wiley, New York, 1966).

——: 'Omoriori: Smeller of Witches', *Natural History*, LXVII, 1958, pp. 142–147.

——: 'Socialization, Social Structure and Intersocial Images', H. Kelman, (ed.), *International Behaviour: A Social Psychological Analysis*, (Holt, Rinehart and Winston, New York), pp. 43–68.

——: 'Wealth and Power in Gusiiland', P. J. Bohannon, (ed.),

Markets in Africa, (Northwestern University Press, Evanston, 1962).

———: 'Witchcraft and Sorcery in a Gusii Community', J. Middleton and E. H. Winter, (eds.), *Witchcraft and Sorcery in East Africa*, (Routledge, Kegan Paul, London, 1963).

Leys, N. M.: *A Last Chance in Kenya*, (Hogarth Press, London, 1931).

———: *Kenya*, (Hogarth Press, London, 1931).

Linton, Ralph: *Acculturation in Seven American Indian Tribes*, (Peter Smith, Gloucester, Mass., 1962).

———: 'Nativistic Movements', *American Anthropologist*, XLV, 1943, pp. 230–240.

Lipset, S. M.: *Agrarian Socialism: The Cooperative Commonwealth Federation in Saskatchewan*, (University of California Press, Berkeley, 1950).

Lloyd-Jones, W.: *K.A.R.: Being an Unofficial Account of the Origin and Activities of the King's African Rifles*, (Arrowsmith, London, 1926).

Lonsdale, J. M.: 'Political Associations in Western Kenya', *Protest and Power in Black Africa*, Robert I. Rotberg and Ali A. Mazrui, (eds.), (Oxford University Press, New York, 1970).

———: 'A Political History of Nyanza 1883–1945', Unpublished Ph.D. thesis, Cambridge University, June, 1964.

———: 'Rural Resistance and Mass Political Mobilization Among the Luo of Western Kenya', Paper read at East African Institute of Social Research Conference, Makerere, University, Kampala, Uganda, December, 1965.

———: 'Some Origins of Nationalism in East Africa' *Journal of African History*, IX, 1, 1968, pp. 119–146.

Mair, Lucy: *Witchcraft*, (World Universal Library, London, 1969).

Mannes, Marya: *More in Anger*, (J. B. Lippincott, Philadelphia, 1958).

Marco Surveys Ltd.: *A Baseline Survey of Factors Affecting Agricultural Development in Three Areas of Kenya*, Nairobi, 1965.

Marwick, N. G.: 'Another Modern Anti-Witchcraft Movement in East Central Africa', *Africa*, XX, 2, April, 1950, pp. 100–112.

Mayer, P.: 'Gusii Bridewealth, Law and Custom', *Rhodes Livingstone Papers*, XVIII, (Oxford University Press, London, 1950).

———: 'Gusii Initiation Ceremonies', *Journal of the Royal Anthropological Institute*, 83, 1953a, pp. 9–39.

——: 'The Lineage Principle in Gusii Society', *International African Institute Memorandum XXIV*, (Oxford University Press, London, 1949).

——: Privileged Obstruction of Marriage Rites Among the Gusii', *Africa*, 20, 1950a, pp. 113–125.

Melland, F. H. and Cholmeley, E. H.: *Through the Heart of Africa*, (Houghton Mifflin, Boston, 1912).

Middleton, J. (ed.): *Gods and Rituals*, (The Natural History Press, New York, 1967).

——: (ed.): *Magic, Witchcraft and Curing*, (The Natural History Press, New York, 1967).

——: (ed.): *Myth and Cosmos*, (The Natural History Press, New York, 1967).

Mitchell, P.: *African Afterthoughts*, (Hutchinson, London, 1954).

Mitchell, R. C.: 'Religious Protest and Social Change: The Origins of the Aladura Movement in Western Nigeria', *Protest and Power in Black Africa*, Robert I. Rotberg and Ali A. Mazrui, (eds.), (Oxford University Press, New York, 1970), pp. 458–496.

—— and Turner, H. W.: *A Bibliography of Modern African Religious Movements*, (Northwestern University Press, Evanston, 1966).

Mooney, J.: *The Ghost-Dance Religion*, (University of Chicago Press, Chicago, 1965).

Moore, B.: *Social Origins of Dictatorship and Democracy*, (Beacon Press, Boston, 1966).

Moore, Henry T.: 'Innate Factors in Radicalism and Conservatism', *Journal of Abnormal Psychology*, XX, 1925, pp. 234–244.

Moyse-Bartlett, H.: *The King's African Rifles: A Study in the Military History of East and Central Africa, 1890–1945*, (Gale and Polden, Aldershot, 1956).

Mungeam, G. H.: *British Rule in Kenya 1895–1912: the Establishment of Administration in the East African Protectorate*, (Clarendon Press, Oxford, 1966).

Nadel, S. F.: 'Witchcraft in Four African Societies: An Essay in Comparison', *American Anthropologist*, 54, January-March, 1952, pp. 18–29.

Nottingham, E. K.: *Religion and Society*, (Random House, New York, 1954).

Nyangweso, (Pseud.): 'Cult of Mumbo in Central and South Kavirondo', *The Journal of East African and Uganda Natural History*, X, 38, May-August, 1930, pp. 13–17.

Ogot, B. A.: 'British Administration in the Central Nyanza District, 1900–1960', *Journal of African History*, IV, 2, 1963, pp. 249–274.

——: *History of the Southern Luo*, Vol. I, (East African Publishing House, Nairobi, 1967).

Oliver, R.: *The Missionary Factor in East Africa*, (Longmans, Green & Co., London, 1967).

—— and Fage, J. D.: *A Short History of Africa*, (Penguin, London, 1962).

Orther, J.: 'An Account of the Political and Religious Tenets of the "Watu wa Misambwa" ', (typescript copy), Catholic Mission Archives, Kibabii, 28 May, 1948.

Osogo, J.: *A History of the Baluyia*, (Oxford University Press, Nairobi, 1966).

——: *Nabongo Mumia*, (East African Literature Bureau, Nairobi, 1967).

Owuor, H. A.: 'Spirit Possession Among the Luo of Central Nyanza, Kenya' (typescript copy), East African Institute of Social Research Library, Makerere University, Kampala, Uganda.

Parrinder, G.: *Religion in an African City*, (Oxford University Press London, 1953).

——: *Witchcraft, European and African*, (Faber and Faber, London, 1963).

Pinard, Maurice: *The Rise of a Third Party*, (Prentice-Hall, Englewood Cliffs, 1971).

Ranger, T. O.: 'Connections Between Primary Resistance Movements and Modern Mass Nationalism in East and Central Africa', Paper read at University of East Africa Social Science Conference, Makerere University, Kampala, Uganda, December, 1966.

——: 'Witchcraft Eradication Movements in Central and Southern Tanzania and their Connection with the Maji Maji', Paper read at University of East Africa Social Science Conference, Dar es Salaam, Tanzania, November, 1966.

Rawcliffe, D. H.: *The Struggle for Kenya*, (Victor Golancz, London, 1954).

Raymaekers, P.: 'L'Eglise de Jesus-Christ sur La Terre Par le Prophete Simon Kimbangu: Contribution a L'Etude des Mouvements Messianiques dans le Bas Congo', *Zaire*, XIII, 7, pp. 675–756.

Richards, A. I.: 'A Modern Movement of Witchfinders', *Africa*, VIII, 4, October, 1935, pp. 448–461.

Richards, E.: *Fifty Years in Nyanza 1906–1956*, (Acme Press, Nairobi, 1956).

Robinson, R. E. and Gallagher, J.: 'The Partition of Africa', *The New Cambridge Modern History*, XI, Cambridge, 1962.

Ronald, O.: *The Missionary Factor in East Africa*, (Longmans, London, 1952).

Rosberg, C. G. and Nottingham, J.: *The Myth of 'Mau Mau'*, (Praeger, New York, 1966).

——: 'Political Conflict and Change in Kenya', *Transition in Africa*, Gwendolyn Carter and Robert Brown, (eds.), (Boston University Press, Boston, 1958).

Rotberg, Robert I.: 'The Lenshina Movement of Northern Rhodesia', *Rhodes-Livingstone Institute Journal*, pp. 63–78.

——: 'Psychological Stress and the Question of Identity: Chilembwe's Revolt Reconsidered', *Protest and Power in Black Africa*, Robert I. Rotberg and Ali A. Mazrui, (eds.), (Oxford University Press, New York, 1970).

Schwartz, Marc J., Turner, V. W. and Tuden, Arthur: *Political Anthropology*, (Aldine, Chicago, 1966).

Seaton, H.: *Lion in the Morning*, (John Murray, London, 1963).

Shepperson, George: 'The Comparative Study of Millenarian Movements', *Millenial Dreams in Action*, Sylvia L. Thrupp, (ed.), (Mouton, The Hague, 1962), pp. 44–52.

——: 'The Politics of African Church Separatist Movements in British Central Africa, 1892–1914', *Africa*, XXIV, 3, July, 1954, pp. 233–246.

—— and Thomas, P.: *Independent African*, (Edinburgh University Press, Edinburgh, 1958).

Smelser, N. J.: 'Mechanisms of Change and Adjustment to Change', *Industrialization and Society*, B. F. Hoselitz and W. E. Moore, (eds.), (UNESCO-Mouton, The Hague, 1963).

——: *Theory of Collective Behavior*, (The Free Press, New York, 1962).

——: 'Toward a Theory of Modernization' *Social Change*, A. Etzioni and E. Etzioni, (eds.), (Basic Books, New York, 1964), pp. 258–274.

Sorrenson, M. P. K.: *Land Reform in the Kikuyu Country*, (Oxford University Press, Nairobi, 1967).

——: *Origins of European Settlement in Kenya*, (Oxford University Press, Nairobi, 1968).

Sundkler, B. G. M.: *Bantu Prophets in South Africa*, (Oxford University Press, London, 1961).

——: *The Christian Ministry in Africa*, (SCM Press, London, 1962).

Swantz, M. J.: 'The Spirit Possession Cults and their Social Setting in a Zaramo Coastal Community', Paper read at University of East Africa Social Science Conference, University College, Dar es Salaam, Tanzania, 1968.

Talmon, Yonina: 'Pursuit of the Millennium: The Relation between Religious and Social Change', *European Journal of Sociology*, III, 1962, pp. 125–148.

Thomson, Joseph: *Through Masailand*, (Low, Marston, Searle and Rivington, London, 1885).

Thrupp, S. L. (ed.): *Millennial Dreams in Action*, (Mouton, The Hague, 1962).

Thurnwold, R.: 'The African in Transition: Some Comparisons with Melanesia', *Africa*, XI, 1935, pp. 174–186.

Turnbull, C. M.: *The Lonely African*, (Simon & Schuster, New York, 1962).

Turner, H. W.: *African Independent Church: The Life and Faith of the Church of the Lord*, Aladura, Vol. II, (Clarendon Press, Oxford, 1967).

Turner, Ralph H. and Killian, Lewis M.: *Collective Behavior*, (Prentice-Hall, Englewood Cliffs, 1957).

Usher-Wilson, L. C.: 'Bishop's Study of "Dini ya Misambwa": First Published Account of Dangerous African Movement', *East Africa and Rhodesia*, 1414 and 1416, November, 1951, pp. 282–283, 345–346.

Vicariate of Kisumu, 'Exposition of Chief Articles of Dini ya Misambwa', Kisumu, 6, April 1948, (typescript report).

Wagner, G.: 'The Abaluyia of Kavirondo', *African Worlds*, D. Forde, (ed.), (Oxford University Press, London, 1965), pp. 27–54.

——: *The Bantu of North Kavirondo*, (Oxford University Press, London 1949).

——: 'The Political Organization of the Bantu in Kavirondo', *African Political Systems*, M. Fortes and E. E. Evans-Pritchard, (eds.), (Oxford University Press, London, 1967), pp. 197–236.

Wallace, A. F. C.: *Religion: An Anthropological View*, (Random House, New York, 1966).

357

Wallis, W. B.: *Messiahs: Their Role in Civilization*, (American Council of Public Affairs, Washington, D.C., 1943).

Ward, B. E.: 'Some Observations on Religious Cults in Ashanti', *Africa*, XXVI, 1, January, 1956, pp. 47–61.

Weber, M.: *The Methodology of the Social Sciences*, (The Free Press, Glencoe, 1949).

Welbourn, F. B.: *East African Rebels: A Study of Some Independent Churches*, (SCM Press, London, 1961).

——: *Religion and Politics in Uganda 1952–1962*, (East African Publishing House, Nairobi, 1965).

Welbourn, F. B. and Ogot, B. A.: *A Place to Feel at Home*, (Oxford University Press, London, 1966).

Welime, J. D. W.: 'Dini ya Msambwa', Paper read at East African Institute of Social Research Conference, Makerere University, Kampala, Uganda, January, 1967.

Were, G. S.: *A History of the Abaluyia of Western Kenya, c. 1500–1930*, (East African Publishing House, Nairobi, 1967).

——: 'Dini ya Msambwa: A Reassessment', Paper read at University of East Africa Social Science Conference, Makerere University, Kampala, December, 1966.

Whisson, M. G.: *Change and Challenge*, (Christian Council of Kenya, Nairobi, 1964).

——: 'The Rise of Asembo and the Curse of Kakia', Paper read at East African Institute of Social Research Conference, Makerere University, Kampala, Uganda, 1961.

——: 'The Will of God and the Wiles of Men', Paper read at the East African Institute of Social Research Conference, Makerere University, Kampala, Uganda, January, 1962.

Woddis, J.: *Africa, the Lion Awakes*, (Lawrence and Wishart, London, 1961).

Wolf, E. R.: *Peasants*, (Prentice-Hall, Englewood Cliffs, 1966).

Wood, S.: *Kenya: The Tensions of Progress*, (Oxford University Press, London, 1962).

Worsley, P. M.: 'Millenarian Movements in Melanesia', *Rhodes-Livingstone Institute*, XXI, March, 1957, pp. 18–31. Also Bobbs-Merril Reprint Series, A–171.

——: *The Trumpet Shall Sound*, (MacGibbon and Kee, London, 1957).

Yinger, J. M.: *Religion, Society and the Individual*, (Macmillan, New York, 1957).

Young, C.: *Politics in the Congo*, (Princeton University Press, Princeton, 1965).

———: 'Rebellion and the Congo', *Protest and Power in Black Africa*, Robert I. Rotberg and Ali A. Mazrui, (eds.), (Oxford University Press, New York, 1957).

Zaretsky, I. I.: *Bibliography on Spirit Possession and Spirit Membership*, (Northwestern University Press, Evanston, 1966).

Government Documents: Kenya

Annual Reports of the following Districts, Departments and Provinces:

Baringo District.

Central Kavirondo, North Kavirondo and South Kavirondo Districts. In 1949 the name was changed to Nyanza. Thenceforth known as Nyanza District Reports.

Trans Nzoia District.

Uasin Gishu District.

Native Affairs Department Reports, 1923–1938.

African Affairs, Annual Report, 1948 *et seq*.

Nyanza Province.

Rift Valley Province.

Colonial Reports, Annual, British East African Protectorate. London, 1905–1920.

Colonial Reports, Annual, Colony and Protectorate of Kenya. London, 1921–1938, 1946–1960.

Court Records for Criminals Case No. 434 of 1964 held in the Resident Magistrate's Court at Kisumu.

Historical Survey of the Origins and Growth of Mau Mau. (The Corfield Report), Cmd. 1030 (1960).

Humphrey, N. *The Liguru and the Land: Sociological Aspects of Some Agricultural Problems of North Kavirondo. 1947.*

Kenya Population Census 1962. Advance Report of Volumes I and II (1964).

Report of the Commission of Inquiry into the Affray at Kolloa, Baringo, 1950.

Report of the East African Commission, 1924. Cmd. 2387, 1925.

Report of the Kenya Land Commission. Cmd. 4556, 1934.

Provincial and District Political Records including Intelligence Reports, Handing-Over Reports.

East African Newspapers and Periodicals
  Daily Nation.
  East Africa and Rhodesia.
  East African Standard.
  Reporter.
  Sunday Nation.
  The Times East Africa.
  Uganda Argus.

Index

agents of social control, listed 65; and Mumbo 65–71, 84; and Msambwa 126–130, 254–260, 262–267; and mass society theory 244; *see also* British, determinants, missionaries

Andersson, E., on protest movements 5; on messianic movements 8

Apter, D., on traditional in politics 144

Baeta, C. G., on protest movements 9–10

Balandier, G., on protest movements 5

Barnett, D. L., on Mau Mau 243

Barrett, D. B., on protest movements 12

Brett, E. A., on settlement 110

British, the colonization of Kenya 1; and protest movements 4, 5–6 12–15, 126–130; penetration of Gusiiland 23–33, 44–45, 59–61; expeditions 24–30, 88–95, 293–294; political reorganization 30–31, 95–100; policies 32–33, 103–110, 164, 205n.136; and Luhya 76, 89–117; and Mumbo 80–82; and Pokot 208–218; and Msambwa 262–267, 293–296, 297; *see also* agents of social control, determinants, land

Bukusu, *see* Dini ya Msambwa, Luhya

Bukusu Union 178, and Msambwa 186, 187–195; *see also* Nabwana

Campbell, A., ideology of a movement 220

Carothers, J. C., and Mau Mau 13; on Masinde 168

Carrier Corps, effect on Gusii 32–33; as determinant of Mumbo 79–80; and squatting 106

Churchill, W., on penetration of Gusiiland 28–29

Cohn, N., on millenarian movements 7, 244–245, 250n.20

Cult of Mumbo, *see* Mumbo

determinants 4–16, 224–249, 292–302; structural 76–79, 292–295; multiple strains as 79–82, 295–297; exacerbating factors 82, 297–299; mobilization 83–84, 229–247, 300–302; *see also* agents of social control

de Wolf, J. J., on Msambwa 7, 10, 198, 284, 285; on squatters 235

Dini ya Msambwa, *see* Msambwa

Fernandez, J. W., on protest movements 6

Foran, W. R., on penetration of Gusiiland 25, 27

Gluckman, M., on bullets-to-water belief 158

Gusfield, J., on mass society theory 242

Gusii, British penetration and 23–31, 59–61, 80–82; composition 24; *see also* Mumbo

Hobley, C. W., on Bukusu 92–94

Hobsbawm, E. J., on protest movements 5; on millenarianism 7–8; on peasant movements 152

Hodgkin, T., on protest movements 76–77

Hoffer, E., on radical protest 231; on mass society theory 241

Huxley, E., on Msambwa 13–14

Iliffe, J., on Maji Maji Rebellion 11–12

Kenyatta, Jomo, 9, 192, 269, 270, 285

Khaoya, Israel, and Msambwa 143, 269

Kikuyu, 9, 23, 60, 190; and Msambwa 84–85, 254, 266–267, 286; and KCA 107, 115; and KAU 191–192, 198; and squatting 232, 243

Killian, L. M., on mass society theory 20n.45, 241

Kipkorir, B., on Msambwa support 10, among Pokot 14

Kolloa Affray, *see* Pokot

Kornhauser, W., on mass society theory 236, 241

La Barre, W., on charisma 11

La Fontaine, J. S., on religion 133, 194; on Msambwa 198

land, colonial policy on 103–110, 112–113, 170–178, 257; as reason for protest 220, 227–229, 296–297; *see also* squatters

Lanternari, V., on protest movements 5

361

structural determinants 76–79; multiple strains 79–82; execerbating factors 82; mobilization 83–84; and Msambwa 137, 254, 258, 300 *see also* agents of social control, protest movements

Nabwana, Pascal, on Mau Mau 193; and Bukusu Union 186, 187, 188, 189, 190, 191, 206n.159

Nakimayu, Donisio, Msambwa and 139, 155, 302n.3; as mission convert 221

nativistic movements, Linton on 8, Mumbo as 23, 62; Msambwa as 133, 137–144; *see also* protest movements

Ochieng' W. R. on Gusii 60

Ogot, B. A. on independent churches 9; on Mumbo 13, 51; on Gusii 60

Owuor, H. A. on Mumbo 51

Pinard, M. ideology of a movement 220

Pkech, Lucas leader of Msambwa among Pokot 10-11, 14, 209–217, 259

Pokot Msambwa among 10–11, 128, 208–218, 220–221

protest movements, causes and definition 3, 4–12, 15–16; in Kenya 5–6, 12–15; stereotype 14–15; reasons for 224–240; radical character of 224–240; *see also* individual authors

radical protest 244–240

Rosberg, C. and Nottingham, J., on protest movements 5

Schlosser, K., on protest movements 6–7

Shepperson, G., on protest movements 5, 9

Smelser, N., on collective behaviour theory 133

Sorrenson, M. P. K., on Mumbo 13;

squatters, settlement of 105–108; economics of 230–240, 241; KCA and 240; and labourers 250n. 33, 251n. 36

Sundkler, B. G. M., independent churches 11, 141

van Wing, J., on protest movements 5

Wafula, Samson, original Msambwa member 124; on Msambwa 139, 141, 144; and Bukusu Union 188; later phase of Msambwa and 269, 272, 273, 279

Walumoli, Joasch, Msambwa and 143, 144, 155, 279; Misango and 289; on Mau Mau 193; as mission convert 221; home of 200–201n. 30

Wagner, G., on Luhya religion 135

Wambaa, R. M. and King, K., on squatters 106

Weber, M., on leadership 143

Wekuke, Benjamin, as founder member of Msambwa 124–125; on Msambwa 137, 144, 145; and Bukusu Union 193; as mission convert 221; Msambwa and 248, 280, 279; Misango and 288–289

Welbourn, F. B., on protest movements 5; on independent churches 9

Welime, J. D. W., on Msambwa 198, 284

Wolf, E. R., on peasants 263, definition of peasants 3–4

Worsley, P., on protest movements 5; on cargo cults 8

Prepared for press, designed and published by Oxford University Press, Eastern Africa Branch, P.O. Box 72532, Electricity House, Harambee Avenue, Nairobi and printed by Kenya Litho Ltd., P.O. Box 40775, Changamwe Road, Nairobi, on paper manufactured by Pan African Paper Mills, P.O. Box 535, Webuye, Kenya.